COLLECTANEA HERMETICA

Hermetic Arcanum of Penes Nos Unda Tagi

The Pymander of Hermes

A Short Enquiry Concerning the Hermetic Art
by A Lover of Philalethes

An Introduction to Alchemy and Notes

Æsch Mezareph or Purifying Fire
A Chymico-Kabalistic Treatise Collected from the
Kabala Denudata or Knorr Von Rosenroth

Somnium Scipionis

The Vision of Scipio Considered as a
Fragment of the Mysteries

The golden Verses of Pythagoras

The Symbols of Pythagoras

The Chaldæan Oracles of Zoroaster

Euphrates or the Waters of the East

William Wynn Westcott

(Supreme Magus of the Rosicrucian Society, Master of the Quatuor Coronati Lodge.)

ISBN 1-56459-260-X

Request our FREE CATALOG of over 1,000
Rare Esoteric Books
<u>Unavailable Elsewhere</u>

Alchemy, Ancient Wisdom, Astronomy, Baconian, Eastern-Thought, Egyptology, Esoteric, Freemasonry, Gnosticism, Hermetic, Magic, Metaphysics, Mysticism, Mystery Schools, Mythology, Occult, Philosophy, Psychology, Pyramids, Qabalah, Religions, Rosicrucian, Science, Spiritual, Symbolism, Tarot, Theosophy, *and many more!*

Kessinger Publishing Company

Collectanea Hermetica

EDITED BY

W. WYNN WESTCOTT, M.B., D.P.H.

(Supreme Magus of the Rosicrucian Society,
Master of the Quatuor Coronati Lodge.)

VOLUME I.

AN ENGLISH TRANSLATION OF THE

HERMETIC ARCANUM

OF

PENES NOS UNDA TAGI.

1623

WITH A PREFACE AND NOTES BY

'SAPERE AUDE", FRA. R.R. ET A.C.

PREFACE

TO THE

"COLLECTANEA HERMETICA."

HERMETIC students find very great difficulty in securing copies of the old Rosicrucian tracts and other notable volumes of occult lore, and I have been urged by many earnest members of the Rosicrucian Society to undertake the Editorship of a series of small volumes, which are to provide some of the texts of the greatest value in Hermetic research. Among my personal friends and fellow-students are many who have made a long study of the Occult Sciences, of the Kabalah, of Alchemy, and of the Higher Magic, and these have assured me of their support in this undertaking. The Notes which are added to each volume are partly taken from mediæval commentators, and are partly those of my coadjutors. The Societas Rosicruciana, as an Institution, is not answerable for the opinions expressed; all responsibility falling upon the actual writers.

The Notes are intended to assist those who have made some progress in the study of Hermetic Philosophy; to the casual reader they may be as incomprehensible as the text itself, and where the general reader finds a simple definite statement, such is probably a *Reveiling* and not a *Revelation*.

W. W. W.

Arcanum Hermeticæ Philosophicæ Opus.

IN QUO OCCULTA NATURÆ ET ARTIS CIRCA LAPIDIS PHILOSOPHORUM MATERIAM ET OPERANDI MODUM CANONICE ET ORDINATE FIUNT MANIFESTA.

Opus authoris anonymi,

PENES NOS UNDA TAGI.

MDCXXIII.

THE SECRET WORK

OF THE

HERMETIC PHILOSOPHY

WHEREIN THE SECRETS OF NATURE AND ART CONCERNING THE MATTER OF THE PHILOSOPHERS' STONE AND THE MANNER OF WORKING ARE EXPLAINED IN AN AUTHENTIC AND ORDERLY MANNER.

The Work of an Anonymous Author,

PENES NOS UNDA TAGI.

EDITED BY "SAPERE AUDE."

PREFACE

TO THE

"ARCANUM."

The *Arcanum Hermeticum* has been chosen for the first volume of the *Collectanea Hermetica*, because since its first publication in 1623, in the Latin language, no alchymic tract has been more widely read, and no other has been so often reprinted, alike in Latin, German, French and English.

The author, Jean d'Espagnet, was sometime President of the Parliament of Bordeaux, he flourished from 1600 to 1630, and obtained a great reputation as an Hermetic philosopher and alchymist. Two of his alchymic works are alone extant; *Enchiridion Physicæ Restitutæ*, and *Arcanum Philosophiæ Hermeticæ;* of these, the former treats of those theories of chemical constitution upon which the possibility of Transmutation of Metals depends, and the latter of the Practice of Alchymy. The *Arcanum* was first published in 1623 in France; five subsequent French editions in the original Latin are known, and an edition in the French tongue was printed in 1651 from the translation of Jean Bachon. Several editions were also published at Geneva, Kiel, Lubeck, Tubingen and Leipzig. The works of Espagnet are also included in Manget's *Bibliotheca Chemica Curiosa* and in the *Bibliotheca Chemica* of Albineus.

Jean d'Espagnet followed the usual Rosicrucian custom of using a motto instead of his name when publishing Hermetic books. The *Hermetic Arcanum* is signed " Penes nos unda Tagi;" he also at times added the motto, " Spes mea in Agno est." These mottoes are anagrams. Each contains the letters of " Espagnet," and the two taken together contain also the letters of " Deus (IHVH with the Shin interposed) omnia in nos," but there are two letters over, " A s." The French biographer says, in error, that only one letter, an " E "—his initial—remains over.

Espagnet was not only an Alchymist, but a Mystic as well; he contributed a preface and a sonnet to a work by Pierre de Lancre, entitled *Tableau de l'inconstance des mauvaises Anges,* 1612. He is also notable as having taken a leading part in the prosecution of persons who were supposed to be black magicians, living in the district called Les Landes and among the Pyrenees; but this action appears to have been the result of his position in the Parliament of Bordeaux.

He ornamented the façade of his house in the Rue de Bahutiers, at Bordeaux, with allegorical sculptures and devices; the house has been destroyed, but these ornaments are still to be seen preserved in the gardens of the mayoral residence.

As a natural philosopher, Jean d'Espagnet declined to be led by the notions of Aristotle, and preferred those of the Alexandrian schools. He postulated the ideal of one material universal basis, or *hyle*, from which all varieties of matter have been evolved by stages of development, a necessary doctrine for one who taught the mutual convertibility of the so-called chemical elementary substances. He also insisted upon the importance of representing all manifestation as separable into three worlds, elementary, celestial, and archetypal; this division is related to the scheme of the Four Worlds of the Kabalists, by a concentration which is recognized by such philosophers. He taught the origin of created things from the chaos of the first matter, which under the energetic impulse of the Divine Force, proceeds from stage to stage of development into heterogeneity. He recognized three stages of matter, the subtle, the mean, and the gross: analogous to the airy, moist, and earthy natures of the Hermetists. Upon these bases his *Enchiridion* is almost a text-book of Rosicrucian Philosophy.

The *Arcanum* describes at considerable length, and with obvious good faith, the procedure of one school of Alchymists in the search for the secret of the Stone Philosophical, and it formulates the stages of the work so that he or she who *can read* may run. Yet it must be confessed that he has well succeeded in *reveiling*, as well as *revealing*, the secret of what was meant by the Prima Materia and the real nature alike of *The* Sulphur, *The* Salt, and *The* Mercury.

Such a work as the *Arcanum*, written by one who knows, is not sent to print, to teach the *public*, to show a cheap and easy way to wealth and luxury, or to assist coiners of spurious moneys, but is intended as a treasure house in which those who have devoted life and love to the quest may find stored up the data and experiences of such as have trodden the Path and have borne tribulation and persecution, counting all loss to be gain in their progress to success and to the possession of that Stone of the Wise, which when obtained can indeed transmute the things of the material world, but does also equally work upon all higher planes, and enables an Adept to soar unheeding into worlds of joy, wisdom, and exultation, which are unseen, unknown, and inconceivable to ordinary mortals, who have chosen the alternative of physical contentment and material happiness.

The original Latin title is given at the first page, together with an English translation.

The German edition of 1685, Leipzig, was entitled: *Das geheime Werck der Hermetischen Philosophie, von Joannes d'Espagnet. Anagr-e-in ļu. mut. Penes nos unda Tagi.* This has an additional preface, and cap. 138 is numbered 137. "Joannes" must be taken as "Joannus."

An English translation was made by James Hasolle, Qui est Mercuriophilus Anglicus; this is the anagram and pseudonym of Elias Ashmole, famous as an antiquary. Copies of his third edition of 1650 are not uncommon. The present editor of the *Hermetic Arcanum* had at first intended to reprint Ashmole's version in its entirety, but a comparison with the original Latin has induced him to make a revision of Ashmole's translation, because he discovered many important inaccuracies, and also because in some places the language was more forcible and plain than our present delicate manners would appreciate.

S. A. is responsible for most of the Notes; a few are from Sigismund Bacstrom, Frater R.R. et A.C., and others are from the marginal references of an anonymous Adept writing in 1710.

SAPERE AUDE.

THE HERMETIC ARCANUM.

CANON I.

THE beginning of this Divine Science is the fear of the Lord[1] and its end is charity and love toward our Neighbour; the all-satisfying Golden Crop is properly devoted to the rearing and endowing of temples and hospices; for whatsoever the Almighty freely bestoweth on us, we should properly offer again to him. So also Countries grievously oppressed may be set free; prisoners unduly held captive may be released, and souls almost starved may be relieved.

2. The light of this knowledge is the gift of God, which by His will He bestoweth upon whom He pleaseth. Let none therefore set himself to the study hereof, until having cleared and purified his heart,[2] he devote himself wholly unto God, and be emptied of all affection and desire unto the impure things of this world.

3. The Science of producing Nature's grand Secret, is a perfect knowledge of universal Nature and of Art concerning the Realm of Metals; the Practice thereof is conversant with finding the principles of Metals by Analysis, and after they have been made much more perfect to conjoin them otherwise than they have been before, that from thence may result a catholic Medicine, most powerful to perfect imperfect Metals, and for restoring sick and decayed bodies, of any sort soever.

4. Those that hold public Honours and Offices or be

always busied with private and necessary occupations, let them not strive to attain unto the acmé of this Philosophy; for it requireth the whole man[3], and being found, it possesseth him, and he being possessed, it debarreth him from all other long and serious employments, for he will esteem other things as strange, and of no value unto him.

5. Let him that is desirous of this Knowledge, clear his mind from all evil passions, especially pride[4], which is an abomination to Heaven, and is as the gate of Hell; let him be frequent in prayer[5] and charitable[6]; have little to do with the world[7]; abstain from company keeping; enjoy constant tranquillity[8]; that the Mind may be able to reason more freely in private and be highly lifted up[9]; for unless it be kindled with a beam of Divine Light, it will not be able to penetrate these hidden mysteries of Truth.

6. The Alchymists who have given their minds to their well-nigh innumerable Sublimations, Distillations, Solutions, Congelations, to manifold Extraction of Spirits and Tinctures, and other Operations more subtle than profitable, and so have distracted themselves by a variety of errors, as so many tormentors, will never be inclined again by their own Genius to the plain way of Nature and light of Truth; from whence their industrious subtilty hath twined them, and by twinings and turnings, as by the Lybian Quicksands, hath drowned their entangled Wits: the only hope of safety for them remaineth in finding out a faithful Guide[10] and Master[11], who may make the Sun clear and conspicuous unto them and free their eyes from darkness.

7. A studious Tyro of a quick wit, constant mind, inflamed with the study of Philosophy, very skilful in natural Philosophy, of a pure heart, complete in manners, mightily devoted to God, though ignorant of practical Chymistry, may with confidence enter into the highway of Nature and peruse the Books of the best Philosophers; let him seek out an ingenious and

sedulous Companion for himself, and not despair of obtaining his desire.

8. Let a Student of these secrets carefully beware of reading or keeping company with false Philosophers[12]; for nothing is more dangerous to a learner of any Science, than the company of an unskilled or deceitful man by whom erroneous principles are stamped as true, whereby a simple and credulous mind is seasoned with false Doctrine.

9. Let a Lover of truth make use of few Authors, but of the best note and experienced truth; let him suspect things that are quickly understood, especially in Mystical Names and Secret Operations[13]; for truth lies hid in obscurity; for Philosophers never write more deceitfully—than when plainly, nor ever more truly—than when obscurely.

10. As for the Authors of chiefest note, who have discoursed both acutely and truly of the secrets of Nature and hidden Philosophy, Hermes and Morienus Romanus amongst the Ancients are in my judgment of the highest esteem; amongst the Moderns, Count Trevisan, and Raimundus Lullius are in greatest reverence with me; for what that most acute Doctor hath omitted, none almost hath spoken; let a student therefore peruse his works, yea let him often read over his Former Testament, and Codicil, and accept them as a Legacy of very great worth. To these two volumes let him add both his volumes of Practice, out of which works all things desirable may be collected, especially the truth of the First Matter, of the degrees of Fire, and the Regimen of the Whole, wherein the final Work is finished, and those things which our Ancestors so carefully laboured to keep secret. The occult causes of things, and the secret motions of nature, are demonstrated nowhere more clearly and faithfully. Concerning the first and mystical Water of the Philosophers he hath set down few things, yet very pithily.

11. As for that Clear Water sought for by many, found by so few, yet obvious and profitable unto all,

which is the Basis of the Philosophers' Work, a noble Pole, not more famous for his learning than subtilty of wit, who wrote anonymously, but whose name notwithstanding a double Anagram hath betrayed[14], hath in his Novum Lumen Chymicum, Parabola and Ænigma, as also in his Tract on Sulphur, spoken largely and freely enough; yea he hath expressed all things concerning it so plainly, that nothing can be more satisfactory to him that desireth knowledge.

12. Philosophers do usually express themselves more pithily in types and enigmatical figures (as by a mute kind of speech) than by words; see for example, Senior's Table, the Allegorical Pictures of Rosarius, the Pictures of Abraham Judaeus in Flamel, and the drawings of Flamel himself[15]; of the later sort, the rare Emblems of the most learned Michael Maiërus wherein the mysteries of the Ancients are so fully opened, and as new Perspectives they present antiquated truth, and though designed remote from our age yet are near unto our eyes, and are perfectly to be perceived by us.

13. Whosoever affirmeth that the Philosophers' grand Secret is beyond the powers of Nature and Art, he is blind because he ignores the forces of Sol and Luna.

14. As for the matter of their hidden Stone, Philosophers have written diversely; so that very many disagreeing in Words, do nevertheless very well agree in the Thing; nor doth their different speech argue the science ambiguous or false, since the same thing may be expressed with many tongues, by divers expressions, and by a different character, and also one and many things may be spoken of after diverse manners.

15. Let the studious Reader have a care of the manifold significations of words, for by deceitful windings, and doubtful, yea contrary speeches (as it should seem), Philosophers wrote their mysteries, with a desire of veiling and hiding, yet not of sophisticating or destroying the truth; and though their writings abound with ambiguous and equivocal words; yet about none do they more contend than in hiding their Golden Branch.

> Quem tegit omnis
> Lucus; et obscuris claudant convallibus umbræ[16].

> Which all the groves with shadows overcast,
> And gloomy valleys hide.

Nor yieldeth it to any Force, but readily and willingly will follow him, who

> Maternas agnoscit aves,
> . . geminæ cui forte Columbæ
> Ipsa sub ora viri cœlo venere volantes[17].

> Knows Dame Venus Birds .
> And him to whom of Doves a lucky pair
> Sent from above shall hover 'bout his Ear.

16. Whosoever seeketh the Art of perfecting and multiplying imperfect Metals, beyond the nature of Metals, goes in error, for from Metals the Metals are to be derived; even as from Man, Mankind; and from an Ox only, is that species to be obtained.

17. Metals, we must confess, cannot be multiplied by the instinct and labour of Nature only; yet we may affirm that the multiplying virtue is hid in their depths, and manifested itself by the help of Art: In this Work, Nature standeth in need of the aid of Art; and both do make a perfect whole.

18. Perfect Bodies as Sol and Luna are endued with a perfect seed; and therefore under the hard crust of the perfect Metals the Perfect Seed lies hid; and he that knows how to take it out by the Philosophers' Solution, hath entered upon the royal highway; for—

> . In auro
> Semina sunt auri, quamvis abstrusa recedant
> Longius.

> In Gold the seeds of Gold do lie,
> Though buried in Obscurity.

19. Most Philosophers have affirmed that their Kingly Work is wholly composed of Sol and Luna; others have thought good to add Mercury to Sol; some have chosen Sulphur and Mercury; others have attributed no small part in so great a Work to Salt mingled

with the other two. The very same men have professed that this Clear Stone is made of one thing only, sometimes of two, or of three, at other times of four, and of five; and yet though writing so variously upon the same subject, they do nevertheless agree in sense and meaning.

20. Now that (abandoning all blinds) we may write candidly and truly, we hold that this entire Work is perfected by two Bodies only; to wit, by Sol and Luna rightly prepared, for this is the mere generation which is by nature, with the help of Art, wherein the union of male and female doth take place, and from thence an offspring far more noble than the parents is brought forth.

21. Now those Bodies must be taken, which are of an unspotted and incorrupt virginity[19]; such as have life and spirit in them[20]; not extinct as those that are handled by the vulgar; for who can expect life from dead things; and those are called impure which have suffered combination; those dead and extinct which (by the enforcement of the chief Tyrant of the world[21]) have poured out their soul with their blood by Martyrdom; flee then a fraticide from which the most imminent danger in the whole Work is threatened.

22. Now Sol is Masculine, forasmuch as he sendete forth active and energizing seed; Luna is Feminine or Negative and she is called the Matrix of Nature, because she receiveth the sperm, and fostereth it by monthly provision, yet doth Luna not altogether want in positive or active virtue[22].

23. By the name of Luna Philosophers understand not the vulgar Moon, which also may be positive in its operation, and in combining acts a positive part. Let none therefore presume to try the unnatural combination of two positives, neither let him conceive any hope of issue from such association; but he shall join Gabritius to Beia[23], and offer sister to brother infirm union, that from thence he may receive Sol's noble Son.

24. They that hold Sulphur and Mercury to be the First Matter of the Stone, by the name of Sulphur they understand Sol; by Mercury the Philosophic Luna; so (without dissimulation) good Lullius[24] adviseth his friend, that he attempt not to work without Mercury and Luna for Silver; nor without Mercury and Sol for Gold.

25. Let none therefore be deceived by adding a third to two: for Love admitteth not a third; and wedlock is terminated in the number of two; love further extended is not matrimony.

26. Nevertheless Spiritual love polluteth not any virgin; Beia might therefore without fault (before her betrothal to Gabritius) have felt spiritual love, to the end that she might thereby be made more cheerful, more pure, and fitter for union.

27. Procreation is the end of lawful Wedlock. Now that the progeny may be born more vigorous and active, let both the combatants be cleansed from every ill and spot, before they are united in marriage. Let nothing superfluous cleave unto them[25], because from pure seed comes a purified generation, and so the chaste wedlock of Sol and Luna shall be finished when they shall enter into combination, and be conjoined, and Luna shall receive a soul from her husband by this union; from this conjunction a most potent King shall arise, whose father will be Sol and his mother Luna.

28. He that seeks for a physical tincture without Sol and Luna, loseth both his cost and pains: for Sol afforded a most plentiful tincture of redness, and Luna of whiteness, for these two only are called perfect; because they are filled with the substance of purest Sulphur, perfectly clarified by the skill of nature. Let thy Mercury therefore receive a tincture from one or other of these luminaries; for anything must of necessity possess a tincture before it can tinge other bodies.

29. Perfect metals contain in themselves two things which they are able to communicate to the imperfect metals. Tincture and Power of fixation; for pure metals, because they are dyed and fixed with pure

B

Sulphur to wit both white and red, do therefore perfectly tincture and fix, if they be fitly prepared with their proper Sulphur and Arsenic: otherwise they have not strength for multiplying their tincture.

30. Mercury is alone among the imperfect metals, fit to receive the tincture of Sol and Luna in the work of the Philosophers' Stone, and being itself full of tincture can tinge other metals in abundance; yet ought it (before that) to be full of invisible Sulphur, that it may be the more coloured with the visible tincture of perfect bodies, and so repay with sufficient Usury.

31. Now the whole tribe of Philosophers do much assert and work mightily to extract Tincture out of gold: for they believe that Tincture can be separated from Sol, and being separated increases in virtue but—

> Spes tandem Agricolas vanis eludit aristis.
>
> Vain hope, at last the hungry Plough-man cheats
> With empty husks, instead of lusty meats.

For it is impossible that Sol's Tincture can at all be severed from his natural body, since there can be no elementary body made up by nature more perfect than gold, the perfection whereof proceedeth from the strong and inseparable union of pure colouring Sulphur with Mercury; both of them being admirably pre-disposed thereunto by Nature; whose true separation nature denieth unto Art. But if any liquor remaining be extracted (by the violence of fire or waters) from the Sun, it is to be reputed a part of the body made liquid or dissolved by force. For the tincture followeth its body, and is never separated from it. That is a delusion of this Art, which is unknown to many Artificers themselves.

32. Nevertheless it may be granted, that Tincture may be separable from its body, yet (we must confess) it cannot be separated without the corruption of the tincture: as when Artists offer violence to the gold destroying by fire, or use Aqua fortis, thus rather cor-

roding than dissolving. The body therefore if despoiled of its Tincture and Golden Fleece, must needs grow base, and as an unprofitable heap turn to the damage of its Artificer, and the Tincture thus corrupted can only have a weaker operation.

33. Let Alchymists in the next place cast their Tincture into Mercury, or into any other imperfect body, and as strongly conjoin both of them as their Art will permit; yet shall they fail of their hopes in two ways. First, because the Tincture will neither penetrate nor colour beyond Nature's weight and strength; and therefore no gain will accrue from thence to recompense the expense and countervail the loss of the body spoiled, and thus of no value; so—

> Cum labor in damno est, crescit mortalis egestas.
>
> Want is poor mortal's wages, when his toil
> Produces only loss of pain and oil.

Lastly, that debased Tincture applied to another body will not give that perfect fixation and permanency required to endure a strong trial, and resist searching Saturn.

34. Let them therefore that are desirous of Alchemy, and have hitherto followed impostors and mountebanks, found a retreat, spare no time nor cost, and give their minds to a work truly Philosophical, lest the Phrygians be wise too late, and at length be compelled to cry out with the prophet, "*Strangers have devoured his strength.*"[26]

35. In the Philosophers' work more time and toil than cost is expended: for he that hath convenient matter, need be at little expense; besides, those that hunt after great store of money, and place their chief end in wealth, they trust more to their riches, than their own art. Let, therefore, the too credulous tyro beware of pilfering pickpockets, for while they promise golden mountains, they lay in wait for gold; they demand bright gold (*viz.*, money beforehand), because they walk in evil and darkness.

36. As those that sail between Scylla and Charybdis[27]

are in danger from both sides: unto no less hazard are they subject who pursuing the prize of the Golden fleece are carried between the uncertain Rocks of the Sulphur and Mercury of the Philosophers. The more acute students by their constant reading of grave and credible Authors, and by the radiant sunlight, have attained unto the knowledge of Sulphur, but are at a stand at the entrance of their search for the Philosophers' Mercury; for Writers have twisted it with so many windings and meanderings, involved it with so many equivocal names, that it may be sooner met with by the force of the Seeker's intuition, than be found by reason or toil.

37. That Philosophers might the deeper hide their Mercury in darkness, they have made it manifold, and placed their Mercury (yet diversely) in every part and in the forefront of their work, nor will he attain unto a perfect knowledge thereof, who shall be ignorant of *any* part of the Work.

38. Philosophers have acknowledged their Mercury to be threefold; to wit, after the absolute preparation of the First degree, the Philosophical sublimation, for then they call it "Their Mercury," and "Mercury Sublimated."

39. Again, in the Second preparation, that which by Authors is styled the First (because they omit the First) Sol being now made crude again,[28] and resolved into his first matter, is called the Mercury of such like bodies, or the Philosophers' Mercury; then the matter is called Rebis,[29] Chaos, or the Whole World, wherein are all things necessary to the Work, because that only is sufficient to perfect the Stone.

40. Thirdly, the Philosophers do sometimes call Perfect Elixir and Colouring Medicine—Their Mercury, though improperly; for the name of Mercury doth only properly agree with that which is volatile; besides that which is sublimated in every region of the work, they call Mercury: but Elixir—that which is most fixed cannot have the simple name of Mercury; and therefore

they have styled it " Their Mercury" to differentiate it from that which is volatile. A straight way is only laid down for some to find out and discern so many Mercuries of the Philosophers, for those only—

>—Quos aequus amavit
> Jupiter, aut ardens evexit ad aethera virtus.[30]

>—Whom just and mighty Jove
> Advanceth by the strength of love;
> Or such who brave heroic fire,
> Makes from dull Earth to Heaven aspire.

41. The Elixir is called the Philosophers' Mercury for the likeness and great conformity it hath with heavenly Mercury; for to this, being devoid of elementary qualities, heaven is believed to be most propitious; and that changeable Proteus[31] puts on and increaseth the genius and nature of other Planets, by reason of opposition, conjunction, and aspect. In like manner this uncertain Elixir worketh, for being restricted to no proper quality, it embraceth the quality and disposition of the thing wherewith it is mixed, and wonderfully multiplieth the virtues and qualities thereof.

42. In the Philosophical sublimation or first preparation of Mercury, Herculean labour must be undergone by the workman; for Jason had in vain attempted his expedition to Colchos without Alcides.

> Alter in auratam nota de vertice pellem
> Principium velut ostendit, quod sumere possis;
> Alter onus quantum subeas.[32]

> One from on high a Golden Fleece displays
> Which shews the Entrance, another says
> How hard a task you'll find.

For the entrance is warded by horned beasts, which drive away those that approach rashly thereunto, to their great hurt; only the ensigns of Diana[33] and the Doves of Venus are able to assuage their fierceness, if the fates favour the attempt.

43. The Natural quality of Philosophical Earth and

the tillage thereof, seems to be touched upon by the poet in this verse;

> Pingue solum primis ex templo a mensibus anni
> Fortes invertant Tauri,
>   Tunc Zephyro putris se gleba resolvit.[34]

> Let sturdy oxen when the year begins
> Plough up the fertile soil,
> For Zephyrus then destroys the sodden clods.

44. He that calleth the Philosophers' Luna or their Mercury, the common Mercury, doth wittingly deceive, or is deceived himself; so the writings of Geber teach us, that the Philosophers' Mercury is Argent vive, yet not of the common sort, but extracted out of it by the Philosophers' skill.[35]

45. The Philosophers' Mercury is not Argent vive in its proper nature, nor in its whole substance, but is only the middle and pure substance thereof, which thence hath taken its origin and has been made by it. This opinion of the grand Philosophers is founded on experience.

46. The Philosophers' Mercury hath divers names, sometimes it is called Earth; sometimes Water, when viewed from a diverse aspect; because it naturally ariseth from them both. The earth is subtle, white and sulphurous, in which the elements are fixed and the philosophical gold is sown; the water is the water of life, burning, permanent, most clear, called the water of gold and silver; but this Mercury, because it hath in it Sulphur of its own, which is multiplied by art, deserves to be called the Sulphur of Argent vive. Last of all, the most precious substance is Venus, the ancient Hermaphrodite, glorious in its double sex.

47. This Argent vive is partly natural, partly unnatural; its intrinsic and occult part hath its root in nature, and this cannot be drawn forth unless it be by some precedent cleansing, and industrious sublimation; its extrinsic part is preternatural and accidental. Separate, therefore, the clean from the unclean, the sub-

stance from the accidents, and make that which is hid, manifest, by the course of nature; otherwise you make no further progress, for this is the foundation of the whole work and of nature.

48. That dry and most precious liquor doth constitute the radical moisture of metals, wherefore by some of the ancients it is called Glass; for glass is extracted out of the radical moisture closely inherent in ashes which offer resistance, except to the hottest flame; notwithstanding our inmost or central Mercury discovers itself by the most gentle and kindly (though a little more tedious) fire of nature.

49. Some have sought for the latent Philosophical earth by Calcination, others by Sublimation; many among glass, and some few between vitriol and salt, even as among their natural vessels; others enjoin you to sublime it out of lime and glass. But we have learned of the Prophet that "*In the beginning God created the Heaven and the Earth, and the Earth was without form and void, and darkness was upon the face of the Deep, and the spirit of God moved upon the Waters, and God said, Let there be Light, and there was Light; and God saw the Light that it was good, and he divided the light from the darkness, etc.*"[36] *Joseph's* blessing spoken of by the same Prophet will be sufficient to a wise man. "*Blessed of the Lord be his Land, for the Apples of Heaven, for the dew, and for the Deep that liveth beneath: for the Apples of fruit both of sun and moon, for the top of the ancient mountains, for the Apples of the everlasting hills, etc.,*"[37] pray the Lord from the bottom of thy heart (my son) that he would bestow upon Thee a portion of this blessed earth.

50. Argent vive is so defiled by original sin,[38] that it floweth with a double infection; the first it hath contracted from the polluted Earth, which hath mixed itself therewith in the generation of Argent vive, and by congelation hath cleaved thereunto; the second borders upon the dropsy and is the corruption of intercutal[39] Water, proceeding from thick and impure water; mixed with the clear, which nature was not able to squeeze

out and separate by constriction; but because it is extrinsic, it flies off with a gentle heat. The Mercury's leprosy infesting the body, is not of its root and substance, but accidental, and therefore separable from it; the earthly part is wiped off by a warm wet Bath and the Laver of nature; the watery part is taken away by a dry bath with that gentle fire suitable to generation. And thus by a threefold washing and cleansing the Dragon putteth off his old scales and ugly skin is renewed in beauty.

51. The Philosophical sublimation of Mercury is completed by two processes; namely by removing things superfluous from it, and by introducing things which are wanting. In superfluities are the external accidents, which in the dark sphere of Saturn do make cloudy glittering Jupiter. Separate therefore the leaden colour of Saturn which cometh up out of the water until Jupiter's purple Star[40] smile upon thee. Add hereunto the Sulphur of nature, whose grain and Ferment it hath in itself, so much as sufficeth it; but see that it be sufficient for other things also. Multiply therefore that invisible Sulphur of the Philosophers until the Virgin's milk come forth: and so the First Gate is opened unto thee.

52. The entrance of the Philosophers' garden is kept by the Hesperian Dragon, which being put aside, a Fountain of the clearest water proceeding from a sevenfold spring floweth forth on every side of the entrance of the garden; wherein make the Dragon drink thrice the magical number of Seven, until having drunk he put off his hideous garments; then may the divine powers of light-bringing Venus and horned Diana, be propitious unto thee.

53. Three kinds of most beautiful flowers are to be sought, and may be found in this Garden of the wise:[41] Damask-coloured Violets, the milk-white Lily, and the purple and immortal flower of love, the Amaranth. Not far from that fountain at the entrance, fresh Violets do first salute thee, which being watered by streams from

the great golden river, they put on the most delicate colour of the dark Sapphire; then Sol will give thee a sign. Thou shall not sever such precious flowers from their roots until thou make the Stone; for the fresh ones cropped off have more juice and tincture; and then pick them carefully with a gentle and discreet hand; if the Fates frown not, this will easily follow, and one White flower being plucked, the other Golden one will not be wanting; let the Lily and the Amaranth succeed with still greater care and longer labour.

54. Philosophers have their sea also, wherein small fishes plump and shining with silver scales are generated; which he that shall entangle, and take by a fine and small net shall be accounted a most expert fisherman.

55. The Philosophers' Stone is found in the oldest mountains, and flows from everlasting brooks; those mountains are of silver, and the brooks are e'en of gold: from thence gold and silver and all the treasures of Kings are produced.

56. Whosoever is minded to obtain the Philosophers' Stone, let him resolve to take a long peregrination, for it is necessary that he go to see both the Indies, that from thence he may bring the most precious gems and the purest gold.

57. Philosophers extract their stone out of seven stones, the two chief whereof are of a diverse nature and efficacy; the one infuseth invisible Sulphur, the other spiritual Mercury; that one induceth heat and dryness, and this one cold and moisture: thus by their help, the strength of the elements is multiplied in the Stone; the former is found in the Eastern coast, the latter in the Western: both of them have the power of colouring and multiplying, and unless the Stone shall take its first Tincture from them it will neither colour nor multiply.

58. Recipe then the Winged Virgin very well washed and cleansed, impregnated by the spiritual seed of the first male, and fecundated in the permanent glory of her untouched virginity, she will be discovered by her

cheeks dyed with a blushing colour; join her to the second, by whose seed she shall conceive again and shall in time bring forth a reverend off-spring of double sex, from whence an immortal Race of most potent Kings shall gloriously arise.

59. Keep up and couple the Eagle and Lion[42] well cleansed in their transparent cloister, the entry door being shut and watched, lest their breath go out, or the air without do privily get in. The Eagle shall snap up and devour the Lion in this combination; afterwards being affected with a long sleep, and a dropsy occasioned by a foul stomach, she shall be changed by a wonderful metamorphosis into a coal black Crow, which shall begin to fly with wings stretched out, and by his flight shall bring down water from the clouds, until being often moistened, he put off his wings of his own accord, and falling down again he be changed into a most White Swan. Those that are ignorant of the causes of things may wonder with astonishment when they consider that the world is nothing but a continual Metamorphosis; they may marvel that the seeds of things perfectly digested should end in greatest whiteness. Let the Philosopher imitate Nature in his work.

60. Nature proceedeth thus in making and perfecting her works, that from an inchoate generation it may bring a thing by divers means, as it were by degrees, to the ultimate term of perfection: she therefore attaineth her end by little and little, not by leaps; confining and including her work between two extremes; distinct and severed as by spaces. The practice of Philosophy, which is the imitator of Nature, ought not to decline from the way and example of Nature in its working and direction to find out its happy stone, for whatsoever is without the bounds of Nature is either an error or is near one.

61. The extremes of the Stone are natural Argent vive and perfect Elixir: the middle parts which lie between, by help whereof the work goes on, are of three sorts; for they either belong unto matter, or operations,

or demonstrative signs: the whole work is perfected by these extremes and means.

62. The material means of the Stone are of divers kinds, for some are extracted out of others successively: The first are Mercury Philosophically sublimated, and perfect metals, which although they be extreme in the work of nature, yet in the Philosophical work they supply the place of means: of the former the seconds are produced; namely the four elements, which again are circulated and fixed: of the seconds, the third is produced, to wit, Sulphur, the multiplication whereof doth terminate the first work: the fourth and last means are leaven or ointments[43] weighed with the mixture of the things aforesaid, successively produced in the work of the Elixir. By the right ordering of the things aforesaid, the perfect Elixir is finished, which is the last term of the whole work, wherein the Philosophers' Stone resteth as in its centre, the multiplication whereof is nothing else than a short repetition of the previous operations.

63. The operative means (which are also called the Keys of the Work) are four: the first is Solution or Liquefaction; the second is Ablution; the third Reduction; the fourth Fixation. By Liquefaction bodies return into their first form, things concocted are made raw again, and the combination between the position and negative is effected, from whence the Crow is generated: lastly the Stone is divided into four confused elements, which happeneth by the retrogradation of the Luminaries. The Ablution teacheth how to make the Crow white, and to create the Jupiter of Saturn, which is done by the conversion of the Body into Spirit. The Office of Reduction is to restore the soul to the stone exanimated, and to nourish it with dew and spiritual Milk, until it shall attain unto perfect strength. In both these latter operations the Dragon rageth against himself, and by devouring his tail, doth wholly exhaust himself, and at length is turned into the Stone. Lastly, the operation of the Fixation fixeth both the White and the Red Sulphurs upon

their fixed body, by the mediation of the spiritual tincture; it decocteth the Leaven or Ferment by degrees, ripeneth things unripe, and sweeteneth the bitter. In fine, by penetrating and tincturing the flowing Elixir it generateth, perfecteth, and lastly, raiseth it up to the height of sublimity.

64. The Means or demonstrative signs are Colours, successively and orderly affecting the matter and its affections and demonstrative passions, whereof there are three special ones (as critical) to be noted; to these some add a Fourth. The first is black, which is called the Crow's head, because of its extreme blackness, whose crepusculum[44] sheweth the beginning of the action of the fire of nature and solution, and the blackest midnight sheweth the perfection of liquefaction, and confusion of the elements. Then the grain putrefies and is corrupted, that it may be the more apt for generation. The white colour succeedeth the black, wherein is given the perfection of the first degree, and of the White Sulphur. This is called the blessed stone; this Earth is white and foliated, wherein Philosophers do sow their gold. The third is Orange colour, which is produced in the passage of the white to the red, as the middle, and being mixed of both is as the dawn with his saffron hair, a forerunner of the Sun. The fourth colour is Ruddy and Sanguine, which is extracted from the white fire only. Now because whiteness is easily altered by any other colour before day it quickly faileth of its candour. But the deep redness of the Sun perfecteth the work of Sulphur, which is called the Sperm of the male, the fire of the Stone, the King's Crown, and the Son of Sol, wherein the first labour of the workman resteth.

65. Besides these decretory signs which firmly inhere in the matter, and shew its essential mutations, almost infinite colours appear, and shew themselves in vapours, as the Rainbow in the clouds, which quickly pass away and are expelled by those that succeed, more affecting the air than the earth: the operator must have a gentle

care of them, because they are not permanent, and proceed not from the intrinsic disposition of the matter, but from the fire painting and fashioning everything after its pleasure, or casually by heat in slight moisture.

66. Of the strange colours, some appearing out of time, give an ill omen to the work: such as the blackness renewed; for the Crow's young ones having once left their nest are never to be suffered to return. Too hasty Redness; for this once, and in the end only, gives a certain hope of the harvest; if therefore the matter become red too soon it is an argument of the greatest aridity, not without great danger, whtch can only be averted by Heaven alone forthwith bestowing a shower upon it.

67. The Stone is exalted by successive digestions, as by degrees, and at length attaineth to perfection. Now four Digestions agreeable to the four abovesaid Operations or Governments do complete the whole work, the author whereof is the fire, which makes the difference between them.

68. The first digestion operateth the solution of the Body, whereby comes the first conjunction of male and female, the commixtion of both seeds, putrefaction, the resolution of the elements into homogeneous water, the eclipse of the Sun and Moon in the head of the Dragon, and lastly it bringeth back the whole World into its ancient Chaos, and dark abyss. This first digestion is as in the stomach, of a melon colour and weak, more fit for corruption than generation.

69. In the second digestion the Spirit of the Lord walketh upon the waters; the light begins to appear, and a separation of waters from the waters occurs; Sol and Luna are renewed; the elements are extracted out of the chaos, that being perfectly mixed in Spirit they may constitute a new world; a new Heaven and new Earth are made; and lastly all bodies become spiritual. The Crow's young ones changing their feathers begin to pass into Doves; the Eagle and Lion embrace one another in an

eternal League of amity. And this generation of the World is made by the fiery Spirit descending in the form of Water, and wiping away Original sin; for the Philosophers' Water is Fire, which is moved by the exciting heat of a Bath. But see that the separation of Waters be done in Weight and Measure, lest those things that remain under Heaven be drowned under the Earth, or those things that are snatched up above the Heaven, be too much destitute of aridity.

> Hic, sterilem exiguus ne deferat humor arenam,[45]
> Here let slight moisture leave a barren Soil.

70. The third digestion of the newly generated Earth drinketh up the dewy Milk, and all the spiritual virtues of the quintessence, and fasteneth the quickening Soul to the body by the Spirit's mediation. Then the Earth layeth up a great Treasure in itself, and is made like the coruscating Moon, afterwards like to the ruddy Sun; the former is called the Earth of the Moon, the latter the Earth of the Sun; for both of them are begot of the copulation of them both; neither of them any longer feareth the pains of the Fire, because both want all spots; for they have been often cleansed from sin by fire, and have suffered great Martyrdom, until all the Elements are turned downwards.

71. The Fourth digestion consummateth all the Mysteries of the World, and the Earth being turned into most excellent leaven, it leaveneth all imperfect bodies because it hath before passed into the heavenly nature of quintessence. The virtue thereof flowing from the Spirit of the Universe is a present Panacea and universal medicine for all the diseases of all creatures. The digestions of the first work being repeated will open to thee the Philosophers' secret Furnace. Be right in thy works, that thou mayest find God favourable, otherwise the ploughing of the Earth will be in vain; Nor

> Illa seges demum votis respondet avari[46]
> Agricolæ—

> Will the expected Harvest e'er requite
> The greedy husbandman.

72. The whole Progress of the Philosophers' work is nothing but Solution and Congelation; the Solution of the body, and Congelation of the Spirit; nevertheless there is but one operation of both: the fixed and volatile are perfectly mixed and united in the Spirit, which cannot be done unless the fixed body be first made soluble and volatile. By reduction is the volatile body fixed into a permanent body, and volatile nature doth at last change into a fixed one, as the fixed nature had before passed into volatile. Now so long as the Natures were confused in the Spirit, that mixed spirit keeps a middle Nature between Body and Spirit, Fixed and Volatile.

73. The generation of the Stone is made after the pattern of the Creation of the World; for it is necessary, that it have its Chaos and First matter, wherein the confused Elements do fluctuate, until they be separated by the fiery Spirit; they being separated, the Light Elements are carried upwards, and the heavy ones downwards: the light arising, darkness retreats: the waters are gathered into one place and the dry land appears. At length the two great Luminaries arise, and mineral, vegetable and animal are produced in the Philosophers' Earth.

74. God created Adam out of the mud of the Earth, wherein were inherent the virtues of all the Elements, of the Earth and Water especially, which do more constitute the sensible and corporeal heap: Into this Mass God breathed the breath of Life, and enlivened it with the Sun of the Holy Spirit. He gave Eve for a Wife to Adam, and blessing them he gave unto them a Precept and the Faculty of multiplication. The generation of the Philosophers' Stone, is not unlike the Creation of Adam, for the Mud was made of a terrestrial and ponderous Body dissolved by Water, which deserved the excellent name of Terra Adamica, wherein

all the virtues and qualities of the Elements are placed. At length the heavenly Soul is infused thereinto by the medium of the Quintessence and Solar influx, and by the Benediction and Dew of Heaven; the virtue of multiplying *ad infinitum* by the intervening copulation of both sexes is given it.

75. The chief secret of this work consisteth in the manner of working, which is wholly employed about the Elements: for the matter of the Stone passeth from one Nature into another, the Elements are successively extracted, and by turns obtain dominion; everything is agitated by the circles of *humidum* and *siccum*,[47] until all things be turned downwards, and there rest.

76. In the work of the Stone the other Elements are circulated in the figure of Water, for the Earth is resolved into Water, wherein are the rest of the Elements; the Water is Sublimated into Vapour, Vapour retreats into Water, and so by an unwearied circle, is the Water moved, until it abide fixed downwards; now *that* being fixed, all the elements are fixed. Thus into it they are resolved, by it they are extracted, with it they live and die; the Earth is the Tomb, and last end of all.

77. The order of Nature requireth that every generation begin from *humidum* and *in humidum*. In the Philosophers' work, Nature is to be reduced into order,[48] that so the matter of the Stone which is terrestrial, compact and dry, in the first place may be dissolved and flow into the Element of Water next unto it, and then Saturn will be generated of Sol.

78. The Air succeeds the Water, drawn about by seven circles or revolutions, which is wheeled about with so many circles and reductions, until it be fixed downwards, and Saturn being expelled, Jupiter may receive the Sceptre and Government of the Kingdom, by whose coming the Philosophers' Infant is formed, nourished in the womb, and at length is born; resembling the splendour of Luna in her beautiful and serene countenance.

79. The Fire executes the courses of the Nature of

the Elements, extreme Fire assisting it; of the hidden is made the manifest; the Saffron dyeth the Lily; Redness possesseth the cheeks of the blushing Child now made stronger. A Crown is prepared for him against the time of his Reign. This is the consummation of the first work, and the perfect rotation of the Elements, the sign whereof is, when they are all terminated in Siccum, and the body void of Spirit lieth down, wanting pulse and motion; and thus all the Elements are finally resolved into Terra.

80. Fire placed in the Stone is Nature's Prince, Sol's Son and Vicar, moving and digesting matter and perfecting all things therein, if it shall attain its liberty, for it lieth weak under a hard bark; procure therefore its freedom that it may succour thee freely; but beware that thou urge it not above measure, for being impatient of tyranny it may become a fugitive, no hope of return being left unto thee; call it back therefore by courteous words, and keep it prudently.

81. The first mover of nature is External Fire, the Moderator of Internal Fire, and of the whole Work; Let the Philosopher therefore very well understand the government thereof, and observe its degrees and points; for from thence the welfare or ruin of the work dependeth. Thus Art helpeth Nature, and the Philosopher is the Minister of both.

82. By these two Instruments of Art and Nature, the Stone lifteth itself up from Earth to Heaven with great ingenuity, and slideth from Heaven to Earth, because the Earth is its Nurse, and being carried in the womb of the wind, it receiveth the force of the Superiors and Inferiors.

83. The Circulation of the Elements is performed by a double Whorl, by the greater or extended, and the less or contracted. The Whorl extended fixeth all the Elements of the Earth, and its circle is not finished unless the work of Sulphur be perfected. The revolution of the minor Whorl is terminated by the extraction and preparation of every Element. Now in this Whorl

there are three Circles placed, which always and variously move the Matter, by an Erratic and Intricate Motion, and do often (seven times at least) drive about every Element, in order succeeding one another, and so agreeable, that if one shall be wanting the labour of the rest is made void. These Circulations are Nature's Instruments, whereby the Elements are prepared. Let the Philosopher therefore consider the progress of Nature in the Physical Tract[49], more fully described for this very end.

84. Every Circle hath its proper Motion, for all the Motions of the Circles are conversant about the subject of *Humidum* and *Siccum*, and are so concatenated that they produce the one operation, and one only consent of Nature: two of them are opposite, both in respect of their causes and the effects; for one moveth upwards, drying by heat; another downwards, moistening by cold; a third carrying the form of rest and sleep by digesting, induceth the cessation of both in greatest moderation.

85. Of the three Circles, the first is Evacuation, the labour of which is in extracting the superfluous *Humidum*, and also in separating the pure, clean and subtle, from the gross and terrestrial dregs. Now the greatest danger is found in the motion of this Circle, because it hath to do with things Spiritual and makes Nature plentiful.

86. Two things are chiefly to be taken heed of in moving this Circle; first, that it be not moved too intensely; the other, that it be not moved for too long a time. Motion accelerated raiseth confusion in the matter, so that the gross, impure and undigested part may fly out together with the pure and subtle, and the Body undissolved be mixed with the Spirit, together with that which is dissolved. With this precipitated motion the Heavenly and Terrestrial Natures are confounded, and the Spirit of the Quintessence, corrupted by the admixture of Earth is made dull and invalid. By too long a motion the Earth is too much evacuated

of its Spirit, and is made so languishing, dry and destitute of Spirit, that it cannot easily be restored and recalled to its Temperament. Either error burneth up the Tincture, or turneth it into flight.

87. The Second Circle is Restoration; whose office is to restore strength to the gasping and debilitated body by Potion. The former Circle was the Organ of sweat and labour, but this of restoration and consolation. The action of this is employed in the grinding and mollifying the Earth (Potter-like), that it may be the better mixed.

88. The motion of this Circle must be lighter than that of the former, especially in the beginning of its Revolution, lest the Crow's young ones be drowned in nest by a large flood, and the growing world be drowned by a deluge. This is the Weigher and Assayer of Measures, for it distributeth Water by Geometrical Precepts. There is usually no greater Secret found in the whole practice of the Work than the firm and justly weighed Motion of this Circle; for it informeth the Philosophers' Infant and inspireth Soul and Life into him.

89. The Laws of this Circle's motions are, that it run about gently: and by little and little, and sparingly let forth itself, lest that by making haste it fall from its measure, and the Fire inherent be overwhelmed with the Waters, the Architect of the Work grow dull, or also be extinguished: that meat and drink be administered by turns, to the end there may be a better Digestion made, and the best temperament of *Humidum* and *Siccum*; for the indissoluble colligation of them both is the End and Scope of the Work. Furthermore see, that you add so much by Watering, as shall be found wanting in assaying, that Restoration may restore so much of the lost strength by corroborating, as Evacuation hath taken away by debilitating.

90. Digestion, the last Circle, acteth with silent and insensible Motion; and therefore it is said by Philosophers, that it is made in a secret furnace; it decocteth

the Nutriment received, and converteth it into the Homogeneous parts of the body. Moreover, it is called Putrefaction; because as meat is corrupted in the Stomach before it passeth into Blood and similar parts; so this operation breaketh the Aliment with a concocting and Stomach heat and in a manner makes it to putrefy that it may be the better Fixed, and changed from a Mecurial into a Sulphurous Nature. Again, it is called Inhumation,[50] because by it the Spirit is inhumated, as a dead man buried in the ground. But because it goeth most slowly, it therefore needeth a longer time. The two former Circles do labour especially in dissolving, this in congealing although all of them work in both ways.

91. The Laws of this Circle are, that it be moved by the Feverish and most gentle heat of Dung, lest that the things volatile fly out, and the Spirit be troubled at the time of its strictest Conjunction with the Body, for then the business is perfected in the greatest tranquillity and ease; therefore we must especially beware lest the Earth be moved by any Winds or Showers. Lastly, as this third Circle may always succeed the second straightways and in due order, as the second the first: so by interrupted works and by course those three erratic Circles do complete one entire circulation, which often reiterated doth at length turn all things into Earth, and makes similarity between opposites.

92. Nature useth Fire, so also doth Art after its example, as an Instrument and Mallet in cutting out its works. In both operations therefore Fire is Master and Perfector. Wherefore the knowledge of Fire is most necessary for a Philosopher, without which as another Ixion (condemned to labour in vain) he shall turn about the Whorl of Nature to no purpose.

93. The name Fire is Equivocal amongst Philosophers; for sometimes it is used by Metonymy for heat; and so there be as many fires as heats. In the Generation of Metals and Vegetables Nature acknowledgeth a Three-fold Fire; to wit, Celestial, Terrestrial and

Innate. The First flows from Sol as its Fountain into the Bosom of the Earth; it stirreth up Fumes, or Mercurial and Sulphurous vapours, of which the Metals are created, and mixeth itself amongst them; it stirreth up that torpid fire which is placed in the seeds of Vegetables, and addeth fresh sparks unto it, as a spur to vegetation. The Second lurketh in the bowels of the Earth, by the Impulse and action whereof the Subterraneous vapours are driven upwards as through pores and pipes, and thrusts outwards from the Centre towards the surface of the Earth, both for the composition of Metals, where the Earth swelleth up, as also for the production of Vegetables, by putrefying their seeds, by softening and preparing them for generation. The third Fire, *viz.*, Innate is also indeed Solar; it is generated of a vapid smoke of Metals, and also being infused with the monthly provision grows together with the humid matter, and is retained as in a Prison; or more truly, as form is conjoined with the mixed body; it firmly inhereth in the seeds of Vegetables, until being solicited by the point of its Father's rays it be called out, then Motion intrinsically moveth and informeth the matter, and becomes the Moulder and Dispenser of the whole Mixture. In the generation of Animals, Celestial Fire doth insensibly co-operate with the Animal, for it is the first Agent in Nature; for the heat of the female answereth to Terrestrial Fire; when the Seed putrefies, this warmth prepareth it. For truly the Fire is implanted in the Seed; then the Son of Sol disposeth of the matter, and being disposed, he informeth it.

94. Philosophers have observed a three-fold Fire in the matter of their work, Natural, Unnatural, and Contra-Natural. The Natural they call the Fiery Celestial Spirit Innate, kept in the profundity of matter, and most strictly bound unto it, which by the sluggish strength of metal grows dull, until being stirred up and freed by the Philosophers' discretion and external heat, it shall have obtained a faculty of moving its body dissolved, and so it may inform its humid matter, by Un-

folding Penetration, Dilatation and Congelation. In every mixed body Natural Fire is the Principle of Heat and Motion. Unnatural Fire they name that which being procured and coming from without is introduced into the matter artificially; that it may increase and multiply the strength of the natural heat. The Fire Contrary to Nature they call that which putrefieth the Compositum, and corrupteth the temperament of Nature. It is imperfect, because being too weak for generation, it is not carried beyond the bounds of corruption: such is the Fire or heat of the menstruum: yet it hath the name improperly of Fire against Nature, because in a manner it is according to Nature, for although it destroys the specific form, and corrupteth the matter, yet it disposeth it for reproduction.

95. It is more credible nevertheless that the corrupting Fire, called Fire against Nature, is not different from the Innate, but the first degree of it, for the order of nature requireth, that Corruption should precede Generation: the fire therefore that is innate, agreeable to the Law of Nature, performeth both, by exciting both successively in the matter: the first of corruption more gentle stirred up by feeble heat to mollify and prepare the body: the other of generation more forcible, moved by a more vehement heat, to animate and fully inform the Elementary body disposed of by the former. A double Motion doth therefore proceed from a double degree of heat of the same fire; neither is it to be accounted a double Fire, for far better may the name of " Fire contrary to Nature " be given to violent and destructive fire.

96. Unnatural Fire is converted into Natural or Innate Fire by successive degrees of Digestion, and increaseth and multiplieth it. Now the whole secret consisteth in the multiplication of Natural Fire, which of itself is not able to Work above its proper strength, nor communicate a perfect Tincture to imperfect Bodies; for although it be sufficient to itself, yet hath it not any further power; but being multiplied by the unnatural,

which most aboundeth with the virtue of multiplying, doth act far more powerfully, and reacheth itself beyond the bounds of Nature—colouring strange and imperfect bodies, and perfecting them, because of its plentiful Tincture, and the abstruse Treasure of multiplied Fire.

97. Philosophers call their Water, Fire, because it is most hot, and indued with a Fiery Spirit; again, Water is called Fire by them, because it burneth the bodies of perfect Metals more than common fire doth, for it perfectly dissolveth them, whereas they resist our Fire, and will not suffer themselves to be dissolved by it; for this cause it is also called Burning Water. Now that Fire of Tincture is hid in the belly of the Water, and manifests itself by a double effect, *viz.*, of the body's Solution and Multiplication.

98. Nature useth a double Fire in the Work of generation, Intrinsic and Extrinsic; the former being placed in the seeds and mixtures of things, is hid in their Centre; and as a principle of Motion and Life doth move and quicken the body. But the latter, Extrinsic, whether it be poured down from Heaven or Earth, raiseth the former, as drowned with sleep, and compels it to action; for the vital sparks implanted in the seeds stand in need of an external motor, that they may be moved and act.

99. It is even so in the Philosophers' work; for the matter of the Stone possesseth his Interior Fire, which is partly Innate, partly also is added by the Philosophers' Art, for those are united and come inward together, because they are homogeneous: the internal standeth in need of the external, which the Philosopher administereth according to the Precepts of Art and Nature; this compelleth the former to move. These Fires are as two Wheels, whereof the hidden one being moved by the visible one, it is moved sooner or later; and thus Art helpeth Nature.

100. The Internal Fire is the middle agent between the Motor and the Matter; whence it is, that as it is

moved by that, it moveth this; and if so be it shall be driven intensely or remissly, it will work after the same manner in the matter. The Information of the whole Work dependeth of the measure of External Fire.

101. He that is ignorant of the degrees and points of external Fire, let him not start upon the Philosophical Work; for he will never obtain light out of darkness, unless the heats pass through their middle stages, like the Elements, whose Extremes are not converted, but only their Means.

102. Because the whole work consisteth in Separation and perfect Preparation of the Four Elements, therefore so many grades of Fire are necessary thereunto; for every Element is extracted by the degree of Fire proper to it.

103. The four grades of Heat are called the heat of the Water Bath, the heat of Ashes, of Coals, and of Flame, which is also called "Optetic:" every grade hath its degrees, two at least, sometimes three; for heat is to be moved slowly and by degrees, whether it be increased or decreased; so that Matter, after Nature's example, may go on by degrees and willingly unto formation and completion; for nothing is so strange to Nature as that which is violent. Let the Philosopher opound for his consideration the gentle access and recess of the Sun, whose Light and Lamp bestoweth its heat to the things of the world, according to the times and Laws of the Universe, and so bestoweth a certain temperament upon them.

104. The first degree of the Bath of Heat is called the heat of a Fever; the second, of Dung. The first degree of the second grade is the simple heat of Ashes, the second is the heat of Sand. Now the degrees of Fire, Coals and Flame want a proper Name, but they are distinguished by the operation of the intellect, according to their intensity.

105. Three grades only of Fire are sometimes found amongst Philosophers, *viz.*, the Water Bath, of Ashes and of Flame: which latter comprehendeth the Fire of

Coals and of Flame: the Heat of Dung is sometimes distinguished from the Heat of the Bath in degree. Thus for the most part Authors do involve the light in darkness, by the various expressions of the Philosophers' Fire; for the knowledge thereof is accounted amongst their chief secrets.

106. In the White Work, because three Elements only are extracted, Three degrees of Fire do suffice; the last, to wit the "Optetic," is reserved for the Fourth Element, which finisheth the Red Work. By the first degree the eclipse of Sol and Luna is made; by the second the light of Luna begins to be restored; by the third Luna attaineth unto the fulness of her splendour; and by the fourth Sol is exalted into the highest apex of his glory. Now in every part the Fire is administered according to the rules of Geometry; so that the Agent may answer to the disposition of the Patient, and their strength be equally poised betwixt themselves.

107. Philosophers have very much insisted upon secrecy in regard to their Fire, they scarce have been bold to describe it, but shew it rather by a description of its qualities and properties, than by its name: as that it is called Airy Fire, Vaporous, Humid and Dry, Clear or Star-like; because it may easily by degrees be increased or remitted as the Artificer pleaseth. He that desireth more of the knowledge of Fire may be satisfied by the Works of Lullius[51], who hath opened the Secrets of Practice to worthy minds candidly.

108. Of the conflict of the Eagle and the Lion also they write diversely, because the Lion is the strongest animal, and therefore it is necessary that more Eagles act together (three at least, or more, even to ten) to conquer him: the fewer they are, the greater the contention, and the slower the Victory; but the more Eagles, the shorter the Battle, and the plundering of the Lion will more readily follow. The happier number of seven Eagles may be taken out of Lullius, or of nine out of Senior.[52]

109. The Vessel wherein Philosophers decoct their

work is twofold; the one of Nature, the other of Art; the Vessel of Nature which is also called the Vessel of Philosophy is the Earth of the Stone, or the Female or Matrix, whereinto the sperm of the Male is received, putrefies, and is prepared for generation; the Vessel of Nature is of three sorts, for the secret is decocted in a threefold Vessel.

110. The First Vessel is made of a transparent Stone, or of a stony Glass, the form thereof some Philosophers have hid by a certain Enigmatic description; sometimes affirming that it is compounded of two pieces, to wit, an Alembic and a Bolt-head; sometimes of three, at other times of the two former with the addition of a Cover.

111. Many have feigned the multiplying of such like Vessels to be necessary to the Philosophical Work, calling them by divers names with a desire of hiding the secret by a diversity of operations; for they called it Dissolvent of solutions; Putrefactory for putrefaction; Distillatory for distillation; Sublimatory for sublimation; Calcinatory for calcination, &c.

112. But all deceit being removed we may speak sincerely, one only Vessel of Art sufficeth to terminate the Work of either Sulphur; and another for the Work of the Elixir; for the diversity of digestions requireth not the change of Vessels; yea we must have a care lest the Vessel be changed or opened before the First work be ended.

113. You shall choose a form of glass Vessel round in the bottom (or cucurbit), or at least oval, the neck a hand's breadth long or more, large enough, with a straight mouth made like a Pitcher or Jug, continuous and unbroken and equally thick in every part, that it may resist a long, and sometimes an acute Fire: The cucurbit is called a Blind-head because its eye is blinded with the Hermetic seal, lest anything from without should enter in, or the Spirit steal out.

114. The second Vessel of Art may be of Wood, of the trunk of an Oak, cut into two hollow Hemispheres,

wherein the Philosophers' Egg may be cherished till it be hatched; of which see the Fountain of Trevisan.[53]

115. The third Vessel Practitioners have called their Furnace, which keeps the other Vessels with the matter and the whole work: this also Philosophers have endeavoured to hide amongst their secrets.

116. The Furnace which is the Keeper of Secrets, is called Athanor, from the immortal Fire, which it always preserveth; for although it afford unto the Work continual Fire, yet sometimes unequally, which reason requireth to be administered more or less according to the quantity of matter, and the capacity of the Furnace.

117. The matter of the Furnace is made of Brick, or of daubed Earth, or of Potter's clay well beaten and prepared with horse dung, mixed with hair, so that it may cohere the firmer, and may not be cracked by long heating; let the walls be three or four fingers thick, to the end that the furnace may be the better able to keep in the heat and withstand it.

118. Let the form of the Furnace be round, the inward altitude of two feet or thereabouts, in the midst whereof an Iron or Brazen plate must be set, of a round Figure, about the thickness of a Penknife's back, in a manner possessing the interior latitude of the Furnace, but a little narrower than it, lest it touch the walls; it must lean upon three or four props of Iron fixed to the walls, and let it be full of holes, that the heat may be the more easily carried upwards by them, and between the sides of the Furnace and the Plate. Below the Plate let there be a little door left, and another above in the walls of the Furnace, that by the Lower the Fire may be put in, and by the higher the temperament of the heat may be sensibly perceived; at the opposite part whereof let there be a little window of the Figure of a Rhomboid fortified with glass, that the light over against it may shew the colours to the eye. Upon the middle of the aforesaid plate, let the Tripod of secrets be placed with a double Vessel. Lastly, let the Furnace

be very well covered with a shell or covering agreeable unto it, and take care that the little doors be always closely shut, lest the heat escape.

119. Thus thou hast all things necessary to the First Work, the end whereof is the generation of two sorts of Sulphur; the composition and perfection of both may be thus finished.

THE PRACTICE OF THE SULPHUR.

Take a Red Dragon, courageous, warlike, to whom no natural strength is wanting; and afterwards seven or nine noble Eagles (Virgins), whose eyes will not wax dull by the rays of the Sun: cast the Birds with the Beast into a clear Prison and strongly shut them up; under this let a Bath be placed, that they may be incensed to fight by the warmth; in a short time they will enter into a long and harsh contention, until at length about the 45th day or the 50th the Eagles begin to prey upon and tear the beast to pieces, which dying will infect the whole Prison with its black and direful poison, whereby the Eagles being wounded, they will also be constrained to give up the ghost. From the putrefaction of the dead Carcasses a Crow will be generated, which by little and little will put forth its head, and the Heat being somewhat increased it will forthwith stretch forth its wings and begin to fly; but seeking chinks from the Winds and Clouds, it will long hover about; take heed that it find not any chinks. At length being made white by a gentle and long Rain, and with the dew of Heaven it will be changed into a White Swan, but the new born Crow is a sign of the departed Dragon. In making the Crow White, extract the Elements, and distil them according to the order prescribed, until they be fixed in their Earth, and end in Snow-like and most subtle dust, which being finished thou shalt enjoy thy first desire, the White Work.

120. If thou intendest to proceed further to the Red, add the Element of Fire, which is not needed for

the White Work: the Vessel therefore being fixed, and the Fire strengthened by little and little through its grades, force the matter until the occult begin to be made manifest, the sign whereof will be the Orange colour arising: raise the Fire to the Fourth degree by its degrees, until by the help of Vulcan, purple Roses be generated from the Lily, and lastly the Amaranth dyed with the dark Redness of blood: but thou mayest not cease to bring out Fire by Fire, until thou shalt behold the matter terminated in most Red ashes, imperceptible to the touch. This Red Stone may rear up thy mind to greater things, by the blessing and assistance of the holy Trinity.

121. They that think they have brought their work to an end by perfect Sulphur, not knowing Nature or Art, and to have fulfilled the Precepts of the secret, are much deceived, and will try Projection in vain; for the Praxis of the Stone is perfected by a double Work; the First is the creation of the Sulphur; the Second is the making of the Elixir.

122. The aforesaid Philosophers' Sulphur is most subtle Earth, most hot and dry, in the belly whereof the Fire of Nature abundantly multiplied is hidden. Therefore it deserveth the name of the Fire of the Stone, for it hath in itself the virtue of opening and penetrating the bodies of Metals, and of turning them into its own temperament and producing its like, wherefore it is called a Father and Masculine seed.

123. That we may leave nothing untouched, let the Students in Philosophy know that from that first Sulphur, a second is generated which may be multiplied *ad infinitum*: let the wise man, after he hath got the everlasting mineral of that Heavenly Fire, keep it diligently. Now of what matter Sulphur is generated, of the same it is multiplied, a small portion of the first being added, yet as in the Balance. The rest, a tyro may see in Lullius[54], it may suffice only to point to this.

124. The Elixir is compounded of a threefold matter,

namely, of Metallic Water or Mercury sublimated as before; of Leaven White or Red, according to the intention of the Operator; and of the Second Sulphur, all by Weight.

125. There are Five proper and necessary qualities in the perfect Elixir, that it be fusible, permanent, penetrating, tincturing, and multiplying; it borroweth its tincture and fixation from the Leaven; its penetration from the Sulphur; its fusion from Argent vive, which is the medium of conjoining Tinctures; to wit of the Ferment and Sulphur; and its multiplicative virtue from the Spirit infused into the Quintessence.

126. Two perfect Metals give a perfect Tincture, because they are dyed with the pure Sulphur of Nature, and therefore no Ferment of Metals may be sought except these two bodies; therefore dye thy Elixir White and Red with Luna and Sol; Mercury first of all receives their Tincture, and having received it, doth communicate it to others.

127. In compounding the Elixir take heed you change not or mix any thing with the Ferments, for either Elixir must have its proper Ferment, and desireth its proper Elements; for it is provided by Nature that the two Luminaries have their different Sulphurs and distinct tinctures.

128. The Second work is concocted as the First, in the same or a like Vessel, the same Furnace, and by the same degrees of fire, but is perfected in a shorter time.

129. There are three humours in the Stone, which are to be extracted successively; namely, Watery, Airy, and Radical; and therefore all the labour and care of the Workman is employed about the humour, neither is any other Element in the Work of the Stone circulated beside the humid one. For it is necessary, in the first place, that the Earth be resolved and melted into humour. Now the Radical humour of all things, accounted Fire, is most tenacious, because it is tied to the Centre of Nature, from which it is not easily separated; extract, therefore, these three humours

slowly and successively; dissolving and congealing them by their Whorls, for by the multiplied alternative reiteration of Solution and Congelation the Whorl is extended and the whole work finished.

130. The Elixir's perfection consisteth in the strict Union and indissoluble Matrimony of Siccum and Humidum, so that they may not be separated, but the *Siccum* may flow with moderate heat into the *Humidum*, abiding every pressure of Fire. The sign of perfection is that if a very little of it be cast in above the Iron or Brazen Plate while very hot, it flow forthwith without smoke.

Let three weights of Red Earth or of Red Ferment, and a double weight of Water and Air well ground up be mixed together. Let an Amalgama be made like Butter, or Metalline Paste, so that the Earth being mollified may be insensible to the touch. Add one weight and a half of Fire; let these be transferred to the Vessel and exposed to a Fire of the first degree; most closely sealed; afterwards let the Elements be extracted out of their degrees of Fire in their order, which being turned downwards with a gentle motion they may be fixed in their Earth, so as nothing Volatile may be raised up from thence; the matter at length shall be terminated in a Stone, Illuminated, Red and Diaphanous; a part whereof take at pleasure, and having cast it into a Crucible with a little Fire by drops give it to drink its Red Oil and incerate it,[55] until it be quite melted, and do flow without smoke. Nor mayest thou fear its flight, for the Earth being mollified with the sweetness of the Potion will retain it, having received it, within its bowels: then take the Elixir thus perfected into thine own power and keep it carefully. In God rejoice, and be silent.

132. The order and method of composing and perfecting the white Elixir is the same, so that thou usest the white Elements only in the composition thereof; but the body of it brought to the term of decoction will end in the plate; white, splendid, and crystal-like, which

incerated with its White Oil will be fused. Cast one weight of either Elixir, upon ten times its weight of Argent-vive well washed and thou wilt admire its effect with astonishment.

133. Because in the Elixir the strength of Natural Fire is most abundantly multiplied by the Spirit infused into the Quintessence, and the depraved accidents of bodies, which beset their purity and the true light of Nature with darkness, are taken away by long and manifold sublimations and digestions; therefore Fiery Nature freed from its Fetters and fortified with the aid of Heavenly strength, works most powerfully, being included in this our Fifth Element: let it not therefore be a wonder, if it obtain strength not only to perfect imperfect things, but also to multiply its force and power. Now the Fountain of Multiplication is in the Prince of the Luminaries, who by the infinite multiplication of his beams begetteth all things in this our Orb, and multiplieth things generated by infusing a multiplicative virtue into the seeds of things.

134. The way of multiplying the Elixir is threefold: By the first; R, Mingle one weight of Red Elixir, with nine times its weight of Red Water, and dissolve it into Water in a Vessel suitable for Solution; the matter being well dissolved and united coagulate it by decoction with a gentle Fire, until it be made strong into a Ruby or Red Lamel, which afterwards incerate with its Red Oil, after the manner prescribed until it melt and flow; so shalt thou have a medicine ten times more powerful than the first. The business is easily finished in a short time.

135. By the Second manner. R, What Portion thou pleasest of thy Elixir mixed with its Water, the weights being observed; seal it very well in the Vessel of Reduction, dissolve it in a Bath, by inhumation; being dissolved, distil it separating the Elements by their proper degrees of fire, and fixing them downwards, as was done in the first and second work, until it become a Stone; lastly, incerate it and Project it. This is the

longer, but yet the richer way, for the virtue of the Elixir is increased even an hundred fold; for by how much the more subtle it is made by reiterated operations, so much more both of superior and inferior strength it retaineth, and more powerfully operateth.

136. Lastly, take one Ounce of the said Elixir multiplied in virtue and project it upon an hundred of purified Mercury, and in a little time the Mercury made hot amongst burning Coals will be converted into pure Elixir; whereof if thou castest every ounce upon another hundred of the like Mercury, Sol will shine most purely to thine eyes. The multiplication of White Elixir may be made in the same way. Study the virtues of this Medicine to cure all kinds of diseases, and to preserve good health, as also other uses thereof, out of the Writings of Arnold of Villa Nova[56], Lullius and of other Philosophers.

137. The Significator of the Philosopher will instruct him concerning the Times of the Stone, for the first Work " ad Album " must be terminated in the House of Luna; the Second, in the second House of Mercury. The first Work " ad Rubeum," will end in the Second House of Venus, and the last in the other Regal Throne of Jupiter, from whence our most Potent King shall receive a Crown decked with most precious Rubies:

Sic in se sua vestigia volvitur Annus.

Thus doth the winding of the circling Year
Trace its own Foot-steps, and the same appear.

138. A Three-Headed Dragon keepeth this Golden Fleece; the first Head proceedeth from the Waters, the second from the Earth, the third from the Air; it is necessary that these three heads do end in One most Potent, which will devour all the other Dragons; then a way is laid open for thee to the Golden Fleece. Farewell! diligent Reader; in Reading these things invocate the Spirit of Eternal Light; Speak little, Meditate much, and Judge aright.[57]

The Times of the Stone.

The interpretation of The Philosophers' Significator. To every Planet two Houses were assigned by the Ancients, Sol and Luna excepted; whereof the planet Saturn hath his two houses adjoining. Philosophers in handling their Philosophical work, begin their years in Winter, to wit; the Sun being in Capricorn, which is the former House of Saturn; and so come towards the right hand. In the Second place the other House of Saturn is found in Aquarius, at which time Saturn, *i.e.*, the Blackness of the work of the Magistery begins after the forty-fifth or fiftieth day. Sol coming into Pisces the work is black, blacker than black, and the head of the Crow begins to appear. The third month being ended, and Sol entering into Aries, the sublimation or separation of the Elements begin. Those which follow unto Cancer make the Work White. Cancer addeth the greatest whiteness and splendour, and doth perfectly fill up all the days of the Stone, or white Sulphur, or the Lunar work of Sulphur; Luna sitting and reigning gloriously in her House. In Leo, the Regal Mansion of the Sun, the Solar work begins, which in Libra is terminated into a Ruby Stone or perfect Sulphur. The two signs Scorpio and Sagittarius which remain are required for the completing of the Elixir. And thus the Philosophers' admirable offspring taketh its beginning in the Reign of Saturn, and its end and perfection in the Dominion of Jupiter.

NOTES.

1. Due reverence for Divine powers is an absolute necessity in the search for occult wisdom, and can alone lead any student in safety to success in the arts of High Magic.

2. Theosophic Eastern teaching (as well as Western Hermetic ritual) insists upon mental and moral as well as bodily purity in every candidate for esoteric instruction.

3. A warning that complete success can hardly be achieved, unless the student is able to devote himself entirely to the pursuit of the occult sciences. *Non omnia possumus omnes.*

4. A warning against spiritual pride; the besetting sin of one who has gone up some steps of the mystic ladder, and who realizes for the first time that there is something he can teach, as well as so much that he has to learn.

5. "Orare est laborare" is the true motto of the Hermetist. Work inspired by enthusiasm and the will to progress, so as to fit oneself to raise others, is ideal prayer in action.

6. If you freely receive knowledge and power you must freely give: the epigram attributed to a fellow student was, "I give, I give; but the more I give, the more do I receive."

7. James i. 27, "Keep himself unspotted from the world," it is more easy to remain clean away from a dirty world; yet if one can keep clean amid the turmoil of a city, such conduct is deserving of a higher reward than is due to a clean but ascetic life.

8. In tranquillity alone can meditation be fertile the flower can only bloom in the calm after the violence of the storm of contest with the passions.

9. In peaceful meditation is the opportunity of that aspiration to the Divine which *may* lead to union (even if momentary) with the Higher and Divine Genius—the Light that *may* light every man that cometh into the world.

10. A teacher and guide is almost an absolute necessity in the Higher Magic; not to drag on the pupil, but to point out the path that has been trodden with success, and to warn against tempting bye-paths with meretricious attractions, but "whose splendour is but seeming." Among the Rosicrucians each Adept was authorized and encouraged to choose one or more pupils to follow in his steps and to take up the mantle and wand when his time came to lay them down.

11. Apart from the help of a Master, it is nearly always found that a fellow student is a great help to progress. A few there are who succeed most in solitary study; others are much helped by the presence of a responsive zeal and reflected desire. A trio of students has also a certain advantage. History has but few examples of two fellow students of the same sex achieving great results: but there are many instances of great progress and high results from the combined work of a truly high minded woman and man developing by mutual and reciprocal interaction; the female providing knowledge by intuition, and the male formulating and developing the practical aspect of the matter. Even in the preliminary grades of mystic study the same result is obtained: unrestrained and unconventional social and intellectual communion may (in the absolute absence of passion) lead to rapid mental and spiritual progress. Compare the narratives of Moses and Miriam, Paul and Thecla, Theon and Hypatia, Flamel and Pernelle, Gichtel and Sophia, Anna Kingsford and her still living *collaborateur*. Analogy supports

the proposition, through all the forms of the manifested universe; wherever the Dyad is developed, the presence of the contrasted forces alone leads to a due result.

12. Beware of false guides: perhaps it is wisest to add, follow only one path at once; even if it be granted that two parallel paths exist, and that they meet farther on—yet it is most easy to attempt one only; still the attempt to traverse both at once is not absolutely forbidden, either by the chiefs of the Western or Eastern Schools.

13. Whenever a student happens upon a very definite assertion in a book certainly the work of a high adept, it is generally safe to seek further; for the ancient writers, when they did publish, never threw pearls of learning away, although willing to tender them to earnest students.

14. Michael Sendivogius; the anonymous inscription on his books was "Author sum qui *Divi Leschi Genus Amo*." The last four words form an anagram of his name; he flourished 1604-46; his chief works are *Novum Lumen*, *De Sulphure*, *Lucerna Salis*, *de Lapide*, *Dialogus Mercurii* and *Epistolæ*.

15. Flamel's work has been reprinted with a preface by W. Wynn Westcott. Nicolas Flamel flourished 1357-1413.

16. See Virgil. *Æneid* vi. 138. The original has "*hunc*" not "*quem*."

17. Virgil. *Æneid* vi. 190-193.

18. See the *Chrysopœia* of Aurelius Augurellus, liber x.; this author died 1514.

19. By these words is meant that the chemical substances used should be quite pure, otherwise the adulterations will hinder the desired result.

20. Probably meaning freshly prepared; perhaps what the modern chemist calls " in a nascent state."

21. Death, the inevitable changer, Siva.

22. In almost all cases where sexual symbolism is used, any principle which is positive to that which is inferior, is also negative or female to that which is superior.

23. These names vary with different authors—Gabritius is also called Gabertius and Gabricus. Beia also is Beya. As brother and sister they mean positive and negative. See David Laqueus. *Harmonia Chemica;* and the dicta of Arislæus in the *Turba Philosophorum.* Gabritius is the fixed and Beia the volatile.

24. Raymond Lully. *Prior Testamentum*, cap. 62.

25. See Note 19.

26. Hosea vii. 9.

27. The rocks of Scylla and the whirlpool of Charybdis lie on either side of the strait between Sicily and Italy.

28. Query, dissolved.

29. *Rebis* is generally explained as that which is "double," or is hermaphrodite, or is the result of the union of two substances.

30. Virgil. *Æneid* vi. 129, 130.

31. The planet Mercury is said in Astrology to act by influence upon other planets in aspect with it, rather than with independent force.

32. See the *Chrysopœia* of Augurellus, 2.

33. Ensigns of Diana and the Doves of Venus: query purity and love on the spiritual plane; or is the reference to Silver on the material plane. For some notes on Alchymy on the spiritual plane, see *Alchymy*, by Sapere Aude.

34. Virgil. *Georgics*, Book I., lines 64, 65, 44.

35. See Cap. 4, libr. 1., of the *Perfect Magistery* of Geber; he lived about A.D. 830.

36. See Genesis i. verses 1 to 4.

37. See Deut. xxxiii. v. 13 to 16. These words differ from the version of the English Bible. For "apples of Heaven," read "precious things." For "the apple of fruit both of the sun and moon," read "the precious fruits brought forth by the sun, and the precious things put forth by the moon." For "the top," read "the chief things." The Hebrew word translated "apple" is MGD. Parkhurst gives "precious fruits." The Hebrew word for "top" or "chief things" is RASh, meaning head, chief or beginning. Godfrey Higgins laboured to teach that it also meant "wisdom:" it is the first word of Genesis, preceded by a Beth-B-RAShITh.

38. This means adulteration, impurity from its mineral origin.

39. Or interstitial, intimately combined with it; yet such as can be easily driven off by a suitable heat.

40. Compare this purple Jovian star with the purple flower of love, the Amaranth in paragraph 53. There is a scale of colours in which Jupiter is Violet.

41. A versification of this beautiful passage may be found in Ainsworth, as spoken by the Sylph appearing to Ruggieri.

42. Note the change from she to he, negative to positive in this paragragh. Nothing is more realistic than sexual symbolism, but one has to exclude it as far as possible for the sake of the Pharisee reader.

43. Let the practical Alchymist note this word, and indeed the whole paragraph, and remember that there is *a* butter besides butter.

44. That is twilight, gloom of evening, the first darkening.

45. Virgil. *Georgics.* I., 70.
46. Virgil. *Georgics.* I., 47.
47. That is "moist" and "dry."

48. Note this order—earth, water, air, fire; and back to earth. See end of paragraph 79.

49. See the *Enchiridion* in Manget's *Bibliotheca*, liber. III., section 3.

50. From *humus* the ground, earth or soil.

51. Raymond Lully was martyred in Africa, 1315.

52. Senior: very little is known of this author; his name is not in the list of Lenglet de Fresnoy.

53. Bernard, Count of Treves; died about 1490. His chief works are, *Natural Philosophy of Metals*, *The Secret Work of Chymia*, and *La Parole délaissée*.

54. His most valued works are *Lullii Testamentum*, *Codicillus seu Vade Mecum aut Cantilena* and *Practica*.

55. Definition of some terms. Inceration must not be confused with incineration, which means reducing to ashes by means of heat. Inceration implies the gradual addition of a liquid (as our mercury) to a solid powder (as our sulphur), until the mixture is of the consistence of *wax*, of which the Latin word is *cera*. See Rulandus.

Cohobation is a process of continuous volatilization and condensation of a volatile liquid in a closed vessel subjected to heat.

Anger: when it is written that you are not to provoke anger, it is meant, do not overheat the matter.

The Goose of Hermogenes is the solvent of the Philosophers, which Bernard of Treves calls the Gate of the Palace of the King.

56. Arnold of Villanova, died 1310; his chief works are *Novum Lumen*, *Flos Florum*, *Rosarium*, *Liber Perfectionis*, *Speculum Alchymiæ*, and *Arcanum Philosophicum*.

57. The original Latin work ends with paragraph 138; the English edition of Elias Ashmole has an additional chapter by I. C. Chymierastes: this has no Alchymic value and is but an apology for Hermes, that he was not a Christian.

Collectanea Hermetica

EDITED BY

W. WYNN WESTCOTT,
M.B. Lond., D.P.H.

*(Supreme Magus of the Rosicrucian Society,
Master of the Quatuor Coronati Lodge.)*

VOLUME II.

THE PYMANDER
OF
HERMES

WITH A PREFACE BY THE EDITOR

PREFACE

This volume contains the English translation by Dr. Everard, 1650, of seventeen tracts (of which the *Pymander* is one) attributed to Hermes Trismegistos, otherwise Mercurius Termaximus, or in the Egyptian language, Thoth, or Taautes or Tat. Of this Hermes no reliable historical details have come down to us, but many of the ancient authors have referred to Hermes as an inspired teacher who instructed the priests and rulers of the Egyptian nation at a time almost certainly anterior to that commonly associated with Moses. It has been asserted by men who have been called learned, that this Hermes was really identical with Enoch, and by others he has been identified as Gautama—the Buddha. If the name HERMES be taken and the suffix ES be neglected, and the word formed of the letters H, R, M, be traced through Chaldee, Coptic, Greek and Latin forms, an analogy will be observed between Hermes, and Hiram the hero of the myth of Freemasonry, a symbolical system of morals and theosophy which is but a reconstruction of a portion of the Ancient Mysteries. Now the Mysteries of Egypt, named Osirian, Serapian and Isiac, are the most ancient known to us, and were the parents of the Eleusinian Mysteries of the Greeks. All these Mysteries were initiations, or forms of Esoteric instruction relating to theosophy, properly so-called, that is the knowledge of divine powers and beings, and the connection between Man and the Divine Source from which he is animated and inspired. Now the tracts which have come down to us, associated with the name of Hermes as their author, are all concerned with that arcane wisdom which was developed in three directions:—Theosophy,—religious and ethical teaching; Alchymy—the relation of the material to the spiritual and the transmutations of the former into the latter; and Magic—the employment of the higher powers latent in man upon the physical plane. In the Hermetic tracts these several objects are not kept distinct, but on the contrary, are almost invariably combined;

hence the great value to a true student of Occultism of these very ancient writings. It is not of course asserted that the *Pymander* or other Hermetic work has come down to us in its original form, but it is contended that although varied in many a line and possibly in many a doctrine by the Neo-Platonists and Alexandrian school, and perhaps in later days by Christian philosophers, the *Pymander, Aureus*, etc., do yet enshrine the very old Egyptian ideals, and are almost the only remains now existing of the Wisdom of the hierophants of the Nile valley.

Kenealy has asserted that the name Hermes meant in the ancient Egyptian language—an interpreter, and in a certain sense the later Hermes of the Greeks and the Mercurius of the Romans conveyed the same notion; this author, in his quaint conceit of Twelve Saviours, places Hermes under the name of Thoth as the Sixth Messiah, and assigns to him the era of 1800 years before Christ.

This Thoth, as an Egyptian divinity, is often represented as a human form with an Ibis head; now the bird Ibis was notable as being the great destroyer of snakes, and the snake as apart from the regal serpent, was an emblem of evil, sin and error; hence the Snake Destroyer fits in well with the character of Hermes as a Teacher of divine truths, which would serve to crush and beat down evil thoughts and actions.

The earliest record of the title Trismegistos, as applied to this Egyptian sage, is found in Greek authors who lived some four centuries B.C. The Neo-Platonists, who were of Greek culture, looked upon Hermes as the embodied LOGOS, or Word or Manifestation of the Divine Spirit. The title may have had reference to his mastery over the Three Divine sciences—Theosophy, Alchymy and Magic—as indeed is stated in paragraph twelve of the Emerald Tablet assigned to him, of which the words following are an old Latin version: *Itaque vocatus sum Hermes Trismegistus, habens tres partes divinæ philosophiæ totius mundi*—that is "possessing the three parts of the divine philosophy of the whole world."

The name Pymander is of Greek and not Egyptian type; it is variously spelled Pimander and Poemandres. Its derivation appears to be from *poimēn*—a shepherd, and *anēr*, genitive plural *andrōn*, and so the Guide of Man, Shepherd of men, and is nearly equivalent to Messiah. In this tract the Pymander is giving instruction to Hermes the sage, n the capacity of Divine teacher to human pupil. A parallel conception is seen in the Bhagavad Gita, where Krishna teaches Arjuna.

Blavatsky in *The Secret Doctrine* refers to the *Pymander* as the "Thought Divine," the Inspired Teacher of that Race—Vol. I., 63; and again at page 74, she speaks of Pymander as "the oldest and most spiritual of the Logoi of the Western continent." She also notices the possibility of a Hebrew derivation from PI, meaning a mouth, and command, or instruction. I observe that Parkhurst associates with this word, the Greek *Phemi*—to speak, so perhaps another form of title may be Phemander—one who spoke to man.

There are two other persons mentioned in the *Pymander*; these are Tat assumed to be a son of Hermes, and Asclepius a grandson.

The *Pymander* has been many times printed, but it is a very difficult volume to obtain. Recent editions have been those of Hargrave Jennings, 1884, a reprint of Everard's English version; John David Chambers, Edinburgh, 1882, a new translation from the Greek; and that of L. Ménard, Paris, 1867.

Of earlier date are the Greek text of C. Parthey Berolins, 1854; an Italian version by C. Lenzoni, 1548; a German edition by J. Scheible, 1855; a French translation, François de Fois, 1579. The earliest Latin edition is that of Marsilius Ficinus, 1471, followed by Franciscus Patricius, 1593; Flussas, 1574; H. Rosselus, 1630; and 1676; and others contained in volumes associated with the writings of Lucius Apuleius of Madaura, and with the books attributed to Jamblichus of Chalcis.

The present edition is a *facsimile* reprint of the translation of the Rev. Dr. Everard from an Arabic text, of which there were two editions published in 1650 and 1657 respectively; this edition is from the earlier one. No alteration has been made except in the mode of spelling of a few words, the archaic form of which in the original would, it was feared, distract the reader's attention from the subject. It is preceded by a preface by J. F., whose name is unknown. The second edition was a reprint of the *Pymander*, and contained in addition an English translation of fifteen chapters of *Asclepius* with a commentary.

Very little is known of the Rev. John Everard, D.D., but Alsager Vian states that he was born about 1575 and died about 1650. He entered the Church and remained a minister for many years, but was frequently suspended, sometimes for heretical doctrines and at others on account of political sermons. It is most probable that he was in truth a Neo-Platonist at heart and was also a disciple of the German mystic Tauler. His original works contain many quotations from Plato, Proclus and Plotinus.

With these notes I leave this Preface, without any attempt to comment on or explain the subject matter of the *Pymander*, believing that it will be better for a student to read and assimilate what he can from the original, rather than to read the work through my spectacles, or those of any other fellow student.

Should the present volume be found to supply a want, the remaining tracts attributed to Hermes will be reproduced in a succeeding volume of this series of "COLLECTANEA HERMETICA".

W. WYNN WESTCOTT.

THE
DIVINE PYMANDER
OF
HERMES MERCURIUS TRISMEGISTUS
IN XVII. BOOKS

Translated formerly out of the *Arabick* into *Greek*, and thence into *Latine*, and *Dutch*, and now out of the Original into *English*;

By that Learned Divine

DOCTOR EVERARD

THE TITLES OF THESE BOOKS
OF
HERMES TRISMEGISTUS.

	The Preface of J. F."	11
1.	His First Book	15
2.	Poemander	21
3.	The Holy Sermon	32
4.	The Key	34
5.	That God is not Manifest, and yet most Manifest	44
6.	That in God alone is Good	49
7.	The Secret Sermon in the Mount of Regeneration, & the Profession of Silence	53
8.	That the Greatest Evil in Man, is the not Knowing of God	62
9.	A Universal Sermon to Asclepius	64
10.	The Mind to Hermes	70
11.	Of the Common Mind to Tat	80
12.	Hermes Trismegistus, his Crater or Monas	90
13.	Of Sense and Understanding	95
14.	Of Operation and Sense	100
15.	Of Truth to His Son Tat	106
16.	That none of the Things that are, can Perish	111
17.	To Asclepius, to be Truly Wise	114

TO THE READER.

Judicious Reader,

This Book may justly challenge the first place for antiquity, from all the Books in the World, being written some hundreds of years before *Moses* his time, as I shall endeavour to make good. The Original (as far as is known to us) is *Arabic*, and several Translations thereof have been published, as *Greek*, *Latin*, *French*, *Dutch*, *etc.*, but never *English* before. It is pity the* Learned Translator had not lived, and received himself, the honour, and thanks due to him from *Englishmen* for his good will to, and pains for them, in translating a Book of such infinite worth, out of the Original, into their Mother-tongue.

Concerning the Author of the Book itself, Four things are considerable, *viz.*, His Name, Learning, Country, and Time.

1. The name by which he was commonly styled, is *Hermes Trismegistus*, *i.e.*, *Mercurius ter Maximus*, or, The thrice greatest Intelligencer. And well might he be called *Hermes*, for he was the first Intelligencer in the World (as we read of) that communicated Knowledge to the sons of Men, by Writing, or Engraving. He was called Ter Maximus, for some Reasons, which I shall afterwards mention.

2. His Learning will appear, as by his Works; so by the right understanding the Reason of his Name.

3. For his Country, he was King of Egypt.

4. For his Time, it is not without much Controversy, betwixt those that write of this Divine, ancient

* Doctor Everard.

Author, what time he lived in. Some say he lived after *Moses* his time, giving this slender Reason for it, *viz.*, Because he was named *Ter Maximus;* for being preferred* (according to the *Egyptian* Customs) being chief Philosopher, to be chief of the Priesthood; and from thence, to be chief in Government, or King. But if this be all their ground, you must excuse my dissent from them, and that for this reason, Because according to the most learned of his† followers, he was called *Ter Maximus;* for having perfect, and exact Knowledge of all things contained in the World; which things he divided into Three Kingdoms (as he calls them), *viz.*, *Mineral, Vegetable, Animal;* which Three, he did excel in the right understanding of; also, because he attained to, and transmitted to Posterity (although in an Ænigmatical, and obscure style) the Knowledge of the Quintessence of the whole Universe (which Universe, as I said before, he divided into Three Parts) otherwise called, The great *Elixir* of the Philosophers; which is the Receptacle of all Celestial and Terrestrial Virtues; which Secret, many ignorantly deny, many have chargeably sought after, yet few, but some, yea, and *Englishmen*‡ have happily found. The Description of this great Treasure, is said to be found engraved upon a *Smaragdine* Table, in the Valley of *Ebron*, after the Flood. So that the Reason before alleged to prove this Author to live after *Moses*, seem invalid; neither doth it any way appear, that he lived in *Moses* his time, although it be the opinion of some, as of *Iohn Functius*, who saith in his Chronology, That he lived Twenty-one years before the *Law* was given by *Moses* in the Wilderness: But the Reasons that he, and others give, are far

* Franciscus Flussas.

† Geber, Paracelsus; Henricus Nollius in *Theoria Philosophiæ Hermeticæ, tractatu priimo*.

‡ Ripley, Bacon, Norton, etc.

weaker than those that I shall give, for his living before *Moses* his time. My reasons for that, are these:—

First, Because it is rec eived amongst the Ancients, that he was the first that invented the Art of communicating Knowledge to the World, by Writing or Engraving. Now if so, then in all probability he was before *Moses;* for it is said of *Moses* that he was from* his childhood, skilled in all the *Egyptian* Learning, which could not well have been without the help of Literature, which we never read of any before that invented by *Hermes.*

Secondly, he is said by† himself, to be the son of *Saturn* and by‡ others to be the Scribe of *Saturn.* Now *Saturn* according to Historians, lived in the time of *Sarug, Abraham's* great Grand-Father. I shall but take in *Suidas* his judgment, and so rest satisfied, that he did not live only before, but long before *Moses;* His words are these¶, *Credo Mercurium Trismegistum sapientem Egyptium floruisse ante Pharaonem.*

In this Book, though so very old, is contained more true knowledge of God and Nature, tahn in all the Books in the World besides, I except only Sacred Writ; And they that shall judiciously read it, and rightly understand it, may well be excused from reading many Books; the Authors of which, pretend so much to the knowledge of the Creator, and Creation. If God ever appeared in any man, he appeared in him, as it appears by this Book. That a man who had not the benefit of his Ancestors' knowledge, being as I said before, The first inventor of the Art of Communicating Knowledge to Posterity by writing, should be so high a Divine, and so deep a Philosopher, seems to be a thing more of God than of Man; and therefore it was the opinion of some‖ That he came from Heaven, not born upon Earth. There is contained in this Book, that true Philosophy,

---

* Acts vii. 22.   † Chapter x.   ‡ Sanchoniathon.
¶ Suidas.   ‖ Goropius Becanus.

without which, it is impossible ever to attain to the height, and exactness of Piety, and Religion. According to this Philosophy, I call him a Philosopher, that shall learn and study the things that are, and how they are ordered, and governed, and by whom, and for what cause, or to what end; and he that doth so, will acknowledge thanks to, and admire the Omnipotent Creator, Preserver, and Director of all these things. And he that shall be thus truly thankful, may truly be called Pious and Religious: and he that is Religious, shall more and more know where and what the Truth is: And learning that, he shall yet be more and more Religious.

The glory and splendour of Philosophy, is an endeavouring to understand the chief Good, as the Fountain of all Good: Now how can we come near to, or find out the Fountain, but by making use of the Streams as a conduct to it? The operations of Nature, are Streams running from the Fountain of Good, which is God. I am not of the ignorant, and foolish opinion of those that say, The greatest Philosophers are the greatest Atheists: as if to know the works of God, and to understand his goings forth in the Way of Nature, must necessitate a man to deny God. The* Scripture disapproves of this as a sottish tenet, and experience contradicts it: For behold! Here is the greatest Philosopher, and therefore the greatest Divine.

Read understandingly this ensuing Book (and for thy help thou mayest make use of that voluminous† Commentary written upon it) then it will speak more for its Author, than can be spoken by any man, at least by me.

                      Thine in the love
                            of the Truth,
                                  J. F

* Job   † Hanbal Offeli alabar.

HERMES TRISMEGISTUS
THE FIRST BOOK.

---

1. O my Son, write this first Book, both for Humanity's sake, and for Piety towards God.

2. For there can be no Religion more true or just, than to know the things that are; and to acknowledge thanks for all things, to him that made them, which thing I shall not cease continually to do.

3. What then should a man do, O Father, to lead his life well, seeing there is nothing here true?

4. Be Pious and Religious, O my Son, for he that doth so, is the best and highest Philosopher; and without Philosophy, it is impossible ever to attain to the height and exactness of Piety or Religion.

5. But he that shall learn and study the things that are, and how they are ordered and governed, and by whom and for what cause, or to what end, will acknowledge thanks to the Workman as to a good Father, an excellent Nurse and a faithful Steward, and he that gives thanks shall be Pious or Religious, and he that is Religious shall know both where the truth is, and what it is, and learning that, he will be yet more and more Religious.

6. For never, O Son, shall or can that Soul which while it is in the Body lightens and lifts up itself to know and comprehend that which is Good and True, slide back to the contrary; for it is infinitely enamoured thereof, and forgetteth all Evils; and when it hath learned and known its Father and progenitor it can no more Apostatize or depart from that Good.

7. And let this, O Son, be the end of Religion and Piety; whereunto when thou art once arrived, thou shalt both live well, and die blessedly, whilst thy Soul is not ignorant whether it must return and fly back again.

8. For this only, O Son, is the way to the Truth, which our Progenitors travelled in; and by which, making their Journey, they at length attained to the Good. It is a Venerable way, and plain, but hard and difficult for the Soul to go in that is in the Body.

9. For first must it war against its own self, and after much Strife and Dissention it must be overcome of one part; for the Contention is of one against two, whilst it flies away and they strive to hold and detain it.

10. But the victory of both is not like; for the one hasteth to that which is Good, but the other is a neighbour to the things that are Evil; and that which is Good, desireth to be set at Liberty; but the things that are Evil, love Bondage and Slavery.

11. And if the two parts be overcome, they become quiet, and are content to accept of it as their Ruler; but if the one be overcome of the two, it is by them led and carried to be punished by its being and continuance here.

12. This is, O Son, the Guide in the way that leads thither; for thou must first forsake the Body before thy end, and get the victory in this Contention and Strifeful life, and when thou hast overcome, return.

13. But now, O my Son, I will by Heads run through the things that are: understand thou what I say, and remember what thou hearest.

14. All things that are, are moved; only that which is not, is unmovable.

15. Every Body is changeable.

16. Not every Body is dissolvable.

17. Some Bodies are dissolvable.

18. Every living thing is not mortal.

19. Not every living thing is immortal.

20. That which may be dissolved is also corruptible.
21. That which abides always is unchangeable.
22. That which is unchangeable is eternal.
23. That which is always made is always corrupted.
24. That which is made but once, is never corrupted, neither becomes any other thing.
25. First, God; Secondly, the World; Thirdly, Man.
26. The World for Man, Man for God.
27. Of the Soul, that part which is Sensible is mortal, but that which is Reasonable is immortal.
28. Every essence is immortal.
29. Every essence is unchangeable.
30. Every thing that is, is double.
31. None of the things that are stand still.
32. Not all things are moved by a Soul, but every thing that is, is moved by a Soul.
33. Every thing that suffers is Sensible, every thing that is Sensible suffereth.
34. Every thing that is sad rejoiceth also, and is a mortal living Creature.
35. Not every thing that joyeth is also sad, but is an eternal living thing.
36. Not every Body is sick; every Body that is sick is dissolvable.
37. The Mind in God.
38. Reasoning (or disputing or discoursing) in Man.
39. Reason in the Mind.
40. The Mind is void of suffering.
41. No thing in a Body true.
42. All that is incorporeal, is void of Lying.
43. Every thing that is made is corruptible.
44. Nothing good upon Earth, nothing evil in Heaven.
45. God is good, Man is evil.
46. Good is voluntary, or of its own accord.
47. Evil is involuntary or against its will.
48. The Gods choose good things, as good things.

49. Time is a Divine thing.
50. Law is Humane.
51. Malice is the nourishment of the World.
52. Time is the Corruption of Man.
53. Whatsoever is in Heaven is unalterable.
54. All upon Earth is alterable.
55. Nothing in Heaven is servanted, nothing upon Earth free.
56. Nothing unknown in Heaven, nothing known upon Earth.
57. The things upon Earth communicate not with those in Heaven.
58. All things in Heaven are unblameable, all things upon Earth are subject to Reprehension.
59. That which is immortal, is not mortal: that which is mortal is not immortal.
60. That which is sown, is not always begotten; but that which is begotten always, is sown.
61. Of a dissolvable Body, there are two Times, one from sowing to generation, one from generation to death.
62. Of an everlasting Body, the time is only from the Generation.
63. Dissolvable Bodies are increased and diminished.
64. Dissolvable matter is altered into contraries; to wit, Corruption and Generation, but Eternal matter into its self, and its like.
65. The Generation of Man is Corruption, the Corruption of Man is the beginning of Generation.
66. That which off-springs or begetteth another, is itself an offspring or begotten by another.
67. Of things that are, some are in Bodies, some in their *Ideas*.
68. Whatsoever things belong to operation or working, are in a Body.
69. That which is immortal, partakes not of that which is mortal.
70. That which is mortal, cometh not into a Body

immortal, but that which is immortal, cometh into that which is mortal.

71. Operations or Workings are not carried upwards, but descend downwards.

72. Things upon Earth do nothing advantage those in Heaven, but all things in Heaven do profit and advantage the things upon Earth.

73. Heaven is capable and a fit receptacle of everlasting Bodies, the Earth of corruptible Bodies.

74. The Earth is brutish, the Heaven is reasonable or rational.

75. Those things that are in Heaven are subjected or placed under it, but the things on Earth, are placed upon it.

76. Heaven is the first Element.

77. Providence is Divine Order.

78. Necessity is the Minister or Servant of Providence.

79. Fortune is the carriage or effect of that which is without Order; the Idol of operation, a lying fantasy or opinion.

80. What is God? The immutable or unalterable Good.

81. What is Man? An unchangeable Evil.

82. If thou perfectly remember these Heads, thou canst not forget those things which in more words I have largely expounded unto thee; for these are the Contents or Abridgment of them.

83. Avoid all Conversation with the multitude or common People, for I would not have thee subject to Envy, much less to be ridiculous unto the many.

84. For the like always takes to itself that which is like, but the unlike never agrees with the unlike: such Discourses as these have very few Auditors, and peradventure very few will have, but they have something peculiar unto themselves.

85. They do rather sharpen and whet evil men to their maliciousness, therefore it behoveth to avoid the

multitude and take heed of them as not understanding the virtue and power of the things that are said.

86. How dost Thou mean, O Father?

87. Thus, O Son, the whole Nature and Composition of those living things called Men, is very prone to Maliciousness, and is very familiar, and as it were nourished with it, and therefore is delighted with it. Now this wight if it shall come to learn or know, that the world was once made, and all things are done according to Providence and Necessity, Destiny, or Fate, bearing Rule over all: Will he not be much worse than himself, despising the whole because it was made. And if he may lay the cause of evil upon Fate or Destiny, he will never abstain from any evil work.

88. Wherefore we must look warily to such kind of people, that being in ignorance, they may be less evil for fear of that which is hidden and kept secret.

THE END OF THE FIRST BOOK

THE SECOND BOOK.

CALLED

"POEMANDER."

My Thoughts being once seriously busied about the things that are, and my Understanding lifted up, all my bodily Senses being exceedingly holden back, as it is with them that are very heavy of sleep, by reason either of fulness of meat, or of bodily labour. Me thought I saw one of an exceeding great stature, and an infinite greatness call me by my name, and say unto me, "What wouldest thou Hear and See? or what wouldest thou Understand, to Learn, and Know?"

2. Then said I, "Who art Thou?" "I am," quoth he, "Poemander, the mind of the Great Lord, the most Mighty and absolute Emperor: I know what thou wouldest have, and I am always present with thee."

3. Then said I, "I would Learn the Things that are, and Understand the Nature of them and know God." "How?" said he. I answered, "That I would gladly hear." Then he, "Have me again in thy mind, and whatsoever thou wouldst learn, I will teach thee."

4. When he had thus said, he was changed in his Idea or Form and straightway in the twinkling of an eye, all things were opened unto me: and I saw an infinite Sight, all things were become light, both sweet and exceedingly pleasant; and I was wonderfully delighted in the beholding it.

5. But after a little while, there was a darkness made in part, coming down obliquely, fearful and hideous, which seemed unto me to be changed into a

Certain Moist Nature, unspeakably troubled, which yielded a smoke as from fire; and from whence proceeded a voice unutterable, and very mournful, but inarticulate, insomuch that it seemed to have come from the Light.

6. Then from that Light, a certain Holy Word joined itself unto Nature, and out flew the pure and unmixed Fire from the moist Nature upward on high; it is exceeding Light, and Sharp, and Operative withal. And the Air which was also light, followed the Spirit and mounted up to Fire (from the Earth and the Water) insomuch that it seemed to hang and depend upon it.

7. And the Earth and the Water stayed by themselves so mingled together, that the Earth could not be seen for the Water, but they were moved, because of the Spiritual Word that was carried upon them.

8. Then said Poemander unto me, "Dost thou understand this Vision, and what it meaneth?" "I shall know," said I. Then said he, "I am that Light, the Mind, thy God, who am before that Moist Nature that appeareth out of Darkness, and that Bright and Lightful Word from the Mind is the Son of God."

9. "How is that?" quoth I. "Thus," replied he, "Understand it, That which in thee Seeth and Heareth, the Word of the Lord, and the Mind, the Father, God, Differeth not One from the Other, and the Unison of these is Life."

TRISMEG. I thank thee. PIMAND. But first conceive well the Light in thy mind and know it.

10. When he had thus said, for a long time we looked steadfastly one upon the other, insomuch that I trembled at his Idea or Form.

11. But when he nodded to me, I beheld in my mind the Light that is in innumerable, and the truly indefinite Ornament or World; and that the Fire is comprehended or contained in or by a most great Power, and constrained to keep its station.

12. These things I understood, seeing the word of

Pimander; and when I was mightily amazed, he said again unto me, "Hast thou seen in thy mind that Archetypal Form, which was before the interminated and Infinite Beginning?" Thus Pimander to me. "But whence," quoth I, "or whereof are the Elements of Nature made?" PIMANDER: "Of the Will and Counsel of God; which taking the Word, and beholding the beautiful World (in the Archetype thereof) imitated it, and so made this World, by the principles and vital Seeds or Soul-like productions of itself."

13. For the Mind being God, Male and Female, Life and Light, brought forth by his Word; another Mind, the Workman: Which being God of the Fire, and the Spirit, fashioned and formed seven other Governors, which in their Circles contain the Sensible World, whose Government or Disposition is called Fate or Destiny.

14. Straightway leaped out, or exalted itself from the downward born Elements of God, the Word of God into the clean and pure Workmanship of Nature, and was united to the Workman, Mind, for it was Consubstantial; and so the downward born Elements of Nature were left without Reason, that they might be the only Matter.

But the Workman, Mind, together with the Word, containing the Circles and Whirling them about, turned round as a Wheel his own Workmanships, and suffered them to be turned from an indefinite Beginning to an undeterminable End; for they always begin where they end.

16. And the Circulation or running round of these, as the Mind willeth, out of the lower or downward-born Elements brought forth unreasonable or brutish creatures, for they had no reason, the Air flying things, and the Water such as swim.

17. And the Earth and the Water was separated, either from the other, as the Mind would: and the Earth brought forth from herself such Living Creatures

as she had, four-footed and creeping Beasts, wild and tame.

18. But the Father of all things, the Mind being Life and Light, brought forth Man, like unto himself, whom he loved as his proper Birth, for he was all beauteous, having the Image of his Father.

19. For indeed God was exceedingly enamoured of his own Form or Shape, and delivered unto it all his own Workmanships. But he seeing and understanding the Creation of the Workman in the whole, would needs also himself Fall to Work, and so was separated from the Father, being in the sphere of Generation or operation.

20. Having all Power, he considered the Operations or Workmanships of the Seven; but they loved him, and every one made him partaker of his own Order.

21. And he learning diligently and understanding their Essence, and partaking their nature, resolved to pierce and break through the Circumference of the Circles, and to understand the Power of him that sits upon the Fire.

22. And having already all power of mortal things, of the Living, and of the unreasonable Creatures of the World, stooped down and peeped through the Harmony, and breaking through the strength of the Circles, so shewed and made manifest the downward-born Nature, the fair and beautiful Shape or Form of God.

23. Which when he saw, having in itself the unsatiable Beauty and all the Operation of the Seven Governors, and the Form or Shape of God, he Smiled for love, as if he had seen the Shape or Likeness in the Water, or the shadow upon the Earth of the fairest Human form.

24. And seeing in the Water a shape, a shape like unto himself in himself he loved it, and would cohabit with it; and immediately upon the resolution, ensued the Operation, and brought forth the unreasonable Image or Shape.

25. Nature presently laying hold of what it so much loved, did wholly wrap herself about it, and they were mingled, for they loved one another.

26. And for this cause, Man above all things that live upon Earth, is double; Mortal because of his Body, and Immortal because of the substantial Man: For being immortal, and having power of all things, he yet suffers mortal things, and such as are subject to Fate or Destiny.

27. And therefore being above all Harmony, he is made and become a servant to Harmony. And being Hermaphrodite, or Male and Female, and watchful, he is governed by and subjected to a Father, that is both Male and Female and watchful.

28. After these things, I said: "Thou art my Mind and I am in love with Reason."

29. Then said Pimander, "This is the Mystery that to this day is hidden, and kept secret; for Nature being mingled with Man brought forth a Wonder most wonderful; for he having the Nature of the Harmony of the Seven, from him whom I told thee, the Fire and the Spirit, Nature continued not, but forthwith brought forth seven Men all Males and Females and sublime, or on high, according to the Natures of the Seven Governors."

30. "And after these things, O Pimander," quoth I, "I am now come into a great desire, and longing to hear, do not digress, or run out."

31. But he said, "Keep silence, for I have not yet finished the first speech."

32. TRISM. Behold, I am silent.

33. PIMAND. The Generation therefore of these Seven was after this manner, the Air being Feminine and the Water desirous of Copulation, took from the Fire its ripeness, and from the æther Spirit; and so Nature produced bodies after the Species and Shape of men.

34. And Man was made of Life and Light into Soul and Mind, of Life the Soul, of Light the Mind.

35. And so all the Members of the Sensible World, continued unto the period of the end, bearing rule, and generating.

36. Hear now the rest of that speech, thou so much desirest to hear.

37. When that Period was fulfilled, the bond of all things was loosed and untied by the Will of God; for all living Creatures being Hermaphroditical, or Male and Female, were loosed and untied together with Man; and so the Males were apart by themselves and the Females likewise.

38. And straightway God said to the Holy Word, Increase in Increasing, and Multiply in Multitude all you my Creatures and Workmanships. And let Him that is endued with Mind, know Himself to be Immortal; and that the cause of Death is the Love of the Body, and let Him Learn all Things that are.

39. When he had thus said, Providence by Fate and Harmony, made the mixtures, and established the Generations, and all things were multiplied according to their kind, and he that knew himself, came at length to the Superstantial of every way substantial good.

40. But he that through the Error of Love, loved the Body, abideth wandering in darkness, sensible, suffering the things of death.

41. TRISM. But why do they that are ignorant sin so much, that they should therefore be deprived of immortality.

42. PIMAND. Thou seemest not to have understood what thou hast heard.

43. TRISM. Peradventure I seem so to thee, but I both understand and remember them.

44. PIMAND. I am glad for thy sake, if thou understoodest them.

45. TRISM. Tell me, why are they worthy of death, that are in death?

46. PIMAND. Because there goeth a sad and dismal darkness before its Body; of which darkness is the

moist Nature, of which moist Nature, the Body consisteth in the sensible World, from whence death is derived. Hast thou understood this aright?

47. TRISM. But why or how doth he that understands himself, go or pass into God?

48. PIMAND. That which the Word of God said, say I: Because the Father of all things consists of Life and Light, whereof Man is made.

49. TRISM. Thou sayest very well.

50. PIMAND. God and the Father is Light and Life, of which Man is made. If therefore thou learn and believe thyself to be of the Life and Light, thou shalt again pass into Life.

51. TRISM. But yet tell me more, O my Mind, how I shall go into Life.

52. PIMAND. God saith, Let the Man endued with a Mind, mark, consider, and know himself well.

53. TRISM. Have not all Men a mind?

54. PIMAND. Take heed what thou sayest, for I the Mind come unto men that are holy and good, pure and merciful, and that live piously and religiously; and my presence is a help unto them. And forthwith they know all things, and lovingly they supplicate and propitiate the Father; and blessing him, they give him thanks, and sing hymns unto him, being ordered and directed by filial Affection, and natural Love: And before they give up their Bodies to the death of them, they hate their Senses, knowing their Works and Operations.

55. Rather I that am the Mind itself, will not suffer the Operations or Works, which happen or belong to the body, to be finished and brought to perfection in them; but being the Porter and Door-keeper, I will shut up the entrances of Evil, and cut off the thoughtful desires of filthy works.

56. But to the foolish, and evil, and wicked, and envious and covetous, and murderous, and profane, I am far off giving place to the avenging Demon, which applying unto him the sharpness of fire, tormenteth

such a man sensibly, and armeth him the more to all wickedness, that he may obtain the greater punishment.

57. And such a one never ceaseth, having unfulfillable desires and unsatiable concupiscences, and always fighting in darkness for the Demon afflicts and tormenteth him continually, and increaseth the fire upon him more and more.

58. TRISM. Thou hast, O Mind, most excellently taught me all things, as I desired; but tell me moreover, after the return is made, what then?

59. PIMAND. First of all, in the resolution of the material Body, the Body itself is given up to alteration, and the form which it had, becometh invisible; and the idle manners are permitted, and left to the Demon, and the Senses of the Body return into their Fountains, being parts, and again made up into Operations.

60. And Anger and Concupiscence go into the brutish or unreasonable Nature; and the rest striveth upward by Harmony.

61. And to the first Zone it giveth the power it had of increasing and diminishing.

62. To the second, the machination or plotting of evils, and one effectual deceit or craft.

63. To the third, the idle deceit of Concupiscence.

64. To the fourth, the desire of Rule, and unsatiable Ambition.

65. To the fifth, profane Boldness, and headlong rashness of Confidence.

66. To the sixth, Evil and ineffectual occasions of Riches.

67. And to the seventh Zone, subtle Falsehood always lying in wait.

68. And then being made naked of all the Operations of Harmony it cometh to the eighth Nature, having its proper power, and singeth praises to the Father with the things that are, and all they that are present rejoice, and congratulate the coming of it; and being made like to them with whom it converseth, it heareth

also the Powers that are above the eighth Nature, singing praise to God in a certain voice that is peculiar to them.

69. And then in order they return unto the Father, and themselves deliver themselves to the powers, and becoming powers they are in God.

70. This is the Good, and to them that know to be deified.

71. Furthermore, why sayest thou, What resteth, but that understanding all men, thou become a guide, and way-leader to them that are worthy ; that the kind of Humanity or Mankind, may be saved by God ?

72. When Pimander had thus said unto me, he was mingled among the Powers.

73. But I giving thanks, and blessing the Father of all things, rose up, being enabled by him, and taught the Nature, of the Nature of the whole and having seen the greatest sight or spectacle.

74. And I began to Preach unto men, the beauty and fairness of Piety and Knowledge.

75. O ye People, Men, born and made of the Earth, which have given Yourselves over to Drunkenness, and Sleep, and to the Ignorance of God, be Sober, and Cease your Surfeit, whereto you are allured, and invited by Brutish and Unreasonable Sleep.

76. And they that heard me, come willingly, and with one accord, and then I said further.

77. Why, O Men of the Off-spring of the Earth, why have you delivered Yourselves over unto Death, having Power to Partake of Immortality ; Repent and Change your Minds, you that have together Walked in Error, and have been Darkened in Ignorance.

78. Depart from that dark Light, be Partakers of Immortality, and Leave or Forsake Corruption.

79. And some of Them That Heard Me, mocking and scorning, went away and delivered themselves up to the way of death.

80. But others, casting themselves down before my

feet, besought me that they might be taught; but I causing them to rise up, became a guide of mankind, teaching them the reasons how, and by what means they may be saved. And I sowed in them the words of Wisdom, and nourished them with Ambrosian Water of Immortality.

81. And when it was Evening, and the Brightness of the same began wholly to go down, I commanded them to give thanks to God; and when they had finished their thanksgiving, everyone returned to his own lodging.

82. But I wrote in myself the bounty and beneficence of Pimander; and being filled with what I most desired, I was exceeding glad.

83. For the sleep of the Body was the sober watchfulness of the mind; and the shutting of my eyes the true Sight, and my silence great with child and full of good; and the pronouncing of my words, the blossoms and fruits of good things.

84. And thus came to pass or happened unto me, which I received from my mind, that is, Pimander, the Lord of the Word; whereby I became inspired by God with the Truth.

85. For which cause, with my Soul, and whole strength, I give praise and blessing unto God the Father.

86. Holy is God the Father of All Things.

87. Holy is God Whose Will is Performed and Accomplished by His Own Powers.

88. Holy is God, that Determineth to be Known, and is Known of His Own, or Those that are His.

89. Holy art Thou, that by Thy Word hast established all Things.

90. Holy art Thou of Whom all Nature is the Image.

91. Holy art Thou Whom Nature hath not Formed.

92. Holy art Thou that art Stronger than all Power.

93. Holy art Thou, that art Greater than all Excellency.

94. Holy art Thou, Who art Better than all Praise.

95. Accept these Reasonable Sacrifices from a Pure Soul, and a Heart stretched out unto Thee.

96. O Thou Unspeakable, Unutterable, to be Praised with Silence!

97. I beseech Thee, that I may never Err from the Knowledge of Thee, Look Mercifully upon Me, and Enable Me, and Enlighten with this Grace, those that are in Ignorance, the Brothers of my Kind, but Thy Sons.

98. Therefore I Believe Thee, and Bear Witness, and go into the Life and Light.

98. Blessed art Thou, O Father, Thy Man would be Sanctified with Thee, as Thou hast given Him all Power.

THE END OF THE SECOND BOOK.

THE THIRD BOOK

CALLED

"THE HOLY SERMON."

The glory of all things, God and that which is Divine, and the Divine Nature, the beginning of things that are.

2. God, and the Mind, and Nature, and Matter, and Operation, or Working and Necessity, and the End and Renovation.

3. For there were in the Chaos, an infinite darkness in the Abyss or bottomless Depth, and Water, and a subtle Spirit intelligible in Power; and there went out the Holy Light, and the Elements were coagulated from the Sand out of the moist Substance.

4. And all the Gods distinguished the Nature full of Seeds.

5. And when all things were interminated and unmade up, the light things were divided on high. And the heavy things were founded upon the moist sand, all things being Terminated or Divided by Fire; and being sustained or hung up by the Spirit they were so carried, and the Heaven was seen in Seven Circles.

6. And the Gods were seen in their Ideas of the Stars, with all their Signs, and the Stars were numbered, with the Gods in them. And the Sphere was all lined with Air, carried about in a circular motion by the Spirit of God.

7. And every God by his internal power, did that which was commanded him; and there were made four footed things, and creeping things, and such as live in

the Water, and such as fly, and every fruitful Seed, and Grass, and the Flowers of all Greens, and which had sowed in themselves the Seeds of Regeneration.

8. As also the Generations of men to the knowledge of the Divine Works, and a lively or working Testimony of Nature, and a multitude of men, and the Dominion of all things under Heaven and the knowledge of good things, and to be increased in increasing, and multiplied in multitude.

9. And every Soul in flesh, by the wonderful working of the Gods in the Circles, to the beholding of Heaven, the Gods, Divine Works, and the Operations of Nature; and for Signs of good things, and the knowledge of the Divine Power, and to find out every cunning workmanship of good things.

10. So it beginneth to live in them, and to be wise according to the Operation of the course of the circular Gods; and to be resolved into that which shall be great Monuments; and Remembrances of the cunning Works done upon Earth, leaving them to be read by the darkness of times.

11. And every generation of living flesh, of Fruit, Seed, and all Handicrafts, though they be lost, must of necessity be renewed by the renovation of the Gods, and of the Nature of a Circle, moving in number; for it is a Divine thing, that every world temperature should be renewed by nature, for in that which is Divine, is Nature also established.

THE END OF THE FRAGMENTS OF THE THIRD BOOK.

Very Imperfect.

THE FOURTH BOOK

CALLED

"THE KEY."

YESTERDAY's Speech, O Asclepius, I dedicated to thee, this day's it is fit to dedicate to Tat, because it is an Epitome of those general speeches that were spoken to him.

2. God therefore, and the Father, and the Good, O Tat, have the same Nature, or rather also the same Act and Operation.

3. For there is one name or appellation of Nature and Increase which concerneth things changeable, and another about things unchangeable, and about things unmoveable, that is to say, Things Divine and Human; every one of which, himself will have so to be; but action or operation is of another thing, or elsewhere, as we have taught in other things, Divine and Human, which must here also be understood.

4. For his Operation or Act, is his Will, and his Essence, to Will all Things to be.

5. For what is God, and the Father, and the Good, but the Being of all things that yet are not, and the existence itself, of those things that are?

6. This is God, this is the Father, this is the Good, whereunto no other thing is present or approacheth.

7. For the World, and the Sun, which is also a Father by Participation, is not for all that equally the cause of Good, and of Life, to living Creatures: And if this be so, he is altogether constrained by the Will of

the Good, without which it is not possible, either to be, or to be begotten or made.

8. But the Father is the cause of his Children, who hath a will both to sow and nourish that which is good by the Son.

9. For Good is always active or busy in making; and this cannot be in any other, but in him that taketh nothing, and yet willeth all things to be; for I will not say, O Tat, making them; for he that maketh is defective in much time, in which sometimes he maketh not, as also of quantity and quality; for sometimes he maketh those things that have quantity and quality and sometimes the contrary.

10. But God is the Father, and the Good, in being all things; for he both will be this, and is it, and yet all this for himself (as is true) in him that can see it.

11. For all things else are for this, it is the property of Good to be known: This is the Good, O Tat.

12. TAT. Thou hast filled us, O Father, with a sight both good and fair, and the eye of my mind is almost become more holy by the sight or spectacle.

13. TRISM. "I Wonder not at It, for the Sight of Good is not like the Beam of the Sun, which being of a fiery shining brightness, maketh the eye blind by his excessive Light, that gazeth upon it; rather the contrary, for it enlighteneth, and so much increaseth the light of the eye, as any man is able to receive the influence of this intelligible clearness.

14. For it is more swift and sharp to pierce, and innocent or harmless withal, and full of immortality, and they that are capable and can draw any store of this spectacle, and sight do many times fall asleep from the Body, into this most fair and beauteous Vision; which thing Celius and Saturn our Progenitors obtained unto.

15. TAT. I would we also, O Father, could do so.

16. TRISM. I would we could, O Son; but for the present we are less intent to the Vision, and cannot yet open the eyes of our minds to behold the incorruptible,

and incomprehensible Beauty of that Good: But then shall we see it, when we have nothing at all to say of it.

17. For the knowledge of it, is a Divine Silence, and the rest of all the Senses; For neither can he that understands that understand anything else, nor he that sees that, see any thing else, nor hear any other thing, nor in sum, move the Body.

18. For shining steadfastly upon, and round about the whole Mind it enlighteneth all the Soul; and loosing it from the Bodily Senses and Motions, it draweth it from the Body, and changeth it wholly into the Essence of God.

19. For it is Possible for the Soul, O Son, to be Deified while yet it Lodgeth in the Body of Man, if it Contemplate the Beauty of the Good.

20. Tat. How dost thou mean deifying, Father?

21. Trism. There are differences, O Son, of every Soul.

22. Tat. But how dost thou again divide the changes?

23. Trism. Hast thou not heard in the general Speeches, that from one Soul of the Universe, are all those Souls, which in all the world are tossed up and down, as it were, and severally divided? Of these Souls there are many changes, some into a more fortunate estate, and some quite contrary; for they which are of creeping things, are changed into those of watery things and those of things living in the water, to those of things living upon the Land; and Airy ones are changed into men, and human Souls, that lay hold of immortality, are changed into Demons.

24. And so they go on into the Sphere or Region of the fixed Gods, for there are two choirs or companies of Gods, one of them that wander, and another of them that are fixed. And this is the most perfect glory of the Soul.

25. But the Soul entering into the Body of a Man, if it continue evil, shall neither taste of immortality, nor is partaker of the good.

26. But being drawn back the same way, it returneth into creeping things. And this is the condemnation of an evil Soul.

27. And the wickedness of a Soul is ignorance; for the Soul that knows nothing of the things that are, neither the Nature of them, nor that which is good, but is blinded, rusheth and dasheth against the bodily Passions, and unhappy as it is, not knowing itself, it serveth strange Bodies, and evil ones, carrying the Body as a burthen, and not ruling, but ruled. And this is the mischief of the Soul.

28. On the contrary, the virtue of the Soul is Knowledge; for he that knows is both good and religious, and already Divine.

29. TAT. But who is such a one, O Father?

30. TRISM. He that neither speaks, nor hears many things; for he, O Son, that heareth two speeches or hearings, fighteth in the shadow.

31. For God, and the Father, and Good, is neither spoken nor heard.

32. This being so in all things that are, are the Senses, because they cannot be without them.

33. But Knowledge differs much from Sense; for Sense is of things that surmount it, but Knowledge is the end of Sense.

34. Knowledge is the gift of God; for all Knowledge is unbodily but useth the Mind as an Instrument, as the Mind useth the Body.

35. Therefore both intelligible and material things go both of them into bodies; for, of contraposition, That is Setting One against Another, and Contrariety, all Things must Consist. And it is impossible it should be otherwise.

36. TAT. Who therefore is this material God?

37. TRISM. The fair and beautiful world, and yet it is not good; for it is material and easily passible, nay, it is the first of all passible things; and the second of the things that are, and needy or wanting somewhat

else. And it was once made and is always, and is ever in generation, and made, and continually makes, or generates things that have quantity and quality.

38. For it is moveable, and every material motion is generation; but the intellectual stability moves the material motion after this manner.

39. Because the World is a Sphere, that is a Head, and above the head there is nothing material, as beneath the feet there is nothing intellectual.

40. The whole universe is material; The Mind is the head, and it is moved spherically, that is like a head.

41. Whatsoever therefore is joined or united to the Membrane or Film of this head, wherein the Soul is, is immortal, and as in the Soul of a made Body, hath its Soul full of the Body; but those that are further from that Membrane, have the Body full of Soul.

42. The whole is a living wight, and therefore consisteth of material and intellectual.

43. And the World is the first, and Man the second living wight after the World; but the first of things that are mortal and therefore hath whatsoever benefit of the Soul all the others have: And yet for all this, he is not only not good, but flatly evil, as being mortal.

44. For the World is not good as it is moveable; nor evil as it is immortal.

45. But man is evil, both as he is moveable, and as he is mortal.

46. But the Soul of Man is carried in this manner, The Mind is in Reason, Reason in the Soul, the Soul in the Spirit, the Spirit in the Body.

47. The Spirit being diffused and going through the veins, and arteries, and blood, both moveth the living Creature, and after a certain manner beareth it.

48. Wherefore some also have thought the Soul to be blood, being deceived in Nature, not knowing that first the Spirit must return into the Soul, and then the blood is congealed, the veins and arteries emptied, and

then the living thing dieth: And this is the death of the Body.

49. All things depend of one beginning, and the beginning depends of that which is one and alone.

50. And the beginning is moved, that it may again be a beginning; but that which is one, standeth and abideth, and is not moved.

51. There are therefore these three, God the Father; and the Good, the World and Man: God hath the World, and the World hath Man; and the World is the Son of God, and Man as it were the Offspring of the World.

52. For God is not ignorant of Man, but knows him perfectly, and will be known by him. This only is healthful to man; the Knowledge of God: this is the return of Olympus; by this only the Soul is made good, and not sometimes good, and sometimes evil, but of necessity Good.

53. TAT. What meanest thou, O Father?

54. TRISM. Consider, O Son, the Soul of a Child, when as yet it hath received no dissolution of its Body, which is not yet grown, but is very small; how then if it look upon itself, it sees itself beautiful, as not having been yet spotted with the Passions of the Body, but as it were depending yet upon the Soul of the World.

55. But when the Body is grown and distracteth, the Soul it engenders Forgetfulness, and partakes no more of the Fair and the Good, and Forgetfulness is Evilness.

56. The like also happeneth to them that go out of the Body: for when the Soul runs back into itself the Spirit is contracted into the blood and the Soul into the Spirit; but the Mind being made pure, and free from these clothings; and being Divine by Nature, taking a fiery Body rangeth abroad in every place, leaving the Soul to judgment, and to the punishment it hath deserved.

57. TAT. Why dost thou say so, O Father, that the Mind is separated from the Soul, and the Soul from the

Spirit? When even now thou saidst the Soul was the Clothing or Apparel of the Mind, and the Body of the Soul.

58. TRISM. O Son, he that hears must co-understand and conspire in thought with him that speaks; yea, he must have his hearing swifter and sharper than the voice of the speaker.

59. The disposition of these Clothings or Covers, is done in an Earthly Body; for it is impossible, that the Mind should establish or rest itself, naked, and of itself; in an Earthly Body; neither is the Earthly Body able to bear such immortality; and therefore that it might suffer so great virtue the Mind compacted as it were, and took to itself the passible Body of the Soul, as a Covering or Clothing. And the Soul being also in some sort Divine, useth the Spirit as her Minister and Servant, and the Spirit governeth the living thing.

60. When therefore the Mind is separated, and departeth from the earthly Body, presently it puts on its Fiery Coat, which it could not do having to dwell in an Earthly Body.

61. For the Earth cannot suffer fire, for it is all burned of a small spark; therefore is the water poured round about the Earth, as a Wall or defence, to withstand the flame of fire.

62. But the Mind being the most sharp or swift of all the Divine Cogitations, and more swift than all the Elements, hath the fire for its Body.

63. For the Mind which is the Workman of all, useth the fire as his instrument in his Workmanship; and he that is the Workman of all, useth it to the making of all things, as it is used by man, to the making of Earthly things only; for the Mind that is upon Earth, void, or naked of fire, cannot do the business of men, nor that which is otherwise the affairs of God.

64. But the Soul of Man, and yet not every one, but that which is pious and religious, is Angelical and Divine. And such a Soul, after it is departed from the

Body, having striven the strife of Piety, becomes either Mind or God.

65. And the strife of Piety is to know God, and to injure no Man, and this way it becomes Mind.

66. But an impious Soul abideth in its own essence, punished of itself, and seeking an earthly and human Body to enter into.

67. For no other Body is capable of a Human Soul, neither is it lawful for a Man's Soul to fall into the Body of an unreasonable living thing: for it is the Law or Decree of God, to preserve a Human Soul from so great a contumely and reproach.

68. TAT. How then is the Soul of Man punished, O Father; and what is its greatest torment.

69. HERM. Impiety, O my Son; for what Fire hath so great a flame as it? Or what biting Beast doth so tear the Body as it doth the Soul.

70. Or dost thou not see how many evils the wicked Soul suffereth, roaring and crying out, I am Burned, I am Consumed, I know not what to Say, or Do, I am Devoured, Unhappy Wretch, of the Evils that compass and lay hold upon me; Miserable that I am, I neither See nor Hear anything.

71. These are the voices of a punished and tormented Soul, and not as many; and thou, O Son, thinkest that the Soul going out of the Body grows brutish or enters into a Beast: which is a very great Error, for the Soul punished after this manner.

72. For the Mind, when it is ordered or appointed to get a fiery Body for the services of God, coming down into the wicked Soul, torments it with the whips of Sins, wherewith the wicked Soul being scourged, turns itself to Murders, and Contumelies, and Blasphemies, and divers Violences, and other things by which men are injured.

73. But into a pious Soul, the Mind entering, leads it into the Light of Knowledge.

74. And such a Soul is never satisfied with singing

praise to God, and speaking well of all men; and both in words and deeds, always doing good in imitation of her Father.

75. Therefore, O Son, we must give thanks, and pray, that we may obtain a good mind.

76. The Soul therefore may be altered or changed into the better, but into the worse it is impossible.

77. But there is a communion of Souls, and those of Gods, communicate with those of men; and those of men, with those of Beasts.

78. And the better always take of the worse, Gods of Men, Men of brute Beasts, but God of all: For he is the best of all, and all things are less than he.

79. Therefore is the World subject unto God, Man unto the World and unreasonable things to Man.

80. But God is above all, and about all; and the beams of God are operations; and the beams of the World are Natures; and the beams of Man are Arts and Sciences.

81. And Operations do act by the World, and upon man by the natural beams of the World, but Natures work by the Elements, and man by Arts and Sciences.

82. And this is the Government of the whole, depending upon the Nature of the One, and piercing or coming down by the One Mind, than which nothing is more Divine, and more efficacious or operative; and nothing more uniting, or nothing is more One. The Communion of Gods to Men, and of Men to God.

83. This is the Bonus Genius, or good Demon, blessed Soul that is fullest of it! and unhappy Soul that is empty of it!

84. TAT. And wherefore Father?

85. TRISM. Know Son, that every Soul hath the Good Mind; for of that it is we now speak, and not of that Minister of which we said before, That he was sent from the Judgment.

86. For the Soul without the Mind, can neither do,

nor say any thing; for many times the Mind flies away from the Soul, and in that hour the Soul neither seeth nor heareth, but is like an unreasonable thing; so great is the power of the Mind.

87. But neither brooketh it an idle or lazy Soul, but leaves such a one fastened to the Body, and by it pressed down.

88. And such a Soul, O Son, hath no mind, wherefore neither must such a one be called a Man.

89. For man is a Divine living thing, and is not to be compared to any brute Beast that lives upon Earth, but to them that are above in Heaven, that are called Gods.

90. Rather, if we shall be bold to speak the truth, he that is a man indeed, is above them, or at least they are equal in power, one to the other, For none of the things in Heaven will come down upon Earth, and leave the limits of Heaven, but a man ascends up into Heaven, and measures it.

91. And he knoweth what things are on high, and what below, and learneth all other things exactly.

92. And that which is the greatest of all, he leaveth not the Earth, and yet is above: So great is the greatness of his Nature.

93. Wherefore we must be bold to say, That an Earthly Man is a Mortal God, and That the Heavenly God is an Immortal Man.

94. Wherefore, by these two are all things governed, the World and Man; but they and all things else, of that which is One.

THE END OF THE FOURTH BOOK.

THE FIFTH BOOK.

"THAT GOD IS NOT MANIFEST AND YET MOST MANIFEST."

1. This Discourse I will also make to thee, O Tat, that thou mayest not be ignorant of the more excellent Name of God.

2. But do thou contemplate in thy Mind, how that which to many seems hidden and unmanifest, may be most manifest unto thee.

3. For it were not all, if it were apparent, for whatsoever is apparent, is generated or made; for it was made manifest, but that which is not manifest is ever.

4. For it needeth not to be manifested, for it is always.

5. And he maketh all other things manifest, being unmanifest as being always, and making other things manifest, he is not made manifest.

9. Himself is not made, yet in fantasy he fantasieth all things, or in appearance he maketh them appear, for appearance is only of those things that are generated or made, for appearance is nothing but generation.

7. But he is that One, that is not made nor generated, is also unapparent and unmanifest.

1 But making all things appear, he appeareth in all and by all; but especially he is manifested to, or in those things wherein himself listeth.

9. Thou therefore, O Tat, my Son, pray first to the Lord and Father, and to the Alone and to the One, from whom is one to be merciful to thee, that thou mayest knowest and understand so great a God; and

that he would shine one of his beams upon thee in thy understanding.

10. For only the Understanding sees that which is not manifest or apparent, as being itself not manifest or apparent; and if thou canst, O Tat, it will appear to the eyes of thy Mind.

11. For the Lord, void of envy, appeareth through the whole world. Thou mayest see the intelligence, and take it in thy hands, and contemplate the Image of God.

12. But if that which is in thee, be not known or apparent unto thee, how shall he in thee be seen, and appear unto thee by the eyes?

13. But if thou wilt see him, consider and understand the Sun, consider the course of the Moon, consider the order of the Stars.

14. Who is he that keepeth order? for all order is circumscribed or terminated in number and place.

15. The Sun is the greatest of the Gods in heaven, to whom all the heavenly Gods give place, as to a King and potentate; and yet he being such a one, greater than the Earth or the Sea, is content to suffer infinite lesser stars to walk and move above himself; whom doth he fear the while, O Son?

16. Every one of these Stars that are in Heaven, do not make the like, or an equal course; who is it that hath prescribed unto every one, the manner and the greatness of their course?

17. This Bear that turns round about its own self; and carries round the whole World with her, who possessed and made such an Instrument.

18. Who hath set the Bounds to the Sea? who hath established the Earth? for there is some body, O Tat, that is the Maker and Lord of these things.

19. For it is impossible, O Son, that either place, or number, or measure, should be observed without a Maker.

20. For no order can be made by disorder or disproportion.

21. I would it were possible for thee, O my Son, to have wings, and to fly into the Air, and being taken up in the midst, between Heaven and Earth, to see the stability of the Earth, the fluidness of the Sea, the courses of the Rivers, the largeness of the Air, the sharpness or swiftness of the Fire, the motion of the Stars; and the speediness of the Heaven, by which it goeth round about all these.

22. O Son, what a happy sight it were, at one instant, to see all these, that which is unmovable moved, and that which is hidden appear and be manifest.

23. And if thou wilt see and behold this Workman, even by mortal things that are upon Earth, and in the deep, consider, O Son, how Man is made and framed in the Womb; and examine diligently the skill and cunning of the Workman, and learn who it was that wrought and fashioned the beautiful and Divine shape of Man; who circumscribed and marked out his eyes? who bored his nostrils and ears? who opened his mouth? who stretched out and tied together his sinews? who channelled the veins? who hardened and made strong the bones? who clothed the flesh with skin? who divided the fingers and the joints? who flatted and made broad the soles of the feet? who digged the pores? who stretched out the spleen, who made the heart like a Pyramis? who made the Liver broad? who made the Lights spungy, and full of holes? who made the belly large and capacious? who set to outward view the more honourable parts and hid the filthy ones.

24. See how many Arts in one Matter, and how many Works in one Superscription, and all exceedingly beautiful, and all done in measure, and yet all differing.

25. Who hath made all these things? what Mother? what Father? save only God that is not manifest? that made all things by his own Will.

26. And no man says that a statue or an image is made without a Carver or a Painter, and was this Work-

manship made without a Workman? O great Blindness, O great Impiety, O great Ignorance.

27. Never, O Son Tat, canst thou deprive the Workmanship of the Workman, rather it is the best Name of all the Names of God, to call him the Father of all, for so he is alone; and this is his work to be the Father.

28. And if thou wilt force me to say anything more boldly, it is his Essence to be pregnant, or great with all things, and to make them.

29. And as without a Maker, it is impossible that anything should be made, so it is that he should not always be, and always be making all things in Heaven, in the Air, in the Earth, in the Deep, in the whole World, and in every part of the whole that is, or that is not.

30. For there is nothing in the whole World, that is not himself both the things that are and the things that are not.

31. For the things that are, he hath made manifest; and the things that are not, he hath hid in himself.

32. This is God that is better than any name; this is he that is secret; this is he that is most manifest; this is he that is to be seen by the Mind; this is he that is visible to the eye; this is he that hath no body; and this is he that hath many bodies, rather there is nothing of any body, which is not He.

33. For he alone is all things.

34. And for this cause He hath all Names, because He is the One Father; and therefore He hath no Name, because He is the Father of all.

35. Who therefore can bless thee, or give thanks for thee, or to thee.

36. Which way shall I look, when I praise thee? upward? downward? outward? inward?

37. For about thee there is no manner, nor place, nor anything else of all things that are.

38. But all things are in thee; all things from thee,

thou givest all things, and takest nothing; for thou hast all things and there is nothing that thou hast not.

39. When shall I praise thee, O Father; for it is neither possible to comprehend thy hour, nor thy time?

40. For what shall I praise thee? for what thou hast made, or for what thou hast not made? for those things thou hast manifested, or for those things thou hast hidden?

41. Wherefore shall I praise thee as being of myself, or having anything of mine own, or rather being another's?

42. For thou art what I am, thou art what I do, thou art what I say.

43. Thou Art All Things, and there is Nothing Else Thou Art Not.

44. Thou Art Thou, All that is Made, and All that is not Made.

45. The Mind that Understandeth.

46. The Father that Maketh and Frameth.

47. The Good that Worketh.

48. The Good that doth All Things.

49. Of the Matter, the most subtle and slender part is Air, of the Air the Soul, of the Soul the Mind, of the Mind God.

The End of the Fifth Book.

THE SIXTH BOOK.
THAT IN GOD ALONE IS GOOD.

1. Good, O Asclepius, is in nothing but in God alone; or rather God himself is the Good always.
2. And if it be so, then must he be an Essence or Substance void of all motion and generation; but nothing is void or empty of him.
3. And this Essence hath about or in himself a Stable, and firm Operation, wanting nothing, most full, and giving abundantly.
4. One thing is the Beginning of all things, for it giveth all things; and when I name the Good, I mean that which is altogether and always Good.
5. This is present to none, but God alone; for he wanteth nothing, that he should desire to have it, nor can anything be taken from him; the loss whereof may grieve him; for sorrow is a part of evilness.
6. Nothing is stronger than he, that he should be opposed by it; nor nothing equal to him, that he should be in love with it; nothing unheard of to be angry, with nothing wiser to be envious at.
7. And none of these being in his Essence, what remains, but only the Good?
8. For as in this, being such an Essence, there is none of the evils; so in none of the other things shall the Good be found.
9. For in all other things, are all those other things as well in the small as the great; and as well in the particulars as in this living Creature the greater and mightiest of all.
10. For all things that are made or generated are

full of Passion, Generation itself being a Passion; and where Passion is there is not the Good; where the Good is, there is no Passion; where it is day, it is not night, and where it is night, it is not day.

11. Wherefore it is impossible, that in Generation should be the Good, but only in that which is not generated or made.

12. Yet as the Participation of all things is in the Matter bound, so also of that which is Good. After this manner is the World good, as it maketh all things, and in the part of making or doing it is Good, but in all other things not good.

13. For it is passible, and movable, and the Maker of passible things.

14. In Man also the Good is ordered (or Taketh Denomination) in comparison of that which is evil; for that which is not very evil, is here good; and that which is here called Good, is the least particle, or proportion of evil.

15. It is impossible therefore, that the Good should be here pure from Evil; for here the Good groweth Evil, and growing Evil, it doth not still abide Good; and not abiding Good it becomes Evil.

16. Therefore in God alone is the Good, or rather God is the Good.

17. Therefore, O Asclepius, there is nothing in men (or among Men) but the name of Good, the thing itself is not, for it is impossible; for a material Body receiveth (or Comprehendeth), is not as being on every side encompassed and coarcted with evilness, and labours, and griefs, and desires, and wrath, and deceits, and foolish opinions.

18. And in that which is the worst of all, Asclepius, every one of the forenamed things, is here believed to be the greatest good, especially that supreme mischief the pleasures of the Belly, and the ring-leader of all evils; Error is here the absence of the Good.

19. And I give thanks unto God, that concerning

the knowledge of Good, put this assurance in my mind, that it is impossible it should be in the World.

20. For the World is the fulness of evilness; but God is the fulness of Good, or Good of God.

21. For the eminencies of all appearing Beauty, are in the Essence more pure, more sincere, and peradventure they are also the Essence of it.

22. For we must be bold to say, Asclepius, that the Essence of God, if he have an Essence, is that which is fair or beautiful; but no good is comprehended in this World.

23. For all things that are subject to the eye, are Idols, and as it were shadows; but those things that are not subject to the eye, are ever, especially the Essence of the Fair and the Good.

24. And as the eye cannot see God, so neither the Fair, and the Good.

25. For these are the parts of God that partake the Nature of the whole, proper, and familiar unto him alone, inseparable, most lovely, whereof either God is enamoured, or they are enamoured of God.

26. If thou canst understand God, thou shalt understand the Fair, and the Good which is most shining, and enlightening, and most enlightened by God.

27. For that Beauty is above comparison, and that Good is inimitable, as God himself.

28. As therefore thou understandest God, so understand the Fair and the Good, for these are incommunicable to any other living Creatures because they are inseparable from God.

29. If thou seek concerning God, thou seekest or askest also of the Fair, for there is one way that leads to the same thing, that is Piety with Knowledge.

30. Wherefore, they that are ignorant, and go not in the way of Piety, dare call Man Fair and Good, never seeing so much as in a dream, what Good is; but being enfolded and wrapped upon all evil, and believing that the evil is the Good, they by that means, both use it

unsatiably, and are afraid to be deprived of it; and therefore they strive by all possible means, that they may not only have it, but also increase it.

31. Such, O Asclepius, are the Good and Fair things of men, which we can neither love nor hate, for this is the hardest thing of all, that we have need of them, and cannot live without them.

The End of the Sixth Book.

THE SEVENTH BOOK.

HIS SECRET SERMON IN THE MOUNT OF REGENERATION, AND THE PROFESSION OF SILENCE.

To His Son Tat.

1. TAT. In the general Speeches, O Father, discoursing of the Divinity, thou speakest enigmatically, and didst not clearly reveal thyself, saying, That no man can be saved before Regeneration.

2. And when I did humbly entreat thee, at the going up the Mountain after thou hadst discoursed unto me, having a great desire, to learn this Argument of Regeneration; because among all the rest, I am ignorant only of this thou toldst me thou wouldst impart it unto me, when I would estrange myself from the World: whereupon I made myself ready, and have vindicated the understanding that is in me, from the deceit of the World.

3. Now then fulfil my defects, and as thou saidst instruct me of Regeneration, either by word of mouth or secretly; for I know not, O Trismegistus, of what Substance, or what Womb or what Seed a Man is thus born.

4. HERM. O Son, this Wisdom is to be understood in silence, and the Seed is the true Good.

5. TAT. Who soweth it, O Father? for I am utterly ignorant and doubtful.

6. HERM. The Will of God, O Son.

7. And what manner of Man is he that is thus born? for in this point, I am clean deprived of the Essence that understandeth in me.

8. HERM. The Son of God will be another, God made the universe, that in everything consisteth of all powers.

9. TAT. Thou tellest me a Riddle, Father, and dost not speak as a Father to his Son.

10. HERM. Son, things of this kind are not taught, but are by God, when he pleaseth, brought to remembrance.

11. TAT. Thou speakest of things strained, or far fetched, and impossible, Father; and therefore I will directly contradict them.

12. HERM. Wilt thou prove a stranger, Son, to thy Father's kind.

13. Do not envy me, Father, or pardon me, I am thy Natural Son; discourse unto me the manner of Regeneration.

14. HERM. What shall I say, O my Son? I have nothing to say more than this, that I see in myself an unfeigned sight or spectacle, made by the mercy of God, and I am gone out of myself into an immortal body, and am not now what I was before, but was begotten in Mind.

15. This thing is not taught, nor is it to be seen in this formed Element; for which the first compound form was neglected by me; and that I am now separated from it; for I have both the touch and the measure of it, yet am I now estranged from them.

16. Thou seest, O Son, with thine eyes; but though thou look never so steadfastly upon me, with the Body, and bodily sight, thou canst not see, nor understand what I am now.

17. TAT. Thou hast driven me, O Father, into no small fury and distraction of mind, for I do not now see myself.

18. HERM. I would, O Son, that thou also wert gone out of thyself, like them that dream in their sleep.

19. TAT. Then tell me this, who is the Author and Maker of Regeneration?

20. HERM. The child of God, one Man by the Will of God.

21. TAT. Now, O Father, thou hast put me to silence for ever and all my former thoughts have quite left and forsaken me, for I see the greatness, and shape of all things here below, and nothing but falsehood in them all.

22. And since this mortal Form is daily changed, and turned by this time into increase, and diminution, as being falsehood; what therefore is true, O Trismegistus?

23. TRIS. That, O Son, which is not troubled, nor bounded; not coloured, not figured, not changed; that which is naked, bright, comprehensible only of itself, unalterable, unbodily.

24. TAT. Now I am mad, indeed, Father; for when I thought me to have been made a wise man by thee, with these thoughts thou hast quite dulled all my senses.

25. HERM. Yet is it so, as I say, O Son, He that Looketh Only upon that which is carried upward as Fire, that which is carried downward as Earth, that which is moist as Water, and that which bloweth or is subject to blast as Air; how can he sensibly understand that which is neither hard, nor moist, nor tangible, nor perspicuous, seeing it is only understood in power and operation; but I beseech and pray to the Mind which alone can understand the Generation, which is in God.

26. TAT. Then am I, O Father, utterly unable to do it.

27. HERM. God forbid, Son, rather draw or pull him unto thee (or Study to Know Him) and he will come, be but Willing, and it shall be done; quiet (or make idle) the Senses of the Body, purging thyself from unreasonable brutish torments of matter.

28. TAT. Have I any revengers or tormentors in myself, Father?

29. HERM. Yes, and those, not a few, but many and fearful ones.

30. TAT. I do not know them, Father.

31. HERM. One Torment, Son, is Ignorance, a second, Sorrow, a third, Intemperance, a fourth Concupiscence, a fifth, Injustice, a sixth, Covetousness, a seventh, Deceit, an eighth, Envy, a ninth, Fraud or Guile, a tenth, Wrath, an eleventh, Rashness, a twelfth, Maliciousness.

32. They are in number twelve, and under these many more; some which through the prison of the body, do force the inwardly placed Man to suffer sensibly.

33. And they do not suddenly, or easily depart from him, that hath obtained mercy of God; and herein consists, both the manner and the reason of Regeneration.

34. For the rest, O Son, hold thy peace, and praise God in silence, and by that means, the mercy of God will not cease, or be wanting unto us.

35. Therefore rejoice, my Son, from henceforward, being purged by the powers of God, to the Knowledge of the Truth.

36. For the revelation of God is come to us, and when that came all Ignorance was cast out.

37. The knowledge of Joy is come unto us, and when that comes, Sorrow shall fly away to them that are capable of it.

38. I call unto Joy, the power of Temperance, a power whose Virtue is most sweet; Let us take her unto ourselves, O Son, most willingly, for how at her coming hath she put away Intemperance.

39. Now I call the fourth, Continence, the power which is over Concupiscence. This, O Son, is the stable and firm foundation of Justice.

40. For see, how without labour, she hath chased away injustice and we are justified, O Son, when Injustice is away.

41. The sixth Virtue which comes into us, I call Communion, which is against Covetousness.

42. And when that (Covetousness) is gone, I call

Truth; and when she cometh, Error and Deceit vanisheth.

43. See, O Son, how the Good is fulfilled by the access of Truth; for by this means, Envy is gone from us; for Truth is accompanied with the Good, together also with Life and Light.

44. And there came no more any torment of Darkness, but being overcome, they are all fled away suddenly, and tumultuarily.

45. Thou hast understood, O Son, the manner of Regeneration; for upon the coming of these Ten, the Intellectual Generation is perfected, and then it driveth away the twelve; and we have seen it in the Generation itself.

46. Whosoever therefore hath of Mercy obtained this Generation which is according to God, he leaving all bodily sense, knoweth himself to consist of divine things, and rejoiceth, being made by God stable and immutable.

47. TAT. O Father, I conceive and understand, not by the sight of mine eyes, but by the Intellectual Operation, which is by the Powers. I am in Heaven, in the Earth, in the Water, in the Air, I am in living Creatures, in the Plants, in the Womb, everywhere.

48. Yet tell me further, this one thing, How are the torments of Darkness, being in number Twelve, driven away and expelled by the Ten powers. What is the manner of it, Trismegistus?

49. HERM. This Tabernacle, O Son, consists of the Zodiacal Circle; and this consisting of twelve numbers, the Idea of one; but all formed Nature admit of divers Conjugations to the deceiving of Man.

50. And though they be different in themselves, yet are they united in practice (as for example, Rashness is inseparable from Anger) and they are also indeterminate: Therefore with good Reason, do they make their departure, being driven away by the Ten powers; that is to say, By the dead.

51. For the number of Ten, O Son, is the Begetter of Souls. And there Life and Light are united, where the number of Unity is born of the Spirit.

52. Therefore according to Reason, Unity hath the number of Ten, and the number of Ten hath Unity.

53. TAT. O Father, I now see the Universe, and myself in the Mind.

54. HERM. This is Regeneration, O Son, that we should not any longer fix our imagination upon this Body, subject to the three dimensions, according to this Speech which we have now commented. That we may not at all calumniate the Universe.

55. TAT. Tell me, O Father, This Body that consists of Powers shall it ever admit of any Dissolution?

56. HERM. Good words, Son, and speak not things impossible; for so thou shalt sin, and the eye of thy mind grow wicked.

57. The sensible Body of Nature is far from the Essential Generation; for that is subject to Dissolution, but this not; and that is mortal, but this immortal. Dost thou not know that thou art born a God and the Son of the One, as I am.

58. TAT. How fain would I, O Father, hear that praise given by a Hymn, which thou saidst, thou heardst from the Powers when I was in the Octonary.

59. HERM. As Pimander said by way of Oracle to the Octonary, Thou dost well, O Son, to desire the Solution of the Tabernacle, for thou art purified.

60. Pimander, the Mind of absolute Power and Authority, hath delivered no more unto me, than those that are written; knowing that of myself, I can understand all things, and hear, and see what I will. And he commanded me to do those things that are good; and therefore all the Powers that are in me sing.

61. TAT. I would hear thee, O Father, and understand these things.

62. HERM. Be quiet, O Son, and now hearken to that harmonious blessing and thanksgiving: the hymn

of Regeneration, which I did not determine to have spoken of so plainly, but to thyself in the end of all.

63. Wherefore this is not taught, but hid in silence.

64. So then, O Son, do thou standing in the open Air, worship looking to the North Wind, about the going down of the Sun, and to the South, when the Sun ariseth; And now keep silence, Son.

The Secret Song.
The Holy Speech.

65. Let all the Nature of the world entertain the hearing of this Hymn.

66. Be opened, O Earth, and let all the Treasure of the Rain be opened.

67. You Trees tremble not, for I will sing and praise the Lord of the Creation, and the All and the One.

68. Be opened you Heavens, ye Winds stand still, and let the Immortal Circle of God receive these words.

62. For I will sing, and praise him that created all things, that fixed the Earth, and hung up the Heavens, and commanded the sweet Water to come out of the Ocean; into all the World inhabited, and not inhabited, to the use and nourishment of all things, or men.

70. That commanded the fire to shine for every action, both to Gods and Men.

71. Let us altogether give him blessing, which rideth upon the Heavens, the Creator of all Nature.

72. This is he that is the Eye of the Mind, and Will accept the praise of my Powers.

73. O all ye Powers that are in me, praise the One and the All.

74. Sing together with my Will, all you Powers that are in me.

75. O Holy Knowledge, being enlightened by thee, I magnify the intelligible Light, and rejoice in the Joy of the Mind.

76. All my Powers sing praise with me, and thou my Continence, sing praise my Righteousness by me; praise that which is righteous.

77. O Communion which is in me, praise the All.

78. By me the Truth sings praise to the Truth, the Good praiseth the Good.

79. O Life, O Light from us, unto you comes this praise and thanksgiving.

80. I give thanks unto thee, O Father, the operation or act of my Powers.

81. I give thanks unto thee, O God, the power of my operations.

82. By me thy Word sings praise unto thee, receive by me this reasonable (or verbal) sacrifice in words.

83. The powers that are in me cry these things, they praise the All, they fulfil thy Will; thy Will and Counsel is from thee unto thee.

84. O All, receive a reasonable Sacrifice from all things.

85. O Life, save all that is in us: O Light enlighten, O God the Spirit; for the Mind guideth or feedeth the Word; O Spirit bearing Workman.

86. Thou art God, thy Man crieth these things unto thee through by the Fire, by the Air, by the Earth, by the Water, by the Spirit, by thy Creatures.

87. From eternity I have found (means to) bless and praise thee, and I have what I seek, for I rest in thy Will.

88. TAT. O Father, I see thou hast sung this Song of praise and blessing with thy whole Will; and therefore have I put and placed it in my World.

89. HERM. Say in thy intelligible World, O Son.

90. TAT. I do mean in my Intelligible World, for by thy Hymn and Song of Praise my mind is enlightened: and gladly would I send from my Understanding a Thanksgiving unto God.

91. HERM. Not rashly, O Son.

92. TAT. In my mind, O Father.

93. HERM. Those things that I see and contemplate, I infuse into thee; and therefore say, thou son Tat, the Author of thy succeeding Generations, I send unto God these reasonable Sacrifices.

94. O God, Thou art the Father, Thou art the Lord, Thou art the Mind, accept these reasonable Sacrifices which Thou requirest of Me.

95. For all things are done as the Mind willeth.

96. Thou, O Son, send this acceptable Sacrifice to God, the Father of all things; but propound it also, O Son, by Word.

97. TAT. I thank thee, Father, thou hast advised and instructed me thus to give praise and thanks.

98. HERM. I am glad, O Son, to see the Truth bring forth the Fruits of Good things, and such immortal branches.

99. And learn this of me: Above all other virtues entertain Silence, and impart unto no man, O Son, the tradition of Regeneration, lest we be reputed Calumniators; For we both have now sufficiently meditated, I in speaking, thou in hearing. And now thou dost intellectually know thyself and our Father.

THE END OF THE SEVENTH BOOK.

THE EIGHTH BOOK

OF

HERMES TRISMEGISTUS.

THAT THE GREATEST EVIL IN MAN, IS, THE NOT KNOWING GOD.

---

1. Whither are you carried, O Men, drunken with drinking up the strong Wine of Ignorance? which seeing you cannot bear: Why do you not vomit it up again?

2. Stand, and be sober, and look up again with the eyes of your heart; and if you cannot all do so, yet do as many as you can.

3. For the malice of Ignorance surroundeth all the Earth, and corrupteth the Soul, shut up in the Body not suffering it to arrive at the Havens of Salvation.

4. Suffer not yourselves to be carried with the great stream, but stem the tide, you that can lay hold of the Haven of Safety, and make your full course towards it.

5. Seek one that may lead you by the hand, and conduct you to the door of Truth and Knowledge, where the clear Light is that is pure from Darkness, where there is not one drunken, but all are sober and in their heart look up to him, whose pleasure it is to be seen.

6. For he cannot be heard with ears, nor seen with eyes, nor expressed in words; but only in mind and heart.

7. But first thou must tear to pieces and break through the garment thou wearest; the web of Ignorance, the foundation of all Mischief; the bond of Corruption; the dark Coverture; the living Death; the

sensible Carcass, the Sepulchre, carried about with us; the domestical Thief which in what he loves us, hates us, envies us.

8. Such is the hurtful Apparel, wherewith thou art clothed, which draws and pulls thee downward by its own self; lest looking up, and seeing the beauty of Truth, and the Good that is reposed therein, thou shouldst hate the wickedness of this garment, and understand the traps and ambushes, which it hath laid for thee.

9. Therefore doth it labour to make good those things that seem and are by the Senses, judged and determined; and the things that are truly, it hides, and envelopeth in such matter, filling what it presents unto thee, with hateful pleasure, that thou canst neither hear what thou shouldst hear, nor see what thou shouldst see.

THE END OF THE EIGHTH BOOK.

THE NINTH BOOK
OF
HERMES TRISMEGISTUS.
A Universal Sermon to Asclepius.

---

1. HERM. All that is moved, O Asclepius, is it not moved in some thing, and by some thing?
2. ASCLEP. Yes, indeed.
3. HERM. Must not that, in which a thing is moved, of necessity be greater than the thing that is moved?
4. Of necessity.
5. And that which moveth, is it not stronger than that which is moved?
6. ASCLEP. It is stronger.
7. HERM. That in which a thing is moved, must it not needs have a Nature, contrary to that of the thing that is moved?
8. ASCLEP. It must needs.
9. HERM. Is not this great World a Body, than which there is no greater?
10. ASCLEP. Yes, confessedly.
11. HERM. And is it not solid, as filled with many great Bodies, and indeed, with all the Bodies that are?
12. ASCLEP. It is so.
13. HERM. And is not the World a Body, and a Body that is moved.
14. ASCLEP. It is.
15. HERM. Then what kind of a place must it be, wherein it is moved, and of what Nature? Must it not

be much bigger, that it may receive the continuity of Motion? and lest that which is moved should for want of room, be stayed, and hindered in the Motion?

16. ASCLEP. It must needs be an immense thing, Trismegistus, but of what Nature.

17. HERM. Of a contrary Nature, O Asclepius; but is not the Nature of things unbodily, contrary to a Body.

18. ASCLEP. Confessedly.

19. HERM. Therefore the place is unbodily; but that which is unbodily, is either some Divine thing or God himself. And by some thing Divine, I do not mean that which was made or begotten.

20. If therefore it be Divine, it is an Essence or Substance; but if it be God, it is above Essence; but he is otherwise intelligible.

21. For the first, God is intelligible, not to himself, but to us, for that which is intelligible, is subject to that which understandeth by Sense.

22. Therefore God is not intelligible to himself, for not being any other thing from that which is understood, he cannot be understood by himself.

23. But he is another thing from us, and therefore he is understood by us.

24. If therefore Place be intelligible, it is not Place but God, but if God be intelligible, he is intelligible not as Place, but as a capable Operation.

25. Now everything that is moved, is moved, not in or by that which is moved, but in that which standeth or resteth, and that which moveth standeth or resteth, for it is impossible it should be moved with it.

26. ASCLEP. How then, O Trismegistus, are those things that are here moved with the things that are moved? for thou sayest that the Spheres that wander are moved by the Sphere that wanders not.

27. HERM. That, O Asclepius, is not a moving together, but a countermotion, for they are not moved after a like manner, but contrary one to the other; and

contrariety hath a standing resistance of motion for resistance is a staying of motion.

28. Therefore the wandering Spheres being moved contrarily to that Sphere which wandereth not, shall have one from another contrariety standing of itself.

29. For this Bear which thou seest neither rise nor go down, but turning always about the same; dost thou think it moveth or standeth still?

30. ASCLEP. I think it moves, Trismegistus.

31. What motion, O Asclepius?

32. ASCLEP. A motion that is always carried about the same.

33. But the Circulation which is about the same, and the motion about the same, are both hidden by Station; for that which is about the same forbids that which is above the same, if it stand to that which is about the same.

34. And so the contrary motion stands fast always, being always established by the contrariety.

35. But I will give thee concerning this matter, an earthly example that may be seen with eyes.

36. Look upon any of these living Creatures upon Earth, as Man for example, and see him swimming; for as the Water is carried one way, the reluctation or resistance of his feet and hands is made a station to the man, that he should not be carried with the Water, nor sink underneath it.

37. ASCLEP. Thou hast laid down a very clear example, Trismegistus.

38. HERM. Therefore every motion is in station, and is moved of station.

39. The motion then of the World, and of every material living thing, happeneth not to be done by those things that are without the World, but by those things within it, a Soul, or Spirit, or some other unbodily thing, to those things which are without it.

40. For an inanimated Body, doth not now, much less a Body if it be wholly inanimate.

41. ASCLEP. What meaneth thou by this, O Trismegistus, Wood and Stones, and all other inanimate things, are they not moving Bodies?

42. HERM. By no means, O Asclepius, for that within the Body which moves the inanimate thing, is not the Body, that moves both as well the Body of that which beareth, as the Body of that which is born; for one dead or inanimate thing, cannot move another; that which moveth, must needs be alive if it move.

43. Thou seest therefore how the Soul is surcharged, when it carrieth two Bodies.

44. And now it is manifest, that the things that are moved are moved in something, and by something.

45 ASCLEP. The things that are, O Trismegistus, must needs be moved in that which is void or empty, Vacuum.

46. Be advised, O Asclepius, for of all the things that are, there is nothing empty, only that which is not, is empty and a stranger to existence or being.

47. But that which is, could not be if it were not full of existence, for that which is in being or existence can never be made empty.

48. ASCLEP. Are there not therefore some things that are empty, O Trismegistus, as an empty Barrel, an empty Hogshead, an empty Well, an empty Wine-Press, and many such like?

49. HERM. O the grossness of thy Error, O Asclepius, those things that are most full and replenished, dost thou account them void and empty.

50. ASCLEP. What may be thy meaning, Trismegistus?

51. HERM. Is not the Air a Body?

52. ASCLEP. It is a Body.

53. HERM. Why then this Body doth it not pass through all things that are and passing through them, fill them? and that Body doth it not consist of the mixture of the four? therefore all those things which thou callest empty are full of Air.

54. Therefore those things that thou callest empty,

thou oughtest to call them hollow, not empty, for they exist and are full of Air and Spirit.

55. ASCLEP. This reason is beyond all contradiction, O Trismegistus, but what shall we call the Place in which the whole Universe is moved?

56. HERM. Call it incorporeal, O Asclepius.

57. ASCLEP. What is that incorporeal or unbodily?

58. HERM. The Mind and Reason, the whole, wholly comprehending itself, free from all Body, undeceivable, invisible, impassible from a Body itself, standing fast in itself, capable of all things, and that favour of the things that are.

59. Whereof the Good, the Truth, the Archetypal Light, the Archetype of the Soul, are as it were Beams.

60. ASCLEP. Why then, what is God?

61. HERM. That which is none of these things, yet is, and is the cause of Being to all; and every one of the things that are; for he left nothing destitute of Being.

62. And all things are made of things that are, and not of things that are not; for the things that are not, have not the nature to be able to be made; and again, the things that are, have not the nature never to be, or not to be at all.

63. ASCLEP. What dost thou then say at length, that God is?

64. HERM. God is not a Mind, but the Cause that the Mind is; not a Spirit, but the Cause that the Spirit is; not Light, but the Cause that Light is.

65. Therefore we must worship God by these two Appellations which are proper to him alone, and to no other

66. For neither of all the other, which are called Gods, nor of Men, nor Demons, or Angels, can anyone be, though never so little, good, save only God alone.

67. And this He is, and nothing else; but all other things are separable from the nature of Good.

68. For the Body and the Soul have no place that is capable of or can contain the Good.

69. For the greatness of Good, is as great as the

Existence of all things, that are both bodily and unbodily, both sensible and intelligible.

70. This is the Good, even God.

71. See therefore that thou do not at any time, call ought else Good, for so thou shalt be impious, or any else God, but only the Good, for so thou shalt again be impious.

72. In Word it is often said by all men the Good, but all men do not understand what it is; but through Ignorance they call both the Gods, and some men Good, that can never either be or be made so.

73. Therefore all the other Gods are honoured with the title and appellation of God, but God is the Good, not according to Heaven, but Nature.

74. For there is one Nature of God, even the Good, and one kind of them both, from whence are all kinds.

75. For he that is Good, is the giver of all things, and takes nothing and therefore God gives all things and receives nothing.

76. The other title and appellation, is the Father, because of his making all things; for it is the part of a Father to make.

77. Therefore it hath been the greatest and most Religious care in this life, to them that are wise, and well-minded, to beget children.

78. As likewise it is the greatest misfortune and impiety for any to be separated from men, without children; and this man is punished after death by the Demons, and the punishment is this, To have the Soul of this childless man, adjudged and condemned to a Body, that neither hath the nature of a man, nor of a woman, which is an accursed thing under the Sun.

79. Therefore, O Asclepius, never congratulate any man that is childless; but on the contrary, pity his misfortune, knowing what punishment abides, and is prepared for him.

80. Let so many, and such manner of things, O Asclepius, be said as a certain precognition of all things in Nature.

THE END OF THE NINTH BOOK.

THE TENTH BOOK

OF

HERMES TRISMEGISTUS.

The Mind to Hermes.

1. Forbear thy speech, O Hermes Trismegistus, and call to mind those things that are said: but I will not delay to speak what comes into my mind, since many men have spoken many things, and those very different, concerning the Universe and Good; but I have not learned the Truth.
2. Therefore, the Lord make it plain to me in this point; for I will believe thee only, for the manifestation of these things.
3. Then said the Mind how the case stands.
4. God and all.
5. God, Eternity, the World, Time, Generation,
6. God made Eternity, Eternity the World; the World Time, and Time Generation.
7. Of God, as it were the Substance, is the Good, the Fair, Blessedness, Wisdom.
8. Of Eternity, Identity, or Selfness.
9. Of the World, Order.
10. Of Time, Change.
11. Of Generation, Life, and Death.
12. But the Operation of God, is Mind and Soul.
13. Of Eternity, Permanence, or Long-lasting, and Immortality.
14. Of the World, Restitution, and Decay or Destruction.
15. Of Time, Augmentation and Diminution.

16. And of Generation, Qualities.
17. Therefore Eternity is in God.
18. The World in Eternity.
19. Time in the World.
20. And Generation in Time.
21. And Eternity standeth about God.
22. The World is moved in Eternity.
23. Time is determined in the World.
24. Generation is done in Time.
25. Therefore the Spring and Fountain of all things is God.
26. The Substance Eternity.
27. The Matter is the World.
28. The Power of God is Eternity.
29. And the Work of Eternity is the World not yet made, and yet ever made by Eternity.
30. Therefore shall nothing be at any time destroyed, for Eternity is incorruptible.
31. Neither can anything perish, or be destroyed in the World, the World being contained and embraced by eternity.
32. But what is the Wisdom of God? Even the Good, and the Fair and Blessedness, and every Virtue, and Eternity.
33. Eternity therefore put into the Matter Immortality and Everlastingness; for the Generation of that depends upon Eternity, even as Eternity doth of God.
34. For Generation and Time, in Heaven, and in Earth, are of a double Nature; in Heaven they are unchangeable and incorruptible, but on Earth they are changeable and corruptible.
35. And the Soul of Eternity is God; and the Soul of the World Eternity; and of the Earth, Heaven.
36. God is in the Mind, the Mind in the Soul, the Soul in the Matter, all things by Eternity.
37. All this Universal Body, in which are all Bodies, is full of Soul, the Soul full of Mind, the Mind full of God.

38. For within he fills them, and without he contains them, quickening the Universe.

39. Without he quickens this perfect living thing the World, and within all living Creatures.

40. And above in Heaven he abides in Identity or Selfness, but below upon Earth he changeth Generation.

41. Eternity comprehendeth the World, either by Necessity, or Providence, or Nature.

42. And if any man shall think any other thing, it is God that actuateth, or operateth this All.

43. But the operation or Act of God, is power insuperable, to which none may compare anything, either Human or Divine.

44. Therefore, O Hermes, think none of these things below, or the things above, in any wise like unto God, for if thou dost thou errest from the Truth.

45. For nothing can be like the unlike, and only and One; nor mayest thou think, that he hath given of his Power to any other thing.

46. For who after him can make anything, either of Life, or Immortality; of Change or of Quality, and himself what other thing should he make.

47. For God is not idle, for then all things would be idle; for all things are full of God.

48. But there is not anywhere in the world such a thing as Idleness; for Idleness is a name that implieth a thing void or empty, both of a Doer and a thing done.

49. But all things must necessarily be made or done both always and according to the nature of every place.

50. For he that maketh or doth is in all things, yet not fastened or comprehended in anything, nor making or doing one thing, but all things.

51. For being an active or operating Power and sufficient of himself for the things that are made, and the things that are made are under him.

52. Look upon, through me, the World is subject to thy sight, and understand exactly the Beauty thereof.

53. A Body immarcessible, than the which, there is nothing more ancient, yet always vigorous and young.

54. See also the seven Worlds set over us, adorned with an everlasting Order, and filling Eternity, with a different course.

55. For all things are full of Light, but the Fire is nowhere.

56. For the friendship and commixture of contraries and unlike became Light shining from the Act or Operation of God, the Father of all Good, the Prince of all Order, and the Ruler of the seven Worlds.

57. Look also upon the Moon, the forerunner of them all, the Instrument of Nature, and which changeth the Matter here below.

58. Behold the Earth, the middle of the whole, the firm and stable Foundation of the Fair World, the Feeder and Nurse of Earthly things.

59. Consider moreover, how great the multitude is of immortal living things, and of mortal ones also; and see the Moon going about in the midst of both, to wit, of things immortal and mortal.

60. But all things are full of Soul, and all things are properly moved by it; some things about the Heaven, and some things about the Earth, and neither of those on the right hand to the left; nor those on the left hand to the right; nor those things that are above, downward; nor those things that are below, upwards.

61. And that all these things are made, O beloved Hermes, thou needst not learn of me.

62. For they are Bodies, and have a Soul, and are moved.

63. And that all these should come together into one, it is impossible without some thing, to gather them together.

64. Therefore there must be some such ones, and he altogether One.

65. For seeing that the motions are divers, and many, and the Bodies not alike, and yet one ordered

swiftness among them all; It is impossible there should be two or more Makers.

66. For one order is not kept by many.

67. But in the weaker, there would be jealousy of the stronger and thence also Contentions.

68. And if there were one Maker of mutable and mortal living wights, he would desire also to make immortal ones, as he that were the Maker of immortal ones, would do to make mortal.

69. Moreover also, if there were two, the Matter being one, who should be chief, or have the disposing of the facture?

70. Or if both of them, which of them the greater part?

71. But think thus that every living Body hath its consistence of Matter and Soul; and of that which is immortal, and that which is mortal, and unreasonable.

72. For all living Bodies have a Soul; and those things that are not living are only matter by itself.

73. And the Soul likewise of itself drawing near her Maker, is the Cause of Life and Being and Being the cause of Life, is after a manner, the cause of immortal things.

74. How then are mortal wights, other from immortal?

75. Or how cannot he make living wights that causeth immortal things and immortality?

76. That there is some Body that doth these things it is apparent, and that he is also one, it is most manifest.

77. For there is one Soul, one Life and one Matter.

78. Who is this? Who can it be? Other than the One God.

79. For whom else can it benefit, to make living things, save only God alone?

80. There is therefore one God.

81. For it is a ridiculous thing to confess the World to be one Sun, one Moon, one Divinity; and yet to have I know not how many gods.

82. He therefore being One, doth all things in many things.

83. And what great thing is it for God to make Life and Soul, and Immortality, and Change, when thy self dost so many things?

84. For thou both seest, speakest and hearest, smellest, tastest and touchest, walkest, understandest, and breathest.

85. And it is not one that seeth, and another that heareth, and another that speaketh, and another that toucheth, and another that smelleth, and another that walketh, and another that understandeth, and another that breatheth, but One that doth all these things.

86. Yet neither can these things possibly be without God.

87. For as thou, if thou shouldst cease from doing these things, were not a living wight; so if God should cease from those, he were not (which is not lawful to say) any longer God.

88. For if it be already demonstrated, that nothing can be idle or empty, how much more may be affirmed of God?

89. For if there be any thing which he doth not do, then is he (if it were lawful to say so) imperfect.

90. Whereas feeling he is not idle, but perfect, certainly he doth all things.

91. Now give thy self unto me, O Hermes, for a little while thou shalt the more easily understand, that it is the necessary work of God that all things should be made or done that are done or were once done, or shall be done.

92. And this, O best Beloved, is life.

93. And this is the Fair.

94. And this is the Good.

95. And this is God.

96. And if thou wilt understand this by work also, mark what happens to thy self, when thou wilt generate.

97. And yet this is not like unto him; for he is not

sensible of pleasure, for neither hath he any other Fellow-workman.

98. But being himself the only Workman he is always in the Work, himself being that which he doth or maketh.

99. For all things, if they were separated from him, must needs fall and die, as there being no life in them.

100. And again, if all things be living wights, both which are in Heaven, and upon Earth; and that there be one Life in all things which are made by God, and that is God, then certainly all things are made, or done by God.

101. Life is the union of the Mind and the Soul.

102. But death is not the destruction of those things that were gathered together, but a dissolving of the Union.

103. The Image therefore of God is Eternity, of Eternity the World, of the World the Sun, of the Sun, Man.

104. But the people say, That changing is Death, because the Body is dissolved, and the Life goeth into that which appeareth not.

105. By this discourse, my dearest Hermes, I affirm as thou hearest, That the World is changed, because every day part thereof becomes invisible; but that it is never dissolved.

106. And these are the Passions of the World, Revolutions and Occultations, and Revolution is a turning, but Occultation is Renovation.

107. And the World being all formed, hath not the forms lying without it, but itself changeth in itself.

108. Seeing then the World is all formed, what must he be that made it? for without form he cannot be.

109. And if he be all formed, he will be kept like the World, but if he have but one form, he shall be in this regard less than the World.

110. What do we then say that he is? we will not raise any doubts by our speech; for nothing that is doubtful concerning God, is yet known.

111. He hath therefore one Idea which is proper to him, which because it is unbodily is not subject to the sight, and yet shews all forms by the Bodies.

112. And do not wonder, if there be an incorruptible Idea.

113. For they are like the Margents of that Speech which is in writing; for they seem to be high and swelling, but they are by nature smooth and even.

114. But understand well this that I say, more boldly, for it is more true; As a man cannot live without life, so neither can God live, not doing good.

115. For this is, as it were, the Life and Motion of God, to move all things, and quicken them.

116. But some of the things I have said, must have a particular explication; Understand then what I say.

117. All things are in God, not as lying in a place; for Place is both a Body, and unmoveable, and those things that are there placed, have no motion.

118. For they lie otherwise in that which is unbodily, than in the fantasy or to appearance.

119. Consider him that contains all things, and understand, that nothing is more capacious, than that which is incorporeal, nothing more swift, nothing more powerful, but it is most capacious, most swift and most strong.

120. And judge of this by thyself, command thy Soul to go into India, and sooner than thou canst bid it, it will be there.

121. Bid it likewise pass over the Ocean, and suddenly it will be there; Not as passing from place to place, but suddenly it will be there.

122. Command it to fly into Heaven, and it will need no Wings, neither shall anything hinder it; not the fire of the Sun, not the Aether, not the turning of the Spheres, not the bodies of any of the other Stars, but cutting through all, it will fly up to the last, and furthest Body.

123. And if thou wilt even break the whole, and see

those things that are without the World (if there be any thing without) thou mayest.

124. Behold how great power, how great swiftness thou hast! Canst thou do all these things, and cannot God?

125. After this manner therefore contemplate God to have all the whole World to himself, as it were all thoughts, or intellections.

126. If therefore thou wilt not equal thy self to God, thou canst not understand God.

127. For the like is intelligible by the like.

128. Increase thy self into an immeasurable greatness, leaping beyond every Body; and transcending all Time, become Eternity and thou shalt understand God: If thou believe in thyself that nothing is impossible, but accountest thy self immortal, and that thou canst understand all things, every Art, every Science and the manner and custom of every living thing.

129. Become higher than all height, lower than all depths, comprehend in thy self, the qualities of all the Creatures, of the Fire, the Water, the Dry and Moist; and conceive likewise, that thou canst at once be everywhere in the Sea, in the Earth.

130. Thou shalt at once understand thy self, not yet begotten in the Womb, young, old, to be dead, the things after death, and all these together as also times, places, deeds, qualities, quantities, or else thou canst not yet understand God.

131. But if thou shut up thy Soul in the Body and abuse it, and say, I understand nothing, I can do nothing, I am afraid of the Sea, I cannot climb up into Heaven, I know not who I am, I cannot tell what I shall be; what hast thou to do with God; for thou canst understand none of those Fair and Good things; be a lover of the Body, and Evil.

132. For it is the greatest evil, not to know God.

133. But to be able to know and to will, and to hope, is the straight way, and Divine way, proper to

the Good; and it will everywhere meet thee, and everywhere be seen of thee, plain and easy, when thou dost not expect or look for it; it will meet thee, waking, sleeping, sailing, travelling, by night, by day, when thou speakest, and when thou keepest silence.

134. For there is nothing which is not the Image of God.

135. And yet thou sayest, God is invisible, but be advised, for who is more manifest than He.

136. For therefore hath he made all things, that thou by all things mayest see him.

137. This is the Good of God, this is his Virtue, to appear, and to be seen in all things.

138. There is nothing invisible, no, not of those things that are incorporeal.

139. The Mind is seen in Understanding, and God is seen in doing or making.

140. Let these things thus far forth, be made manifest unto thee, O Trismegistus.

141. Understand in like manner, all other things by thy self, and thou shalt not be deceived.

THE END OF THE TENTH BOOK.

THE ELEVENTH BOOK

OF

HERMES TRISMEGISTUS.

OF THE COMMON MIND TO TAT.

1. The Mind, O Tat, is of the very Essence of God, if yet there be any Essence of God.
2. What kind of Essence that is, he alone knows himself exactly.
3. The Mind therefore is not cut off, or divided from the essentiality of God, but united as the light of the sun.
4. And this mind in men, is God, and therefore are some men Divine, and their Humanity is near Divinity.
5. For the good Demon called the Gods immortal men, and men mortal Gods.
6. But in the brute Beasts, or unreasonable living wights, the Mind is their Nature.
7. For where there is a Soul, there is the Mind, as where there is Life, there is also a Soul.
8. In living Creatures therefore, that are without Reason, the Soul is Life, void of the operations of the Mind.
9. For the Mind is the Benefactor of the Souls of men, and worketh to the proper Good.
10. And in unreasonable things it co-operateth with the Nature of everyone of them, but in men it worketh against their Natures.
11. For the Soul being in the Body, is straightway

made Evil by Sorrow, and Grief and Pleasure or Delight.

12. For Grief and Pleasure flow like Juices from the compound Body, whereinto, when the Soul entereth, or descendeth, she is moistened and tincted with them.

13. As many Souls therefore, as the Mind governeth or over-ruleth, to them it shows its own Light, resisting their prepossessions or presumptions.

14. As a good Physician grieveth the Body, prepossessed of a disease, by burning or lancing it for health's sake.

15. After the same manner also, the Mind grieveth the Soul, by drawing it out of Pleasure, from whence every disease of the Soul proceedeth.

16. But the great Disease of the Soul is Atheism, because that opinion followeth to all Evil and no Good.

17. Therefore the Mind resisting it procureth Good to the Soul, as a Physician health to the Body.

18. But as many Souls of Men, as do not admit or entertain the Mind for their Governor, do suffer the same thing that the Soul of unreasonable living things.

19. For the Soul being a Co-Operator with them, permits or leaves them to their concupiscences, whereunto they are carried by the torrent of their Appetite, and so tend to brutishness.

20. And as Brute Beasts, they are angry without reason, and they desire without reason, and never cease, nor are satisfied with evil.

21. For unreasonable Angers and Desires, are the most exceeding Evils.

22. And therefore hath God set the Mind over these, as a Revenger and Reprover of them.

23. TAT. Here, O Father, that discourse of Fate or Destiny which thou madest to me, is in danger to be overthrown; For if it be fatal for any man to commit Adultery or Sacrilege or do any evil, he is punished also, though he of necessity do the work of Fate or Destiny.

24. HERM. All things, O Son, are the work of Fate, and without it, can no bodily thing, either Good or Evil, be done.

25. For it is decreed by Fate, that he that doth any evil, should also suffer for it.

26. And therefore he doth it, that he may suffer that which he suffereth, because he did it.

27. But for the present let alone that speech, concerning Evil and Fate, for at other times we have spoken of it.

28. Now our discourse is about the Mind, and what it can do, and how it differs, and is in men such a one, but in brute Beasts changed.

29. And again, in Brute Beasts it is not beneficial, but in men by quenching both their Anger and Concupiscences.

30. And of men thou must understand some to be rational or governed by reason, and some irrational.

31. But all men are subject to Fate, and to Generation, and Changes, for these are the beginning and end of Fate or Destiny.

32. And all men suffer those things that are decreed by Fate.

33. But rational men, over whom as we said, the Mind bears rule, do not suffer like unto other men; but being free from viciousness, and being not evil, they do suffer evil.

34. TAT. How sayest thou this again, Father? An Adulterer, is he not evil? a Murderer, is he not evil? and so all others.

35. HERM. But the rational man, O Son, will not suffer for Adultery, but as the Adulterer, nor for Murder, but as the Murderer.

36. And it is impossible to escape the Quality of Change, as of Generation, but the Viciousness, he that hath the Mind, may escape.

37. And therefore, O Son, I have always heard the good Demon say, and if he had delivered it in writing,

he had much profited all mankind: For he alone, O Son. as the first born, God, seeing all things, truly spake Divine words. I have heard him say sometimes, That all Things are one thing, Especially Intelligible Bodies, or that all Especially Intelligible Bodies are one.

38. We live in Power, in Act and in Eternity.

39. Therefore a good Mind, is that which the Soul of him is.

40. And if this be so, then no intelligble thing differs from intelligible things.

41. As therefore it is possible, that the Mind, the Prince of all things; so likewise, that the Soul that is of God, can do whatsoever it will.

42. But understand thou well, for this Discourse I have made to the question which thou askest of me before, I mean concerning Fate and the Mind.

43. First, if, O Son, thou shalt diligently withdraw thy self from all Contentious speeches, thou shalt find that in Truth, the Mind, the Soul of God bears rule over all things, both over Fate and Law and all other things.

44. And nothing is impossible to him, no not of the things that are of Fate.

45. Therefore, though the Soul of man be above it, let it not neglect the things that happen to be under Fate.

46. And these thus far, were the excellent sayings of the good Demon.

47. TAT. Most divinely spoken, O Father, and truly and profitably, yet clear this one thing unto me.

48. Thou sayest, that in brute Beasts the Mind worketh or acteth after the manner of Nature, co-operating also with their (impetus) inclinations.

49. Now the impetuous inclinations of brute Beasts, as I conceive, are Passions. If therefore the Mind do co-operate with these impetuous Inclinations, and that they are the Passions in brute Beasts, certainly the Mind is also a Passion, conforming itself to Passions.

50. HERM. Well done, Son, thou askest nobly, and yet it is just that I should answer thee.

51. All incorporeal things, O Son, that are in the Body, are possible, nay, they are properly Passions.

52. Everything that moveth is incorporeal; everything that is moved is a Body; and it is moved into the Bodies by the Mind. Now motion is Passion, and there they both suffer; as well that which moveth, as that which is moved, as well that which ruleth, as that which is ruled.

53. But being freed from the Body, it is freed likewise from Passion.

54. But especially, O Son, there is nothing impassible, but all things are passible.

55. But Passion differs from that which is passible, for that (Passion) acteth but this suffers.

56. Bodies also of themselves do act, for either they are unmovable, or else are moved; and which soever it be, it is a Passion.

57. But incorporeal things do always act, or work, and therefore they are passible.

58. Let not therefore the appellations or names trouble thee, for Action and Passion are the same thing, but that it is not grievous to use the more honourable name.

59. TAT. O Father. thou has delivered this Discourse most plainly.

60. HERM. Consider this also, O Son, That God hath freely bestowed upon man, above all other living things, these two, to wit, Mind and Speech, or Reason, equal to immortality.

61. These if any man use, or employ upon what he ought, he shall differ nothing from the Immortals.

62. Yea, rather going out of the Body, he shall be guided and led by them, both into the Choir and Society of the Gods, and blessed Ones.

63. TAT. Do not other living Creatures use Speech O Father?

64. HERM. No, Son, but only Voice; now Speech and Voice do differ exceeding much; for Speech is common to all men, but Voice is proper unto every kind of living thing.

65. TAT. Yea, but the Speech of men is different. O Father, every man according to his Nation.

66. HERM. It is true, O Son, they do differ: Yet as man is one so is Speech one also; and it is interpreted and found the same, both in Egypt, Persia, and Greece.

67. But thou seemest unto me, Son, to be ignorant of the Virtue or Power, and Greatness of Speech.

68. For the blessed God, the good Demon said or commanded the Soul to be in the Body, the Mind, in the Soul, the Word, or Speech, or Reason in the Mind, and the Mind in God, and that God is the Father of them all.

69. Therefore the Word is the Image of the Mind, and the Mind of God, and the Body of the Idea, and the Idea of the Soul.

70. Therefore of the Matter, the subtlest or smallest part is Air, of the Air the Soul, of the Soul the Mind, of the Mind God.

71. And God is about all things, and through all things, but the Mind about the Soul, the Soul about the Air, and the Air about the Matter.

72. But Necessity, and Providence, and Nature, are the Organs or Instruments of the World, and of the Order of Matter.

73. For of those things that are intelligible, every one is but the Essence of them in Identity.

74. But of the Bodies of the whole, or universe, every one is many things.

75. For the Bodies that are put together, and that have, and make their changes into other, having this Identity, do always save and preserve the uncorruption of the Identity.

76. But in every one of the compound Bodies, there is a number

77. For without number it is impossible there should be consistence or constitution, or composition, or dissolution.

78. But Unities do both beget and increase Numbers, and again being dissolved, come into themselves.

79. And the Matter is One.

80. But this whole World, the great God, and the Image of the Greater, and united unto him, and conserving the Order and Will of the Father, is the fulness of Life.

81. And there is nothing therein, through all the Eternity of the Revolutions, neither of the whole, nor of the parts which doth not live.

82. For there is nothing dead, that either hath been, or is, or shall be in the World.

83. For the Father would have it as long as it lasts, to be a living thing; and therefore it must needs be God also.

84. How therefore, O Son, can there be in God, in the Image of the Universe, in the fulness of Life, any dead things?

85. For dying is corruption, and corruption is destruction.

86. How then can any part of the incorruptible be corrupted, or of God be destroyed?

87. TAT. Therefore, O Father, do not the living things in the World die, though they be parts thereof.

88. HERM. Be wary in thy Speech, O Son, and not deceived in the names of things.

89. For they do not die, O Son, but as compound Bodies they are dissolved.

90. But dissolution is not death; and they are dissolved, not that they may be destroyed, but that they may be made new.

91. TAT. What then is the operation of Life? Is it not Motion?

92. HERM. And what is there in the World unmovable? Nothing at all, O Son.

93. TAT. Why, doth not the Earth seem unmovable to thee, O Father?

94. HERM. No, but subject to many motions, though after a manner it alone be stable.

95. What a ridiculous thing it were, that the Nurse of all things should be unmovable, which beareth and bringeth forth all things.

96. For it is impossible, that anything that bringeth forth, should bring forth without Motion.

97. And a ridiculous question it is, Whether the fourth part of the whole, be idle: For the word immovable, or without Motion, signifies nothing else, but idleness.

98. Know generally, O Son, That whatsoever is in the World is moved either according to Augmentation or Diminution.

99. But that which is moved, liveth also, yet it is not necessary, that a living thing should be or continue the same.

100. For while the whole World is together, it is unchangeable, O Son, but all the parts thereof are changeable.

101. Yet nothing is corrupted or destroyed, and quite abolished but the names trouble men.

102. For Generation is not Life, but Sense; neither is Change Death, but Forgetfulness, or rather Occultation, and lying hid.

Or better thus.

For Generation is not a Creation of Life, but a Production of Things to Sense, and making them Manifest. Neither is Change Death, but an Occultation or Hiding of that which was.

103. These things being so, all things are Immortal, Matter, Life, Spirit, Soul, Mind, whereof every living thing consisteth.

104. Every living thing therefore is Immortal, because of the Mind, but especially Man, who both receiveth God, and converseth with him.

105. For with this living wight alone is God

familiar; in the night by dreams, in the day by Symbols or Signs.

106. And by all things doth he foretell him of things to come, by Birds, by Fowls, by the Spirit, or Wind, and by an Oak.

107. Wherefore also Man professeth to know things that have been, things that are present, and things to come.

108. Consider this also, O Son, That every living Creature goeth upon one part of the World, Swimming things in Water, Land wights upon the Earth, Flying Fowls in the Air.

109. But Man useth all these, the Earth, the Water, the Air, and the Fire, nay, he seeth and toucheth Heaven by his Sense.

110. But God is both about all things, and through all things, for he is both Act and Power.

111. And it is no hard thing, O Son, to understand God.

112. And if thou wilt also see him, look upon the Necessity of things that appear, and the Providence of things that have been, and are done.

113. See the Matter being most full of Life, and so great a God moved with all Good, and Fair, both Gods, and Demons, and Men.

114. TAT. But these, O Father, are wholly Acts or Operations.

115. HERM. If they be therefore wholly Acts or Operations, O Son, by whom are they acted or operated, but by God?

116. Or art thou ignorant, that as the parts of the World, are Heaven, and Earth, and Water, and Air; after the same manner the Members of God, are Life, and Immortality, and Eternity, and Spirit, and Necessity, and Providence, and Nature, and Soul, and Mind, and the Continuance or Perseverance of all these which is called Good.

117. And there is not any thing of all that hath been, and all that is, where God is not.

118. TAT. What in the Matter, O Father?

119. HERM. The Matter, Son, what is it without God, that thou shouldst ascribe a proper place to it?

120. Or what dost thou think it to be? peradventure some heap that is not actuated or operated.

121. But if it be actuated, by whom is it actuated? for we have said, that Acts or Operations, are the parts of God.

122. By whom are all living things quickened? and the Immortal, by whom are they immortalized? the things that are changeable, by whom are they changed?

123. Whether thou speak of Matter, or Body, or Essence, know that all these are acts of God.

124. And that the Act of Matter is materiality, and of the Bodies corporality, and of Essence essentiality; and this is God the whole.

125. And in the whole, there is nothing that is not God.

126. Wherefore about God, there is neither Greatness, Place, Quality, Figure, or Time; for he is All, and the All, through all, and about all.

127. This Word, O Son, worship and adore. And the only service of God, is not to be evil.

THE END OF THE ELEVENTH BOOK.

THE TWELFTH BOOK
OF
HERMES TRISMEGISTUS.
His Crater or Monas.

---

1. The Workman made this Universal World, not with his Hands, but his Word.
2. Therefore thus think of him, as present everywhere, and being always, and making all things, and one above, that by his Will hath framed the things that are.
3. For that is his Body, not tangible, nor visible, nor measurable, nor extensible, nor like any other body.
4. For it is neither Fire, nor Water, nor Air, nor Wind, but all these things are of him, for being Good, he hath dedicated that name unto himself alone.
5. But he would also adorn the Earth, but with the Ornament of a Divine Body.
6. And he sent Man an Immortal and a Mortal wight.
7. And Man had more than all living Creatures, and the World, because of his Speech, and Mind.
8. For Man became the spectator of the Works of God, and wondered, and acknowledged the Maker.
9. For he divided Speech among all men, but not Mind, and yet he envied not any; for Envy comes not thither, but is of abode here below in the Souls of men, that have not the Mind.
10. TAT. But wherefore, Father, did not God distribute the Mind to all men?
11. Because it pleased him, O Son, to set that in the middle among all souls as a reward to strive for.

12. TAT. And where hath he set it?
13. HERM. Filling a large Cup or Bowl therewith, he sent it down, giving also a Cryer or Proclaimer.
14. And he commanded him to proclaim these things to the souls of men.
15. Dip and wash thyself, thou that art able, in this Cup or Bowl; Thou that believest, that thou shalt return to him that sent this Cup; thou that acknowledgest whereunto thou wert made.
16. As many therefore as understood the Proclamation, and were baptised or dowsed into the Mind, these were made partakers of Knowledge, and became perfect men, receiving the Mind.
17. But as many as missed of the Proclamation, they received Speech, but not Mind, being ignorant whereunto they were made, or by whom.
18. But their senses are just like to brute Beasts, and having their temper in Anger and Wrath, they do not admire the things worthy of looking on.
19. But wholly addicted to the pleasures and desires of the Bodies, they believe that man was made for them.
20. But as many as partook of the gift of God, these, O Tat, in comparison of their works, are rather immortal than mortal men.
21 Comprehending all things in their Mind, which are upon the Earth, which are in Heaven, and if there be anything above Heaven.
22. And lifting up themselves so high, they see the Good, and seeing it, they account it a miserable calamity to make their abode here.
23. And despising all things bodily and unbodily, they make haste to the One and Only.
24. Thus, O Tat, is the Knowledge of the Mind, the beholding of Divine Things, and the Understanding of God, the Cup itself being Divine.
25. TAT. And I, O Father, would be baptised and drenched therein.
26. HERM. Except thou first hate thy body, O Son,

thou canst not love thy self; but loving thy self, thou shalt have the Mind, and having the Mind, thou shalt also partake the Knowledge or Science.

27. TAT. How meanest thou that, O Father?

28. HERM. Because it is impossible, O Son, to be conversant about things Mortal and Divine.

29. For the things that are, being two Bodies, and things incorporeal, wherein is the Mortal and the Divine, the Election or Choice of either is left to him that will choose; For no man can choose both.

30. And of which soever the choice is made, the other being diminished or overcome, magnifieth the act and operation of the other.

31. The choice of the better therefore is not only best for him that chooseth it, by deifying a man; but it also sheweth Piety and Religion towards God.

32. But the choice of the worse destroys a man, but doth nothing against God; save that as Pomps or Pageants, when they come abroad, cannot do any thing themselves, but hinder; after the same manner also do these make Pomps or Pageants in the World, being seduced by the pleasures of the Body.

33. These things being so, O Tat, that things have been, and are so plenteously ministered to us from God; let them proceed also from us, without any scarcity or sparing.

34. For God is innocent or guiltless, but we are the causes of Evil, preferring them before the Good.

35. Thou seest, O Son, how many Bodies we must go beyond, and how many choirs of Demons, and what continuity and courses of Stars, that we may make haste to the One, and only God.

36. For the Good is not to be transcended, it is unbounded and infinite; unto itself without beginning, but unto us, seeming to have a beginning, even our knowledge of it.

37. For our knowledge is not the beginning of it, but shews us the beginning of its being known unto us.

38. Let us therefore lay hold of the beginning and we shall quickly go through all things.

39. It is indeed a difficult thing, to leave those things that are accustomable, and present, and turn us to those things that are ancient, and according to the original.

40. For these things that appear, delight us, but make the things that appear not, hard to believe, or the Things that Appear not, are Hard to believe.

41. The things most apparent are Evil, but the Good is secret, or hid in, or to the things that appear; for it hath neither Form nor Figure.

42. For this cause it is like to itself, but unlike every thing else; for it is impossible, that any thing incorporeal, should be made known, or appear to a Body.

43. For this is the difference between the like and the unlike, and the unlike wanteth always somewhat of the like.

44. For the Unity, Beginning, and Root of all things, as being the Root and Beginning.

45. Nothing is without a beginning, but the Beginning is of nothing, but of itself; for it is the Beginning of all other things.

46. Therefore it is, seeing it is not from another beginning.

47. Unity therefore being the Beginning, containeth every number, but itself is contained of none, and begetteth every number, itself being begotten of no other number.

48. Every thing that is begotten (or made) is imperfect, and may be divided, increased, diminished.

49. But to the perfect, there happeneth none of these.

50. And that which is increased, is increased by Unity, but is consumed and vanished through weakness, being not able to receive the Unity.

51. This Image of God, have I described to thee, O Tat, as well as I could; which if thou do diligently

consider, and view by the eyes of thy mind, and heart, believe me, Son, thou shalt find the way to the things above, or rather the Image itself will lead thee.

52. But the spectacle or sight, hath this peculiar and proper; Them that can see, and behold it, it holds fast and draws unto it, as they say, the Loadstone doth Iron.

THE END OF THE TWELFTH BOOK.

THE THIRTEENTH BOOK
OF
HERMES TRISMEGISTUS.
Of Sense and Understanding.

---

1. Yesterday, Asclepius, I delivered a perfect Discourse; but now I think it necessary, in suite of that, to dispute also of Sense.
2. For Sense and Understanding seem to differ, because the one is material, the other essential.
3. But unto me, they appear to be both one, or united, and not divided in men, I mean.
4. For in other living Creatures, Sense is united unto Nature but in men to Understanding.
5. But the Mind differs from Understanding, as much as God from Divinity.
6. For Divinity is from or under God, and Understanding from the Mind, being the sister of the Word or Speech, and they the Instruments one of another.
7. For neither is the Word pronounced without Understanding, neither is Understanding manifested without the Word.
8. Therefore Sense and Understanding do both flow together into a man, as if they were infolded one within another.
9. For neither is it possible without Sense to Understand, nor can we have Sense without Understanding.
10. And yet it is possible (for the Time being) that the Understanding may understand without Sense, as they that fantasy Visions in their Dreams.
11. But it seems unto me, that both the operations

are in the Visions of Dreams, and that the Sense is stirred up out of sleep, unto awaking.

12. For man is divided into a Body and a Soul; when both parts of the Sense accord one with another, then is the understanding childed, or brought forth by the Mind pronounced.

13. For the Mind brings forth all Intellections or Understandings. Good ones when it receiveth good Seed from God; and the contrary when it receives them from Devils.

14. For there is no part of the World void of the Devil, which entering in privately, sowed the seed of his own proper operation; and the Mind did make pregnant, or did bring forth that which was sown, Adulteries, Murders, Striking of Parents, Sacrileges, Impieties, Stranglings, throwing down headlong, and all other things which are the works of evil Demons.

15. And the Seeds of God are few but Great, and Fair, and Good Virtue, and Temperance, and Piety.

16. And the Piety is the Knowledge of God, whom whosoever knoweth being full of all good things, hath Divine Understanding and not like the Many.

17. And therefore they that have that Knowledge neither please the multitude, nor the multitude them, but they seem to be mad, and to move laughter, hated and despised, and many times also murdered.

18. For we have already said, That wickedness must dwell here, being in her own region.

19. For her region is the Earth, and not the World, as some will sometimes say, Blaspheming.

20. But the Godly or God-worshipping Man laying hold on Knowledge, will despise or tread under all these things; for though they be evil to other men, yet to him all things are good.

21. And upon mature consideration, he refers all things to Knowledge, and that which is most to be wondered at, he alone makes evil things good.

22. But I return again to my Discourse of Sense.

23. It is therefore a thing proper to Man, to communicate and conjoin Sense and Understanding.

24. But every man, as I said before, doth not enjoy Understanding; for one man is material, another essential.

25. And he that is material with wickedness as I said, received from the Devils the Seed of Understanding; but they that are with the Good essentially, are saved with God.

26. For God is the Workman of all things; and when he worketh he useth Nature.

27. He maketh all things good like himself.

28. But these things that are made good, are in the use of Operation, unlawful.

29. For the Motion of the World stirring up Generations, makes Qualities, infecting some with evilness, and purifying some with good.

30. And the World, Asclepius, hath a peculiar Sense and Understanding, not like to Man's, nor so various or manifold, but a better and more simple.

31. For this Sense and Understanding of the World is One, in that it makes all things, and unmakes them again into itself; for it is the Organ or Instrument of the Will of God.

32. And it is so organized or framed, and made for an Instrument by God; that receiving all Seeds into itself from God, and keeping them in itself, it maketh all things effectually and dissolving them, reneweth all things.

33. And therefore like a good Husband-man of Life, when things are dissolved or loosened, he affords by the casting of Seed, renovation to all things that grow.

34. There is nothing that it (the World) doth not beget or bring forth alive; and by its Motion, it makes all things alive.

35. And it is at once, both the Place and the Workman of Life.

36. But the Bodies are from the Matter, in a differ-

ent manner; for some are of the Earth, some of Water, some of Air, some of Fire, and all are compounded, but some are more compounded, and some are more simple.

37. They that are compounded, are the heavier, and they that are less, are the higher.

38. And the swiftness of the Motion of the World, makes the varieties of the Qualities of Generation, for the spiration or influence, being most frequent, extendeth unto the Bodies qualities with one fulness, which is of Life.

39. Therefore, God is the Father of the World, but the World is the Father of things in the World.

40. And the World is the Son of God, but things in the World are the Sons of the World.

41. And therefore it is well called the World, that is an Ornament, because it adorneth and beautifieth all things with the variety of Generation, and indeficiency of Life, which the unweariedness of Operation, and the swiftness of Necessity with the mingling of Elements, and the order of things done.

42. Therefore it is necessarily and properly called the World.

43. For of all living things, both the Sense and the Understanding, cometh into them from without, inspired by that which compasseth them about, and continueth them.

44. And the World receiving it once from God as soon as it was made, hath it still, What Ever it Once Had.

45. But God is not as it seems to some who Blaspheme through superstition, without Sense, and without Mind, or Understanding.

46. For all things that are, O Asclepius, are in God, and made by him, and depend of him, some working by Bodies, some moving by a Soul-like Essence, some quickening by a Spirit, and some receiving the things that are weary, and all very fitly.

47. Or rather, I say, that he hath them not, but I

declare the Truth, He is All Things, not receiving them from without, but exhibiting them outwardly.

48. And this is the Sense and Understanding of God, to move all things always.

49. And there never shall be any time, when any of those things that are, shall fail or be wanting.

50. When I say the things that are, I mean God, for the things that are, God hath; and neither is there anything without him, nor he without anything.

51. These things, O Asclepius, will appear to be true, if thou understand them, but if thou understand them not, incredible.

52. For to understand, is to believe, but not to believe, is not to understand; For my speech or words reach not unto the Truth, but the Mind is great, and being led or conducted for a while by Speech, is able to attain to the Truth.

53. And understanding all things round about, and finding them consonant, and agreeable to those things that were delivered and interpreted by Speech, believeth; and in that good belief, resteth.

54. To them, therefore, that understand the things that have been said of God, they are credible, but to them that understand them not, incredible.

55. And let these and thus many things be spoken concerning Understanding and Sense.

THE END OF THE THIRTEENTH BOOK.

THE FOURTEENTH BOOK

OF

HERMES TRISMEGISTUS.

OF OPERATION AND SENSE.

---

1. TAT. Thou hast well explained these things, Father: Teach me furthermore these things; for thou sayest, that Science and Art were the Operations of the rational, but now thou sayest that Beasts are unreasonable, and for want of reason, both are and are called Brutes; so that by this Reason, it must needs follow that unreasonable Creatures partake not of Science, or Art, because they come short of Reason.

2. HERM. It must needs be so, Son.

3. TAT. Why then, O Father, do we see some unreasonable living Creatures use both Science and Art? as the Pismires treasure up for themselves food against the Winter, and Fowls of the Air likewise make them Nests, and four-footed Beasts know their own Dens.

4. These things they do, O Son, not by Science or Art, but by Nature; for Science or Art are things that are taught, but none of these brute Beasts are taught any of these things.

5. But these things being Natural unto them, are wrought by Nature, whereas Art and Science do not happen unto all, but unto some.

6. As men are Musicians, but not all; neither are all Archers or Huntsmen, or the rest, but some of them have learned something by the working of Science or Art.

7 After the same manner also, if some Pismires

did so, and some not, thou mightest well say, they gather their food according to Science and Art.

8. But seeing they are all led by Nature, to the same thing, even against their wills, it is manifest they do not do it by Science or Art.

9. For Operations, O Tat, being unbodily, are in Bodies, and work by Bodies.

10. Wherefore, O Tat, in as much as they are unbodily, thou must needs say they are immortal.

11. But in as much as they cannot act without Bodies, I say, they are always in a Body.

12. For those things that are to any thing, or for the cause of any thing made subject to Providence or Necessity, cannot possibly remain idle of their own proper Operation.

13. For that which is, shall ever be; for both the Body, and the Life of it, is the same.

14. And by this reason, it follows, that the Bodies also are always, because I affirm: That this corporiety is always by the Act and Operation, or for them.

15. For although earthly bodies be subject to dissolution; yet these bodies must be the Places, and the Organs, and Instruments of Acts or Operations.

16. But Acts or Operations are immortal, and that which is immortal, is always in Act, and therefore also Corporification if it be always.

17. Acts or Operations do follow the Soul, yet come not suddenly or promiscuously, but some of them come together with being made man, being about brutish or unreasonable things.

18. But the purer Operations do insensibly in the change of time, work with the oblique part of the Soul.

19. And these Operations depend upon Bodies; and truly they that are Corporifying come from the Divine Bodies into Mortal ones.

20. But every one of them acteth both about the Body and the Soul, and are present with the Soul, even without the Body.

21. And they are always Acts or Operations, but the Soul is not always in a Mortal Body, for it can be without a Body, but Acts or Operations cannot be without Bodies.

22. This is a sacred speech, Son, the Body cannot Consist without a Soul.

23. TAT. How meanest thou that, Father?

24. HERM. Understand it thus, O Tat, When the Soul is separated from the Body, there remaineth that same Body.

25. And this same Body according to the time of its abode, is actuated or operated in that it is dissolved and becomes invisible.

26. And these things the Body cannot suffer without act or operation, and consequently there remaineth with the Body the same act or operation.

27. This then is the difference between an Immortal Body, and a Mortal one, that the immortal one consists of one Matter, and so doth not the mortal one; and the immortal one doth, but this suffereth.

28. And everything that acteth or operateth is stronger, and ruleth; but that which is actuated or operated, is ruled.

29. And that which ruleth, directeth and governeth as free, but the other is ruled, a servant.

30. Acts or Operations do not only actuate or operate living or breathing or insouled Bodies, but also breathless Bodies, or without Souls, Wood, and Stones, and such like, increasing and bearing fruit, ripening, corrupting, rotting, putrifying, and breaking, or working such like things, and whatsoever inanimate Bodies can suffer.

31. Act or Operation, O Son, is called, whatsoever is, or is made or done, and there are always many things made, or rather all things.

32. For the World is never widowed or forsaken of any of those things that are, but being always carried or moved in itself, it is in labour to bring forth the things that are, which shall never be left by it to corruption.

33. Let therefore every act or operation be understood to be always immortal, in what manner of Body soever it be.

34. But some Acts or Operations be of Divine, some of corruptible Bodies, some universal, some peculiar, and some of the generals, and some of the parts of every thing.

35. Divine Acts or Operations therefore there be, and such as work or operate upon their proper Bodies, and these also are perfect, and being upon or in perfect Bodies.

36. Particular are they which work by any of the living Creatures.

37. Proper, be they that work upon any of the things that are.

38. By this Discourse, therefore, O Son, it is gathered that all things are full of Acts or Operations.

39. For if necessarily they be in every Body, and that there be many Bodies in the World, I may very well affirm, that there be many other Acts or Operations.

40. For many times in one Body, there is one, and a second, and a third, besides these universal ones that follow.

41. And universal Operations, I call them that are indeed bodily, and are done by the Senses and Motions.

42. For without these it is impossible that the Body should consist.

43. But other Operations are proper to the Souls of Men, by Arts, Sciences, Studies, and Actions.

44. The Senses also follow these Operations, or rather are the effects or perfections of them.

45. Understand therefore, O Son, the difference of Operations, it is sent from above.

46. But sense being in the Body, and having its essence from it, when it receiveth Act or Operation, manifesteth it, making it as it were corporeal.

47. Therefore, I say, that the Senses are both

corporeal and mortal, having so much existence as the Body, for they are born with the Body, and die with it.

48. But mortal things themselves have not Sense, as Not consisting of such an Essence.

49. For Sense can be no other than a corporeal apprehension, either of evil or good that comes to the Body.

50. But to Eternal Bodies there is nothing comes, nothing departs; therefore there is no sense in them.

51. TAT. Doth the Sense therefore perceive or apprehend in every Body.

52. HERM. In every Body, O Son.

53. TAT. And do the Acts or Operations work in all things?

54. HERM. Even in things inanimate, O Son, but there are differences of Senses.

55. For the Senses of things rational, are with Reason; of things unreasonable, Corporeal only, but the Senses of things inanimate are passive only, according to Augmentation and Diminution.

56. But Passion and Sense depend both upon one head, or height, and are gathered together into the same, by Acts or Operations.

57. But in living wights there be two other Operations that follow the Senses and Passions, to wit, Grief and Pleasure.

58. And without these, it is impossible that a living wight, especially a reasonable one, should perceive or apprehend.

59. And therefore, I say, that these are the Ideas of Passions that bear rule, especially in reasonable living wights.

60. The Operations work indeed, but the Senses do declare and manifest the Operations, and they being bodily, are moved by the brutish parts of the Soul; therefore I say, they are both maleficial or doers of evil.

61. For that which affords the Sense to rejoice with

Pleasure is straightway the cause of many evils happening to him that suffers it.

62. But Sorrows gives stronger torments and Anguish, therefore doubtless are they both maleficial.

63. The same may be said of the Sense of the Soul.

64. TAT. Is not the Soul incorporeal, and the Sense a Body, Father? or is it rather in the Body.

65. HERM. If we put it in a Body, O Son, we shall make it like the Soul or the Operations, for these being unbodily, we say are in Bodies.

66. But Sense is neither Operation, nor Soul, nor anything else that belongs to the Body, but as we have said, and therefore it is not incorporeal.

67. And if it be not incorporeal it must needs be a Body; for we always say, that of things that are, some are Bodies and some incorporeal.

THE END OF THE FOURTEENTH BOOK.

THE FIFTEENTH BOOK
OF
HERMES TRISMEGISTUS.
OF TRUTH TO HIS SON TAT.

---

1. HERM. Of Truth, O Tat, it is not possible that man being an imperfect wight, compounded of imperfect Members, and having his Tabernacle consisting of different and many Bodies, should speak with any confidence.

2. But as far as it is possible, and just, I say, That Truth is only in the Eternal Bodies, whose very Bodies be also true.

3. The Fire is fire itself only, and nothing else; the Earth is earth itself and nothing else; the air is air itself and nothing else; the water, water itself and nothing else.

4. But our Bodies consist of all these; for they have of the Fire, they have of the Earth, they have of the Water, and Air, and yet there is neither Fire, nor Earth, nor Water, nor Air, nor anything true.

5. And if at the Beginning our Constitution had not Truth, how could men either see the Truth, or speak it, or understand it only, except God would?

6. All things therefore upon Earth, O Tat, are not Truth, but imitations of the Truth, and yet not all things neither, for they are but few that are so.

7. But the other things are Falsehood, and Deceit, O Tat, and Opinions like the Images of the fantasy or appearance.

8. And when the fantasy hath an influence from

above, then it is an imitation of Truth, but without that operation from above, it is left a lie.

9. And as an Image shews the Body described, and yet is not the Body of that which is seen, as it seems to be, and it is seen to have eyes, but it sees nothing, and ears, but hears nothing at all; and all other things hath the picture, but they are false, deceiving the eyes of the beholder, whilst they think they see the Truth, and yet they are indeed but lies.

10. As many therefore as see not Falsehood, see the Truth.

11. If therefore we do so understand, and see every one of these things as it is, then we see and understand true things.

12. But if we see or understand any thing besides, or otherwise than that which is, we shall neither understand, nor know the Truth.

13. TAT. Is Truth therefore upon Earth, O Father?

14. HERM. Thou dost not miss the mark, O Son. Truth indeed is nowhere at all upon Earth, O Tat, for it cannot be generated or made.

15. But concerning the Truth, it may be that some men, to whom God will give the good seeing Power, may understand it.

16. So that unto the Mind and reason, there is nothing true indeed upon Earth.

17. But unto the True Mind and Reason, all things are fantasies or appearances, and opinions.

18. TAT. Must we not therefore call it Truth, to understand and speak the things that are?

19. HERM. But there is nothing true upon Earth.

20. TAT. How then is this true, That we do not know anything true? how can that be done here?

21. HERM. O Son, Truth is the most perfect Virtue, and the highest Good itself, not troubled by Matter, not encompassed by a Body, naked, clear, unchangeable, venerable, unalterable Good.

22. But the things that are here, O Son, are visible,

incapable of Good, corruptible, passible, dissolvable, changeable, continually altered, and made of another.

23. The things therefore that are not true to themselves, how can they be true?

24. For every thing that is altered, is a lie, not abiding in what it is; but being changed it shews us always, other and other appearances.

25. TAT. Is not man true, O Father?

26. HERM. As far forth as he is a Man, he is not true, Son; for that which is true, hath of itself alone its constitution and remains, and abides according to itself, such as it is.

27. But man consists of many things and doth not abide of himself but is turned and changed, age after age, Idea after Idea, or form after form, and this while he is yet in the Tabernacle.

28. And many have not known their own children after a little while, and many children likewise have not known their own Parents.

29. Is it then possible, O Tat, that he who is so changed, is not to be known, should be true? no, on the contrary, he is Falsehood, being in many Appearances of changes.

30. But do thou understand the true to be that which abides the same, and is Eternal, but man is not ever, therefore not True, but man is a certain Appearance, and Appearance is the hightest Lie or Falsehood.

31. TAT. But these Eternal Bodies, Father, are they not true though they be changed?

32. HERM. Everything that is begotten or made, and changed is not true, but being made by our Progenitor, they might have had true Matter.

33. But these also have in themselves, something that is false in regard of their change.

34. For nothing that remains not in itself, is True.

35. TAT. What shall one say then, Father, that only the Sun which besides the Nature of other things, is not changed, but abides in itself, is Truth?

36. HERM. It is Truth, and therefore is he only intrusted with the Workmanship of the World, ruling and making all things whom I do both honour, and adore his Truth; and after the One, and First, I acknowledge him the Workman.

37. TAT. What therefore doth thou affirm to be the first Truth, O Father?

38. HERM. The One and Only, O Tat, that is not of Matter, that is not in a body, that is without Colour, without Figure or Shape, Immutable, Unalterable, which always is; but Falsehood, O Son, is corrupted.

39. And corruption hath laid hold upon all things on Earth, and the Providence of the True encompasseth, and will encompass them.

40. For without corruption, there can no Generation consist.

41. For Corruption followeth every Generation, that it may again be generated.

42. For those things that are generated, must of necessity be generated of those things that are corrupted, and the things generated must needs be corrupted, that the Generation of things being, may not stand still or cease.

43. Acknowledge therefore the first Workman by the Generation of things.

44. Consequently the things that are generated of Corruption are false, as being sometimes one thing, sometimes another: For it is impossible they should be made the same things again, and that which is not the same, how is it true?

45. Therefore, O Son, we must call these things fantasies or appearances.

46. And if we will give a man his right name, we must call him the appearance of Manhood; and a Child, the fantasy or appearance of a Child; an old man, the appearance of an old man; a young man, the appearance of a young man; and a man of ripe age, the appearance of a man of ripe age.

47. For neither is a man, a man; nor a child, a child; nor a young man, a young man; nor an old man, an old man.

48 But the things that pre-exist and that are, being changed are false.

49. These things understand thus, O Son, as these false Operations, having their dependance from above, even of the truth itself.

50. Which being so, I do affirm that Falsehood is the Work of Truth.

THE END OF THE FIFTEENTH BOOK.

THE SIXTEENTH BOOK
OF
HERMES TRISMEGISTUS.

THAT NONE OF THE THINGS THAT ARE, CAN PERISH.

---

1. HERM. We must now speak of the Soul and Body, O Son; after what manner the Soul is Immortal, and what operation that is, which constitutes the Body, and dissolves it.

2. But in none of these is Death, for it is a conception of a name, which is either an empty word, or else it is wrongly called Death (by the taking away the first letter,) instead of Immortal. [Thanatos for Athanatos.]

3. For Death is destruction, but there is nothing in the whole world that is destroyed.

4. For if the World be a second God, and an Immortal living Wight, it is impossible that any part of an Immortal living Wight should die.

5. But all things that are in the World, are members of the World, especially Man, the reasonable living Wight.

6. For the first of all is God, the Eternal and Unmade, and the Workman of all things.

7. The second is the World, made by him, after his own Image and by him holden together, and nourished, and immortalized; and as from its own Father, ever living.

8. So that as Immortal, it is ever living, and ever immortal.

9. For that which is ever living, differs from that which is eternal.

10. For the Eternal was not begotten, or made by another; and if it were begotten or made, yet it was made by itself, not by any other, but it is always made.

11. For the Eternal, as it is Eternal, is the Universe.

12. For the Father himself, is Eternal of himself, but the World was made by the Father, ever living, and immortal.

13. And as much Matter as there was laid up by him, the Father made it all into a Body, and swelling it, made it round like a Sphere, endued it with Quality, being itself immortal, and having Eternal Materiality.

14. The Father being full of Ideas, sowed Qualities in the Sphere, and shut them up, as in a Circle, deliberating to beautify with every Quality, that which should afterwards be made.

15. Then clothing the Universal Body with Immortality, lest the Matter, if it would depart from this Composition, should be dissolved into its own disorder.

16. For when the Matter was incorporeal, O Son, it was disordered, and it hath here the same confusion daily revolved about other little things, endued with Qualities, in point of Augmentation, and Diminution, which men call Death, being indeed a disorder happening about earthly living wights.

17. For the Bodies of Heavenly things have one order, which they have received from the Father at the Beginning, and is by the instauration of each of them, kept indissolveible.

18. But the instauration of earthly Bodies, is their consistence; and their dissolution restores them into indissoluble, that is, Immortal.

19. And so there is made a privation of Sense, but not a destruction of Bodies.

20. Now the third living wight is Man, made after the Image of the World; and having by the Will of the Father, a Mind above other earthly wights.

21. And he hath not only a sympathy with the second God, but also an understanding of the first.

22. For the second God, he apprehends as a body; but the first, he understands as Incorporeal, and the Mind of the Good.

23. Tat. And doth not this living wight perish?

24. Herm. Speak advisedly, O Son, and learn what God is, what the World, what an Immortal Wight, and what a dissolvable One is.

25. And understand that the World is of God and in God; but Man of the World and in the World.

26. The Beginning, and End, and Consistence of all, is God.

The End of the Sixteenth Book.

THE SEVENTEENTH BOOK
OF
HERMES TRISMEGISTUS.

To Asclepius, to be Truly Wise.

---

1. Because my Son Tat, in thy absence, would needs learn the Nature of the things that are: He would not suffer me to give over (as coming very young to the knowledge of every individual) till I was forced to discourse to him many things at large, that his contemplation might from point to point, be more easy and successful.

2. But to thee I have thought good to write in few words, choosing out the principal heads of the things then spoken, and to interpret them more mystically, because thou hast, both more years, and more knowledge of Nature.

3. All things that appear, were made, and are made.

4. Those things that are made, are not made by themselves, but by another.

5. And there are many things made, but especially all things that appear, and which are different, and not like.

6. If the things that be made and done, be made and done by another, there must be one that must make, and do them; and he unmade, and more ancient than the things that are made.

7. For I affirm the things that are made, to be made by another; and it is impossible, that of the things that are made any should be more ancient than all, but only that which is not made.

8. He is stronger, and One, and only knowing all things indeed, as not having any thing more ancient than himself.

9. For he bears rule, both over multitude, and greatness, and the diversity of the things that are made, and the continuity of the Facture and of the Operation.

10. Moreover, the things that are made, are visible, but he is invisible; and for this cause, he maketh them, that he may be visible; and therefore he makes them always.

11. Thus it is fit to understand and understanding to admire and admiring to think thy self happy, that knowest thy natural Father.

12. For what is sweeter than a Natural Father?

13. Who therefore is this, or how shall we know him?

14. Or is it just to ascribe unto him alone, the Title and Appellation of God, or of the Maker, or of the Father, or of all Three? That of God because of his Power; the Maker because of his Working and Operation; and the Father, because of his Goodness.

15. For Power is different from the things that are made, but Act or Operation, in that all things are made.

16. Wherefore, letting go all much and vain talking, we must understand these two things, That Which is Made, and Him Which is the Maker; for there is nothing in the middle, between these Two, nor is there any third.

17. Therefore understanding All things, remember these Two; and think that these are All things, putting nothing into doubt; neither of the things above, nor of the things below; neither of things changeable, nor things that are in darkness or secret.

18. For All things, are but two Things, That which Maketh, and that which is Made; and the One of them cannot depart, or be divided from the Other.

19. For neither is it possible that the maker should

be without the thing made, for either of them is the self-same thing; therefore cannot the One of them be separated from the other, no more than a thing can be separated from itself.

20. For if he that makes be nothing else, but that which makes alone, Simple, Uncompounded, it is of necessity, that he makes the same thing to himself, to whom it is the Generation of him that maketh to be also All that is made.

21. For that which is generated or made, must necessarily be generated or made by another, but without the Maker that which is made, neither is made, nor is; for the one of them without the other, hath lost his proper Nature by the privation of the other.

22. So if these Two be confessed, That which maketh, and that which is made, then they are One in Union, this going before, and that followlng.

23. And that which goeth before, is, God the Maker, and that which follows is, that which is made, be it what it will.

24. And let no man be afraid because of the variety of things that are made or done, lest he should cast an aspersion of baseness, or infamy upon God, for it is the only Glory of him to do, or make All things.

25. And this making, or facture is as it were the Body of God, and to him that maketh or doth, there is nothing evil, or filthy to be imputed, or There is Nothing thought Evil or Filthy.

26. For these are Passions that follow Generation as Rust doth Copper, or as Excrements do the Body.

27. But neither did the Copper-smith make the Rust, nor the Maker the Filth, nor God the Evilness.

28. But the vicissitude of Generation doth make them, as it were to blossom out; and for this cause did make Change to be, as one should say, The Purgation of Generation.

29. Moreover, is it lawful for the same Painter to make both Heaven, and the Gods, and the Earth, and

the Sea, and Men, and brute Beasts, and inanimate Things, and Trees; and is it impossible for God to make these things? O the great madness, and ignorance of men in things that concern God!

30. For men that think so, suffer that which is most ridiculous of all; for professing to bless and praise God, yet in not ascribing to him the making or doing of All things, they know him not.

31. And besides their not knowing him, they are extremely impious against him, attributing unto him Passions, as Pride, or Oversight, or Weakness, or Ignorance, or Envy.

32. For if he do not make or do all things, he is either proud or not able, or ignorant, or envious, which is impious to affirm.

33. For God hath only one Passion, namely Good; and he that is good is neither proud, nor impotent, nor the rest, but God is Good itself.

34. For Good is all power, to do or make all things, and every thing that is made, is made by God, that is by the Good and that can make or do all things.

35. See then how he maketh all things, and how the things are done, that are done, and if thou wilt learn, hou mayest see an Image thereof, very beautiful, and like.

36. Look upon the Husbandman, how he casteth Seeds into the Earth, here Wheat, there Barley, and elsewhere some other Seeds.

37. Look upon the same Man, planting a Vine, or an Apple-Tree, or a Fig-Tree, or some other Tree.

38. So doth God in Heaven sow Immortality, in the Earth Change in the whole Life, and Motion.

39. And these things are not many, but few, and easily numbered for they are all but four, God and Generation, in which are all things.

THE END OF THE SEVENTEENTH BOOK.

FINIS.

Collectanea Hermetica

EDITED BY

Dr. Wynn Westcott,

S.M. of the Soc. Ros. in Ang., Master of the Quatuor Coronati Lodge.

VOLUME III.

A Short Enquiry concerning the

Hermetic Art

BY

A LOVER OF PHILALETHES.

London, 1714.

Preface by

NON OMNIS MORIAR

An Introduction to Alchemy
and Notes by S. S. D. D.

NOTE BY THE EDITOR OF THE SERIES.

The first volume of the *Collectanea Hermetica* has been well received; indeed the *Hermetic Arcanum* of Jean d' Espagnet could not fail to interest Alchymic students. There could be no doubt that the second volume of the series, *The Divine Pymander*, of Hermes Trismegistus, would also secure an even greater distribution. In now issuing a reprint of the *Short Enquiry concerning the Hermetic Art*, by A lover of Philalethes, with a Preface by " Non omnis Moriar," and an " Introduction to Alchymy," by my friend, S. S. D. D., great confidence is felt that this third volume will be equally successful.

W. Wynn Westcott, M.B., D.P.H.

PREFACE.

THERE is great reason to believe that this *Enquiry into the Hermetic Art*, first published in 1714, led to the composition of the still more extended and more spiritually conceived volume, the *Suggestive Enquiry into the Hermetic Mystery and Alchemy*, which was published anonymously in 1850. This latter volume, which has for many years been unprocurable, and which cannot yet be reprinted by any one unless with the consent of the survivor of the two authors, is an almost complete review of Alchymy on the spiritual plane.

The volume before us has a distinct reference to the science of Alchymy referred to the plane of human improvement, although it is also definitely concerned with the equally possible, though almost incredible power of transmutation upon the material plane.

This *Short Enquiry* was written with especial reference to the Kabalistic work, now almost unprocurable, the *Æsch Mezareph*, which is a tractate connecting physical alchymy with the Kabalah—so well known to refer to divine, human and cosmic conceptions; and which system of philosophy has been so very largely used by the late Madame Blavatsky to support and corroborate the wonderful system of human and universal genesis partly unveiled in her great work, *The Secret Doctrine* of the adepts of the Eastern World. With her wonderful intuition she perceived that the published and still extant Kabalistic treatises were but debased copies of the more true Chaldee Hebrew doctrine; for she indeed was never entirely initiated into either of the branches of the still extant Kabalistic and Hermetic secret societies. From the Eastern Light which had dawned upon her so generously, she could indeed criticise, but could never fully comprehend the nature of Kabalistic illumination.

Dr. Anna Kingsford, the other eminent modern Theosophist or seeker after the true conception of the Divine, although but slightly familiar with the Indian school of thought, was somewhat fully in communion with the doctrines called Hermetic—or by collateral descent,—Rosicrucian.

The anonymous author of this *Short Enquiry* was definitely a Rosicrucian adept, and although his common name has not transpired, yet his identity was known to the initiated occultists of his day, and the records of his progress inscribed in the unpublished roll of his branch of the Rosicrucian fraternity.

The *Suggestive Enquiry* chose instead of *Æsch Mezareph*, two other ancient discourses upon Alchymy as the text for its instruction; these were the "Aureus, or Golden Tractate of Hermes," and the "Six Keys of Eudoxus," which formed one of three portions of the famous *Hermetic Triumph*, the other two fragments being named the "War of the Knights," and the "Discourse of Eudoxus and Pyrophilus." The earliest edition, known to me, of these curious tracts, is the French translation of "Limojon de Saint Didier," dated 1699; besides this, there is still procurable the English version of 1723.

It is intended to reproduce these curious essays in succession to the *Æsch Mezareph*, which is already in preparation, and which is certain to interest all true students of the occult sciences, because it points out the analogies between alchymic tenets and the allegorical explanation of many passages in the Old Testament of the Hebrews.

In order to assist fellow students in their investigations, I have added here a summary of the *Short Enquiry*, and have prevailed upon the learned Soror S. S. D. D., to contribute an "Introduction to Alchymy," which will be found pregnant with meaning by those who have the divine afflatus, although to the ordinary reader, who takes up an Hermetic book only from curiosity, her essay will need to be studied with the closest attention.

SUMMARY.

THE anonymous author commences with a definition of Alchymy, and proceeds to argue that there must be a sound basis for the science because so many authors of different eras and widely separated countries have all agreed upon the essentials of the doctrine and of the art, and that in many instances almost identical results have been described by adepts wholly unknown to each other, although contemporaneous. He very properly urges that the decision of the truth or error of these doctrines can only be rightly judged by other persons who have actually investigated these researches, and the negative evidence of those who have failed, and the judgment of those who have not searched for themselves, is not any criterion by which such intricate forms of philosophy should be estimated. He further insists that the great learning and lives of pious zeal of many of those who gained success in alchymy should demand an *à priori* confidence in the tenets they demonstrated and sought to unfold. Leaving for the time the thread of the argument, he regrets the failures and wasted energies of many who, in defiance of the warnings of true adepts, and in disregard of the conditions which they laid down as essential to success, yet intruded themselves upon this psycho-spiritual path. He points out especially three requirements which were always insisted upon as necessary to attainment of the summum bonum, *viz.*, a virtuous life, pure and unsullied by sensual enjoyment from birth to the time of trial, a certain freedom from ordinary social and business liabilities, and the inherent power to comprehend the language of symbol and allegory.

He then warmly supports the alleged necessity for the use by alchymists of symbolism and illustration rather than the plain language of exoteric science; remarking most truly that to the pupil who has in himself the power to succeed, the light of intuitive perception will surely dawn, and that so will he be enabled to appreciate the ideals intended to be conveyed, and at the same time will acknowledge the wisdom of such reveiling as is present in the works of the true adepts.

The *Enquiry* then passing superficially to the Assiatic or material plane, yet at all times preserving the actual scheme of spiritual manifestation, considers the grand doctrine of contrast, alluding to the essential differences between Perfect and Imperfect metals, and thus introduces the ideal of the Triune. There are three principles of manifestation and of matter, and even three processes of transmutation. The Universal Solvent or bond of union is then considered, the snowy splendour of Unity standing between the two contrasted forces which form the Dyad. (See the *Sepher Yetzirah*.) This subject is largely commented upon, and allusion is made to the Process even upon the plane of matter, requiring a "Means Mineral" between the two material forms. Many illustrations are then given, notably the doctrines of Sir George Ripley, a Canon of Bridlington, famous alike as a churchman and as a chemist, who formulated the ideal of the Green Lion as a type of the third element—the Means—by which alone could the extremes be knit in perfect association.

Returning once more to the help of the student, the *Enquiry* recommends that such as mean to succeed should study not only *one* real master in his published works, but several; because each author took care that by one book alone the whole secret could not be learned; and that this was not only to stimulate research and cultivate the intuition, but also lest any unworthy person should obtain so great an acquisition as transmutation, which could be misused as well as turned to good account.

Our author then becomes discursive and suggestive and elucidates (or reveils) the meaning and intention of several symbols and paraphrases, such as the terms " Doves of Diana " and the Caduceus of Hermes, and some of the Kabalistic allegories such as the story of Naaman, Elisha and Gehazi.

Becoming still more useful to the learner, our author reverts to the requirements and aims of students, telling them plainly that the Great Secret is almost unattainable by study alone, and that a Master is needed, and that a Master will be forthcoming to him or her who has the inherent faculty of culture upon the Alchymic basis; and finally he ends his discourse by encouraging the learner in his efforts by showing the analogies between the seed of gold reproducing gold, and the grain of wheat by which alone is a crop of Wheat to be obtained. The Solar heat of nature in her working to produce a crop for man's needs and benefit, is also a type of the Hidden Fire by which the alchymist is able to separate the impure from the pure, and to produce the mystic gold from amongst the dross of worldly mind and common matter.

In conclusion, he states, that although the adepts made such free use of allegory, symbol and simile in order to disguise their secret, yet if a man's intuition do but take a firm grasp of one of them, the mystery of a whole series unfolds itself, and the discovery of matters, means and process is achieved, alike on the material plane, and in that higher world where we find Rest in God alone.

N. O. M.; R.R. et A.C.

An Introduction to Alchemy.

By S. S. D. D.

WRITERS on Alchemy are in the habit of making so many prefatory remarks on their own account, that their books stand in very little need of preface; unless indeed, the Editor undertakes to reveal the secrets which the Author is so careful to conceal. I must at once say I am not prepared to do this, but to one thing, I can with advantage call your attention, which is that the study of Alchemy, above all other branches of Occult science, demonstrates the value of Analogy in our search after the real meaning of the mysteries of man and his relation to the Universe. The process of transmutation, which displays a series of colours, recalls the Religion of the Egyptians, symbolising as it did, the blackness of night, the rainbow colours of dawn, the whiteness of noon, and the red glow of evening. The first stage of this symbolism alludes to the blackness of ignorance, the chaotic darkness of men who reject the keys to the secret of the Universe, which are to be found in the rainbow colours; to the vibrations of sound, to scents, tastes, feelings, and subtle psychical impressions. When a man's mind begins to grasp the order and relation of such sense impressions as these, he bids fair to pass from the darkness of ignorance to the white light of wisdom, and perhaps eventually to attain to the imperial purple which clothes the elect.

To do this he must, within himself, possess the divine gift of *wonder*; for it is through this faculty that he raises himself above the cares of life. The man whose curiosity carries him from the contemplation of the manifestation to the contemplation of its causes, is the man whose instincts are preparing him to undertake the Great Work.

Content is fatal; the man who is content with anything, who does not feel in his most successful moments, during the most sacred earthly joys, a keen sense of want and disappointment, can never hope to find the Stone of the Wise—true wisdom and perfect happiness.

The happy are sufficiently rare, however, for me to hope that few of my readers will be deterred from the study of Alchemy by what I have said. We have all been taught to look with horror upon Medusa's head, with the serpents twisting round its face, the terror of which turned all to stone who gazed upon it. But we must, if we would learn the secret wisdom of the ages, learn to long for a glance from those wonderful eyes, which will bestow upon us the gift of indifference to personal joys and sorrows. For the wise man must be as a precious stone; a centre of light to all that approach him; giving joy to others, because he contains the image of the highest joy in himself; desiring nothing from the world, drawing his inspiration from the supernal light—that "Wisdom Goddess" who wears the serpent crowned head upon her shield.

Well has Robert Fludd said, " Be ye changed from dead stones into living philosophical stones. Be equal with God. Ye hear all these things but ye believe not. Oh miserable mortals, who do so anxiously run after your own ruin."

Then the philosopher points out the futility of the ordinary man of petty aims and weak will, never gaining the goal of the higher, or for the matter of that, the lower Alchemy.

" Oh thou miserable one, wilt thou be more happy?

Oh thou proud one, wilt thou be elevated above the circles of this world?

Oh thou ambitious one, wilt thou command in Heaven above this earth, and thy dark body?

Oh ye unworthy, will ye perform all miracles?

Know ye rejected ones, of what nature it is, before ye seek it."

So it comes to the old, old teaching, GNOTHI SEAUTON, Know thyself; until by deep thought and meditation, words have become more than words to thee; until thou hast analyzed them, separated them, transposed them into every conceivable form, and finally extracted from them, their quintessence and spiritual meaning, thou wilt understand no word that the ancient philosophers speak to thee.

Take now the loose meaning attached to such a word as imagination; in these materialistic days it has become synonymous with extravagant fancy, if not with lying: but hear what Paracelsus says of imagination as an occult manifestation of power: "Man has a visible and invisible workshop. The visible one is his body, the invisible one his imagination. . . . The imagination is a sun in the soul of man acting in its own sphere, as the sun in our system acts on the earth. Wherever the latter shines, germs planted in the soil grow, and vegetation springs up; the imagination acts in a similar manner in the soul, and calls forms of life into existence. . . The Spirit is the master, imagination the tool; and the body the plastic material. Imagination is the power by which the will forms sidereal entities out of thoughts, it can produce and cure disease."

Perhaps this passage will give new light to those who have lately treated this faculty with such contempt, in dealing with the subject of hypnotism.

In truth, Imagination is the power of forming images in our minds. It is the development and intensification of an idea, which first exists, is then conceived passively in the thought sphere; then the mind (perceiving the idea can be used) brings desire into play, which is developed into an act of Will, and this converts the passive conception of the idea into an active Imagination. So begins the magical process, the rest it is not for me to divulge.

I will only add on this subject the saying of Eliphaz Levi, that, "The first matter of the Magnum Opus is both within and about us, and the intelligent will, which assimilates light, directs the operations of substantial form, and only employs chemistry as a very secondary instrument."

The *Suggestive Enquiry*, published a century later than the work under our consideration, points out the method which should be employed in the exhaustive analysis of the nature of man, so necessary to the completion of the great work. He says:—

"Metempsychosis takes the human identity (or consciousness) from animal existence to the ethereal elements of its original formation."

That is, in thinking inwardly with calm and philosophic mind we can pass from the manifested life we see and feel, to the motive power of that life; and finally to the cause of the motive power; from the mundane to the supra-mundane; from the intellectual to the intelligible; from the earth to the firmament; from water to the fiery rays of heat emerging from the central light which is the source of all things.

The same book continues, "These elements are the universal fundamentals of nature: only in the Human form can they attain that supremacy of reason which returns to its first cause."

Reason is the light which guides us. Let me hasten to add how necessary it is to distinguish between the false reason, and the Heavenly Reason which we perceive when intuition is purified; and we rise above the lower passions. The false reason is merely an image set up by our unbalanced forces to justify us in evil doing. Well has it been said, that when we find ourselves seeking to justify ourselves by giving reasons for our actions, we have been doing something we are secretly ashamed of.

True Reason is the clear light descending upon us from that which is above all pretence. It was a communion with this faculty, that Saint Thomas à Kempis desired when he told those who would detain him, he must leave them, as one was waiting for him in his cell. False reason seeks to justify itself with much argument; Pure Reason knows Truth, and can afford to be silent.

So continues the *Suggestive Enquiry* "In the Human form only is it possible to comprehend the Divine form; when it has done so by a triplicate growth of Light in the understanding consciously allied, it emanates a fourth form, truthful, godlike, being the express image of its person magically portrayed."

I think I have said enough to show that the Alchemist undertakes no light task. I can hold out no hope of success to those who still retain an absorbing interest in the world. *In* the world Adepts may be, but not *of* it. Alchemy is a jealous mistress, she demands from pupils no less than life; for her sake you must perform the twelve labours of Hercules; for her you must descend into Hell, for her sake you must ascend into Heaven. You must have strength and patience, nothing must terrify you, the joys of Nirvâna must not tempt you; having chosen your work, you must to this end purify yourself from perishable desires, and bring down the light of the shining ones, that it may radiate upon you here on earth. This is the work of the Alchemist; his true ideal is also the highest ideal of Eastern Theosophy; to choose a life that shall bring him in touch with the sorrows of his race rather than accept the Nirvâna open to him; and like other Saviours of the world, to remain manifested as a living link between the supernal and terrestrial natures.

S. S. D. D.—R. R. *et* A. C.

A Short Enquiry Concerning the Hermetic[1] Art.[2]

THIS Art, of bringing all Imperfect Metals to Perfection, hath been asserted for Truth, by Men of almost every Degree, in most Ages of the World; many of whose Books are extant.

They have declared, that they have made and possessed this great Treasure, which not only brings all Imperfect Metals to the Perfection of Sol and Luna[3] (according to the Quality of the Medicine), but healeth all manner of Diseases in Human Bodies, even renewing Youth and prolonging Life.

Those Authors, from Age to Age, have justified one another's Testimony[4]; alledging, as a farther Proof of the Art, that all that have understood it, have written most agreeingly of it, though contemporary, and unknown to one another in Person, or by Writing.

How far these Men's Writings have obtain'd, a very little Enquiry may serve; for most men look upon these (Alchymic) Books only as Cunningly-devised Fables, and the Art itself as altogether impossible.[5]

To which the (Alchymic) Authors answer, That it is not Lawful, nor Commendable to reprobate an Art, by Judges who are ignorant of its Laws as well as the Facts; and that the Ignorant Negative of such, is by no means sufficient to set aside the Affirmative Knowledge of so many Men of Unquestionable Credit, Piety, and Virtue,—supported by Arguments and Circumstances of Uncontestible Force.

From which, together with the Excellency of the

Things themselves (*viz.*, Long Life and Riches, *vide* the "Way to Bliss"*), many have been induced to believe and seek after this Art.

Tis the Melancholy View that I have taken of these Men, that have occasioned the putting my own Thoughts into the Order you find them, hoping no Master will be offended, nor any Inquirer displeased.

When I compare, I say, the variety of these Men's Fortunes, Capacities and other Qualifications, with those the *Philosophers* have laid down for men like to succeed, it fills me with Pity, and makes me almost tremble to rehearse the words of Norton,† *viz.* :—

"That of a Million hardly three,
Were e'er ordain'd for Alchymy."

O sad Tidings to such Men! whose impair'd Healths, injured Fortunes and barren Practice, renders them more unfit every day than other, and instead of attaining that which should crown their Labours with success, are at length in danger of *denying*, if not *cursing* the Art itself.

I would pretty thoroughly enquire from whence this ill success, which attends the generality of Enquirers, proceeds, and accordingly shall mention a few chief Impediments,[6] in my Opinion.

First; But few of those that seek this Art, are qualified according to the *Philosophers* for attaining it; for they assert, That to find it requires the whole Man;‡ as well as that, when found, it possesses him: Also that it is never found of any by Chance or by accidental Tryals, and casual Experiments; and that unless the

---

* An anonymous Alchymic Essay, written in the time of Queen Elizabeth, published by Elias Ashmole, 1658; this famous antiquary also issued Alchymic books under the title of "*James Hasolle, Qui est Mercuriophilus Anglicus.*"

† Author of *Crede Mihi* or *The Ordinall of Alchymy*, written about 1477.

‡ See The *Hermetic Arcanum* of Espagnet, paragraph 4.

Mind* be kindled with a Beam of Divine Light, it will not be able to penetrate this most hidden Science.

These with many more Cautions, are plentifully set down in their Books, on purpose to inform and reform a great many Persons too rashly concern'd in these things; and yet how few take their Advice! undertaking this Study with much less than half the Man; constantly trying Experiments that have no Authority but their own idle Fancy; and consequently have Minds, in respect to this Science, as dark as Midnight.

Then add to these an almost Insuperable Difficulty, (hard enough to be overcome by those that can spare even the whole Man and are very cautious in their Practice, as having a pretty good Understanding of Natural Things in general, and of the Mineral Kingdom in particular) and that is the Subtilty of Stile so peculiar to Hermetick Philosophers.

Of this they often warn us, telling us also, that if it were not for this, they could not disclose, and at the same time hide their Secret. And though this be a Paradox, that at the same time they give light, they darken, yet they affirm it for Truth, with many other things hard enough to be understood; which yet must be understood before any one can profit by them, witness *Geber*,† *Sendivo*,‡ &c.

Also *Norton* has given a hint of this mysterious way of writing,[7] and which indeed sufficiently shews that it will obscure, whether we can discern its Instruction or not, *viz.* :—

" If you consider how the Parts of Works
Be out of Order set by the Old Clerks."

* The Adept, like the poet, is born not made.

† Geber, the Arab alchemist, died about 740 A.D., his real name was Abu Musa Jafar al Sofi.

‡ Michael Sendivogius lived about 1636, was the editor of the *Dialogue between Mercury, Nature and the Alchemist*, and other works designed if not completed by his Master, Alexander Seton.

This breaking to pieces of the several Works, makes it almost impossible for a Tyro to make their Writings Tally; any one part not being rightly apply'd, the whole is incompleat.

Another tells us he has done this, by mixing Unusual Candor with Philosophical Subtilties, in such a manner as would render their Secret safe, tho' openly told; Nor is he wanting to admonish his Reader to be cautious in these things, *viz.*:—

"Yet beware,
That thou mistake not; for I do aver,
A mingled Doctrine these Lines do declare;
For both ways in this Book of mine do claim a share:
Learn to distinguish every Sentence well,
And know to what Work it doth appertain.
This is great Skill, which few, as I can tell,
By all their Reading, yet could e'er attain;
And yet of Theory, this is the main."

Wherefore 'tis obvious, there is no possibility of success, 'till it be learned to which Work their Sayings relate; which indeed is not easie, and is the top of Theory; nor can any speed upon any other, tho' never so finely spun, or fondly embraced.

And though Philosophers do sometimes affirm their Matters to be many, and their Works also; yet they very often, with equal Authority and Truth, assert the contrary; Artephius * saith:—

"Tho' we say in many places, *take this*, and *take that*; yet we mean, that it behoveth thee to take ONE THING.[8] For these things are so set down by the envious Philosophers to deceive the Unwary. Do'st thou, Fool, believe, that we do openly teach the Secret of Secrets? And do'st thou take our Words according to the literal Sound? Know assuredly, he that takes the Words of other Philosophers according to the

---

* Lived about 1160, A.D.; he wrote two works, *On the Philosopher's Stone* and *The Art of Prolonging Life*: they were published in Paris in 1657.

"ordinary Signification and Sound of them, he doth "already wander in the midst of the Labyrinth, having "lost Ariadne's Thread,* and hath as good as appointed "his money to Perdition."

By means of these seeming Contradictions, bolder steps have been taken by some of them in discovering this Art, than otherwise they would have done, and even some have dared to imitate, nay, so much as to repeat.

From hence I infer, That as much has been communicated to the World as can be expected, or that God will yet suffer to be discover'd by Writing. For this Art is declared, by those that have knowingly written of it, to be under his immediate Protection. Likewise that those that come to the Knowledge of it, shall admiringly wonder at its Preservation; and that which will augment their wonder, will be, that so slender a Vail secures it; and which God makes a sufficient Guard against all the Attacks made by the unworthy. *Vide Sendivo*, etc.

Likewise, that as soon as any one discerns[9] the Intention of the Philosophers, from the seeming Sense of the Letter, the dark *Night* of Ignorance will fly away, and a glorious *Morning* of Light and Knowledge will break forth: When *Diana*[10] will unveil herself, Bathing in that most pleasant *Fountain* so much sought.

And that he will find himself in the High Road of Nature which is that *Secret Way* of Philosophers,[11] *viz.*, most *easie*, *delightful* and *speedy*; in which are no Storms, no Heterogeneities, nor any Fire, but the gentle one of Generation.

Norton asserts, That there are but few clerks that comprehend this Work, it being truly Philosophical. And he saith, That in this Work you must not begin with Quicksilver[12] and Metals, as if in another Work you might; which other Work, he adds, if it be done in

---

* Ariadne, daughter of Minos, King of Crete, furnished to Theseus a thread by which to pass through the Labyrinth, and so reach the Minotaur, for the purpose of slaying it.

three Years, would be a blessed Chance, and which belongs to great Men; advising poor Men not to meddle with it, for that Errors in it may be committed above a Hundred ways; that it is a Work of Pain and Labour, as well as full of Perils.

That these things are so, we are sorrowfully confirm'd, by a Modern Author, as is so well known by many. *Intro-Apert.**

Now as their Works differ, so their Waters[13] or Mercuries differ also; for if you would calcine a perfect Metal, it must be done with Mercury; but if you would dissolve an imperfect Body (*which is in the way to Perfection*) it must be done with *Mercurial Water*, which is the Dew or Rain Water of Philosophers.

The perfect Body[14] is calcin'd with a gross Humidity, and by a tedious Labour; but the imperfect Body is dissolved and purified in a much more subtile Mercury, by an easie Fire and little Toil.

And tho' this subtile Menstruum be the Mercury of the imperfect Body, yet it will (for a certain purpose) dissolve *Sol*, as warm water dissolves Ice, and will make its Body a mere Spirit.

This is the Fountain† of Chymical or Hermetick Philosophy, concerning which it is said—

"He that exactly knows the Magistery of this Water, "no Words, or Secrets of Philosophers, Sayings, Writ- "ings or Enigmas, will be concealed from him. And "further, that it is stupendous in its Virtues, and the "things out of which it is immediately drawn, are most "secret above all others; also the means of extracting "it most wonderful. In the Knowledge of which, all "their Fires, Weights and Regimens lie hid."

The same Author affirms, that none can imagine its

---

* By Eirenæus Philalethes, whose name is unknown; *The Open Entrance to the Shut Palace of the King*, first published at Amsterdam, 1668; a masterly work of very great interest.

† See Bernard of Treves: the Fountain was a symbol specially used by him.

Splendour, except they see it, and then you will think you look upon a certain Celestial Body. Believe me, saith he, I have seen this *Snowy Splendor*.[15]

Sendivo not only confirms the same in Words to this effect, *viz.*, Believe me, for I beheld it, that that Water was as white as Snow, but adds, from whence it was drawn, *viz.*, From the Beams of the *Sun* and *Moon*.[16]

Nor is this said by him only, but by many more; I shall instance a few.

Artephius asserts, That 'tis drawn from the Beams of the Sun and Moon, yea, that this dissolving Water is the Soul of the Sun and Moon, their moist Fire, and the only Agent in the World for this Art.

The author of *Arcanum Hermeticæ*,* saith, "Let thy "Mercury draw its Original from both these Lights."

Flamel, speaking of the Sun and Moon, saith, "They "are of a Mercurial Source, and Sulphurous Original."

Another, *viz.*, the Author of *The Way to Bliss*, saith: "That as the Sun is the Father of all things, and the "Moon his Wife the Mother, (for he sends not down "these begetting Beams immediately, but through the "Belly of the Moon) and this double Spirit is carry'd in "a Wind and Spirit into the Earth,† to be made up "and nourished."

Which double Spirit or Flame, Geber calls the immediate Matter of Metals.

You very well know, that Hermes himself, as well as most of his Followers, agree in these things; and 'tis our Business to observe wherein they do agree. Arnold‡ says, "In our Imperfect Metal, there are the "Sun, and Moon in Virtue and near Power." The Philosophick Work begins with this Heavenly Mercury, and an imperfect Body purified.

---

* Jean d'Espagnet: see Volume I. of the *Collectanea*.

† Compare the Emerald Tablet of Hermes Tristmegitos.

‡ Arnold of Villanova, born 1245, a physician, a professor at the University of Barcelona.

"There is a pure Matter " (saith another) " which is " the Matter of Gold, containing in itself the Heat that " giveth Increase." (Fire of Generation.) This is lock'd under thick Folds in common Gold; nor is it to be extracted, but by a strong and tedious Decoction, which is a Work liable to many Errors, and hath always occasioned those that wrought in it to complain of the length and trouble of it. But in the other Work, the Body is soon dissolved, by a sweet and kindly Bath, or moist Fire."[17]

As the former Path requires much Pain and Patience to effect the Work, so this requires great Skill and Application to find it out, it being deeply concealed. The Masters of these Secrets do also affirm, that these Works (which are all one in the Beginning) may be conjoin'd, and made their grand Medicine. And I have been informed, that the way of making them one is but slenderly hid. For should they but change some Words (which they affect to use in order to conceal it) of one[18] Syllable, and sometimes of two, for others of three, and sometimes of four or more, it would not be difficult, for a Tyro, to conceive it. And the Reason given for this slender Covering is, that if any one should discern it, and yet be ignorant of the means of both it would be of little avail; and that if he knew the means, he could not long remain ignorant of the Practice. So that the Knowledge of the Means seems absolutely necessary in the first place.

These Norton calls his " Means Mineral," which, he saith, are no other than Magnetia* and Litharge† her Brother. And he asserts that to clarifie them is the foulest Work of all.

And though he makes these means two, yet he tells you how they differ, *viz.*, as a Mother from her Child, or as a Male from a Female: Which we see brings his

* Magnesia, is the oxide of the metal Magnesium, in modern chemistry; this is not what is referred to.

† Litharge, is an impure oxide of lead; this is not here intended.

to the general Doctrine of Philosophers, *viz.*, Agent and Patient, which seems to be their one intention, whatever Skill they use to perplex their Sayings.

Litharge, he says, is a subtil Earth, brown, ruddy, and not bright.

> "Old Fathers called it a thing of vile price,
> For it is nought Worth by way of Merchandise;
> No man that findeth it would bear it away,
> No more than they would an Ounce of Clay."[19]

He likewise saith, it is not to be sold in all Christian Ground, but thou must be fain to make it.

Magnetia is fair and bright, known by few, and is found in High Places as well as in Low and called by Plato, *Titanos*; these are the Materials to make Elixir; and addeth:—

> "This Secret never was before this Day
> So truly shewed, take it for your Prey."

Now to apply these things to the Doctrine of Philosophers; Litharge must be their Brass or Philosophical Sol; Magnetia must be understood to be their Subtil Humidity, or Philosophical Mercury; which is Living and not only so, but Inlivening; Clean and not only so, but cleansing; Volatile, and not only so, but Volatilizing, even the most fixed Body of Sol; and is the Radical Moisture of Metals.

How this is attained, is worthy our Inquiry, and whether they agree in the manner of preparing it, as well as from whence it is to be drawn, *viz.*, From the Sun and Moon; for it seems it must have the Influences of both.

But to collect these Virtues requires a Mean, as Ripley* hath it, speaking of the Green Lion,[19A]

> "He is the mean, the Sun and Moon between, etc."

Also the Author of "Hunting the Green Lion"† saith,

---

* Sir George Ripley, Canon of Bridlington, lived about 1490.

† Name of author unknown. This is a short essay which has been attributed to Lully or his friend Cremer of Westminster.

"The Lion is the Priest, the Sun and Moon the Wed;
Yet they were both born in the Priest's Bed."

By which Green Lion another saith, "All Philoso-"phers understand Green Gold, multiplicable, sper-"matick, and not yet perfected by Nature; Or "Assa Fœtida, because in the very first of this "Operation or Distillation, a white Fume with a "stinking smell exhales." It was by this strong scent that Flammel knew this Subject.

That this agrees with the rest of the Philosophers, I need not enlarge to shew, it being well known to them who read their Books.

This Distillation, Hermes, as well as many others, declares must be made by a gentle Fire, by little and little, with great Discretion, lest the thick be mixed with the thin, the subtile with the gross, or the foul with that which is clean. Lully[*] is very famous for his witty Description of this Operation, under the Figure of Distilling of Wine, which he sometimes also calls Juice of Lunaria, from which he extracts the Sweat with a gentle Fire, in the form of a white Water.

This is also called by other Names, as Adrop, Saturn,[20] Brass, Leprous Gold, and Imperfect Body; and which they all agree lies in great Obscurity, satur-nine and foul, in the making of which there is a great Stink; that 'tis not fixed, a Medium between a Metal, and a Mineral partaking of the Nature of both, and very crude, containing an Argent vive, which is the Basis and Ground-work of their precious Medicine. And thus, saith the Philosopher, you will come to under-stand how Saturn contains the greatest Secret in this Art. This is "The Golden Branch, so much conceal'd, "which all the Groves with Shadows overcast and "gloomy Vallies hide, and which will follow none, but "him that knows Dame Venus's Birds and him to whom "of Doves a lucky Pair," &c.—*Arcanum Hermeticæ*.[†]

[*] Raymond Lully, a Spanish priest, died in 1314, on the coast of Africa, being stoned to death by Mohammedans.

[†] Jean d'Espagnet, see paragraph 15 of the *Hermetic Arcanum*.

The Masters of this Science agree with one Voice in this, *viz.*, That this Matter must be exactly purified, and dissolved into an Argent vive, of such Virtues as are nowhere else possible to be found.

This is performed by a wonderful Cohobation; the Number of which Cohobations are much varied: But in this they all agree, that there must be so many, till a total Dissolution and perfect Purity be known.

The time of doing this, some will have it, is hinted in *Arcanum Hermeticæ* where 'tis said, "Cause the Dragon to "drink Three times the Magical Number Seven, until "being drunk, he put off his hideous Garment."*

Thus, I say, Three times Seven is Twenty-One, which some will interpret Days, and to which some other Philosophers seem to agree; but whether these are One and Twenty Days or Cohobations, he will rightly determine, who shall be blessed with the Knowledge of their "Light bringing Venus, and Horned Diana."—*Arcanum Hermeticæ*.

Likewise the Philosophers agree in the Virtues of this Water, *viz.*, that as it partakes of the Natures of both Sexes, so it acts the part of both, *viz.*, Dissolving and Congealing. For they assert, That it will Congeal itself into a Lunar or a Solar Nature, (according to the design of the Workman) without any addition whatsoever.

There are also some Cautions given concerning Proportion in Compounding the Imperfect Body, as well as with relation to its Dissolution; for that in case of undue Weight or Measure, the Virtue will be much diminished, if not altogether spoiled. But if a due Proportion be observed, and a proper Fire given, the true Sign will follow.

The true Union between the imperfect Leprous Body, and its Water, they have deeply conceal'd, as the Philosophers own, and Searchers find; because as they say, the rest is so easie in the Work of Generation,

---

* See paragraph 52 of the *Hermetic Arcanum*.

that 'tis hardly to be missed, by one that hath attain'd their wonderful Mercury, so united and purified.

Concerning which, they have declared, they have given such hints as are sufficient to an enlightened Mind; and that none shall ever dare to do it more openly, without a Curse from God.

But all have not done it with the same Candor, nor by the same Similes and Enigmas; *The New Light* * under that of Chalibs; *The Way to Bliss*, by that of the Witty Fire of Hermes, and so of the rest, Norton says:—

"Bacon † did it darkly, in his Three Letters all;
But Raimond ‡ better in his Art general."

And since the Readers can expect no better Account from me, concerning the Means and Medium of this Wonderful Union, than the Philosophers have learnt in their Books, I must refer them for more ample Satisfaction and Information therein. For, as Norton saith:—

"Trust not therefore to Reading of one Book,
But in many Authors' Works ye may look.
Liber librum aperit, saith Arnold the great Clerk;
Anaxagoras ¶ said the same for his Work,
Who that slothful is in many Books to see,
Such one in Practice, prompt shall never be."

The Reason he gives for thus Reading and Comparing many Books, is, that

"Every each of them taught but one point, or twain,
Whereby his Fellows were made certain,
How that he was to them a Brother,
For every of them understood each other."

I have mentioned Norton the more, because it appears

---

* *Novum Lumen Chymicum*, by Seton and Sendivogius.

† Bacon, lived about 1270.

‡ Raymond Lully.

¶ A Greek philosopher of the Ionic School, born 500 B.C

to me, that he and his Contemporary Ripley, have written very Learnedly of this Art, and wonderful Agreeingly, through both writ near the same time, and very probably one in England and the other abroad; and for ought I can meet with, were not known to one another at that time. Nor can one suppose that Norton had seen Ripley's *Compound of Alchimy*, since it was written but six years before his *Ordinal*. Books of that kind especially, did not in those days come abroad quickly: Nor doth Norton, when he reckons up some that had written excellently of Proportion, take any notice of Ripley, who beyond all question hath in that excell'd.

This Harmony in Authors, that have written of the Art at the same time, and unknown one to another, a Modern Adept of the same Nation with the two before mentioned, has brought as a convincing Argument (among others) to prove its Being; and which, with me, has great Weight, and seems to serve his purpose.

This Author has profess'd to have outdone all that went before him, discovering such things, he says, as the World was barren enough before, yet his Disciples have much complain'd of their ill success; notwithstanding they have seemed to understand him more fully than the other Philosophers, insomuch that many have concluded his way of proceeding in this Art to be different from many of theirs. Nay, at length some have so ill rewarded his Candor, as to charge him with being ignorant of those things he so solemnly professeth to be true, and of which his Accusers are unworthy.

It seems he foresaw his Readers would thus misconstrue his Writings, and therefore he here and there scatters some necessary Cautions for those that would receive them.

"Nor let any expect," saith he, "Comfortable Doc-
"trine in our Books, who know not the true Keys, by
"which our Matter is brought forth from Darkness into
"the Light: For verily tho' we write for the Inlightening
"a true Son of Art, yet also for the fatal Blinding of all

"such Owls and Bats, who cannot behold the Light of
"the Sun, nor can endure the Splendor of our Moon. To
"such we propound rare Tricks, suiting to their sordid
"Fancy: To the Covetous, an easie way without Ex-
"pence: To the Hasty, Rash and Unstable, multiplicity
"of Distillations.

"In the World our Writings shall prove like a curious
"edged Knife;* to some they shall carve out Dainties, to
"others they shall serve only to cut their Fingers. 'Tis
"the Sign of an Owl,[21] to be blinder, by how much the
"Sun shines brighter.—If thou wilt be heedless, thou
"may'st sooner stumble at our Books, than at any thou
"didst ever read in thy Life. . . Take this from one
"that knows best the Sense of what he has written;
"where we speak most plainly, there be most circum-
"spect, (for we do not go about to betray the Secrets of
"Nature) especially in those places which seem to give
"Receipts so plain as you would desire, suspect either
"a Metaphor, or else be sure that something is sup-
"pressed which thou wilt hardly find (without Inspira-
"tion) of thyself; yet to a Son of Art, we have written
"that which never heretofore was by any reveal'd."

I might add many more Cautions of other Authors, as well as of this, concerning the Difficulties which attend the Reading of their Books; and had not mention'd what I have, but that it appear'd the more necessary to mention some of this Author's because almost every Body has taken up an Opinion, that he is more easily understood than the rest; but how profitably, themselves may judge.

We should not be just to ourselves, if we should be ignorant that when any of them have made a Discovery of this or the other Part of the Work, they have not Balanced it with such Obscurities which are not easily discerned; especially by the Unwary.

And therefore if the Students in this Art, and particularly of this Author's Works, did believe the

---

* Compare, "I come not to send peace, but a sword."

Philosophers had Cunning equal to their Skill and would but take the Advice given by them, they would not have room to Censure the Philosophers but themselves.

For what could anyone have said, more to have deter'd Inquirers from rash Conclusions, either in Theory or Practice, than this Author has done? *viz.*, "Venture not," saith he, "to practice barely upon my "Words: For know that what I have only hinted, is far "more than what I have discover'd; and what I have "declared to thy first Apprehension, most openly, hath "yet its lurking Serpent under the green leaves; I "mean some hidden thing, which thou oughtest to "understand; which thou, being Cocksure at first Blush, "wilt neglect."

The fond Notion which Men have entertained, of understanding this Author's Writing more perfectly or easier than the rest of the Masters is to me an Argument of his great skill in that peculiar way of Writing, which the Hermetick Philosophers profess and value themselves upon, *viz.*, to be able openly to show the Art to the Sons of it, and yet secure it from the unworthy.

That this is true, all their Writings shew; for some of them have learn'd the Art from Books as they own; which could not be, if it were not taught in them. These indeed are very few in comparison to those that Learn it not, though they read the same Books, but not the same things in them. As this Author hath again excellently described such men, *viz.*, "Some I know will serve my Book, as they "have served others; out of it they will read their own "Phantastick Processes, which I never dreamt of, nor "yet are they in Nature. Though we write in English, "yet our Matter will be as hard as Greek to some, who "will think they understand us well, when they miscon-"strue our Meaning most perversely. Nor is it imagin-"able, that they who are Fools in Nature, should be "wise in our Books, which are Testimonies to Nature."

As this Author hath profess'd an extraordinary esteem for Ripley, and (in many things) has imitated his Candour, yet he has so manifestly compounded it with the Craft of Norton, that it is hard to distinguish them, and which well deserves the Cautions he hath given, and his Readers' Care therein.

He has in his Books led us some part of the way under such Philosophical Vails, as have been pretty easily seen through by most that read them with Application; who no sooner discover some of his Metaphors, but overcome with joy, and exalted with an Opinion of their own Abilities, presently cry out, we have found! we have found! And what have they found? Why their way into a Labyrinth.*

For at the end of this short Walk, he hath set up one Metaphor, harder to be understood than all the rest, *viz.*, The Doves of Diana. This stands at the Entrance into a great Labyrinth, in which are abundance of Inquirers rambling at this day; many of them undiscerned by one another.

I have taken several Turns in it myself, wherein one shall meet with very few; for 'tis so large, and almost every one taking a different Path, that they seldom meet.

But finding it a very melancholy Place, I resolved to get out of it, and rather content myself to walk in the little Garden before the Entrance, wherein many things tho' not all, were orderly to be seen. Choosing rather to stay there, and contemplate on the Metaphor set up, than venture again into the Wilderness; in which I heard the Noise and Voices of several strange and devouring Creatures, (some of which I had with difficulty escaped) every one, almost, having a differing Sound.

As this Author seems to have design'd a full stop at the Pillar he hath caused to be erected, and to prevent

---

* There is a portion of the Royal Arch Ceremony of Freemasonry which seems related to this symbolism.—S.A.

Travellers running unawares into that dangerous and dark Wilderness, caused this Inscription to be put upon it, *viz.*, "Learn what Diana's Doves are, which "doth vanquish the Lion by asswaging him; I say, the "green Lion, which is indeed the Babylonian Dragon, "Killing all things with his poison. Then at length learn "to know the Caducean Rod of Mercury, with which he "works wonders;" etc. Therefore I will not step one Step farther without a Guide, for I dread going again into the Labyrinth.

This guide must be a very wise Man, indued with singular Gifts; for he must not only tell me the Interpretation, but the Dream itself; and by this I may judge of his Ability.

For, as Kelly saith, "Let no Man lead, unless he "knows the Way."

Therefore let none mistake my Inquiring the Way, for a Teaching of it. If any do, and suffer by it, they must blame themselves, not me; for I am Inquiring, I say, not Teaching the Way. Masters cannot be deceived, but Searchers may.

We do not find this Enigma of Doves so frequently used as many others, and which also are very difficult to be understood. These figures, I conceive, spring from a Root of Knowledge and Learning, far above the Vulgar's Reach: For, is not this Art, saith one, Cabalistical, and full of Mysteries? So one of these Masters, well versed in Rabinical Learning, has told us what the name of a Dove doth signifie, as well as what it doth not, *viz.*:—" The Name of a Dove[22] is never apply'd to "Metals themselves (which ought to be well observed by "Inquirers, many having erred after this manner) but "the ministering and preparing Natures. And that he "that understands the Nature of the Burnt Offering (for "Purification) will not take Turtles themselves, but two "young Pigeons (which are the Off-spring) or Sons of "the Dove."

And this Secret Pair he rather appropriates to Nogah (Venus) which is the Fifth amongst the Planets; so the

Author of *Arcanum Hermiticæ* calls them the Birds of Venus. Tho' this Cabalist applies the name of Dove to Diana also.*

In the *History of Natural Things*, saith he:—"Luna "is called the Medicine for the White[23]; because she "hath received a Whitening Splendor from the Sun, "which, by a like shining, illustrates and converts into "her own Nature all the Earth—that is the imperfect "Metals: And that place of Isaiah xxx. 26, may be "mystically understood of this, because the Work being "finished, she hath got a Solar Splendor.[24] But in that "state, the place in Canticles vi., 9,[25], belongs to her. "But by the same Name the Matter of the Work is "called; and so indeed, like to the Horned Moon, she is "in the first State of Consistence; and like the full "Moon in the last state of Fluidity and Purity."

In another Place he hath this Passage, speaking of two Birds, which place, I make no doubt, but the Author of *Introit. Apert.* had well considered, if not drawn his early Knowledge from, and of Argent vive, which he calls a Leopard, Water not wetting, and Jordan of the Wise Man, etc. "And he shall have "four Wings of a Bird upon his Back; the four Wings "are of two Birds, which exasperate[26] this Beast with "their feathers, to the intent he may enter and fight the "Lion and the Bear. And Power was given him over "them, that he may overcome them, and extract their "glutinous Blood. Of all these is made one Fourth "Beast, which is frightful and terrible and very strong. ".. Eating and breaking to pieces himself and others; .. "Treading the residue under his Feet."[27]

This Guide I think may be depended upon, having given Demonstration of his Ability, by telling not only the Interpretation, but the Original figure itself.

More I have not met with in my Inquiry, therefore no more can be expected from me concerning this great Stumbling-block, at which so many fall into Error.

* A delightful example of mystification. N. O M.

From these things 'tis very evident, to me, that this Art cannot be found by never so many casual Tryals, or Experiments, without a real Knowledge, as Sendivo has written, *viz.*: "Know for certain also, that this "Art is not placed in Fortune, or casual Invention, but "in real Science; and that there is but this one Matter "in the World, by which, and of which, the Philo-"sopher's Stone is made, *viz.*, the Mercury of the "Philsophers."[28]

Out of what this is made, he teaches in his Treatise of Sulphur, as well as elsewhere. This is that Mercury, saith another, which the returning Sun diffuseth everywhere in the Month of March, or House of Aries; from whence also the Sulphur is to be sought. Which Sulphur, in this Work, saith Sendivo, is indeed instead of the Male; but the Mercury instead of the Female; of the Composition and Acting of these two, are generated the Mercuries of Philosophers. For as they have a double Sulphur, so they have a double Mercury, *viz.*, For the White and for the Red: Which is but seldom, and then very cautiously hinted; and these Mercuries differ, both in Colour and Quality, as may be easily gathered from their Books, by careful Readers.

The Author of *Intro. Apert.* indeed hath taught, that there are two Mercuries to the White, used in two different Works; Asserting that the Acuation of the Mercury for Sol Vulgar, must differ from that of Philosophical Sol. And further, If (saith he) "you shall in "your Decoction of Sol Vulgar, use the same Mercury "which is used in our Sol (tho' both flow from the "same Root in general) and apply that Regimen of Heat "which the Wise Men in their Books have apply'd to "our Stone, thou art, without all doubt, in an Erron-"eous Way: And that is the great Labyrinth in which "almost all young Practitioners are ensnared. For there "is scarce one Philosopher, who in his Writings does not "touch both ways."

In this, we may say of him, he hath not fallen short

of any of them: For he has so interwoven one Work with another, one Regimen with another (by way of Balance, as I said before, for Discoveries) that little less than the Knowledge of all in Theory, will prevent our falling into constant Error, in some of these particulars; even after the Field in general is known: and which happened to himself as he confesses, and which I shall mention, as it falls in my Inquiry.

These (with many more) are the Difficulties which the Inquirers after this Art have to incounter with; and which, one would think, should rather deter, than encourage, many Men from pursuing it as they do: especially considering the adverse Fortune that attends most Men, who prosecute this Study to their dying day; finishing their Lives in Ignorance and Despair. This Melancholy Prospect, I say, should leave such a deep Impression upon us, as to make us more cautiously meddle with this rare and difficult Philosophy; which without a Master or the special Favour of God, is never attain'd. As the Author of the *New Light* informs us, *viz.*, that unless God reveal it by a good Wit, or Friend, 'tis hardly known.

By the last most commonly, by the first most rarely. For as he adds, " Tho' Lully was a man of a subtile " Wit, yet if he had not received the Art from Arnoldus, "certainly he had been like those which find it with "difficulty; and Arnoldus also received it from a Friend: " Every Art and Science is easie to a Master, but not to " a Scholar."

Therefore this Art is easie to none, tho' of never so quick a Wit and Parts, but to those that know it only.

The Cabalist, I have before mentioned, hath lively prefigured, wise and good Men by Elisha; and the foolish Pretenders of this Art, by Gehazi, who was indeed Servant to Elisha; but to what purpose, the History of them, in the Second Book of Kings, sheweth.

Elisha an Example of Natural Wisdom, and a Despiser of Riches: He knew how to correct and make wholesome Poisonous Waters, and to multiply Treasure beyond the common Course of Nature: He could cure the worst Infirmities, nay, even raise the Dead: He knew how and when to blind and open the Eyes of Inquirers, also to punish Mockers, and even make Iron to swim; yea, his very Remains were efficacious after he was dead.

Gehazi labour'd in vain, and remain'd a Servant for ever; never qualified to be a Master, notwithstanding he had the Advantage of conversing with so great a one: He was Covetous, a Lyar and Deceiver; a Prattler, boasting of other Men's Deeds; Conceited and Hasty, thinking he sufficiently understood his Master, when he bids him take his Staff, and lay it upon the Dead Child, presently enterprising, though with an Heterogeneous Matter, and so able to effect nothing not discerning the Law of Nature; but Elisha apply'd a living Homogenous Agent, and then the Dead was raised. And instead of a double Portion of his Master's Knowledge (which Elisha desired and obtained by his Master Elijah) Gehazi got a Leprosie, as the Reward of his Doings.

A great deal might be observed from this History of Elisha and Gehazi, who are Notable Examples of Wise and Good Men, and their Reverse, *viz.*, Foolish and Profane; the last may talk, as Gehazi did, of procuring the supernatural Son of the Wise Man, but without being able to effect it; no more can his Successors, which are not a few even at this Day, who not only succeed him in Qualifications but Success.

The Philosophers agree with one Voice, that one worthy of this Science must be strictly Virtuous, leading a holy Life, or God will not prosper him: He must have a competent Understanding, or he will not be able to conceive: He must be Diligent and Laborious, or he will not be able to work out what he conceives; and he must be private or he will not quietly enjoy that which he works out. To these must be added Patience and Leisure, together with a Competent Fortune; which is the more necessary in this Study, because it requires, as is already said the whole Man to find out the means, and then a careful Application is absolutely necessary to accomplish the Work.

The Philosophers, you very well know, take the liberty of seemingly contradicting themselves, and one another: Sometimes asserting the Work to be very easie; other times that 'tis very difficult or hard. One while, that 'tis short; then again that 'tis very tedious. Again, that 'tis done with little Expense, and an easie Labour; then complaining of the charge and Toil. Sometimes affirming their Matter to be but one only thing, other times that 'tis compounded of several. One while the Work is to be done with a gentle Fire, another time that 'tis not perform'd without a strong. Then again, that 'tis equal, and of the same degree; and yet that 'tis daily increased.

These are the Difficulties with many more that might be named which Inquirers lie under. And yet the Philosophers affirm, they all vanish when the Key of this Art is once attain'd, which is the Chalibs of Philosophers. No longer will a Tyro relish a false Writer, or be to seek to reconcile the true. For that as soon as the first Gate is opened, all the rest will fly open of themselves.

I fear many will be displeased and say, these difficulties are too well known to us already, we want rather to be told how we shall overcome 'em, than have them repeated to us. To these I answer, in the Philosopher's Words, Expound the Philosopher's Writings according to Nature and not to Fancy. Now they say, their stone is nothing else but Gold digested to the highest degree of purity and subtile Fixity. Many consent to this but will plead, that common Gold is not meant. In answer to which I shall add, let them read Sendivo on the Elements of Fire, The Way to Bliss, and others, and consider the Extensibility, Permanency and Purity of the Gold there spoken of. And also let them consider whether 'tis not such Gold they would produce by this Art, as is called common Gold. Then if it be common Gold you would produce, whether common Gold be not the Natural Body for such a Production; as common Man is of producing its own Kind; common Wheat, of Wheat; and so throughout whole Nature.

Common Wheat in a Barn, is as dead as common Gold in a chest; tho' both these have a Life, *i.e.*, of Existence, and Power to increase their Kind; which Life must die, before the Power is brought to Action; and when this is done, they are properly called living Gold, and living Wheat, and not before.

Now, how comes Wheat to be so, we are pretty well appriz'd, *viz.*, tis sown in its proper Vessel, the Earth; it is moistened with its proper Humidity and is digested by its proper Heat, and so it grows and increases.

And if we are to take Nature for our Example, Gold must be proceeded with after the same manner; tho' the Vessel, the Humidity and Heat differ, for a Metal and for a Vegetable, yet both are liable to the Deficiencies and Excess of these things.

For if Wheat hath not a Matrix duly qualified, or hath too much or too little Humidity, and so of Heat, it will succeed accordingly. And so must the other, if Nature be the same in the one as in the other, as no doubt she is; or to what purpose are we so often recommended to the Consideration of Nature. Sendivo bids us follow Nature; waving the many Subtilties of the Philosophers, written to amuse the Unskilful Inquirers.

To conclude on this Head, if every Multiplication is from Seed; that the Perfection of every thing is its attaining a Seminal Virtue; and that nothing has this, which is imperfect of its Kind: Then it will follow, that if there be a Seminal Virtue in Metals, and that all of them are of the same Nature, the Seminal Virtue (that is the power of Multiplying) can be no where but in the most Perfect, which is Gold; *vide* Ars Metallica.

As these things are consonant to Nature, Sound Reason and the Doctrine of Philosophers, even the most envious, I, for my part, shall make them my rule in my Inquiry: Others may do as they please.

And as the Author of the Way to Bliss has not only told us (among many others) where the Seed of Gold lies, *viz.*, in Gold; but how it lies, *viz.*, This Seed of Gold is his whole Body loosened and softened in his own Water; there is all your stuff and Preparation. So he hath also, with the same Candor, shewed us the Water in which it dies, and with which 'tis raised. Where speaking of the Affinity that is known between Gold and Quicksilver (in common Uses) which he calls the grand Mother of the Stone, and Spring of all her Goodness: Wherefore, says he, "When this fine and clean "Body of Quicksilver is made, by Nature and Art, yet "much finer and clearer, and again, as much more pierc-"ing and spiritual, and able to perform it; how much "more readily will she run to her like, and devour it, the "clean, fine and spiritual, that is the Quicksilverypart of "the Metal. And if she do devour it, then it cannot be "lost, but must needs go into a better Nature, even the "Nature we desire."

This, he says, is done by the well-ordering the witty Fire of Hermes, "that here is all the Hardness, here "all the World is blinded all the rest is easie. Search "then this rare kind of Heat; for here is all the Cun-"ning; this is the Key of all; this makes the Seeds and "bringeth forth: Search wisely, and where it is, in the "midst of Heaven and Earth for it is in the midst of "both these places, and yet but one indeed; it is Earthy, "yet Watery, Airy, and very Fiery, etc. He adds, Let "the dew of this starry blood beat about the Womb, "and your seed shall joy and prosper. Muse and conject "well upon my Words, you that are fit and skilled in "Nature, for this is a very Natural Heat; and yet all "the World is blinded. Nay indeed, if a Man would "read little, and think much upon the ways of Nature, "he might easilie hit this Art; and before that, never."

Thus the witty Author, according to the Custom of

all Philosophers, brought us to a full stop, and left us to consider Nature, in order to remove the Remora* that so often stops Inquirers in their career.

'Twas from the Excellency and Virtue of this Fire, no doubt, that the Cabalist I have before mentioned intituled his wonderful Book, *Æsch Mezareph*,† or *Purifying Fire*.

This Fire has lain hid from many, a long time after they knew the Field in general, where the Seed was to be Sown. The fiery Furnace of Philosophers, says one of them, lay hid from me long; but after I knew this, and how it was fitted to its proper Vessel, after a few days I beheld the admirable Brightness of our Water, which being seen, I could not but be amazed.

So Pontanus seems surprised at the wonderful Effects of this Fire, for want of the Knowledge of which he had erred so long and often; and tells us who inform'd him of it, *viz.*, Artephius,[29] whose Book is extant, and read by most Inquirers, tho' not with the same success; some interpreting his Sayings one way, and some another; but few according to the true Sense and Meaning. Whence they have erred and will always err, unless they learn it better; the way to learn it, is but just told above, by the Author of *The Way to Bliss*, which agrees with the Way Pontanus prescribes, *viz.*, They that should read Geber, and all other Philosophers, never so long, could not comprehend it, because that Fire is found by deep and profound Meditation only; and then it may be gather'd from Books, and not before.

We must not only have the Knowledge of this Fire; but, as we are often told, the true Measure of it to its Furnace; both which seem to be remote from the Eyes of the Vulgar: When this is known, the Difficulties that attend the Radical Dissolution of the close and fixed Body of Gold vanish. And before this can be done; this stout fixed Body must be Calcined, and re-

---

* Query, hindrance.

† To be reprinted in a future volume of this series.

duced into as fine a Calx as possible, which is often hinted by Philosophers, but with a design to conceal it. Geber witnesses, that everything Calcined is of easier Solution, because the Parts of the Calcined Body, more subtilated by Fire, are more easily mixed with Water, and turned into Water. Without this previous Calcination, no Solution is found.

Therefore no wonder so many fail in their Attempts, to dissolve Gold in a Generative Way, by working on its Compact and Gross Body; For as the gross Bodies of Sol and Luna are not fit for Dissolution, but only their altered and unctuous Calxes; so Mercury, in its gross Body, is not able to do this, but in its altered more subtile and spiritual Nature; and drawn from its Vitriolick Caverns, acuated with its pure salt and piercing Sulphur, which then overcomes all things, even itself. For it not only dissolves Sol and Luna into its own Nature. but coagulates itself into theirs, true and fixed, by a proper Heat only.

Some may say, All these are so fully taught already, that a bare repeating of them is of no use.

That they are taught already, by the Masters of this Science themselves, is my warrant for repeating of 'em; and if you have already Learn'd these things, you have no Reason to be uneasie; if you have not, tis your advantage to be put in mind of them, even by an Inquirer.

Sad experience sheweth, that but very few of the past or present Searchers, learn those things which they often brag the Philosophers have taught: But at length to cover their own Ignorance, they fall into Arrogance, and blame the Philosophers for hiding of them; as is observed by (the never too much to be admired) Candid Ripley; who, in return, only modestly reproves them, Thus:—

"All Philosophers record and say the same;
But simple Searchers putteth them in blame,
Saying, they hide it; But they are Blameworthy,
Who are no Clerks and meddle with Philosophy."

Here this good Man, in few words, justifies the true

Philosophers, and lays the blame where it ought, *viz.*, on the Unskilful Medlers with Philosophy.

What tho' he has conceal'd the Key of the Art under his green Lion, as others have done under the Doves, Chalibs, secret Fire, etc., some under one figure, some under another, which best answered their purpose, *viz.*, Concealing the Art from the Unworthy. What they have done towards Discovering of it to the Deserving, merits the greatest Acknowledgements, not Censure from Inquirers to whom they declare they are not indebted.

Nor do I affirm, that all these different Terms are synonymous, that behoves the Inquirer to satisfy himself in, from their Writing, whether they are or can be deemed so.

I have ventur'd to call the Green Lion of Ripley the Key of the Work, because his Expositor has as good as called it so. "Learn then," says he, "to "know this Green Lion, and its Preparation, which "is all in all the Art; it's the only Knot; untye it, "and you are as good as Master: For whatever then "remains, is but to know the outward Regimen of the "Fire, for to help on Nature's Internal Work."

And the same Author has expressly called the Chalibs so, *viz.*, I will tell thee (if thou wilt conceive) it is called Chalibs, by the Author of the New Light;[*] and it is the true Principle of the Work, the true Key (as it may be handled) of unlocking the most hidden Secrets of Philosophers.

Again our Chalibs is the true Key of our work, without which the Fire of the Lamp could not be, by any Art, kindled. Which he further describes thus, *viz.*, It is the Minera of Gold, a Spirit very pure, beyond others, etc.

Sendivogius calls this Matter, as well by the Name of Magnet, as Chalibs, *viz.*, To speak more plainly, says he, 'tis our Magnet, which, in our foregoing

[*] Sendivogius.

Treatises, I called Chalibs, or Steel. The Air generates this Magnet, and the Magnet generates or makes out Air to appear and come forth: I have here intirely shewed thee the Truth.

This Author has comprized in few Words what the Author of *Intro. Apert.* has divided into Three Chapters, *viz.*, Chalibs, Magnet, and Air; all which he has Concentrated in a Fourth, *viz.*, Chaos. The Earth, says he, is a heavy Body, the Matrix of Minerals, because it keeps them occultly in itself; altho' it brings to light Trees and animals. The Heaven is that wherein the great Lights, together with the Stars, are rowled about; and it sends down its Virtues through the Air into inferior things.

When he has gone thus far, he, in Imitation of Sendivogius's Skill and Candor, adds, But in the Beginning, all being confounded together, made a Chaos.

Behold! I have faithfully opened to you the Truth; for our Chaos, etc.

O the Harmony and Skill, as well as Candor of these two great Masters! Beg of God that he would make you Discerners and Partakers of these things. Nor let me forget most candid Ripley, who exactly corresponds with these, *viz.*:

"For as of one Mass was made all thing
Right; so must in our Practice be.
In Philosophers Books therefore, who lifts to see,
Our Stone is called the less World One and Three:
Magnesia also of Sulphur, and Mercury,
Proportionate by Nature most perfectly."

Thus we see Ripley's One Mass, Philalethes's Chaos, and Sendivogius's Matter of the Antient Philosophers, are the same; containing Three, *viz.*, Magnet, Chalibs, Air, or Magnesia, Sulphur and Mercury: which also are called by abundance of other Names in Philosophers' Books, *e.g.*, Artephius speaking of the Compound, Magnesia, says, That 'tis compounded,[30] like a Man of Body, Soul and Spirit; which he thus expounds, *viz.*,

"For the Body is the fixed Earth of the Sun, which is
"more than most fine, ponderously lifted up by the force
"of our Divine Water: The Soul is the Tincture of the
"Sun and Moon, proceeding from the Conjunction or
"Communication of these two: But the Spirit is the
"Mineral Virtue of the Two Bodies and the Water, which
"carries the Soul, etc. Again, the Spirit therefore
"pierceth, the Body fixeth, the Soul coupleth, coloureth
"and whiteneth. Of these three united together, is our
"Stone made; that is, of the Sun, and Moon, and Mer-
"cury. Flammel says he could easily give very clear
"Comparisons and Expositions of this Body, Soul and
"Spirit: But then he must of necessity speak things
"which God reserves to reveal unto them that fear and
"love him, and consequently ought not to be written";
yet he is not wanting to concur with Artephius, in
calling them the Sun, Moon and Mercury, and agree-
ing exactly with him in his Exposition.

It would be as it were endless, and indeed needless, to recite all the different Expressions used by Philosophers, who confirm and constantly maintain this Doctrine of Trinity in Unity, under various Modes of Speech, and hard-to-be-understood Similes.

But to keep a little to that of the Green Lion, which is worth our Enquiry: Ripley speaking of its Blood, asserts this Secret to be hid by all Philosophers, *viz.*:

"The said Menstrual is (I say to thee in counsel)
The Blood of our Green Lion, and not of Vitriol:
Dame Venus can the Truth of this thee tell
At the beginning, to Counsel if thou her call.
This Secret is hid by Philosophers great and small.
Which blood drawn out of the Green Lion,
For lack of Heat, had not perfect Digestion."

So the Author of *Arcanum Hermeticæ* saith, the most precious Substance is Venus, the Hermaphrodite of the Antients, glorious (or powerful) in both Sexes.

The Author of *Æsch Mezareph*, speaking of Venus, under the Names Nogah and Hod, which is a necessary Instrument to promote the Metalick Splendor, says, It has more a part of a Male, than Female; and speaking of the Green Lion, he saith, Which, I pray thee, do not think is called so from any other Cause but its Colour: For unless thy Matter shall be green, not only in that immediate State before 'tis reduced into Water, but also after the Water of Gold is made of it. Why 'tis called a Lion, is hinted by another, *viz.*, Having Power to overcome, and reduce Bodies to their first Matter, and to make fixed things volatile and spiritual; whence 'tis fitly called a Lion.

Some there are who derive the Name Green from the Rawness or Unripeness of the Subject, and not from the Colour, *viz.* :—

> "Whose Colour doubtless is not so,
> And that your Wisdom do well know;
> But our Lion wanting Maturity,
> Is called Green, from Unripeness, trust me."
>
> *The Hunting of the Green Lion.*

Another says :—

> "For it is because of its transcendent Force
> It hath, and for the Rawness of its Source,
> Of which the like is no where to be seen,
> That it of them is named their Lion green.
> Our subject is no ways malleable;
> It is metalline, and its Colour sable."
>
> *Sophic Feast.*

These are some more of the seeming Contradictions, which Philosophers warn us not to be deceived with, but to learn to Reconcile. These Difficulties are to be overcome by Meditation only.

Now, let us try whether, or how far, 'tis possible to Reconcile these Contradictions concerning the Green Lion. The Cabalist (much admired by me) says, the Matter is actually green, both before 'tis dissolved and afterwards also: This doth not deny, but confirm, that 'tis spoke of, and considered, in divers States; and then it may not be absurd to suppose, that it may be, and is, described by one in one state and degree of Perfection, and by others in another: By one in its Impurity; by another in its Passage from thence to its Purity (for Ripley says 'tis unclean); and by a third when 'tis Purified. For as Matters, when more or less pure or mature, are of a different Texture, so they also differ in Colour. And 'tis in this Sense, I make no doubt the Philosophers are to be understood, not only with relation to this Subject, but 'Tis not therefore every Matter which is foul or green (as Vitriol is, which Ripley says, Fools take to be their Green Lion) that intitles it to this wonderful Name; no, but it must have all the other Virtues and Powers in it, that are assigned by Philosophers: Which thing lies very obscure, and seemingly base, but it is, in its Purity and exalted Virtue, their Subject of Wonders. To produce which, this fond Minera, they tell us, must be dissolved and exactly purified, in a pure Homogeneal Water, which is its own Blood, as White as Milk; which Name some have rather imposed. This Leprous Body, Sendivo and others have called Saturn, and Saturn's Child; and what some have called Blood and Milk, he calls Urine.

Thus the Masters of this Science take the liberty to express themselves by different Similes, in order to disguise their Secret, which a mental man will discover and improve by, as soon as he shall discern any one of their Intentions; the rest follow in course, tho' varied ever so many ways, as they themselves testifie.

What some have called Blood, Wine, &c., the Author of the *Learned Sophics Feast* calls fiery Water, &c., *viz.*:[31]

"Their Lion green they suffer'd him to prey
On Cadmus Sociates; and when the Fray
Was over, they with Dian's charms him ty'd
Aud made him under Waters to abide,
And washed him clean; and after gave him Wings
To fly, much like a Dragon, whose sharp springs
Of fiery Water, the only way was found
To cause Apollo his Harp-strings to sound.
This is the true Nymph's Bath, which we did try,
And proved to be the Wise Men's Mercury."

Here all Doubts and Difficulties end, when this is

attain'd; so with it I shall finish this Inquiry: Having shewed my Fellow Inquirers, in what manner I have been enchain'd in it; concluding in the Words of the aforesaid Author, *viz.*:

" Happy are they, who shall not miss to find
    The new uprising Sun :[32]
More happy they, who, with renewed Mind,
    In God find Rest alone."

NOTES BY S.S.D.D.

1. *Hermetic;* alluding to Hermes Trismegistos: a mythical Magus who has given his name to many treatises on western Occultism and Alchemy. The names of Hiram King of Tyre, Chiram abif and Hermes have been counterchanged; and the Kabalistic Key applied to the name throws some light on the actual meaning of the Alchemical process,—taking the Hebrew lettering Ch I R M, we get the falling dew containing that principle of life reproduction—nitrogen, working in darkness upon the perfectable body. Also an expert may here discern an allusion to the wonderful power of chlorine on gold. The merest tyro in chemistry knows the famous Aqua Regia of the ancients was a cunningly manufactured liquor bearing a close resemblance to the fluid obtained by the mixture of Nitric acid and Hydrochloric acid.

2. *Art.*—The Hermetic Science being the Ethical side of Western Occultism; the Hermetic art may be regarded as the practical application of the same on all planes, from those of pure reason and exalted consciousness through those of human life down to the most material; from the regeneration and purification of the soul, to the regeneration and purification of the baser metals.

3. *To the perfection of Sol and Luna.*—These words are much in favour with masters of the mysteries who are desirous of hiding their meaning. They are used in a hundred different ways, signifying active and passive; male and female; sudden rapid vibration, and solid resisting substance; gold, and silver; red rust of iron; blue vitriol, *i.e.*, sulphate of copper, green sulpate of iron, and sulphide of antimony. Throughout the Alchemic processes they have been used to denote the force and the substance; the transmutor and the transmuted. And wise is he whose solar power has the penetrating force to discern the truth in the lunar shades with which he is surrounded.

4. *Have justified one another's testimony.*—Here we have a ray of hope, for those who have read many alchemical treatises will find that there are startling agreements in the teachings of some of the best works, such as those of Clavius, Rosenstein, Becker, Ponia and others who give more practical directions than vague writers like Geber, Bacon and Flamel.

5. *The Art altogether impossible.*—The position taken up is natural enough. No man could with reasonable hope of success, hope to transform a fully grown elm tree into an oak, just as impossible would it seem to transmute a lump of copper into a lump of gold. But the Alchemists did not assert this to be possible, until both metals were reduced to one original basic substance, which they call Hylē and which we call Protyle in the mineral, or Protoplasm in the animal world. It was under these circumstances that they asserted transmutation to be possible; and it is in this relation we find the deep significance of the mystical death and resurrections of Osiris, Buddha and Christ. "Unless ye be born again ye cannot enter into the kingdom of perfection;" Unless the imperfect metal is destroyed, it cannot rise again into perfection. See also Eugenius Philalethes in his tract called *Euphrates or the Waters of the East*, printed in 1655.

6. *The chief impediments.*—Three out of a million men, says Norton, may be ordained for Alchemy. Now some light may be thrown on the true nature of the Art by this statement. It is no common gift that is needed, and without delay of argument I may safely assert that the proportions mentioned points at once to the fact that only persons of genius can hope to attain the perfection of this Art of Arts. It is the Art of living in the divine light; the Art of knowing, the Art of "being one" with the highest universal consciousness. No talent will give insight to the man who is unable to bring about this regeneration of his soul; no labour will avail him who has shut out the life of the universe from his little life. The man of genius, the divine artificer of his soul

must make himself, and know himself to be, one with the least of created things, and then and then only will he know what it is to be one with the Creator.

7. *This mysterious way of writing.*—For the guidance of those who propose to study ancient and mediæval writers on Alchemy, I may say that the work naturally divides itself into three parts; and each of these into three processes, decoction, distillation, cohobation. The first part is the preparation of the Body or matter; the second is preparation of the soul or medium; and the third is preparation of the spirit or active principle. Take the three principles of the Alchemists, being the time honoured veils under which truth has been hid. Call the body—sulphur, the soul—salt, and the spirit—mercury. Purify each separately, then must these three become one; they must rise; they must fall; they must circulate in the vessel. And this is the fourth work. This is simple enough and is the mere ordinary process of subliming with heat, cohobating the separated parts, and subliming again until the body becomes spiritual, the spirit become corporified, the impure becomes pure, and nothing is wasted, but all is found in its right place, and the perfection or right proportion is attained.

8. *Take one thing.*—Just as on the human plane you take the one man; and reduce him in thought down to the cell unit, so the alchemists reduced their one substance to its simplest form, and found things all latent therein.

9. That is, as soon as anyone develops his power of intuition, of reading between the lines, and of understanding the oriental passion of allegory that permeates mystical and religious writers, the meaning of many statements, utterly absurd if interpreted literally, will appear plain to the enlightened mind.

10. *Diana.*—The moon goddess, answering to what has of late been called the astral body or aura; the sensitive radiations of which convey impressions to our bodily sense organs. *The Fountain* alludes to the universal source of life and light with which it is the object of the occult student to bring his astral life into touch.

11. *The Secret Way of Philosophers.*—The philosophers know well enough that the first study for mankind is Man; to know thyself is to know nature. To become an adept of power is to possess the key of all the secrets of nature because you possess the key to your own nature.

12. The above explains why in *this* work we do **not** begin with quicksilver.

13. This is the first practical remark, on the subject of metals, in the treatise. It may here be noted that common quicksilver dissolves into a liquid resembling water in appearance if mixed with a proportion of one to ten of nitric acid.

14. *The perfect body.*—Gold undergoes a considerable change when mixed with mercury. The imperfect body mercury can be reduced to subtil water with nitric acid.

15. Very well describes the ordinary corrosive sublimate of commerce.

16. It may here be noted that the sign of Mercury combines the lunar and solar symbols.

17. *Moist fire* describes nothing in nature more accurately than the liquid acids of commerce; but let the student be warned that many authors expressly deny that this is the real meaning of the term.

18. See what is said previously of the words Sol and Luna, note 3.

19. There is an elaborate treatise called "The Privy Seal of Secrets, which upon pain of damnation is not unadvisedly to be broken up nor revealed to any but with great care and many cautions." Circa 1680, in which it is asserted that "the first matter of the philosophers is a lutinous or clayey substance."

19A. *The Green Lion.*—I here reprint an ancient receipt for the manufacture of this mystic animal, or of his prototype:—

R. Sea salt; purify by dissolving it in dew; expose it to the beams of the moon, uncovered in a wide basin; cover it with a glass cover and leave it in the rays of the sun; this repeat during forty nights and days. Put it into a large high glass body; imbibe gradually with very strong and clear distilled vinegar, until it is thoroughly diluted, close it, and set it to putrefy for two or three days in a gentle heat. Distil this per alembic in a sand bath, and the spirit of the vinegar will come over; when the green oil comes, change the receiver quickly. Pour back the distilled vinegar and leave it to putrefy, you will then obtain more green oil by again distilling.

20. "To make Sphæra Saturni Paracelsi. Take salt petre, 2 ounces; potass. carb. 1 ounce; Reg. Ant. Mast $4\frac{1}{2}$ ounces; tartar in crystals, 1 ounce: common salt half an ounce; pulverise separately and mix together. Put the whole into a large crucible and let it melt gently in a wind furnace. Stir with a red hot tobacco pipe and unite ingredients well, pour into an iron cone and you will find your treasure at the bottom."

21. "The Gods made blind (or mad) him whom they doom to destruction." *Quem Deus vult perdere prius dementat*

22. *Dove* in Hebrew is I U N H, pronounced Yoneh, and by Gematria $=10+6+50+5=71=8$; this multiplied by 2 (the 2 doves) $=16$ which again can be reduced to 7, the number of Venus. Doves also being birds signify thë sublimed metal, that is the part which flies upwards under the influence of heat.

23. *Luna* in Hebrew IRCh, pronounced Yaraich.

24. Isaiah xxx. 26. "Moreover the light of the moon shall be as the light of the sun, etc."

25. "My dove my undefiled is but one."

26. The four wings of two birds; taking this Leopard to be Mercury in its aspects of Corrosive Sublimate, which a century or two back was made by dissolving quicksilver in Aqua fortis, *i.e.*, nitric acid, and uniting it with sea salt, containing hydrochloric acid; it is possible to understand the two birds as signifying nitrogen and chlorine gas, which with heat would doubtless "exasperate the beast."

27. The original of these scattered quotations will be found in the Latin *Kabbalah Denudata* of Knorr von

Rosenroth, the *Asch Mezareph* of which is to be republished in this series. This Alchemical portion of the work, the *Asch Mezareph or Refining Fire*, is given by Eliphaz Levi in the *Clef des Mysteres* in disjointed paragraphs, and he asserts it to be the book of *Abraham the Jew*, which revealed so much to Nicholas Flamel, and he exemplifies his explanations of its *inner* meaning with Flamel's well-known plates.

28. *The Mercury of the Philosophers*, Now though the Alchemists did use Mercury, as is proved by Norton's list of materials, yet one thing is asserted by them over and over again, and that is, that the "Mercury of the Philosophers" is not Quicksilver. The passage alluded to, in the *Asch Mezareph*, but not quoted, as the "Treatise on Sulphur," is as follows: "For that sulphur of gold and iron whose extraction is taught by many and is easy; also of gold, iron, and copper, also of gold, iron, copper, and antimony, which are gathered together by vinegar after fulmination out of the lixivium, being changed into a red oil with a moist Hydrargyrum do tinge silver."

29. The words alluded to by Pontanus are in the third chapter of the *Secret Book of Artephius*. "Antimonium est de partibus Saturni, et in omnibus modis habet naturam ejus. Antimonium Saturni, convenit Soli." See Salmon's edition.

30. Compare Note 7.

31. Our author finishes up with a poem which a learned friend of mine would call "As clear as mud." However, I will make an effort to throw light upon some of the riddles it propounds. We have seen the *green lion* may be taken to mean a certain corrosive fluid concocted from sea salt and other ingredients, this must be mixed with the Martial Cadmus and the medicine of purification or Diana. In this mixture sea salt must be used, because it contains the universal Lunar mercury or first Ens of Mercury. Ferrous sulphate or cuprous sulphate should be added to introduce the mercury of copper or iron into the resulting sublimate, indicated by

the wings alluded to in the text. The whole alludes to the making of Sal Alembroth, which contains the secret fire and stirs up matter to action.

32. The New Uprising Sun of course alludes to the material work of gold-making, and the author finishes up by a commendation of the happier state of those who find Rest in God alone. In this connection I may quote from the *Suggestive Enquiry*, printed half a century ago:—
"What imagination is strong or hardy enough to glance into the full faith? *To be* the understanding of that Light of which all nature is the efflux. *To move* one with the First Mover and *be* his will.—Increase thyself into an immeasurable greatness, leaping beyond all bodies, and transcending time, become Eternity, and thou shalt understand God. If thou canst become higher than all height, lower than all depth, thou shalt comprehend in thyself the qualities of all creatures. Conceive likewise that thou can'st at once be everywhere. Learn to know thyself, not yet begotten, young, old, dead, the things after death and all of these together, else thou canst not yet understand God. But if thou hast shut up thy soul, blinding it, fettering it, saying I understand nothing, I can do nothing. I am afraid of the sea; I cannot climb up into Heaven; I know not who I am; I cannot tell what I shall be; What hast thou to do with God? It is the greatest evil not to know that there is a God-power latent in man."

By the "I AM" is signified, in the *Kabalah*, the subjective unity of all; the affirmation that there is one Fountain from which all nature flows. The knowledge of this Identity with nature in its first substance is the source of miracles due to the magical accords of colours, numbers, harmonies and planetary circulations, and all manifestation of vibration. The visible springs from the Invisible. "Human power is limited only by the poverty of its Imagination and the pettiness of its Will."

S. S. D. D.—R. R. et. A. C.

Collectanea Hermetica

EDITED BY

W. WYNN WESTCOTT, M.B., D.P.H.

S. M. of the Soc. Rosic. in Angliâ
W. M. of the Quatuor Coronati Lodge

VOLUME IV.

ÆSCH MEZAREPH

OR

PURIFYING FIRE

A CHYMICO-KABALISTIC TREATISE
COLLECTED FROM THE KABALA DENUDATA
OF KNORR VON ROSENROTH.

Translated by a Lover of Philalethes, 1714

PREFACE, NOTES AND EXPLANATIONS BY
"SAPERE AUDE"

PREFACE.

By Sapere Aude.

The *Æsch Mezareph* or *Ash Metzareph*, is only known to persons of Western Culture from the Latin Translation found in a fragmentary condition in the work entitled *Kabalah Denudata* by Knorr von Rosenroth, published at Sulzbach in 1677-84. These volumes have as a sub-title " The Transcendental, Metaphysical and Theological Doctrines of the Hebrews ", and they enshrine a Latin translation, with part of the Hebrew text and commentaries, of the great *Sohar* or *ZOHAR*, "The Book of Splendour" which is the most famous of all the Hebrew mystical codices of the Kabalah.

Three of the principal tracts of the *Zohar* are now familiar to English readers through the translation of my friend, MacGregor Mathers: his edition of *The Book of Concealed Mystery*, *The Greater Holy Assembly*, and *The Lesser Holy Assembly*, has obtained so great a circulation that I am emboldened to issue this volume, which exemplifies the Kabalistic scheme of Alchymy, as one of the series of *Collectanea Hermetica*. The *Æsch Metzareph* is still extant as a separate treatise in what is called the Hebrew language, but which is more properly Aramaic Chaldee: it was a companion volume to the Chaldean *Book of Numbers* so often referred to by H. P. Blavatsky, and which is no longer to be procured, although I have reason to think that copies still exist in concealment.

The first volume of Rosenroth's work consists entirely of a Kabalistic Lexicon. Upon the title-page is inscribed:—

Apparatus in Librum Sohar
nempe
Loci communes Kabalistici
secundum ordinem Alphabeticum
concinnati, qui Lexici instar esse possunt.

Upon the main title page of the work he describes this portion as collected from five sources:—

    I. Clavis ad Kabalam antiquam: *i.e.*, explicatio et ad debitas Classes Sephiristicas facta distributio omnium nominum et cognominum Divinorum è Libro Pardes.

    II. Liber Schaare Orah seu Portæ Lucis.

    III. Kabala recentior. Rabbi Jizchak Loria.

    IV. Index plurimarum materiarum Cabalisticarum in ipso Libro Sohar propositarum.

    V. Compendium Libri Cabalistico-Chymici, Æsch Metzareph dicti, de Lapide Philosophico.

The *Æsch Metzareph* can be re-constructed from its fragments scattered through this Lexicon, almost in its entirety. This work has been done by *The Lover of Philalethes*, who published the English version of 1714.

The present volume is a Reprint of that English version, in its original form; many corrections however, have been made, and a few changes in spelling and diction introduced in order to avoid archaic forms, leading young students into difficulties. For instance, Kabalah is written instead of Kabbala, because the Hebrew word has only one B, and *ah* represents the Hebrew letter Hé better than the English *a*, which suggests that the word is spelled with the Hebrew aleph.

The Hebrew or Chaldee name of this treatise is spelled thus AShH MTzRP. *The Lover of Philalethes* of 1714 spelled this in English by a diphthong Æ SCH; and in the second word he puts Z for Tz, zain for tzaddi, this leads to confusion and error. The meaning of Ash or Ashah is "fire" or "a fire offering", and metzareph is "cleansing" or "purifying". The whole title refers to "Cleansing Fires", as the mode by which pure gold was obtained in Alchymy, by burning off the dross and so separating the pure from the impure—on the material plane! while the cleansing fire of trial is also a suitable simile for the purification and exaltation of the human soul on the plane of spiritual Alchymy. The words Ash Metzareph, or Æsch Mezareph as Rosenroth spells it, are found in the book of Malachi, cap. 3, v. 2, where it is said that the messenger of the Lord is like a "refiner's fire".

There are in the book many references to other old Hebrew

and Chaldee works, several of these are included in the great collection of tracts called the *Talmud*; of this work there are two great forms, the *Talmud* of Babylon, and that of Jerusalem. The former is the more important, and is more learned and mystical. Among the tracts referred to, are:— Pirke Aboth, PRQI ABUT, Sayings of the Fathers; Baba Kama, BBA QMA, The first Gate; Baba Bathra, BBA BTRA, The Latter Gate; Baba Metsia, BBA MTzIOA, The Middle Gate.

The work *Schaare Orah* mentioned by Rosenroth is the Hebrew SHOR AURH or *Gate of Light* written by Rabbi Joseph Gikatilla ben Abraham.

The *Liber Pardes* of Rosenroth is the book *Sepher Pardesh Rimmonim*, or *Garden of Pomegranates*, its author was Rabbi Moses Cordovero, or Remak, who flourished about 1550.

The value of this treatise is so largely dependent upon the Literal Kabalah and the method of Gematria, or the mutual conversion between letters and numbers that it is wise to introduce here a table of the English Letters attributed to the Hebrew Letters and Numbers. The system followed is that conventional one laid down in Wynn Westcott on "Numbers", which has also been adopted in each of the previous volumes of the series of *Collectanea Hermetica*. The system is only an approximation to the true rendering of Hebrew into English; as for example I is adopted for Yod, but some authors use I or Y or J; and for Ayin, O is adopted which has sometimes the force of Ay and O, and at others of Gn, when used as a consonant.

Aleph	Beth	Gimel	Daleth	Heh	Vau
A	B	G	D	H	V
1	2	3	4	5	6
Zain	Cheth	Teth	Yod	Kaph	Lamed
Z	CH	TH	I	K	L
7	8	9	10	20	30
Mem	Nun	Samech	Ayin	Peh	Tzaddi
M	N	S	O	P	Tz
40	50	60	70	80	90
	Qoph	Resh	Shin	Tau	
	Q	R	SH	T	
	100	200	300	400	

The special final Letters are not used as numerals in the *Æsh Metzareph*.

The *Æsh Metzareph* is almost entirely Alchymical in its teachings, and is suggestive rather than explanatory in its words. The allegorical method of teaching runs through it, and the similes have to be kept carefully in mind, otherwise confusion will result. Several Alchymic processes are set out, but not in such a way that they could be carried out by a neophyte; any attempt to do so would discover that something vital was missing at one stage or other.

But although the *Æsh Metzareph* is not a manual of practical Alchymy, yet an attentive study of its statements considered with accurate relation to the numerical allusions, may give some true conclusions as to the materia and agents to be employed in the several forms of Transmutation.

The nominal Christian of narrow views will see in this tract a confirmation of his opinion, that Alchymy is an unholy art and prompted by the Evil One; and there is perhaps no book which contains more Scripture verses referred to as illustrating the means and aims of Alchymy; so that perhaps such a one may point to this work as the brightest example of the assertion that "the Devil can quote even Holy Scripture to his purpose."

CONTENTS.

CHAPTER		PAGE
I.	ELISHA. NAAMAN. THE TWO SYSTEMS OF ALLOTTING THE SEPHIROTH TO THE ALCHYMIC PRINCIPLES AND METALS	9
II.	GOLD, ITS TEN VARIETIES, AND THE KAMEA OF 6	13
III.	SILVER, REFERRED TO THE TEN SEPHIROTH; ITS KAMEA OF 9	20
	IRON, THE ANIMAL FORMS; ITS KAMEA OF 5	23
IV.	TIN IS RELATED TO JUPITER; ITS KAMEA OF 4	27
V.	BRASS, ITS DECAD; ITS KAMEA OF 7 ...	29
	RELATED TO VENUS	32
VI.	LEAD, CHOKMAH; ITS DECAD; ITS KAMEA OF 3	33
	ARIAH, THE LIONS, NAAMAN	35
	ANTIMONY	37
VII.	JARDEN; THE RIVER JORDAN, ITS SYMBOLISM	38
	JESOD, QUICKSILVER, THE EDOMITE WIFE; ITS KAMEA OF 8	38
VIII.	JUNEH, THE DOVE	43
	JARACH, THE MOON	43
	GOPHRITH, SULPHUR	44

ÆSCH-MEZAREPH;[1]

OR

PURIFYING FIRE.

CHAPTER I.[2]

ELISHA[3] was a most notable Prophet, an Example of Natural Wisdom, a Despiser of Riches, (as the History of the Healing of Naaman sheweth, 2 Kings, c. 5, v. 16) and therefore truly Rich. According to what is said in Pirke Aboth,[4] *viz.*, Who is Rich? He that rejoiceth in his Portion, cap. 4. For so the true Physician of impure Metals hath not an outward Show of Riches, but is rather like the Tohu[5] of the first Nature, empty and void. Which Word is of equal Number with the Word Elisha, *viz.*, 411. For it is a very true saying in Baba Kama[6], fol. 71. col. 2. The thing which causeth Riches, (such as Natural Wisdom) is supplied instead[7] of Riches.

Learn therefore to purify Naaman, coming from the North, out of Syria, and acknowledge the power of Jordan: Which is as it were Jar-din[8] that is the River of Judgment flowing out of the North.

And remember that which is said in Baba Bathra, fol. 25, col. 2. He that will become Wise, let him live in the South; and he that will grow Rich, let him turn himself toward the North, etc. Although in the same place Rabbi Joshua Ben Levi says, let him live always in the South, for whilst he becomes Wise, at the same time he becomes Rich. "Length of Days is in her right hand, and in her left, Riches and Honour." Prov., c. 3, v. 16. So thou wilt not desire other Riches.

But know, that the Mysteries of this Wisdom, differ not from the superior Mysteries of the Kabalah. For such as is the Consideration of the Predicaments in Holiness, the same is also in Impurity; and the same Sephiroth which are in Atziluth,[9] the same are in Assiah,[10] yea, the same in that Kingdom, which is commonly called the Mineral Kingdom; although their Excellency is always greater upon the spiritual plane. Therefore the Metallic Root here possesseth the place of Kether,[11] which hath an occult Nature, involved in great obscurity, and from which all Metals have their Origin; even as the Nature of Kether is hidden, and the other Sephiroth flow from thence.

Lead hath the place of Chokmah, because Chokmah immediately proceeds from Kether, as it immediately comes from the Metallic Root, and in Ænigmatic similes, it is called the "Father" of the following Natures.

Tin possesseth the place of Binah, shewing Age, by its Greyness, and shadowing forth Severity and Judicial Rigour, by its Crackling.

Silver is placed under the Classis of Chesed, by all the Masters of the Kabalah, chiefly for its Colour and Use.

Thus far the White Natures. Now follow the Red.

Gold is placed under Geburah, according to the most common Opinion of the Kabalists; Job in c. 37, v. 22, also tells us that gold cometh from the north,[12] not only for its Colour, but for the sake of its Heat and Sulphur.

Iron is referred to Tiphereth,[13] for he is like a Man of War, according to Exod., c. 15, v. 2, and hath the Name of "Seir Anpin," from his swift Anger, according to Psalm 2, v. ult., "kiss the son lest he be angry."

Netzach and Hod are the two Median places of the

Body, and the Seminal Receptacles, and refer to the Hermaphroditic Brass. So also the two Pillars of the Temple of Solomon (referring to these two Sephiroth) were made of Brass, 1 Kings, c. 7, v. 15.

Jesod is Argent vive. For to this, the name "Living" is Characteristically given; and this Living Water is in every case the Foundation of all Nature and of the Metallic Art.

But the true Medicine of Metals is referred to Malkuth, for many Reasons; because it represents the rest of the Natures under the Metamorphoses of Gold and Silver, right and left, Judgment and Mercy,[15] concerning which we will speak more largely elsewhere.

Thus I have delivered to thee the Key to unlock many Secret Gates, and have opened the door to the inmost adyta of Nature. But if anyone hath placed those things in another order, I shall not contend with him, inasmuch as all systems tend to the one truth.

For it may be said, the three Supernals are the Three Fountains of Metallic things. The thick water is Kether, Salt is Chokmah, and Sulphur is Binah; for known reasons. And so the Seven Inferior will represent the Seven Metals, *viz*., Gedulah and Geburah, Silver and Gold; Tiphereth, Iron; Netzach and Hod, Tin and Copper; Jesod, Lead; and Malkuth will be the Metallic Woman, and the Luna of the Wise Men; and the Field into which the Seeds of secret Minerals ought to be cast, that is the Water of Gold, as this Name (Mezahab[16]) occurs, Genesis, c. 36, v. 39.

But know, my Son, that such Mysteries are hid in these things as no Tongue may be permitted to utter. But I will not offend any more with my Tongue, but will keep my Mouth *with a Bridle*, Psalm 39, v. 2.

---

[17]Gehazi the Servant of Elisha, is the type of the vulgar Students of Nature, who contemplate the *Valley*

and Depths of Nature, but do not penetrate into her Secrets.

Hence they Labour in vain, and remain Servants for ever. They give Counsel about procuring the Son of the Wise Men whose Generation exceeds the Power of Nature, but they can add nothing to assist in his Generation, 2 Kings, c. 4, v. 14 (for which purpose a Man like Elisha is required). For Nature doth not open her Secrets to them, v. 26, but contemns them, v. 30, and the Raising of the Dead is impossible to them, v. 31. They are Covetous, cap. 5, v. 20; Liars, v. 22; Deceivers, v. 25; Prattlers of other Men's Deeds, 2 Kings, c. 8, v. 4-5, and instead of Riches, contract a Leprosy themselves, that is Disease, Contempt and Poverty, v. 27. For the word Gehazi,[18] and the word Chol, Prophane or Common, have both the same Number.[19]

CHAPTER II.

[1]In Metallic things, Geburah is of the Class to which Gold is referred; which has again its Decad; (*i.e.*, Ten Orders or Degrees). So that,

1. Chethem,[2] that is, pure fine Gold, is referred to the Kether thereof; which, Canticles, c. 5, v. 11, is referred to the Head.

2. Batzar,[3] Gold, is referred to Chokmah, as though laid up in strongholds, Job, c. 22, v. 24, 25, and c. 36, v. 19.

3. Charutz,[4] Prov., c. 8, v. 10, is referred to Binah, from the digging of it; which Name belongs to the Feminine Gender.

4. Zahab Shachut,[5] that is, fine and drawn Gold, 2 Chron., c. 9, v. 15, because it hath the Analogy to the Thread of Chesed.

5. Zahab,[6] alone, is referred to Geburah, because Gold cometh from the North, Job, c. 37, v. 22.

6. Paz,[7] and Zahab Muphaz,[8] are referred to Tiphereth, 1 Kings, c. 10, v. 18; Psalm, c. 21, v. 4, and 19, v. 11; and Daniel, c. 10, v. 5.[9] For so Tiphereth and Malkuth are compounded in the Golden Throne, 1 Kings, c. 10, v. 18; also when it is called a Vessel of Gold, Job, c. 28, v. 17; a Crown of Gold, Psalm 21, v. 3; Bases of Gold, Cant., c. 5, v. 15.

7. Zahab Sagur,[10] is referred to Netzach, that is Gold shut up, 1 Kings, c. 4, v. 20, 21, Job, c. 28, v. 15, to wit, to bring forth Seed.

8. Zahab Parvajim,[11] is referred to Hod; 2 Chron., c. 3, v. 6, 1 Kings, c. 6, v. 20, from its likeness to the Blood of Young Bullocks, for this kind is Red at the left Hand.

9. `Zahab Tob,[12] is referred to Jesod, that is good Gold, Gen., c. 2, v. 12, for this kind is called good, after the manner of a good Man.

10. But Zahab Ophir,[13] is referred to Malkuth, Job, c. 22, v. 24, for it is the Name of a Land (or Earth) as called so from Ashes. See also 1 Chronicles, c. 29, v. 4.

And[14] now concerning the Name Zahab, I will lead thee into the Cave of the hidden Matter, and will shew thee the Treasuries of Solomon[15] mentioned in Nehemiah, c. 13, v. 13, viz., the Perfection of Stones, Exodus, c. 26, v. 6.

Come See! There are many places, to which Gold is referred, viz., Geburah and Binah, and other special Places, where the Species of Gold are disposed by one thus, by another other ways. But now I represent to thee the Nature of Gold in Tiphereth.

Neither can you object out of the Zohar or Tikkunim. For know, that in this place ought to be understood Tiphereth, of the Measure or Degree of Geburah. And it is a great Mystery, because Tiphereth commonly contains Iron under it, from whence we seek Gold.

This is the Sol or Sun[16] of Nature and Art, whose lesser Number is ten, the Symbol of all Perfection; Which Number by Gematria also shews you the lesser Number of Tiphereth; likewise the word Atah[17] belonging to the same in its lesser computation.

Mingle therefore Iron and Clay, Daniel, c. 2, v. 33, and thou shalt have the Foundation of Gold.

This is that Gold, to which is attributed the Notion of Tetragrammaton,[18] Exodus, c. 32, v. 5, in the History of the Calf, which was to be ground to powder, and thrown upon the Waters, v. 20, whence you shall see seven kinds of Gold immediately following one another in the Work.

First, simple Gold, which is called Zahab barely; for it is truly Gold, tho' not digged out of the Earth; nor destroyed by the Violence of the Fire, but living, rising out of the Waters; sometimes of a Black, sometimes of a Yellowish, and often like a Peacock's Colour; going back of its own accord into the Waters, and this may be called Zahab Saba,[19] as tho' you should say, Sabi, the Gold of Captivity, because 'tis newly captured, and shut up in its Prison; where it keeps a Fast of Forty Days and Nights, that you know not what is become of it, Exodus, c. 32, v. 1; for there is then no External appearance, even as Moses was hidden and they knew not what had become of him.

Secondly, it becomes Zahab Shacuth as though killed and slain, for it dies and its corpse putrefies and grows black: then it is under Judgment and the Shells rule it, and the powers of the name of 42 letters[20] fulfil their time upon it.

Thirdly, but then follows Zahab Ophir, as tho' you should say Aphar,[21] for it is of the Colour of Ashes; which time the twenty-two Letters of the Alphabet will determine for you.

Fourthly, it become Zahab Tob, because it is good to Colour, tho' not of the Colour of Gold, but Silver. This may be called Chethem. For it may be so called, according to Lam., c. 4, v. 1.[22] How shall Gold be coloured with Redness, and Hacchethem Hattob,[23] *i. e.*, good Silver be changed? And thence is referred that text in Job, c. 22, v. 24, and put it upon Opher, he would have said Opheret,[24] Lead, Batsar, Silver, that is this White Gold. For from hence you shall have Silver. And to Silver when it shall be in the state of a Stone, add Nachlim,[25] Rivers of Metallic Waters; from whence you shall have Ophir, that is Gold of Ophir, which was accounted the best. Now you shall have the Number of the great Name Ehejeh;[26] for thou shalt possess, after twenty-one days, these things. If thou wilt now open thy Treasure,[27] open it; but it shalt yet only give Silver as Stones, 1 Kings, c. 10, v. 27.

But if thou desire more, let thy Gold be,

Fifthly, Zahab Sagur, *i.e.*, Shut-up Gold: Let it remain in the Prison, in the Place of its Maturation, in the Bowels of the Earth of the Wise Men all the time of the Decumbiture of Ezekiel, c. 4, v. 6.[28] And thy Gold shall become the

Sixth, Jarak Rak,[29] *i.e.*, Yellow Gold, like Zahab Parvajim. These are the thirty Men, Judges, c. 14, v. 19, whom Sampson slew. For this being done,

Seventhly, Your Gold will be Paz and Muphaz and Uphaz; being strengthened to Conquer and Colour all imperfect Metals.

This is that Charutz, that sharp pointed (or penetrating) thing; which Job, c. 41, v. 30, says ought to be cast upon Clay, *i.e.*, imperfect Metals, that hath Cohach, Power to produce Gold: for Tit and Cohach[31] are of equal Numbers. And make it to boil like a deep pot, a Sea of thick Metallic Waters; and it shall become like a Vessel of Paint: But after that it shall make the Path to shine, v. 31-32. Blessed be the Name of the Glory of his Kingdom for ever and ever.

I write these things, I the insignificant one, according to my slender knowledge, who have earnestly sought out secret things, to the healing of all Creatures. But that which moved me thereto is spoken in Sohar Heæsinu, fol. 145, cap. 580, concerning the Office of a Physician, that I should not desist from the good and right Way until I should find the best Medicine: And the Words are these;

It is written, Deut., c. 32, v. 10, "He found him in Desert land and in the waste howling Wilderness; he led him to find the causes, and made him understand and kept him as the apple of his eye. And rightly because he hath compelled all the Cortices to serve him." Thus far was it written in the Book of Kartanæus the

Physician. And then he drew from this Text various Observations necessary to a wise Physician about the Cure of the Patient, lying in the Chamber of sickness, Genesis, c. 39, v. 20, where the Captives of the King may worship the Lord of the World. For when a prudent Physician comes, he finds him in the Land of the Desert, and in the Wilderness of the Howling Solitude, which are as the Diseases afflicting him, and finds him in the Captivity of the King.

Here it may be objected that it is not lawful to cure him, because the Holy One, Who is Blessed for ever, hath caused him to be ill and as if a captive. But this is not so; for David says, Psalm 41, v. 2, "Blessed is he who considereth (the curing of) the poor; the Lord will preserve him and keep him alive." For he is poor who lies in the House of Sickness; and if the Physician be wise that Holy One, who is blessed for ever, loads him with Blessings, in reference to him, whom he cures. That Physician finds him in the Land of the Desert, that is ill, etc. And what is to be done for him; Rabbi Eleasar hath told us: Hitherto we have heard nothing of that Physician, nor of his Book; except that once a certain Merchant told me that he heard his Father say, that in his time there was a certain Physician, who having seen a Patient, presently said, "this one will live and that one will die"; and that it was reported of him, that he was a just and true Man fearing Sin; and that, if any Man could not procure those things he needed, he would buy them for him, and freely supply his necessities; and that it was said, there was not so nice a Man in the whole World, and that he did more with his Prayers, than with his Hands. And when we supposed this Man to be the very same Physician, the Merchant made reply, Certainly his Book is in my Hands, having been left to me as an Inheritance by my Father; and all the Sayings of that Book are hidden in the Mystery of the Law: And in it we do find profound Secrets, and many Medicines; which notwithstanding, is not lawful to apply to any, except to him that feareth Sin, etc. Rabbi Eleasar said, Lend it to me. He replied, I will, so as to shew to you the Power of the Sacred Light. And you have heard (said Rabbi Eleasar) that Book was in my Hands twelve months, and we found in it sublime and precious Lights, etc., and we have found in it various sorts of Medicines, ordered according to the Prescriptions of the Law, and the profound Secrets, etc. And we said, Blessed be the Holy and Merciful One, Who bestoweth a share of Wisdom upon Men from the Supernal Wisdom. Thus far here.

These things moved me to seek the like good and secret Books; and from the good Hand of my God I found that which I now teach to thee. And the Camea[31] of this Metal is altogether wonderful, for it consists of six times six Partitions, everywhere wonderfully shewing the Virtue of the Letter Vau,[32] related to Tiphereth. And all the Columns and Lines, as well from the bottom to the top, as from the right to the left, and from one Angle to another, give the same Sum; and thou mayest vary the same *ad infinitum*. And the various totals always observe this principle, that their lesser Number is always 3, 9, or 6; and again, 3, 9 or 6; and so on. Concerning which I could reveal many things to thee.

Now I add this Example, which shows as the total of a line the number 216 of Arjeh[33] our wonderful Lion, 14 times, which is the Name Zahab, Gold. Compute and be Rich.

19

11	63	5	67	69	1
13	21	53	55	15	59
37	27	31	29	45	47
35	39	43	41	33	25
49	57	19	17	51	23
71	9	65	7	3	61

(S. A. adds in the Notes the true Magic Square of the Planet Sol.)

CHAPTER III.

CHESEPH,[1] Silver is referred to Gedulah on account of its whiteness which denotes Mercy and Pity. In Raja Meh. it is said that by 50 silver shekels, Deut., c. 22, v. 29, is understood Binah, Understanding, but when from 50 portals it inclines to the side of Gedulah—see the book Pardes Rimmonim, tract 23, c. 11.

Cheseph, Silver, in Metallic things Rabbi Mordechai writes thus:

Let the Red Minera[2] of Silver be taken, let it be ground very finely; add an Ounce and a half[3] of the Calx of Luna to six Ounces of it. Let it be placed in a Sand bath in a Vial sealed. Let there be given a small Fire for the first Eight Days, lest its Radical Humidity be burnt up. The second Week, one degree stronger; and the third yet stronger; and on the fourth, that the sand may not be red hot, but so that when Water is dropped upon it, it may hiss. Then on the top of the Glass, thou shalt have a White Matter, which is the Materia Prima or tinging Arsenic,[4] being the living Water of Metals, which all Philosophers call dry Water, or their Vinegar. Let this be purified thus: Take of the Crystalline Matter sublimed; Let it be ground upon a Marble, with an equal part of Calx of Luna, and let it be put into a Vial sealed, and set in a Sand bath again, the first two Hours with a gentle Fire, the second with a stronger, and the third with one yet more violent, and increased till the Sand will hiss, and our Arsenic will be sublimed again, the starry Beams being sent forth. And since a quantity of this is required thou shalt augment it thus:

Take six Ounces of this, and an Ounce and a half of the most pure Filings of Luna, and make an Amalgama, and let them be digested in a Vial in hot Ashes, till all the Luna be dissolved, and converted into Arsenical Water.

Take an Ounce and a half of this Spirit, and place it in a closed Vial: Let this be put into hot Ashes, and it will ascend and descend; which heat continue, till it leaves off Sweating, and it lies at the bottom the Colour of Ashes. Thus the matter is dissolved and putrefied.

Take one part of this Cinereous Matter, and half a part of the aforesaid Water, let them be mixed and sweat in a Glass, as before, which will happen in about Eight Days; when the Cinereous Earth shall begin to wax white, take it out, and let it be imbibed with five Washings of its Lunar Water, and digested as before. Let it be imbibed the third time, with five Ounces of the same Water, and coagulated as before, for Eight Days. The fourth Imbibition requires seven Ounces of the Lunar Water. And the Sweating being ended, this Preparation is finished.

Now for the White Work. Take 21 Drachms of this White Earth, 14 Drachms of the Lunar Water, 10 Drachms of Calx of most pure Luna; mix them upon a marble slab and commit them to Coagulation, till they grow hard; imbibe it with three parts of its own Water, till it hath drank up this Portion; and repeat that so often, till it flow on a Copper Plate, made red hot, without Smoke; and then thou shalt have the Tincture for the White, which thou mayest increase by the means aforesaid.

For the Red, you must use Calx of Sol, and a stronger Fire; and 'tis a work of about four months. Thus this author.

Let this be compared with the Writing of the Arab Philosopher (Geber), where he writes very fully of the Arsenical Matter.

Chesed,[5] in the Metallic Kingdom, is Luna, *Nemine Contradicente*. And so the Lesser Number of Gedulah is as that of Sama,[6] or Sima. Silver is referred to in Prov., c. 16, v. 16, and c. 17, v. 3, and also Psalm 12, v. 7, and Job, c. 28, v. 1. Silver is also found allotted to each one of the Sephirotic Decad, thus see the c. 38 of Exodus, v. 17 and 19, where Silver forms the Chapiters of the Pillars representing Kether or the summit. While Silver is compared with Chokmah, in Proverbs, c. 2, v. 4, and to Binah, in Prov., c. 16, v. 16.

Gedulah is manifest out of the History of Abraham, where Silver is always preferred, Gen, c. 13, v. 2, and c. 23, v. 15, 16, and c. 24, v. 35, 53.

Geburah is shewed, when Silver is put in the Fire, Prov., c. 17, v. 3, and Num., c. 31, v. 21. Psalm 66, v. 10. Prov., c. 27, v. 21. Isaiah, c. 48, v. 10. Ezek., c. 22, v. 22. Zech., c. 13, v. 9. Mal., c. 3, v. 3.

Tiphereth is the Breast of the Statue, in Dan., c. 2, v. 32.

Netzach is a Vein of Silver, in Job, c. 28, v. 1.

Hod are the Silver Trumpets, Num., c. 10, v. 2.

Jesod is found in Prov., c. 10, v. 20, and Malkuth, in Psalm 12, v. 6.

The Camea of this Metal represents nine times nine Squares, showing the same sum twenty times, *viz.*, 369, and in its lesser Number 9, which all the Variations shew, though they should be a thousand times a thousand; because this Chesed (which is Mercy) endureth for ever. Psalm 136, v. 1.

37	78	29	70	21	62	13	54	5
6	38	79	30	71	22	63	14	46
47	7	39	80	31	72	23	55	15
16	48	8	40	81	32	64	24	56
57	17	49	9	41	73	33	65	25
26	58	18	50	1	42	74	34	66
67	27	59	10	51	2	43	75	35
36	68	19	60	11	52	3	44	76
77	28	69	20	61	12	53	4	45

Barzel,[7] Iron; in the Natural Science, this Metal is the middle Line, reaching from one extreme to the other. This is that Male and Bridegroom, without whom the Virgin is not impregnated. This is that Sol, Sun or Gold of the Wise Men, without whom, the

Moon will be always in Darkness. He that knows his Rays, works in the Day; others grope in the Night.

Parzala,[8] whose lesser number is 12, is of the same account as the Name of that Bloody Animal Dob,[9] a Bear, Whose Number is 12 also.

And this is that Mystical thing, which is written, Dan., 7, 5, " And behold another Beast, a second like unto a Bear, stood on its one side, and it had three Ribs standing out in his Mouth, between his Teeth; and thus they said unto it, Arise, eat much Flesh." The Meaning is, that in order to constitute the Metallic Kingdom, in the second place, Iron is to be taken; in whose Mouth or Opening (which comes to pass in an Earthen Vessel) a threefold Scoria is thrust out, from within its whitish Nature.

Let him eat Batsar,[10] *i.e.*, Flesh, whose lesser Number is 7, that is Puk,[11] that is Stibium, whose lesser Number in like manner is 7.

And indeed much Flesh, because the proportion of this, is greater than of that; and indeed such a proportion as Puk, that is 106, bears to Barzel 239; such shall be the proportion of Iron to Antimony.

But understand the *Flesh of the Lion*, which is the first Animal; whose *Eagle's Wings*, and so much as is very Volatile in him, shall be *drawn out*, and it shall be *lifted up*, and by purifying be separated from its *Earth* or Scoria: And it will stand *on its Feet*; that is, shall get its Consistency, in a Cone; *like a Man* erect and with a shining Countenance, like Moses. For Enos[12] and Moses[13] in full writing by Gematria each give 351. And the Heart of Iron, [for the heart, Leb[14] and iron, Barzel, in their least Number both give 5], (Mineral) *i.e.*, the Tiphereth of Man Mineral shall be given to it.

For even the name of the Star belonging to this, is Edom,[15] which hath the Connotation of a Red Man.

These things being done, the third Beast ought to be taken, which is *as it were a Leopard, i.e.*, Water not wetting; the Garden of the Wise Men; for Nimra[16] a Leopard, and Jardin in their lesser Number, make the same Sum, *viz.*, 12. Such also is the Quickness of this Water, that is not unlike a Leopard upon that account.

And he shall have four Wings of a Bird[17] *upon his Back*, the four Wings are two Birds, which exasperate[18] this Beast with their Feathers, to the intent he may enter and fight with the Bear and Lion; altho' of himself he be volatile and biting enough, and venomous like a Winged Serpent and Basilisk.

And the Beast had four Heads; in which Words are understood four Natures lurking in his Composition, *i.e.*, white, red, green, and watery.

And power was given him over the other Beasts, *i.e.*, the Lion and the Bear, that he may extract their gluten or Blood.

From all these are made one Fourth Beast in the 7th verse, which is *frightful*, *terrible*, and *very strong*: For it casts forth so great Fumes, that at some times there is Peril of Death, if he be handled at undue time and place.

And he hath great Teeth of Iron, because this is one of the Parts and Materials compounding it; *Eating and Breaking* himself, and others to pieces, and *Treading the Residue under his Feet*. That is, of a Nature so violent, that by many bruisings and tramplings, he is as it were tamed at length.

And he had *ten horns*, because he hath the Nature of all the Metallic Numbers.

A little Horn, etc., for out of this is extracted the young King, who hath the Nature of Tiphereth (that is of a Man) but of the Nature or Part of Geburah: For it is that Gold which predominates in the Work of the Wise Men. Thus far the Preparatories.

And now the Beast is to be killed, and his Body to be destroyed and delivered up to the Fire to be burned, etc. For now follows the Regimen of the Fire. Concerning which elsewhere.

The Sword of the Illustrious Naaman is also related to the word Barzel.

Lancea;[19] in the Study of the Metallic Natures, the History of Phinehas, Numbers, c. 25, v. 7, belongs to this place. By the Fornicators are understood the (Masculine) Arsenical Sulphur, and the (feminine) dry Water unduly mixed, together in the Mineral.

By the Spear of Phinehas is meant the Force of Iron acting upon the Matter to cleanse it of Dross: By which Iron,[20] not only is the Arsenical Sulphur killed, but also the Woman herself is at length mortified; so that the Miracle of Phinehas may be fitly applied here. See also the Targum on this Place, *i.e.*, Numbers, c. 25, v. 7. For the Nature of Iron is wonderful, as its Camea (whose lines add up to 65 each way) shews.

It is here given: the Number 5, and its Square (*i.e.*, 25) denote the Feminine Nature, which is corrected by this Metal.

11	24	7	20	3
4	12	25	8	16
17	5	13	21	9
10	18	1	14	22
23	6	19	2	15

CHAPTER IV.

BEDIL,[1] Tin; in Natural Science, this Metal is not greatly used; for as it is derived by Separation, so its Matter remains separate from the Universal Medicine.

Amongst the Planets, Zedek[2] is attributed to it; a white wandering Planet, to which the Gentiles applied an Idolatrous Name, mention whereof is forbidden, see Exodus, c. 22, v. 12, and a greater Extirpation is promised, Hosea, c. 2, v. 17, and Zechariah, c. 13, v. 2.

Amongst the Beasts, no Allegory is better applied to this metal than that, because of its Crackling, it should be called Chazir Mijaar,[3] a Boar out of the Wood, Psalm 80, v. 14, whose Number is 545; which is not only made five times from 109, but in its lesser Number shews a Quinary, as the Name Zedek 194; which Numbers being added, make 14; and they make the Number 5, which twice taken is 10, the lesser Number of the word Bedil, by the two figures of 46 being added together. But five times ten shews the Fifty Gates of Binah,[4] and the first Letter of the Sephira Netzach,[5] which is the Sephirotic Class to which this Metal is referred.

In particular Transmutations, its Sulphurous Nature alone doth not profit, but with other Sulphurs, especially those of the Red[6] Metals, it does reduce thick Waters, duly terrificated into Gold; so also into Silver, if its nature be subtilized into a thin water by Quicksilver which (amalgam) amongst others is made well enough by Tin.

But its viscous and watery Nature may be meliorated into Gold, if it be duly pulverized with the Calx of

Gold through all the Degrees of Fire, for ten Days, and by degrees thrown upon flowing Gold, in the form of little masses, which also I am taught is to be done with Silver. But no man is wise unless his Master is Experience.

I add no more; He that is wise may correct Natures and help by Experiments where they are imperfect.

Kassitera,[7] Tin; See Bedil's Camea,[9] where the Number resulting from every side is Dal[8]; representing the Tenuity and Vileness of this Metal, in all Metallic Operations.

4	14	15	1
9	7	6	12
5	11	10	8
16	2	3	13

CHAPTER V.

Hod,[1] in the Wisdom of Nature, is of the Classis of Brass; for the Colour expresses the Nature of Geburah, which this Sephira contains. And the Use of Brass was for instruments of Praise and Music, 1 Chronicles, c. 15, v. 19. "And Brazen Bows were of Use in War." 2 Samuel, c. 22, v. 35, Job, c. 20, v. 24, and the like, 1 Samuel, c. 17, v. 5, 6, 38.

But as Hod is encompassed with a Serpent, so Nechuseth[2]—Brass is of the same Root with Nachash[3] a Serpent.

The Seventy Talents of Brass of the Oblation, Exodus, c. 38, v. 29, represent Seventy Princes; for about this place is the greatest Force of the Cortices or Shells.[4] Whence in Hod is a degree of Prophetical Representation, as from the Root Nachash comes Nechashim, Enchantments, Numbers, c. 23, v. 23, and c. 21, v. 1. But he that will be curious, may find, that Hod has a special Decad. So also in the History of Brass, from the Law, he may easily gather a Decad.

For may not that Oblation in general from which afterwards Vessels were made for the Tabernacle, Exodus, c. 38, v. 29, be referred to Kether, since all the other degrees spring from this?

Doth not the Laver of Brass, Exodus, c. 30, v. 18, shew the Nature of Chokmah, from which an Influx is let down to all the Inferiors? But the Basis thereof, which also was of Brass, is Binah; for Chokmah resides therein.

Afterwards the Brazen Altar, Exodus, c. 27, v. 2, with its Furniture represents the two Extremes, for the two

Bars in the same place were covered over with Brass; and are as it were the two Arms, Gedulah and Geburah. The Body of the Altar itself, Tiphereth. The four Rings of Brass, to the right and left are Netzach and Hod.

And the Brazen Net, which was instead of a Foundation, is Jesod.

And if you say, that the Altar was to be referred to Malkuth, according to the most common Opinion, which Altar may represent the Notion of a Woman: I answer, 'Tis true according to the general Distribution of the Tabernacle and Temple. But amongst the special Classis of Brass, where all things before incline to the Female, and so also Tiphereth, the Notion of the Male will not be so remote.

For there are yet Adne, Brazen Bases, Exodus, c. 26, v. 37, and c. 27, v. 10, which being as it were the bottom of the Tabernacle, have congruously enough the Nature of Malkuth.

He that would here trace these Mysteries more largely, might easily prolong his Discourse: But a wise Man will in short understand the Foundation.

The wonderful Camea[5] belonging to the Classis of Brass, contains seven times seven Squares; and the Sum of each Line, whether Horizontal, Vertical, or Diagonal, are equal to each other, and to Tzephah[6].

22	47	16	41	10	35	4
5	23	48	17	42	11	29
30	6	24	49	18	36	12
13	31	7	25	43	19	37
38	14	32	1	26	44	20
21	39	8	33	2	27	45
46	15	40	9	34	3	28

As for Example, Here all the Columns make the same Tzephah, 175, as is to be seen above; for the first Column to the right, 4, 29, etc., makes 175, and so the rest to the last towards the left. After the same manner note the uppermost corner 22, (where is the Mystery of the 22[7] Letters) 47, etc., and ending with the number 4, where note the Mystery of the Tetragrammaton[8] and so all to the bottom. Lastly, crosswise from the Angle between the East and South, to the Angle between the West and North, 4, 11, 18, etc., are 175, and from the Angle between the East and North, to the Angle between the West and South, *viz.*, 22, 23, 24, etc., make all 175.

Therefore contemplate these things and thou shalt see an Abyss of Profundity.

Unless thou hadst rather allude to those Coverings, in which Brass was used, Exodus, c. 27, v. 2, 6, etc.

So if No. 1 be omitted, and you begin with line 2, there meets you the Sum Botzatz,[9] 1 Samuel, c. 14, v. 4, writ defectively. If you begin with line 3, you will have the like Sum of 189. If you begin with line 4, then 196. If you begin with line 5, then 203. And so they ascend, exceeding one another by 7^{10}.

But if by a skip you dispose the Numbers 1, and 3, and 5, and 7, and 9, etc., then begin with which you will, you will observe the same Proportion. Also 1, and 4, and 7, and 10, and 13, etc. Also 1, and 5, and 9, and 13. This Septenary Net will always, from every Face, represent the same Sum, whose farther Use I should be able to open elsewhere.

Nechusheth, Brass,[11] see Sohar Pekude, 103, 410, etc., and see Hod as above. Amongst the Planets Nogah,[12] Venus corresponds to it. A necessary Instrument to promote the Metallic Splendour.

Yet it hath more the part of a Male[13] than Female. For do not deceive thyself, to believe a white Splendour is promised to thee, as the word Nogah infers. But Hod ought to receive a Geburic Influence, and gives it also. O, how great is this Mystery.

Learn therefore to lift the Serpent up on high, which is called Nechushtan, 2 Kings, c. 18, v. 4, if thou wouldst cure infirm Natures after the Example of Moses.

CHAPTER VI.

Chokmah,[1] in the Metallic Doctrine, is the Sephira of Lead, or Primordial Salt, in which the Lead of the Wise Men lies hid. But how is so high a Place attributed to lead which is so Ignoble a Metal, and of which there is so seldom Mention made in the Scripture?

But here lies Wisdom! Its several Degrees are kept very secret; hence there is very little mention made of it. But yet here will not be wanting examples of the particular Sephiroth.

For may not that which, in Zech., c. 5, v. 7, is called a Lifted up Talent of Lead, and brought from the deep,[2] represent the grade of Kether? And that which in the same Chapter, v. 8, is spoken concerning the Stone of Lead,[3] it sets before itself the Letter Jod, which is in Chokmah.[4]

Then Ezekiel, c. 27, v. 12, Lead is referred to the place of the congregation, of which type is Binah.

And Amos, c. 7, v. 7, Anak,[5] a Leaden Plummet, denotes the Thread of Chesed. For Anak, with the whole Word, hath 72 the Number of Chesed. But in Numbers, c. 31, v. 22, Lead is reckoned amongst those things which can abide the Fire, will be referred to Geburah.

But Job, c. 19, v. 24, graven with an Iron Pen and Lead[6] are joined together, from whence you have Tiphereth.

But in Ezekiel, c. 22, v. 18, 20, there is the Furnace of Trial, or of Grace, or Furnace of Judgment, in which also is put lead; hence, Netzach and Hod; for thence ought to flow a River of Silver.

And Jeremiah, c. 6, v. 29, the Furnace of Probation; out of which, by the means of Lead, good Silver is looked for.[8] Is not the just Man, and he that justifies, Jesod (*i.e.*, the Foundation)?

But if you seek the bottom of the Sea, look upon Exodus, c. 15, v. 10, where the Notion of Malkuth will occur.

This is that Red Sea, out of which the Salt of Wisdom is extracted, and through which the Ships of Solomon fetched Gold.

Ophereth,[9] in the Doctrine of Natural things, is referred to Wisdom,[10] for a great Treasure of Wisdom lies hid here. And hither is referred the quotation Proverbs, c. 3, v. 19. The Lord in Wisdom hath founded the earth; I say, the Earth, concerning which Job speaks, c. 28, v. 6, which hath Dust of Gold. Where, take notice of the Word Ophereth, *i.e.*, Lead. This Lead, by a Mystical Name is called Chol,[11] because therein lies the System of the whole Universe. For its Figure[12] has below a Circle, the Sign of Universal Perfection, and over the circle is a cross formed of four Daleths, whose Angles meet in one Point; so you may know, that all Quaternity lies here, and the Quaternions of Quaternity: whether you refer to the Elements, or Cortices, or Letters or Worlds.

And in this Lead of the Wise Men, four Elements lie hid, *i.e*, Fire, or the Sulphur of the Philosophers; Air, the Separator of the Waters; the dry Water; and the Earth of the Wonderful Salt.

There are also hid in it the four Cortices, described in Ezekiel, c. 1, v. 4, for in the Preparation of it there will occur to thee the Whirlwind, a great Cloud, and a Fire enfolding itself, and at length the desired Splendour[13] breaks forth.

Also the Natural Sephira of the Tetragrammaton, and the Metal thereof, occurs to thee here. And you will naturally travel through four Worlds in the very Labour; when after the Faction and Formation, laborious enough, there will appear the wonderful creation: after which thou shalt have the Emanation of the desired Natural Light.

And note, that the word Chol, whose Number is 50, multiplied by 15, according to the Number of the Sacred Characteristic Name[14] in the Sephira of Wisdom, will produce the Number of Ophereth, *i.e.*, 750.

Also the Kamea of that Metal is also wonderful, in which the Number 15, *viz.*, the Name Jah, *i.e.*, a form of Jehovah, in a Magic Square of nine Squares (because we are in the ninth Sephira[15]) throughout all its Columns, shows itself after this manner.[16]

4	9	2
3	1	7
8	5	6

The Planet Shabthai[17] denominated from "Rest," because in this Principle is offered the most desired Rest.

And if you shall compute the words Lahab[18] Shabthai, *i.e.*, the point or edge of Saturn, there will arise the Number of the Name Ophereth, *viz.*, Lead.

Arjeh,[19] a Lion, in Natural Science is variously applied.

"For there is Gur Arjeh, a Lion's Whelp;" as Jacob speaks, Genesis, c. 49, v. 9. That word Gur,[20] a Whelp, Numbers 209, and if you add the whole Word in the place of a Unit, it will be 210, which is the Number of the word "Naaman[21] the Syrian, the General of the Army of the King of Aram,[22]" 2 Kings, c. 5, v. 1, by whom is Allegorically to be understood the Matter of the Metallic Medicine, to be purified Seven times[23] in Jordan, which many men, studious in Metallic Affairs, call Gur.[24]

2. And that thou mayest the better understand this Matter, take the Lesser Number of this word Naaman, which is 21, this is equal to the Number of the Name of Kether, which is Ehejeh, 21.[25]

3. The Number of Naaman, with the whole Word, is 211; to which another Name of the Lion is equal, Ari, 211.[26]

4. And so also Arjeh, a Lion is equal in Number to the first word[27] of that wonderful History, 2 Kings, c. 5, v. 1. "And Naaman, etc." For this constitutes 216.

5. Moreover, the word Kephir,[28] a young Lion, and Jerik,[29] agree also in their Number; for each of them give 310. And now it is known in Metallic Mysteries, that at the very Entrance, we meet the Ænigma of the Lion of Green growth, which we call the Green Lion[30]; which, I pray thee, do not think is so-called, from any other Cause but its Colour. For unless thy Matter shall be green, not only in that intermediate state before 'tis reduced into Water, and also after the Water of Gold is made of it, remember that this Universal Dry Process must be amended.

6. The other Names of Lions, are Lebi,[31] which is a Lioness, according to Job, c. 4, v. 11. The Whelps of the Lioness shall separate themselves; Ezekiel, c. 19, v. 2. "Thy Mother being a Lioness lay amongst the Lions;" Nahum, c. 2, v. 12. "A Lioness is there"; v. 13, "The Lion did strangle them for his Lioness."

Also Lish,[32] which denotes a fierce Lion, with long straight hair: as found in Proverbs, c. 30, v. 30. These two Names, in their Lesser Numbers each contain a Septenary, for Lebi numbers 43, which gives 7, and Lish 340, which gives 7 also. To these the Name Puk,[33] Stibium is equal, whose Sum is 106, and its lesser Number is 7, than which nothing could be more plain. Especially if the Sirname of that Mineral be considered, when it is called the Hairy Servant, or he with long hair or Ruddy haired; with many like Names given to it.

7. There is yet another Name of a Lion according to the Masters of the Sanhedrim, in chapter 11, fol. 95, col. 1, *i.e.*, Shachatz;[34] which also the Targum uses; and Psalm 17, v. 12; its Number is 398, in its lesser Number it is 2. And the Chaldaic Word Tzadida[35] shews the same lesser Number 2, being used in Targum, 2 Kings, c. 30, v. 30, Jeremiah, c. 4, v. 30, (instead of the Hebrew Word Puk, which is Antimony) for its sum is 109, which together with the whole Word, is 110, and its lesser Number 2.

8. At length also there meets us the Name of the Black Lion, to wit, Shacal,[36] whose Number is 338, and its lesser Number 5.

Now take the least Number of the word Naaman 210, which is 3, and the least Number of the Chaldaic word Parzel,[37] Iron, which is 2, and you will have 5, the Black Lion.

9. Zahab, Gold, is called by the name Red Lion; and so not only the least Numbers of the Names Lebi and Lish make 14, which Number Zahab hath; but also the least Number of the word Zahab is 5, as I said but now to be equal to Shacal.

But under this Notion is to be understood Gold, either already Mortified, or now at length drawn from the Mines of the Wise Men,—Black in Colour, but Red in Potency.

CHAPTER VII.

JARDEN,[1] denotes a Mineral Water, useful in the cleansing of Metals, and Leprous[2] Minerals. But this Water flows from two sources, whereof one is called Jeor,[3] *i.e.*, a fluid, having the Nature of the Right Hand, and very Bountiful. The other is called Dan,[4] Rigorous and of a sharp Nature.

But it flows through the Salt Sea, which ought to be observed, and at length is thought to be mixed with the Red Sea; which is a Sulphurous Matter, Masculine, and known to all true Artists.

But know thou, that the Name Zachu,[5] *i.e.*, Purity, being multiplied by 8, the Number of Jesod, produces the Number Seder,[7] *i.e.*, Order, which is 264. Which Number is also contained in the word Jarden; thus you may Remember, that at least Eight Orders of Purification are required, before the true Purity follows.

Jesod,[8] in natural things, contains under itself Quicksilver; because this Metal is the Foundation of the whole Art of Transmutation.

And as the Name of El[9], doth insinuate the Nature of Silver, because both belong to the Classis of Chesed, (but here to that Chesed, which is inferior, *viz.*, Jesod). So the name of El Chai, is the same as it were, Cheseph Chai,[10] *i.e.*, Quicksilver.

And so Kokab,[11] a Star, is the Name of the Planet, under whose Government this Matter is, with the whole Word is 49; which same is the Number of El-Chai.

But remember that all Quicksilver doth not conduce to this Work, because the sorts of it differ even as Flax from Hemp or Silk, and you would work on Hemp to no purpose, to make it receive the Tenuity and Splendour of fine Flax.

And there are some that think it a sign of Legitimate Water, if being mixed with Gold, it presently ferments. But the common liquid Mercury, precipitated by Lead, performs this. And what will it do?

Verily I tell thee, there is no other Sign of a true Mercury but this, that in a due heat it invests itself with a Cuticula which is the purest refined Gold; and that in a little space of time, yea, in one night.

This is that which, not without a Mystery, is called Kokab, a Star; because according to the natural Kabalah, Numbers, c. 24, v. 17, out of (the Metal) Jacob comes a Star; or in Plain language the shapes of Rods, and Branches, arise; and from this Star flows this Influence, of which we speak.

This Argent Vive, in the Gemara Tract Gittin, ch. 7, fol. 69, is called Espherica,[12] *i.e.*, Spherical Water, because it flows from the Mundane Sphere.

And in Genesis, c. 36, v. 39, it is called Mehetabel,[13] as tho' it were Mé Hathbula, by changing the order of the Letters, *i.e.*, the Waters of Immersion, because the King is immerged in them to be cleansed.

Or as tho' it were the El Hatob, by a like Change of Letters; the Waters of the good El, or of Living Silver; for Life and Good have equal power, as Death and Evil have the same.

This is called the Daughter of Metred,[14] that is, (as the Targum teaches,) the Gold-maker, Labouring with daily Weariness.

For this Water flows not out of the Earth, nor is digged out of the Mine; but is produced and perfected with great Labour and much Diligence.

This Wife (or female) is also called Me Zahab,[15] the

Waters of Gold, or such a Water as sends forth Gold.

If the Artist be betrothed to her, he will beget a Daughter, who will be the Water of the Royal Bath. Although some would have this Bride to be the Waters that are made out of Gold; which Bride (notwithstanding) poor Men leave to be espoused by great Men.

The Husband of Mehetabel is that Edomite King, and King of Redness, who is called Hadar, Glorious; *viz*., the Beauty of the Metallic Kingdom, which is Gold, Daniel, c. 11, v. 20-29. But such Gold as may be referred to Tiphereth. For Hadar represents 209, which Number also the Tetragrammaton, multiplied by 8, produces, (which is the Number of Circumcision and Jesod[17]) if the whole Word be added as one.

But that thou mayest know, that Tiphereth, of the degree of Geburah, is understood; know thou, that that Number being added to the whole, is also contained in Issac,[18] which in like manner is of the Classis of Gold.

The City of that King is called Pegno,[19] Brightness, from its Splendour, according to Deut., c. 33, v. 2. Which Name, and the Name Joseph,[20] (by which Jesod is meant, have the same Number 156. That you may know that Argent vive is required to the Work; and that the Royal Beauty doth not reside out of this Splendid City.

To this place belongs another Sirname, *i.e.*, Elohim Chajim,[21] as tho' it were called Living Gold; because Elohim and Gold denote the same Measure. But so this Water is called, because it is the Mother and Principle of Living Gold: For all other kinds of Gold are thought to be dead; this only excepted.

Nor will you err, if you shall attribute to it another special name, for it may be called Mekor Majim Chajim[22], that is, a Fountain of Living Water. For, from this Water the King is enlivened, that he may give Life to all Metals and Living Things.

The Kamea[28] of this Water is altogether wonderful, and exhibits in like manner the Number Chai (*i.e.* Living) 18 times, the same Sum in a Magic Square of 64 Squares, which is the Sum of Mezahab, Waters of Gold; being variable, after this manner, to infinity.

8	58	59	5	4	62	63	1
49	15	14	52	53	11	10	56
41	23	22	44	45	19	18	48
32	34	35	29	28	38	39	25
40	26	27	37	36	30	31	33
17	47	46	20	21	43	42	24
9	55	54	12	13	51	50	16
64	2	3	61	60	6	7	57

Here you have the Sum 260, from the bottom to the top, from the right hand to the left, and by the Diagonal; the lesser Number of 260 is 8, the Number of Jesod; as also the Root of the whole Square is 8.

The Symbol of the first Sum is 260, which makes the word Sar,[24] *i.e.*, "he went back," because in going forward the Sum always goes backward through the units.

For Example, if you begin with 2, reckoning the first Column for 8 the Sum will be 268, which is resolved in 7.

If you begin with the 3 (reckoning 8 for the second Column) the Sum will be 276, which resolves into 6. And so of the rest.[25] And so also the number of Purifications increasing, the Weight of thy Water decreases.

CHAPTER VIII.

Juneh, a Dove;[1] amongst the Ænigmas of Natural things, the Name of a Dove is never applied to the Metals themselves, but to the Ministering and Preparing forms of Nature.

He that understands here the Nature of the Burnt Offering[2] will not take Turtles, but two young male Pigeons, or Sons of the Dove, Leviticus, c. 1, v. 14, and c. 12, v. 8, and c. 14, v. 22.

But count the word Beni 62,[3] and 2 for a Pair of Doves, and thence is the number 64 of the word Nogah, which is the Name of the 5th amongst the Planets,[4] and you shall go the true way. Else " labour not to be Rich ; Cease from thy own Wisdom :" Wilt thou cause thine eyes presently to discern it ? That will not be : But the Scholar of the Wise Men maketh to himself Wings, and flieth as an Eagle, even as he doth the Minerals of the Stars[5] to heaven. Prov., c. 23, v. 4, 5.

Jarach,[6] the Moon or Luna[7] in the History of Natural Things is called the " Medicine for the White," because she hath received a Whitening Splendour from the Sun, which by a like shining, illuminates and converts to her own Nature all the Earth, that is the impure Metals.

And the place of Isaiah, c. 30, v. 26, " the moon shall be as the Sun," may be mystically understood of this, because the Work being finished, she hath a solar Splendour ; but in this State, the place of Canticles, c. 6, v. 10, belongs to her,—" fair as the Moon."

By the same Name the Matter of the Work is called: and so indeed it is like to the crescent Moon, in the first State of Consistence; and like to the Full Moon in the last State of Fluidity and Purity. For the words Jarach, the Moon, and Razia, Secrets, also Rabui, a Multitude, have by Gematria the same Numbers, because in this Matter are found the Secrets of Multiplication.

Gophrith[10] is Sulphur; in the Science of Minerals this Principle is referred to Binah, to the left because of its Colour; and to left also, Gold is wont to be referred; and Charutz,[11] a kind of Gold, is also referred to Binah, and being 7 in its lesser Number agrees with that of Gophritha.[12]

Therefore the Gold of Natural Wisdom ought to be Charutz; that is digged out, or the like not excocted. And this is that Sulphur, which hath a fiery Colour, and is penetrating and changing to impure Earths; to wit, Sulphur with Salt, Deut., c. 29, v. 23. Sulphur with Fire, rained down upon the Wicked,—that is the impure Metals, Psalm 11, v. 6.

You must dig up this Sulphur; and it is to be digged out of the Water, that you mayest have Fire obtained from Water.[13] "And if your Ways be right before the Lord, your Iron shall swim upon the Water," 2 Kings, c. 6, v. 6. "Go thy way then to the River Jordan with Elisha"; see v. 4. "But who shall declare the Geburah of the Lord?" Psalm 106, v. 2.

Many seek other Sulphurs, and he that hath entered the "House of the Paths" shall understand them, Proverbs, c. 8, v. 2. For the Sulphurs of Gold and Iron, the Extraction whereof is taught by many, and is easy; also of Gold, Iron and Brass; also of Gold, Iron, Copper and Antimony, which are gathered together after Fulmination by Vinegar, out of the lixivium, which are changed into a Red Oil, with a moist Hydrargyrum,—do tinge Silver. For from Proverbs, c. 21, v. 20, we know there is a Treasure to be desired and also an Oil to be found in the dwelling of a Man of Wisdom.

FINIS.

NOTES BY SAPERE AUDE.

CHAPTER I.

1. Æsch Mezareph, or Cleansing Fire. In Hebrew letters ASh MTzRP, according to the system of transliteration adopted in the volume called *Numbers* written by the Editor of the *Collectanea Hermetica*. ASh is fire and MTzRP is a word meaning "refiner" and "goldsmith," and is from the root TzRP meaning cleanse, purify and refine. The *sch* found here instead of *sh* in the word ASH, betrays the German source of the First Latin Edition.

2. Compare *Kâbalah Denudata*, page 116.

3. Elisha. The Hebrew mode of spelling proper names and words meaning the metals, planets and Sephiroth is very important, as words are also numbers and shew relation. Elisha is spelled ALIShO, that is 411, whose lesser number is 6.

4. Pirke Aboth. The Sayings of the Fathers.

5. Tohu is THU, meaning "void;" see Genesis, c. 1, v. 2.

6. Baba Kama, the "First Gate," a tract of the Talmud.

7. Instead of; the Latin is "est instar divitiarum."

8. Jar-din, the words are IAR DIN, the river Jordan.

9. Atziluth, ATzILUT is the highest World of the Kabalah.

10. Assiah, OShIH is the lowest World of the Kabalah.

11. The Ten Sephiroth now follow in their order:—
Kether, KTR the Crown, the First Sephira.
Chokmah, ChKMH is Wisdom, the Second Sephira.
Binah, BINH is Understanding, the Third Sephira.
Chesed, ChSD is Mercy, the Fourth Sephira.
Geburah, GBVRH is Severity, the Fifth.
Tiphereth, TPART is Beauty, the Sixth.
Netzach, NTzCh is Victory, the Seventh.
Hod, HUD is Splendour, the Eighth.
Jesod, ISUD is Foundation, the Ninth.
Malkuth, MLKUT is the Kingdom.

12. Job states that ZHB, gold comes from the North, but our Bible translates the word Zahab as "fair weather."

13. It is the Microprosopus of metals.

14. Living, the word is ChI.

15. The two columns of the Sephiroth.

16. Mezahab, given as the name of the grandmother of Mehetabel the wife of the Edomite King Hadar. Zahab means gold. These Edomite kings form another mystery.

17. Compare *Kab. Den.*, p. 235.

18. Gehazi is spelled GIChZI; 3, 10, 8, 7, 10 or 38. The mediæval Alchymic authors called him a sophister.

19. Chol, ChL, 38, for Ch is 8 and L is 30; while G is 3, I is 10, Ch is 8, Z is 7 and I is 10; total 38.

Frater Q.S.N. writes:—

The meaning of this portion appears to be that Gehazi represents the Pretender to Alchymy who knowing that transmutation is possible, wastes his own time, and advises a similar waste on the part of others, in attempting processes against natural law and harmony; one metal cannot be directly turned into another, but the path of evolution must be retraced to the hyle or prima materia and then the other line of evolution followed.

CHAPTER II.

1. Compare *Kab. Den.*, page 227.
2. This word is really Ketem, KTM. Canticles, c. 5, v. 11, says "his head is as the most fine gold."
3. Batzar is BTzR, gold in dust.
4. Charutz is ChRUTz, from the root meaning the ore of gold which is "dug out"; native in masses or grains.
5. This name is ZHB ShChUTh; ChUTh means filum, funiculus, or a thread From its ductile, malleable nature, gold can be drawn out. The Kabalah speaks of the Thread of Chesed—the flux of its force to Malkuth; the Thread of Red Colour, the flux from Geburah to Malkuth, related to the kiss on the lips; the Yellow Thread of Tiphereth, related to gold; and lastly, the Spinal Cord of Man, ChUTh H ShDRH, white as silver, passing from above down through Tiphereth. The Golden Thread is Yellow, being a compound of Red and White, Geburah and Gedulah.

N. O. M.

6. Zahab, ZHB; 7, 5, 2 or 14, lesser number 5. Some English references write this word Zeb, it means "shining" or "yellow."
7. Paz; PZ; 80, 7, or 87. Gold as found pure, solid gold as formed into a crown. Psalm 21, v. 3.
8. Zahab Muphaz, ZHB MUPZ; Muphaz means pure.
9. Daniel, c. 10, v. 5, "Gold of Uphaz," the words are KTM AUPZ. Kethem is "concealed."
10. ZHB SGUR, treasured, also fine gold: or perhaps gold shut up, in the bowels of the earth, or in a chemical closed vessel.
11. ZHB PRUIM, Parvahim, appears to be the name of a place: but also LDM means for the blood

of, H the PRV bullock: left hand means "of the Sephirotic tree."

12. ZHB ThUB. Tob is the common adjective for good or pure.

13. ZHB AUPIR, Gold of Ophir, probably Arabia. Gold was not coined until the time of Ezra; before that, as a medium of exchange, it was weighed. For a reference to these sorts of Gold see Buxtorf, Lexicon Hebraicum, 1646, London, page 170, where the student is referred to the Talmudic Joma, 44, 2.

14. Compare *Kab. Den.*, page 301.

15. Solomon. This is an error, for Solomon is ShLMH or Shelomoh, and the name here is Shelemaiah, ShLMIH, who is called "the priest," who was made "treasurer."

16. Sol is ShMSh that is 300, 40, 300, total 640, whose lesser number is 6 and 4 that is 10. A simile of TPART, that is 400, 80, 1, 200 and 400, or 1081, whose lesser number is also 10.

17. Atah is ATH, or 1, 400, 5 or 406, also 10.

18. Because a feast was to be made in honour of the Calf, to the Lord, and the word in Exodus for Lord is here IHVH.

19. Saba or ShBA and Sabi, ShBI, mean captivity.

20. The name of 42 letters is the Hebrew of "Pater Deus, Filius Deus, Spiritus Sanctus Deus, Tres in uno, Unus in tribus."

21. Aphar is APR, meaning ashes or a powder.

22. The word is KTM.

23. Hacchethem ha Tob, HKTM H TUB; Tob means good.

24. Opheret is OPRT, the common Hebrew name of Lead. Batzar, BTzR, is gold, containing silver. Job, c. 22, v. 24, does not in the E.B. say "Put it upon Ophir," but "Thou shalt lay up—the gold of Ophir."

25. Nachlim is NChLIM, plural of Nachal, a stream, river or torrent.

26. Ehejeh, this is also often written in English as Aheie, the letters are AHIH.

27. This is an error, the word is Treasury, closed vessel.

28. That is the 40 days which Ezekiel had to lie on his right side for the iniquity of Judah.

29. That is IRQ RQ.

30. This Cohach is KCh, power, whose number is 28. Tit is ThITh meaning clay, whose number is 9, 10, 9 or 28.

31. The Magic Square given is not the true Square of Sol. This word QMIO, commonly written Kamea, is a Mystical Square, sub-divided into lesser squares by perpendicular and horizontal lines; in each space is placed a number or equivalent letter or letters, so arranged as to give the same total by addition in each line, up and down, or across.

32. Vau corresponds to the English letter V and to the number 6, the number of Sol, and Tiphereth, Beauty, is the sixth Sephira from above.

33. Arjeh, the word is ARIH, that is 1, 200, 10, 5, or 216, meaning a "lion," and the square shows the total of 216 by addition,
    Six times horizontally,
    Six times vertically,
    Twice diagonally,
in all 14 times, the number of ZHB or Gold. The root of ARIH is ARH, to snatch prey. The name ZHB, gold, is related to ZHR, *light, shining, splendour,* as the shining of a golden plate, and AUR is *light;* compare *aurum,* gold, and *aura,* a shining halo: all are related again to Sol.

The true Magic Square or Kamea of Sol, is here given, it contains only all the numbers from 1 to 36.

6	32	3	34	35	1
7	11	27	28	8	30
19	14	16	15	23	24
18	20	22	21	17	13
25	29	10	9	26	12
36	5	33	4	2	31

CHAPTER III.

1. Compare *Kab. Den.*, page 483. Cheseph should be Keseph, the initial is not Cʜ, the word is KSP. Gedulah is GDULH, Magnificence.

2. Red mineral of Silver, there is none; the word should be Quicksilver, whose ores, Oxide and Sulphide, are red, Cinnabar.

3. Some translators say half an ounce only; the Latin words are "Recipe calcis Lunæ unciam semis." El. Lévi says calx of antimony.

4. Arsenic, or Orpiment, or Auripigment; or was it Corrosive Sublimate?

5. Compare *Kab. Den.*, page 359. This word Chesed, CʜSD, has the same reference as the word Gedulah at the commencement of the chapter.

6. SAMA numbering 102, lesser number 3. SIMA numbering 111, lesser number 3.

7. Compare, *Kab. Den.*, page 206. Barzel is BRZL, which is 239, least number 5; iron ores are plentiful in Palestine; some authors write it in English as Berezel—it is from BR, bright, and NZL, to melt, hence cast iron.

8. Parzala is PRZLA, numbering 318, is Chaldee for Iron.

9. Dab is DUB, numbering 12.

10. Batsar is BShR or 502.

11. Puk, the Hebrew is PUK or 80, 6, 20, or 106, which is 7. There must be nearly two and a half times as much antimony as iron.

12. Enos is ANSh; 1, 50, 300, or 351.

13. Moses is MUShH; 40, 6, 300, 5 or 351.

14. Leb is LB or 30, 2 is 32, or 5. Leb means the heart; some English authors write Laib.

15. Edom is ADUM: ADM is red and is the proper name of red man; ADMH is red earth.

16. Nimra is NMRA; 50, 40, 200, 1 or 291 is 12. Jardin is IR DN; 10, 200—4, 50 or 264 is 12. Nimrah was a place in Gilead, Numbers, c. 32, v. 3; and as a common noun means Leopard.

17. Bird is OUQ, and OITh, and TzPUR. "Bird" in Alchymy generally means Sublimations.

18. Compare the *Hermetic Arcanum*, of this Series, section 119.

19. Compare *Kab. Den.*, 683. Lancea, a spear, is in Hebrew RUMCh; called in Numbers, a javelin. Phineas is in Hebrew PINChS, a proper name not easily related to any root.

20. The name Chalybs was also given to iron, it was derived from the nation of Chalybes living on the shores of the Black Sea; they were famous for smelting ores; see Xenophon *Anabasis*, v. 5.

CHAPTER IV.

1. Compare *Kab. Den.*, page 185. Bedil or Badil is BDIL or 46 or 10. This metal is not found native in Palestine.
2. Zedek, TzDQ or 194, and lesser number is 14 and then 5; this is Jupiter.
3. A boar from the wood, Aper de Sylva, is ChZIR MIOR, that is 225 and 320 or 545, whose lesser number is 14 and then 5.
4. The Fifty Gates of Binah or Understanding (see also Chapter III, paragraph 1) may be referred to the Decad of Potencies acting through the Five human senses, but the phrase has a more arcane meaning: the *Theosophical Glossary* says that 50 is a blind, and that the number is 49.
5. Nun is 50.
6. Query Mars and Venus.
7. Compare *Kab. Den.*, page 676. Kassitera is QSThRA, is a Chaldee word meaning Tin.
8. Dal, that is DL or 30 and 4, 34.
9. This is the true Magic Square of Jupiter.

CHAPTER V.

1. Compare *Kab. Den.*, page 271. Hod is the eighth Sephira. The letters are HUD or 5, 6, 4, that is 15, lesser number 6. Hod is found in the same column as Geburah. For brass, query copper.
2. Nechuseth is NCh ShT, it is also used for copper as well as Brass and Bronze, in the Bible.
3. Nachash is NChSh: note that NChShIM means "enchantments."
4. Cortices, shells or Klippoth.
5. This is the true Kamea of Seven.

6. Tzephah, that is TzPH or 90, 80, 5, that is 175, lesser numbers 13 and 4.

7. There are 22 Hebrew letters divided into a triad, heptad and dodecad.

8. Four is the number of the letters of IHVH.

9. Botzatz is BUTzTz, in the English Bible Bozez; it is here written BTzTz, these are 188 and 182.

10. That is by allowing seven for each column, and so adding 7 to the total of column two, 14 to column three, 21 to column 4.

11. Compare *Kab. Den.*, page 570. Nechuseth, Æs, Brass, a return to the subject of the Hermaphroditic Brass, which in a sense is both Hod and Netzach.

12. Nogah is NUGH, Splendour, numbering 64.

13. More a Red male than White female.

14. Nechushtan, the brazen serpent which Moses made, in the likeness of the fiery serpents which were a plague to the people. See Numbers, c. 21, v. 9.

Netzach and Hod are here attributed to Brass, and no mention is made of Copper pure. Now Brass is not a pure metal but is made by fusing together Copper two parts and Zinc one part. Zinc pure as a metal was not apparently known to the Hebrews. Brass is an Hermaphrodite and this is taught in Rosicrucian Colleges in a special Sephirotic manner.

Brass is very frequently mentioned in the O.T., but Copper only once in Ezra, c. 8, v. 27, but even there the word is Nechuseth with the adjective MTzHB, shining. Thomas Thompson says Nechuseth ought to have been translated Copper generally, and refers to Genesis, c. 4, v. 22, when Tubal Cain was a worker in Brass, and hence it was known before the Flood; now the same word Nechuseth, Brass, is said to be dug out of the hills in Deut., c. 8, v. 9, and Brass is never found native.

CHAPTER VI.

1. Compare *Kab. Den.*, page 345. Chokmah, the second Sephira. Lead is commonly in Hebrew Ophereth, OPRT.
2. There is in this place no reference to "brought from the deep;" the Latin of Rosenroth says "in alto deportatum."
3. The reference says "and he cast the weight of the lead upon the mouth" of the ephah.
4. Yod, I is related per Tetragrammaton to Chokmah.
5. Anak is ANK, or 1, 50, 20 is 71 and adding 1 for the whole word is 73; and Chesed, ChSD, is 8, 60, 4, or 72.
6. With an iron pen and lead axe, OTh pen, BRZL iron, OPRT lead.
7. Furnace is KUR.
8. Cupellation of silver by lead.
9. See *Kab. Den.*, page 625. Ophereth is 70, 80, 200, 400, or 750.
10. That is to Chokmah.
11. Kol is KL, 20 and 30 is 50; this word means the "all."
12. That is this author used as a symbol of Lead a circle surmounted by a cross of four equal limbs; other Alchymists use this symbol for Antimony, and for Lead use the symbol of Saturn.
13. A brightness as the colour of amber.
14. This name is Jah; or IH, 10 and 5.
15. That is Jesod the foundation or base.
16. This is the usual Kamea of Saturn.
17. Shabtai, ShBTAI, this is Saturn, 713.
18. Lahab, LHB, 37: means flame or point.
19. Arieh or Arjeh is ARIH, or 1, 200, 16, 5, that is 216.

20. Gur, GUR is 3, 6, 200 or 209, in Latin *catulus*.

21. Naaman, is NOMN or 50, 70, 40, 50, or 210; lesser number 21 and then 3.

22. The English Bible omits the name Aram, which is found in the Hebrew.

23. Seven Purifications almost universal in transmutations, refer to the Regimen of the planets.

24. Authorities differ as to whether Gur is referred to the Matter or to the River.

25. AHIH or 1, 5, 10, 5, which is 21.

26. ARI is 1, 200, 10.

27. Naaman preceded by a Vau, V that is Six.

28. Kephir, KPIR; also said to mean a Lioness.

29. Jerek, IRQ; means green colour, herbaceous.

30. One authority adds here "which must yet become black and red."

31. Lebi, LBIA, or 43 : LB means the heart.

32. LISh, 340.

33. Puk, Stibium is native antimony; is PUK, 80, 6, 20, or 106, becoming 7.

34. Shachatz, ShChTz, or 300, 8, 90 ; a lion greedy of its prey.

35. Tzadida, TzDIDA, 90, 4, 10, 4, 1, or 109, lesser 10 and 1 : add one for the word itself and you get 110 or 2.

36. ShChL, 300, 8, 30, giving 338, and then **lesser** number 14 then 5.

37. PRZL ; 80, 200, 7, 30, or 317 or 11 or 2 : this is Chaldaic for the Hebrew Barzel—iron.

CHAPTER VII.

1. Compare *Kab. Den.*, page 455. Jarden, IRDN, 10, 200, 4, 50, or 264 or 12 or 3. All Latin and English versions here write Jarden, but the word is really the Bible word for the river Jordan.

2. That is impure metallic ores.

3. Jeor, IAR. "Jamin" is the right side.

4. Dan or rather Din, DIN, judgment, severity; or is Dan referred to DN, the name of the Tribe.

5. Zachu, ZKU; 7, 20, 6 or 33.

6. Eight; how is this? Jesod is the Ninth Sephira, yet Jesod is ISUD; 10, 60, 6, 4, or 80, lesser number 8.

7. Seder, order, SDR, 264; which equals 33; Zachu multiplied by 8.

8. Compare *Kab. Den.*, page 441. Jesod, ISUD, the Ninth Sephira.

9. El or Al, AL meaning God, is 31; lesser number is 4 of the Tetragrammaton.

10. Cheseph Chai, that is Silver of Life, Quicksilver or Mercury. KSP ChI, or 160 and 18, that is 178; but AL ChI is 1, 30, 8, 10, or 49.

11. Kokab, KUKB, also referred to the planet Mercury. Kokab is 48 and add one for the name, we get 49.

12. Espherica, ASPIRKA; there is a Chaldee ShPR, a root for globe, roundness.

13. MHIThBAL as though it were MI HThBLA or MI AL HThB. Mehetabel was wife of Hadar, King of Edom.

14. Metred or Matred, MTRD; the Gold Maker. Matred was mother of Mehetabel, the wife of the King of Edom. The Kings and Dukes of Edom, who reigned before there was any King over Israel, constitute a deep mystery.

15. Mezahab or more properly Mi-zahab. MI for MIM, the Hebrew name of water.

16. Hadar, HDR; 5, 4, 200, that is 209. Tetragrammaton is 16, which multiplied by 8 is 208.

17. Jesod is 8 as above. Circumcision is Mulah, MVL; 40, 6, 30 or 76, and does not relate to 8 by Gematria.

18. Isaac, ITzChQ; 10, 90, 8, 100, or 208; means laughter.

19. Pegno or Pau, POU; this O is ayin, which in some words has the sound of "gn."
20. Joseph, IVSP, 156.
21. Elohim Chiim, ALHIM ChIIM, the Deities of the Living Ones; both words are of plural form. Elohim is the plural of El—God, and Chiim the plural of ChI—a living one. Elohim is 86 and Chiim 68, they have the same Lesser Number.
22. Mekor majim chiim, MQUR MIIM ChIIM, Mekor, or rather Mequor, is a Fountain.
23. This is the usual form of the Magic Square of 8 related to Mercury.
24. Sar is SR; 60 and 200 or 260, " declined."
25. As if instead of 8 for the second column and 16 for the third, you add 24 for the fourth you obtain 284, whose lesser number is 14 and then 5; and again 292 becomes 13 or 4.

CHAPTER VIII.

1. Compare *Kab. Den.*, page 430. Or Iunah, or Joneh; a dove is IUNH.
2. Knorr von Rosenroth gives Holocaust.
3. Beni is BNI, sons; 2, 50, 10 or 62.
4. Nogah, NUGH, 64, refers to Venus; it means "external splendour."
5. That is, he volatilizes the metals their representatives.
6. Compare *Kab. Den.*, page 456. Jarach or IRICh, which is 10, 200, 10, 8 or 228.
7. Rosenroth adds here: "She is the Shekinah and whether in decrease or at the full, she is a mystery to the student. This increase and decrease are suggested by the name. Irach is referred to the waning moon, and the name Levanah, LBNH, to the Full Moon, when it resembles pure Incense, as in Exodus, c. 30,

v. 34. Levunah Zakah, LBUNH ZKR, and also the Full Moon hath a white colour, but it accepts white light from the Sun. And six Sephiroth are called the Moons." *Sohar, Jethro,* 35, c. 139.

This Levunah means Frankincense, and the root is LBN, meaning White, Zahah is "consumed by fire."

Irach also means "scent" and "smelling" as well as moon and thence month.

"As Luna receives Light from Sol, so does Malkuth from Tiphereth" says the *Liber Pardesh*.

8. Razia, RZIA; 200, 7, 10, 1 are 218, in Latin "arcana."

9. Rabui, RBUI; 200, 2, 6, 10 are 218, in Latin "a multitude."

10. Compare *Kab. Den.*, page 241. Gophrith; GPRIT, 3, 80, 200, 10, 400 are 693. The substance is found native in Palestine.

11. Charutz, CHRUTz; 8, 200, 6, 90 or 304, whose lesser number is 7.

12. Gophritha, GUPRITA; this is 700; the lesser number being 7 also.

13. See Westcott, *Everburning Lamps of the Ancients*, in regard to II. Maccabees, c. 1, v. 19 to 22, where water is changed into fire.

SUPPLEMENT.

It may be useful to students to add the Chaldee and Hebrew names of some other substances used in Alchymic art.

Clay. Tit, TIT; and Chemar, CHMR.
Earth. Aretz, ARTz; and Adamah, ADMH; and Aphar, APR.
Nitre. Nether, NTR.
Salt. Melach, MLCH.

Sand. Chol, ChUL.
Amber. Chashmal, ChShML.
Dew, Thel, ThL; Latin *Ros*.
Vapour, Steam, Aid, AID.
Ashes, Cinis, APR.
Furnace, TNUR and KBRH and KBShN.
Vinegar, Acetum, ChMO, also means Ferment.
Bath, Balneum, MRChTzT.
Glass, Vitrum, ZKUKIT.
Calx, GIR, also means Chalk, Lime and Mortar.
Quintessence, ChMSh TUShIH.
Dissolve, MSH, and also to Melt.
Putrefaction, RQB, and BASh.
Coagula, QBA. Solve, MUG.
Path, NTIB, in the sense of the 32 Paths of Wisdom.
Divination, QSM.
Magician, ChRThM.
Purification, BRR.
Oil, Oleum, IZHR, from its brightness Zohar.
Black, ChM, AIShUN, ShChR.
White, LBN, TzChR, ChUR and QDR.
Red, ADM, and ShRQ.
Blue, TKLT, also means Perfection.
Green, IRUQ, LCh, RONN and DSh.
Life, CHIIM.
Death, MUT.
Immortality; neither Hebrew nor Chaldee has any such root word.

Collectanea Hermetica

EDITED BY

W. WYNN WESTCOTT, M.B., D.P.H.

VOLUME V.

Somnium Scipionis

TRANSLATED INTO ENGLISH

WITH AN ESSAY

"THE VISION OF SCIPIO CONSIDERED AS A FRAGMENT OF THE MYSTERIES"

By L. O.

The Golden Verses of Pythagoras

By A. E. A.

The Symbols of Pythagoras

By S. A.

SOMNIUM SCIPIONIS.
THE VISION OF SCIPIO

BY

MARCUS TULLIUS CICERO.

CICERO, who was almost the most celebrated orator of antiquity, was born B.C. 107, and was educated by Crassus. He served as a Roman warrior under Sylla, and subsequently became a philosopher. After many years he entered political life, becoming Quæstor of Sicily, then Ædile, and finally Consul. At the last he retired to Tusculum, and was assassinated B.C. 43. He left many classical works, among which are the beautiful essays on "Friendship" and on "Old Age." His only mystical work was the *Somnium Scipionis, or Vision of Scipio*, of which a translation by L. O. is here produced, with an Essay upon its connection with the doctrines taught in the ancient Mysteries.

This Scipio was named Africanus the Younger; he had died in B.C. 128; he was the grandson by adoption of Publius Cornelius Scipio Africanus the Elder. The account of this dream or Vision is put into the mouth of the younger Scipio Africanus, who relates that, in early youth, when he first served in Africa he visited the Court of Masinissa, the steady friend of the Romans, and particularly of the Cornelian family. During the feasts and entertainments of the day, the conversation turned on the words and actions of the first great Scipio. His adopted grandson having retired to rest, the Shade of the departed hero appeared to him in sleep, darkly foretold the future events of his life, and encouraged him to tread in the paths of Patriotism and true glory, by announcing the reward prepared in a future state for those who have served their country faithfully in this life. The scene is laid in the suburban garden of the younger Africanus, and the *dramatis personæ* consist of certain intimate friends and acquaintances.

A few literary and suggestive Notes have been added.

THE VISION OF SCIPIO

Translated by L. O.

When I came to Africa, where, as you know, I was Tribune to the Fourth Legion of soldiers, under the Consul Manius Manilius, nothing appeared to me more desirable than that I should meet Masinissa, a Monarch who had ever been most friendly to our family for just reasons. When I came to him, the old man, having embraced me, wept, and, after a pause, looked up to Heaven: "Ah, thanks," said he, "to Thee I render, Oh highest Sun, and to ye other Celestial companions, in that before I depart this life, I am permitted to behold in my own Kingdom and under these skies P. Cornelius Scipio, whose name itself refreshes me: for, never from my soul has the memory of that best and most invincible of men departed!" Then I inquired of him concerning the affairs of his Kingdom, and he of me respecting our Republic; and our day thus passed in lengthened conference. After a royal entertainment our talk again drew out into the far night, when the old man would speak of nothing save the elder Scipio (Africanus Major): everything about him he remembered, not only his deeds, but even his sayings. When, therefore, we parted to retire to rest, what with the journey and our nocturnal sitting, I was more than usually tired and fell sound asleep.

Whereupon (as I believe arising out of the subject of our talk;—for it often happens that our thoughts and conversation produce some such result in sleep as that which Ennius[3] relates to have happened concerning Homer, whom it appears he was frequently accustomed to meditate upon and to talk about during his waking hours) Africanus appeared to me in a form[4] which I recognised more from his bust than from my knowledge of the man himself. When I recognised him, I trembled indeed: he, however, speaking said, "Take courage and banish fear, O Scipio; commit to memory what I have to say."

"Seest thou yonder City, which, compelled by me to submit to the Roman people, yet renews its former wars, unable to remain at peace? (Here he shewed me Carthage from a certain clear and brilliant spot in the celestial heights, full of stars) and to the assault of which thou comest, as yet a mere boy? This City, in two years from the present time, thou as Consul shalt overthrow, and that hereditary name, which hitherto thou bearest from us, shall belong to thee by thine own exertions. When moreover Carthage has been razed by thee, thou shalt effect thy Triumph and be made Censor; then as Legate thou shalt proceed to Egypt, Syria, Asia and Greece, being made Consul a second time during thy absence, and undertaking thy greatest war, destroy Numantia. But when thou are borne upon the triumphal car to the Capitol, thou shalt find the Republic thrown into confusion by the policy of my grandson.[5] Here, O Africanus, it will be necessary for thee to display to the Fatherland the light of thy spirit, thy genius, and thy wisdom; at this period of thy life I see but darkly the course of thy destiny, though when thine age shall have completed eight times seven circuits and returns of the Sun, thus bringing thee to the fatal epoch of thy life[6] by the natural circuit of these two numbers (each of which is held to be perfect, the one from a different reason to the other); to thee alone and to thy name the whole State will turn; to thee, as Senator, all good people, the Latin allies and the Latins themselves shall turn; thou shalt be the one upon whom the whole salvation of the State shall rest, and, lest misfortune befall, it behoves thee as dictator to firmly establish the Republic if you would escape the impious hands[7] of thy kinsmen:" at this portion of the recital Laelius[8] cried out and the others bitterly lamented, but Scipio, smiling slowly, said: "I beseech you not to arouse me from slumber; peace for a little, and hear the rest."

"But, O Africanus, in order that thou mayest be the more devoted to the welfare of the Republic, mark this well: for all those who have guarded, cherished, and assisted their Fatherland, a particular place in Heaven is assigned, where the blessed enjoy everlasting life. For nothing on earth is more acceptable to that supreme Deity who reigns over the whole Universe, than those assemblages and combinations of men united by Law which we call States; the rulers and preservers whereof coming forth from this place, return thither."

At this point, although I was thoroughly terrified, not so much by the fear of death, as by the treachery of my own kinsmen, I asked notwithstanding whether he himself was really alive and my father Paulus and others whom we believed to be annihilated?

"Yea," said he, "in very truth, those still live who have flown forth from the bonds of the body as from a prison: for indeed, what is called your life, is but a death! Why, dost thou not see thy father Paulus coming to thee?"

At that sight I indeed burst forth into a flood of tears: he, on the other hand, embracing, kissed me and forbade me to weep; and then, when my tears had been repressed, and I began to be able to speak, "Prithee tell me," said I, "most revered and excellent father: Since this is life, as I have heard Africanus say, Why do I tarry upon Earth? Why do I not hasten to come hither to you?"

"It may not be," he replied, "for, unless that Deity who is the Lord of this Universe which thou beholdest, shall liberate thee from the prison of your body,[10] hither approaching, it is not possible to come. For men are born under this Law to be faithful guardians of that Globe which thou seest in the midst of this Universe and which is called the Earth: and a Soul has been given to them from those sempiternal fires which you call Stars and Constellations; these being spherical and globular bodies, animated with divine Souls, pursue their circling orbits with marvellous celerity. Wherefore, O Publius,[12] both by thee and all pious persons, the Soul should be retained in the keeping of the body: not without His command, by whom that Soul is given to you, must it depart from mortal life, lest you should appear to be untrue to that duty to Mankind which has been assigned to you by the Deity. But do thou cultivate justice and piety, O Scipio, following in the steps of thy Grandsire and of myself, who begat thee. These qualities, although excellent among parents and relations, become still more noble when practised towards one's Country: through this life lies the road to Heaven and to the assemblage of those, who have already lived upon earth and now, released from the body, inhabit this place which thou seest (this Sphere shone forth with the most resplendent brightness amid blazing stars) and which, after the Greeks, you call the Milky Way. From this place all other bodies appeared to my gaze exceedingly bright and marvellous. There were, moreover, those Stars which are never seen from Earth: and the magnitude of all of them were such as we have never suspected: among these I beheld the smallest[14] to be the farthest from Heaven and the nearest to Earth, shining with a borrowed Light. Moreover, the spheres of the Stars far transcended the size of the Earth. Thus, the Earth itself already appeared small to me, so that I was grieved to observe how small a part of its surface we in reality occupy."[15]

As I continued to gaze steadfastly, Africanus continuing said, "How long wilt thy mind remain rivetted to the Earth? Dost thou not behold into how glorious a Temple thou art come? Now know that the Universe consists of nine circles or rather Spheres, all connected together, one of which is celestial and the furthest off, embracing all the rest, the supreme Deity preserving and governing the others. In this sphere are traced the eternal revolutions of the Stars and to it are subject the seven spheres which revolve backwards with a contrary motion to that of the Celestial Sphere. The first (of these Seven) Spheres is occupied[17] by the Star which on Earth is called Saturn. Next comes the sphere of that splendid Star, salutary and fortunate to the human race, called Jupiter. Then comes the Red Sphere, terrible to the Earth, which you call Mars. Following beneath these spheres, and in almost the middle region, is placed the Sun, the Leader, Chief and Governor of the other Lights, the mind[18] of the World and the organizing principle,—of such wondrous magnitude that it illuminates and impregnates every part of the Universe with its Light. The Spheres of Venus and Mercury in their respective courses follow the Sun as companions. In the lowest Sphere the Moon revolves illumined by the rays of the Sun. Below this in truth nothing exists which is not subject to death and decay, save indeed the Souls, which by the gift of the Gods are bestowed upon the human race. Above the Moon all things are eternal, but the sphere of the Earth, which occupies a middle place and comes ninth[19] does not move: it is the lowest and to it all ponderable bodies are born by their own gravity."

When I had recovered from my amazement at the sight of these things, "What," said I, "is this sweet and wondrous melody which fills my ears?"

"This," said he, "is that harmony, which, affected by the mingling of unequal intervals, yet notwithstanding in harmonious proportions and with reason so separated, is due to the impulse and movement of the spheres themselves: the light with the heavier tones combined,—the various sounds uniformly going to make up one grand symphony."[20] For, not with silence, can such motions be urged forward, and Nature leads us to the conclusion that the extremes give forth a low note at the one end and a high note at the other. Thus the celestial sphere, whose motion in its starlight course is more rapid, gives forth a sharp and rousing sound: the gravest tone being that of the lunar sphere, which is lowest; but the Earth, the ninth sphere, remains immovable, always fixed in the lowest seat encompassing the middle place of the Universe. Moreover, the motions of those eight spheres which are above the earth, and of which the force of two[21] is the same, cause seven sounds supported by regular intervals; which number is the connecting principle of almost all things. Learned men, having imitated this divine mystery with stringed instruments and vocal harmonies, have won for themselves a return to this place, just as others, who, endowed with superior wisdom, have cultivated the divine sciences even in human life."

"Now to this melody the stopped ears of men have become deaf;[22] nor is there any duller sense in you. Just as at that place which is called Catadupa,[23] where the Nile falls from the highest Mountains, the people living there lose the sense of hearing on account of the magnitude of the sound, so, indeed, such a tremendous volume of sound arises from the rapid revolution of the whole Cosmos that the ears of men are not capable of receiving it, just as you are unable to look straight at the Sun whose rays would blind the eye and conquer the sense."

Filled with wonder at these things, my eyes ever and anon wandered back to Earth.

Hereupon Africanus said: "I perceive that even now you gaze upon the habitation and abode of mortals. But, if it appear as small to thee, as indeed it is, thus seen, strive ever after these heavenly things and lightly esteem those of earth. For what glory or renown really worthy of being sought after canst thou derive from the mouths of men. Thou seest that the earth is inhabited in scattered places confined within narrow limits, such inhabited regions are in themselves mere specks upon its surface with vast wildernesses intervening: and those who dwell upon the earth are not only separated thus, so that no communication is possible amongst them from the one to the other, but they occupy positions partly oblique, partly transverse, partly even opposite to yours; from these you can certainly hope for no glory. Also thou wilt perceive this same earth to be, as it were, circumscribed and encircled by zones, two of which, the most widely separated and situated at each end under the very poles of heaven, are ice-bound as thou seest[24]: while the middle and largest zone is burnt up with the heat of the Sun. Two zones are habitable, one of which lies to the South, those who dwell therein planting footsteps opposite to your own, and having nothing to do with your race. As to the other zone which you inhabit, and which is subject to the North wind, see how very slender a part has to do with you: for the whole surface inhabited by your race, restricted towards the poles and wider laterally, is indeed but a small island surrounded by the sea, which you call on earth the Atlantic, the Great Sea, or Ocean. Yet, notwithstanding its name, it is but small as thou seest. How then is it possible that from these known and cultivated countries either thy name or that of any of us can cross those Caucasian Mountains, which thou seest, or pass beyond the

Ganges? Who, in the remaining parts of the East, in the uttermost regions of the wandering Sun, either in Northern or Southern Climes, will hear thy name? So then, with these parts taken away, dost thou indeed perceive within what narrow limits your glory seeks to spread itself; and how long even will those who sing your praises continue to do so?

"Yea, indeed, if generations hence posterity shall seek to perpetuate the fame of anyone of us handed down from father to son, yet notwithstanding, on account of fire and flood, which will inevitably happen at certain fixed periods[26] of time, we are unable to attain lasting renown, much less eternal glory. Moreover, of what importance are the things which shall be said concerning thee by those to be born hereafter, when no one who existed before will then be alive? More especially, when of those same men who are to come, not one will be able to remember the events of even one year. Now, according to common custom, men usually measure the year merely by the return of the sun, or, in other words, by the revolution of one star. But when the whole of the constellations shall return to the original positions from which they once set forth, thus restoring at long intervals the original configuration of the Heavens, then can that be truly called 'the Great Year,'[27] within which period, I scarcely dare say how many generations of men are comprised. For, just as in time past, when the Soul of Romulus entered into these sacred abodes, the Sun appeared to fail and be extinguished, so when the Sun shall again fail in the same position and at the same time, then, when the Signs of the Zodiac shall have returned to their original position, and the Stars are recalled, the cycle of the Great Year shall be accomplished; of this enormous period of time, know that not a twentieth part has yet passed away.[28]

"Wherefore, if thou despairest of a speedy return to

this quarter, wherein all things are prepared for great and excellent men, pray of what value is that human glory which can scarcely endure the smallest part of one cycle? And so, if you would look on high and fix your gaze on this state and your eternal home, thou shalt pay no heed to vulgar talk, neither allow thy actions to be influenced by the hope of human rewards. True virtue for its own sake should lead thee to real glory. Leave to others the care of ascertaining what they may say of you: they will assuredly speak of you beyond all doubt. Human fame is wholly restricted within these narrow limits which thou seest, and never at any time has anyone gained immortal renown, for that is impossible through the annihilation of men and the oblivion of posterity."[29]

Whereon I said, "If indeed O, Africanus, for those who have deserved well of their country a Path, as it were, lies open to Heaven[30]—although from my youth up I have followed in the footsteps of yourself and my father, and never tarnished your great renown—now nevertheless, with such a prospect before me, I will strive much more vigilantly."

"Strive on," said he, "with the assurance that it is not you who are subject to death, but your body. For thou art not what this form appears to be, but the real man is the thinking principle of each one—not the bodily form which can be pointed out with the finger.[31] Know this, then, that thou art a God,[32] inasmuch as Deity is that which has Will, sensation, memory, foresight, and who so rules, regulates and moves the body to which his charge is committed, just as the supreme Deity does the Universe, and as the Eternal God directs this Universe, which is in a certain degree subject to decay, so a sempiternal Soul moves the frail body.

"Now, that which is always in motion is eternal, whereas that which only communicates motion, and which itself is put in motion by some other cause, must necessarily cease when the motive impulse is withdrawn. Accordingly that alone which moves spontaneously because it is ever all itself, never indeed ceases to move, and is moreover the source of motion in all things. Now a primary cause is not derived from any other cause; for forth from that do all things proceed, and from no other. That which springs from something else cannot be the primary cause, and if this indeed never had a commencement, neither will it ever have an end. For the primal cause once destroyed could neither be generated afresh from any other thing, nor itself produce anything else: for all things must necessarily proceed from the primal cause. This eternal principle of all Motion arises out of that which is moved by itself and of itself, and cannot therefore be born or perish; or else of necessity the whole heavens must collapse, and all Nature come to a standstill, unable any longer to derive the impulse by which it was set in motion at the first.

"Since, accordingly, it is manifest that that is eternal which moves of itself, who will deny this eternal principle to be a natural attribute of Souls. For everything which is moved by an external impulse is inanimate: but that, on the other hand, which energizes from within is truly animated, and this is the peculiar operation of the Soul. If then the Soul is the one thing above all, which is self motive, it certainly is not born, but eternal. Do thou then exercise this Soul of thine in the noblest pursuits: solicitude and care for the welfare of one's country are the best: for, animated and controlled by these sentiments, the Soul passes more swiftly to this sphere—its true home. And this may be the more speedily achieved if, while imprisoned in the body, it shall rise superior to terrestrial limitations, and by the contemplation of those things which are beyond the body, it shall abstract itself to the greatest degree from its earthly tabernacle.

"For the Souls of men who have delivered themselves over to the desires of the body, and of those women who, as abettors, have surrendered themselves, and by the impulse of passions obedient to sensual gratifications, have violated the laws of God and of Man, once liberated from the body, are whirled around this world, and such tortured Souls will not return to this place, save after many centuries."

Here he ceased, and I awoke from sleep.

THE VISION OF SCIPIO CONSIDERED AS A FRAGMENT OF THE MYSTERIES.

By L. O.

"To some he gave the ability of receiving the knowledge of Light, which may be taught, but to others, even when asleep, he extended the fruit of his strength."—SYNESIOS.

As a literary production merely, this is one of the most beautiful and imaginative compositions bequeathed to us by Cicero. A careful examination of the ideas unfolded in its few short pages will prove instructive to every earnest student of the Mysteries—those great Institutions of Antiquity, guardians of a sacred science, the echoes of which still linger herein. This opinion has been entertained by more than one commentator upon the strength of internal evidence, and constitutes the *raison d'être* of the present translation.

The Vision of Scipio is suggestive, resuming as it does so many of the leading conceptions involved in the mystical philosophy of the old world, and, in this respect, it but rarely happens that so much is conveyed in so brief a fragment. To those, however, who have grasped the many beauties of the Magian philosophy, or such traces of it as appear discernible in the lapse of time, any attempt to reconstruct the scattered fragments which remain to us must be welcome, and hence the object of this article is to examine the leading conceptions of the *Somnium*, in order to arrive at a coherent view of the philosophy which underlies it. That philosophy, it is reasonable to conjecture, was alike the system inculcated in the ancient Mysteries of every nation—those Mysteries being considered as the organised endeavour of illuminati to elucidate the great problems of Life and Death, the nature of the Soul and its relation to the Deity.

Men have ever found themselves face to face with these great difficulties, striving to unravel the skein of life with all the poverty of language, and the restrictions of human thought. But human thought alone is powerless for such sublime ascents—a higher faculty of the Soul being requisite. "Strive," says the Zoroastrian* Oracle, "to understand the Intelligible which exists beyond the Mind, with the extended flame of an extended intellect."

The solution of these momentous questions is of the first importance, because of the moral consequences involved; morality being largely modified in scope and direction by the conclusions arrived at in philosophy. Thus the influence of a system of thought purely of the intellect, must obviously differ from that resulting in the case of a Religio-philosophical system: while it is worthy of remark that no influence has proved so powerful in the direction of human affairs—no sentiment so ineradicably implanted in the human breast—as that of Religion. Here lies the supreme bond of union between all human beings—the most highly vitalized sentiment of which humanity is capable.

It seems probable that the Mysteries—which were almost cosmopolitan †—had for object to draw men

* *The Chaldean Oracles* form Volume VI. of this Series.

† Vide *L'immortalité de l'ame chez les anciens Egyptiens*, by Wiedemann.

closer to each other by bonds of union deeper than those of mere worldly interest, and this was only possible by an appeal at once to both the philosophic and religious sides of the nature. Before the instinct of veneration had been dwarfed, as, generally speaking, it has now largely become, and, at a time when the whole activities of the higher mind functioned, so to speak, under the ægis of Religion, it is not surprising that the Mysteries should have exerted an enormous influence in the lands where they were established.

What, it will be asked, was the nature of the revelations vouchsafed to participants, or the benefit to be derived from initiation therein? Our information on this subject is confined to certain meagre historical details, from which we gather that these Institutions professedly existed to celebrate the mythological histories associated with certain divinities. That they were held in universal esteem and treated with profound reverence is certain—a fact which sufficiently points to the serious nature of these activities, and the lofty intentions which animated them. Indeed, it is difficult to understand how any suggestions to the contrary could gain credence in face of the fact that the most cultured and luminous minds in the past have contributed to elucidate our reflections upon this subject—all the resources of poetry and philosophy in the early days of the world being mainly burthened with this one theme in some shape or form.

The best thought of the ancient world was, to a large extent, the Theosophy we know to-day in another dress. From Plato to Proclus, from Homer to Ovid—the thoughts of such men have lived after them, and even if to-day largely misunderstood, they nevertheless succeeded in investing the traditions of their time with a significance which none but a student of the Mysteries can hope to understand.

The peculiar Mythologies of Egypt and Greece respectively were but the machinery of a symbolism, the interpretation of which formed alike the science of the Soul and the system of the Mysteries. Herein lay concealed those great truths which serve to explain the immediate mysteries of our environment, the development and elucidation of which served to enlighten and astonish the Neophyte; these culminating in appropriate theurgic formulæ, conferred a clearer hope of immortality—a perception of the Universal Presence, such as the *Entheast**** alone could derive.

Needless to say that such results are not attainable by any process of thought *per se :* all that thought can do is to dimly apprehend a higher faculty of the Soul—a mode of perception transcending the merely intellectual.

In the Vision of Scipio this higher faculty takes the form of a clairvoyant perception, a marvellous insight superior to all bodily limitations, whereby the consciousness is brought into *rapport* with other worlds than those normally perceived by the senses.

Apuleius, who was initiated into the Isiac Mysteries, thus refers to his experience : " I approached the confines of death, and having trod on the threshold of Proserpine, I returned therefrom, being borne through all the elements. At midnight I saw the Sun shining with its brilliant Light, and I approached the presence of the Gods beneath and the Gods above, and stood near and worshipped them. Behold, I have related to you things of which, though heard by you, you must necessarily remain ignorant."†

Although the initiates themselves appear to have remained true to their trust and we are thus denied a direct statement, professedly expounding the system

---

* A word used by the Neoplatonic writers meaning " Immersed in God."

† *Metamorphosis of Apuleius*, 11th Book.

in question, there yet remain to us a collection of utterances attributed to Zoroaster and others, known as the Zoroastrian Oracles, which were continually appealed to by the ablest commentators* on the Mysteries and are of great assistance in solving this difficult problem. These fragments tersely resume many of the most daring conceptions of mature thinkers and theurgists long ago—conceptions which endow Religion with enterprise and the Soul with God-like attributes. Little wonder then at the old proverb "Man, know thyself,"—when that knowledge involved so much. Such self-knowledge—the most profound homage that man can render to the divinity—was by no means an analysis of the *human self*, but an attempt to consider the principles working in the great Universe around us as all reflected in the total constitution of each human being. It is for this reason that the Vision of Scipio is *apparently* devoted to an exposition of the divine Potencies operating in the Universe around us.

The Gods, in the antient conception, around which so many classic traditions have clustered, were representations through images and similitudes of certain mighty powers, considered to exist between Man and the Supreme Principle: these powers, although rooted in this Principle, were yet regarded as possessing energies distinct from their ineffable cause. "These mighty powers," says Taylor, "are called by the Poets a Golden Chain, on account of their connection with each other and incorruptible nature, ... they are rooted in this Supreme Principle like trees in the Earth, which have a distinct energy of their own at the same time that they energize in conjunction with their cause."†

* *Vide* the writings of Proclus on the Philosophy of Plato, also of Plotinus and Porphyry.

† Taylor's *Miscellany*, p. 129.

But what, it may be asked, about the Supreme Principle of things, that which is so incomparable to its attributes:—was this not lost sight of in the multitude of divinities? "To that God," says Porphyry, "who is above all things, neither external speech ought to be addressed, nor yet that which is inward, when it is defiled by the passion of the soul, but we should venerate him in pure silence and through pure conceptions of his nature."

With this view in mind the student is led to regard the Pantheon of any Nation as a collection of symbols, more or less appropriate, and intended to convey some idea of the totality of divine attributes.

It is moreover comparatively easy to discover certain fundamental similarities which may be said to underlie the great classic Pantheons, and such comparisons clearly indicate a unity of conception which enables us to identify as essentially one and the same the Mystical Systems pervading alike Chaldea and Greece on the one hand, and Egypt on the other.

The divinities of Mythology were symbols;—symbols which translated to the trained perception of the initiate the factors of his great equation, those supramundane forces which are most reverently defined as deific. One in many and many in One. It was the intimate knowledge of these and of the various entities correlated therewith which constituted the "Divine Sciences" to which reference is made in the Vision of Scipio.

These Divine Sciences, by the practice of which wise men have attained release from the gross and the nether, gaining the upper air and endless light, were formulated on Universal Truths, proceeding from Universals to Particulars. The unspeakable harmony in the bosom of the world which causes all things to sympathise with all, justified the Hermetic Axiom,

Qui se cognoscit, in se omnia cognoscit,* and hence our consideration of Macrocosmic truths implies in reality much more than their merely phenomenal observance would seem to warrant.

The nine Spheres alluded to in this Vision, and which for the purposes of study are more properly regarded as either seven or ten—are primal powers and the roots alike of force and form. Hence the "divine sciences" derived from the decimal numeration rest upon a basis of mathematical accuracy—mathematics being an exact science. Here we find the first traces of the Kabalistic Sephiroth,—three Triads of Powers resumed in a Tenth,—the Ennead or procession of nine Gods occurring alike in Chaldean and Egyptian Theology as well as in the Platonic system.†

This idea was no doubt based upon the principle that as the numbers from 1 to 10 formed the base of every possible numerical variation, so every manifested thing in Nature is ultimately referable to these Ten primordial powers, for number guides form and lies at the root of sound. Pursuing this conception further, it will be seen that the linear equivalents of numbers 1 and 2 cannot of themselves produce a concrete form: for the first would be represented by one straight line, and the second by two straight lines, neither of which can enclose a space. These two numbers must therefore ever remain abstractions, and the succeeding number Three become the first concrete expression: on the other hand,

---

* Who knows himself knows all things in himself.

† Compare also the Jupiter, Neptune and Pluto of the Greeks and Romans ruling respectively over three great Realms—Heaven, "The Sea," and Infernal Regions. Also in *Lydus (de Mensibus)* p. 121, Taylor, we read "That the number nine is divine, receiving its completion from three triads, and preserving the summits of Theology according to the Chaldaic philosophy as Porphyry informs us."

the number Ten is a synthetical return to Unity, or the commencement of a fresh series. It is for this reason that the objective powers of manifestation are septenary, and these, corresponding to their geometrical forms, are also allied to colours and sounds, as suggested in the *Somnium*.

These Seven divine forces were anciently supposed to reside in the Planets, the ruling intelligences of which were thus regarded as the Vicegerents of the Sephirotic powers; and the administration not only of the whole physical world, but even of human affairs, came to be attributed to the celestial wanderers.

This Septenate—called also the "Tree of Life"—was traced in every created thing—in the Animal, Vegetable, and Mineral departments. This theoretical procession, from primal natures down to the more complex, also laid the foundation of Alchemy, for some subjects, from the simple integrity of their nature, were considered as peculiarly appropriate vehicula for the Anima Mundi.

It is important to notice in the Vision of Scipio, that the Planets are regarded as in a way distinct from the Spheres within which they energize, and here also lies a conception which will repay attention.* According to Hermetic teaching, everything which has culminated in idea or materiality—in form, *per se*, or its physical expression—is regarded as ensphered, and thereby individualized: such intangible and magnetic circuli are conceived to be forces evolving form—form being static force. Each individual or entity—whether a stone, a plant, an animal, or a man—energizes according to its nature, *i.e.*, gives expression to the archetype of its sphere, and this is the work of evolution: while the

* "According to the Orphic theology, each of the planets is fixed in a luminous ethereal sphere called ολοτης or *Wholeness*, because it is a part with a total subsistence and is analogous to the sphere of the fixed stars." *Metamorphosis of Apuleius*, eleventh book, Taylor's translation.

crown of manifested life is naturally considered to be the production of spiritually perfect man—the form of forms.

In just the same way as the planetary spheres are here said to be comprised within the sphere of the fixed Stars, so all entities are vested in the Anima Mundi in varying degree, according to vehiculum; in the higher kingdoms increased complexity obtains, culminating in the human being—as it is said, " Oh, Man of a daring nature, thou subtil production ! "*

The Unity of the Divine One—" circumscribing the Heavens with convex form "—which is considered to underlie all manifestation, is a necessary conception to the doctrines of Macrocosm and Microcosm, the greater and lesser worlds: that which is a part, of necessity partakes of the nature of the whole, and thus every entity is a microcosm, or little world, reflecting the greater world or macrocosm after a certain formula—but reflection involves reversal. This latter truth, resumed also in the old axiom, " As above, so below, but after another manner," is probably the explanation of more than one incongruity in the *Somnium*.

Man being made in the likeness of the Gods, the planetary forces find their representatives in the constitution of his being, but whereas in macrocosmic action their operation is, as it were, without within—in the human organism it is rather within without, and not only are the Seven great Sephirotic powers distributed throughout the entire human system as a whole, but also the three worlds in Man, *viz.*, the head, the chest, and vital parts, are said to each contain Seven important centres or orifices.†

* See Vol. VI. *The Zoroastrian Oracles.*

† *Vide Sepher Yetzirah*, Westcott, and Mather's *Kabbalah Unveiled* p. 50.

In the ancient conception, the Planets were the presidential heads of the elemental permutations—exciting forces which communicated their own peculiar energies through one or another of the Signs of the Zodiac. To understand the action of the Planets, it is necessary to consider what these Signs of the Zodiac are. The celestial definition is of course familiar to everyone, but that does not throw light on the Chaldean theory. The twelve constellations were related to the three conditions of each of the four elements of the ancients, thus making twelve elemental variations in all: these are not, however, to be confounded with the Fire, Air, Water, and Earth usually recognized under these terms, but to the subtil æthers underlying them, and necessary for the manifestation of the gross elements. Thus the fiery Signs, *viz.*, Aries, Leo, and Sagittarius, were all considered to transmit the influence of subtil Fire, but in three different conditions, these being respectively the Fiery, Watery, and Airy degrees of ætheric Fire—and so on with each of the other elemental triplicities.

In one complete diurnal revolution of the Sun, the successive influences of the whole of these twelve constellations are transmitted around the circuit of our Earth: this would give an *average* time of two hours to each Sign, during which its elemental current would be operative.* These influences are intensified, or the reverse, by the presence or absence of the planets from the Signs, because some planets are considered to harmonize with the elemental vibrations of certain Signs, and *vice versâ*.

This, in its human application, will be the better understood when it is stated that the four elements referred to were especially connected with the constitution of the human being, and the proportion in which these

---

* Compare the Eastern theory of the Tatwas.

mingled would thus regulate the temperament of the individual under the regimen of the planets. According to the Hermetic system, it is only when these ætheric vibrations are disposed with due interval and proper balance that the spirit can be rendered manifest—the dead Osiris be raised to life, and the Lord of this World enter into his Kingdom. Some Souls lack qualities in which others abound, but the perfect man is fully representative. The elemental constitution of the individual is derived from the vivific fountains of Nature's energies: the Zodiacal hierarchies having successively endowed the human race at certain stages of its evolution, under the presidency of the Sephirotic powers.

The history of human evolution passing in its different phases, from the blackness of putrefaction "through all the colours," to the golden glory of spiritual perfection, presents a perfect parallel with the Alchemical process of the "Great Work," with which, indeed, in a major aspect it is identical. The period of the Annus Magnus, or Great Year, comprising 25,868 solar years, or thereabouts, is that of one complete "circulation," for a minor revolution of the Zodiacal powers is both begun and finished within that time. The great celestial phenomena thus become coincident with the progress of the Race, and its final apotheosis approximately predicable.

The Earth is now under the dominion of Sorrow and Sadness: "When, Oh Lord of the Universe, shall she turn from her evil ways, and *again* behold Thy face?"

"The music of the Spheres,"*—a doctrine attributed to Pythagoras (who probably learnt it from the Egyptians)—is another cardinal Mystery tenet: by the skilful blending of these celestial harmonies, we are

---

* *Vide* "Creation by Voice and the *Ennead* of Hermopolis," Maspero.

told, sages achieve their apotheosis. This is an allusion to the secret of the Lagash (mystical speech or incantation) and probably has the same significance as the Seven Thunders of Revelations (accompanied by lightning). As it is written, "Thy splendour, Oh Lord, shall fill the ends of the Universe!" But, in addition to this, the subtil forces of our spiritual being have long been denoted by the Rainbow of Glory, our perception of which is the promise of a new life.

This blessed vision has been vouchsafed to other Seers of the World. Hai Ebn Yokdhan also perceived and described the essences of those Spheres: in each " he saw distinct immaterial essences, like the image of the Sun reflected from one glass to another, according to the order of the Spheres . . . in all he discovered infinite beauty, brightness and pleasure, such as neither eye hath seen, nor ear heard, nor hath it entered into the heart of man . . . except those who have attained it or *experimentally known it.*"*

No wonder then at the exclamation of the younger Scipio, " *Quid moror in terris ? Quin huc ad vos venire propero ?* "†

To so reasonable a suggestion as this the reply given is not one which it is easy to appreciate. Upon this head Plato observes:—" The instruction in the doctrine given in the Mysteries that we human beings are in a kind of prison, and that we ought not to free ourselves from it or seek to escape, appears to me difficult to be understood, and not easy to apprehend."‡

On the other hand, it is of course not clear that the suicide really escapes from his prison by reason of

---

* *Vide Platonist*, Vol. III., p. 335.

† " Why tarry upon the earth ? Why do I not hasten to come to thee ? "

‡ *Phædo* 16.

having put off the material body: the explanation appears to be that the term of our life period is imposed by the astral forces prior to birth, and is therefore not dependent for its determination on physical circumstance during the individual career. The result therefore of such an abrupt termination of human life as that involved by suicide,* would be to transfer the life energies to the astral centres where they would still be operative, thereby enormously intensifying the unimpeded phantasy of excarnate life to which the Soul of the suicide would be subject.

In early life the disciples of the magi learnt to resolve the bonds of proscription, and by loosening the ungirders of the Soul, to enter the immeasurable region.

"Explore the River of the Soul," says the Oracle, "so that, having become a servant to the body, you "may again rise to the order from which you descended, "joining works to sacred reason."

The Magian and Hermetic philosophies appear to have persistently considered the body as the charnel house of the Soul, "occultly intimating that the death of the Soul was nothing more than a profound union with the ruinous bonds of the body."†

Perplexing possibly, but none the less is it a great truth that the exterior and sensuous life is death to the highest energies of the Soul, *for all divine natures are incorporeal.*

This identification of the spiritual and, comparatively speaking, immortal being, with the impermanent and fleeting nature, was overcome by the purifications. The method adopted seems to have been that, after a certain period of rigour of life and practice of the virtues, the latter were, so to speak, confirmed and established by

---

* *Vide Eleusinian and Bacchic Mysteries*, p. 31

† Taylor.

initiation into the Sacred Mysteries. Julian says, "The Oracles of the Gods declare that through purifying ceremonies, not the Soul only, but bodies themselves become worthy of receiving much assistance and health: 'for (say they) the mortal vestment of bitter matter will by these means be preserved.'"*

According to Plato, "Purification is to be derived from the five mathematical disciplines, *viz*., from Arithmetic, Geometry, Stereometry, Music and Astronomy." But the parts of initiation into the sacred Mysteries were also five, and the first of these parts consisted of the purification. "The fifth gradation is the most perfect felicity . . . and according to Plato an assimilation to divinity as far as it is possible to mankind."† It is possible that this five-fold initiation had reference to the regimen of the four elements of the ancients and the Eternal Spirit operating therein.‡

The Hermetic doctrine, which explains and resumes these ideas, considers these four Elements to intervene, as it were, between man and the divine Spirit. They are the Zones immediately penetrated by Souls departing this life, and their period of detention therein is regulated by the past spent life. Some few Souls coming forth pure, traverse these without let or hindrance and others require a long purification therein. The following allegorical fragment of Empedocles, cited by Plutarch, is doubtless a true echo of the ancient Mystery teaching concerning this matter. Speaking of the unpurified Souls which enter these Regions, he thus describes the treatment they undergo: "The ethereal force pursues them towards the Sea. The Sea vomits them forth upon its shores, the Earth in turn flings them upwards

---

* *Julian Orat.* V., p. 334. † *Mathematica*, Theon of Smyrna.
‡ *Vide Hermes in Asclepios*, Part III.

to the untiring Sun, and the Sun again drives them back into the Whirlwind of Space. Thus all the elements toss them from one to another, and all hold them in horror."*

Purity of Soul is therefore a *sine quâ non* to all, who, while yet upon the Earth, would come " forth from the bands of body step by step." But purity itself is not sufficient, it must be accompanied by Intelligence and Will: Intelligence to direct the life to the highest Good, Will to preserve the "equilibrium of balance,"—that steady mean between two opposing forces, which to pursue is indeed difficult.

The exhortation to devote attention to divine things, while faithfully performing the duties of practical life, is one which must echo universal response. The calms of lofty contemplation expand our being, enlarging the purview of life, and the true dignity of the Soul is alone maintained when in alliance with its own divine summit. For not until the Spirit has penetrated beyond the limitations of body, and the mind been raised amid the stately solitudes of the Universal Temple, can the Man be said to be really Man, or the " Mercury of the philosophers " " truly animated."

The value of right motive in the direction of human ife is forcibly exemplified in the *Somnium*, and while the noblest activities in incarnation are recognised to be those which benefit collective interests, yet the fallacy of identifying the self with a life of even political celebrity or warlike achievement for their own sake, is clearly shown; personal fame is but the meteoric gleam flashing at intervals down the avenues of time, and cannot permanently endure. The cataclysms of Water and Fire, which at regular intervals visit our Earth, are vicissitudes too sweeping and vast in their nature to

---

* *Asclepios*, Part X.

permit the unbroken continuity of the human race; these "baptisms" of the two primal elements confirm and initiate each new phase in the great work of the world's perfectionment: marking stages alike in the spiritual history of Mankind.

The human Soul—the child of the Night of time—tends ever to the phenomenal and transient on the one hand, and the noumenal and essential on the other: situated between the divine and the animal, it is assimilable unto either. The channel to the other world is a still-covered way—often impassible, formed of spiritual aspirations—stepping-stones across the River of Lethe. This efflorescence of the human mind opens up a pathway into Heaven, a means whereby the identity may be transferred to the higher spheres by those who, while yet in the body, study the divine science. This off-shoot of the "Tree of Life" was, in the Kabbalistic initiation, resolvable into a septenary of perfections, reflecting the glories of the Seven Heavens, denoted respectively as Wisdom and Understanding, Mercy and Severity, Beauty, Glory and Victory.

The great revelation vouchsafed to the illuminati of all ages, and which has been the constant experience of Seers and initiates throughout the past, is a perception of Light—a brilliance unperceived by the normal senses—compared to which physical illumination is but darkness. It is this LVX AOUR or Limitless Light pervading the primeval vastnesses of Universal Nature, the attainment of which confers unspeakable content upon the "subterranean workers"—dwellers in this material sphere—for it is the divine radix of all things. "The mortal who approaches the Fire shall receive a Light from divinity: for unto the persevering mortal the blessed Immortals are swift!"

NOTES

ON THE

SOMNIUM SCIPIONIS.

1. M. Manilius was introduced as a sharer in the dialogue.
2. The *just causes* were that the elder Scipio had amply rewarded Massinissa, Prince of Numidia, for his fidelity in the Second Punic War.
3. Ennius not only said that Homer used to appear to him in dreams, but also that he was indeed a reincarnation of Homer.
4. That is, his adoptive grandfather appeared to him; but as Africanus the Elder had died when our Scipio was but a year old, he could have had no idea of his personal appearance.
5. Tiberius Gracchus, a Tribune of Rome, died B.C. 133.
6. That is fifty-six years of age.
    Seven was esteemed venerable, holy, divine and motherless. See Westcott on *Numbers*, p. 31. Eight was called Perfect, being the first cube; it is the only evenly even number of the decad.
7. Scipio was found dead in bed in B.C. 128, murdered by order of Caius Gracchus, and it is said that the chamber door was opened by his wife, Sempronia, to give admission to the assassins.
8. Lælius was a character seen as an actor in the vision.

9. Paulus Æmilius, the conqueror of Perseus, son of Philip King of Macedon, was his natural father, but our Scipio was adopted by the son of the Elder Scipio Africanus.

10. A condemnation of suicide, which deprived one of the entry to the Heaven, before mentioned.

11. The heavenly bodies are inhabited by egos in certain states of progress, but not necessarily by men, perhaps by those higher than men.

12. Publius Cornelius Æmilianus Scipio was the full name of the dreamer; Africanus Minor was added by his admirers.

13. This heaven was in the Via Lactea.

14. The Moon, which is not itself a luminary, but is illuminated by the Sun.

15. The Roman Empire was but a small spot of the whole exposed surface of the earth.

16. Eight similar spheres enveloped in a ninth vast and glorious envelope.

17. Note the distinction between the Sphere and the Planet pertaining to it.

18. Mens; in ancient occult works, this word is of far higher import than our word, *mind*. Compare the Chaldaic philosophy in Stanley's *History of Philosophy*.

19. G. R. S. Mead in his remarks on the *Somnium*, calls attention to this paragraph as demonstrating the early existence in Europe of the present Theosophic system. Of the Nine, omitting the first universal sphere, and the last, the Earth, there remain Seven types, which are traced in Man as the Seven human Principles.

20. This is a statement of the Pythagorean doctrine of the "Music of the Spheres," so frequently referred to in occult works. In this consideration refer to the first chapters of the *Timæus* of Plato.

21. G. R. S. Mead suggests Mercury and Venus.

22. The hearing of this Music being constant, is not perceived by men.

23. The Great Cataract.

24. H. P. Blavatsky suggested that at the true poles this was not so.

25. Island: the word is *Insula* in all the Latin versions I have seen. Mead reads *Infula*, a strip.

26. H. P. Blavatsky's Theosophic cosmology states that the dominant races are successively overthrown by alternate cataclysms of water and fire. The words are indeed here "eluviones exustionesque."

27. The Romans knew of this Great Cycle of rather more than 25,000 years. Hipparchus noted the Precession of the Equinoxes, which forms a reason for this cycle.

28. Only about 600 years had passed.

29. Kill out ambition, is the burden of this passage; both Western and Eastern schools of Occult Science dwell on the need of subjugating the lower Self.

30. Even patriotism is not the Highest Path. Compare the Thirty-two Paths of *Sepher Yetzirah*.

31. The constant theme of the Mystic, but one utterly neglected by the man in the street.

32. A truly Rosicrucian idea.

THE GOLDEN VERSES & THE SYMBOLS OF PYTHAGORAS.

THIS most eminent philosopher, the founder of the Italic School, was born about the year 580 B.C., at Samos, an island in the Ægean Sea; he studied in Greece and in Egypt and is said to have visited also India, Persia and Palestine. He settled at Crotona, a notable city of Greek colonization in the south of Italy; here he taught for forty years, but was at last obliged to leave the country on account of the disturbances accompanying a revolution there, he reached Metapontum where he died about the year 500 B.C.

It is said that he left no written works, and all that remains of his doctrine is derived from his pupils and successors. Mnesarchus, his son, and Aristæus, who married his widow, were the immediate successors who carried on the school of philosophy and they were succeeded by Bulagoras, Tidas and Diodorus. At a later date the teachings were continued at three centres, Heraclea, Metapontum and Tarentum.

The oldest authors who have left any record of his teachings are Philolaus, circa 370 B.C.; Archytas of Tarentum; Aristotle, B.C. 322; Theon of Smyrna; Jamblichus of Chalcis; Proclus; Simplicius; and lastly Photius of Constantinople, who lived about 850 A.D., and left a Bibliotheca of ancient philosophy. During the middle ages Meursius, Meibomius, Kircher,

Beroaldus and Marsilius Ficinus reprinted the old remains of the Pythagoreans.

Later editors have been Michael Neander, André Dacier, Thomas Stanley, 1700, and J. C. von Orelli, 1819.

The "Golden Verses" and the "Symbols" enshrine the Pythagorean doctrine in a concise and convenient form; they are the only works extant directly attributed to the great master, but history records that many treatises were written by his pupils to explain his philosophy; such are—Three Treatises, paideutic, politic and physic; the Universe; the Sacred discourse; the Soul; on piety; arithmetic; prognostics; and Magical virtues of herbs.

There are however two short *epistles*, one to Anaximenes and one to Hiero, which are thought to be authentic; and lastly, there is a short paragraph on the letter Y as a symbol of human life.

The Notes are chiefly gleaned by A.E.A. and by S. A. from the commentaries of Hierocles, who lived about 330, from Jamblichus of Chalcis, 320, and André Dacier, whose treatise is dated 1706, of which there is an English edition of 1707, by N. Rowe.

S. A.

THE GOLDEN VERSES OF PYTHAGORAS

Translated by A. E. A.

1. FIRST worship the immortal gods as the Law ordains.
2. Reverence thy oath, and next, the illustrious heroes.
3. Then supplicate the good terrestrial demons, with proper offerings.
4. Honour also thy parents, and those most nearly related to thee.
5. Of other men, make him thy friend who is most distinguished by virtue.
6. Listen to his kind words, and copy his good deeds.
7. Do not hate thy friend for a small fault.
8. Now, Power is a near neighbour to necessity.
9. Know these things; accustom thyself to be the master of thy Passions:
10. First gluttony, then sloth, luxury, and anger.
11. Do no shameful act in private with thyself, nor with another:
12. And above all things respect thyself.
13. In the next place be just both in deed and word.
14. And let it not be thy habit to behave thyself in any matter thoughtlessly,

15. But consider this,—that all must die.
16. And that as the good things of Fortune may be acquired, so also they may be lost.
17. As to those calamities which befall men through Divine Fortune,
18. If thou suffer, suffer in patience, and resent them not.
19. Do thy best to remedy them, and bear in mind,
20. That Destiny does not give the largest share to good men.
21. Many sorts of reasonings, good and bad, are to be found amongst men;
22. But be not disturbed by them, nor allow them to harass thee.
23. But if anything false of thee be put forth, bear it patiently.
24. Listen now carefully to what I am about to tell thee.
25. Let no one ever seduce thee by his words or acts,
26. Nor make thee do what is not seemly.
27. Deliberate before doing, in order that what thou doest may not be foolish.
28. For it is the part of a stupid man to speak and act without thought.
29. But do thou act so that thou shalt not be troubled by the result.
30. Do nothing also which thou dost not understand,
31. But learn all that thou shouldest know, and so thou shalt lead a pleasant life.
32. Neglect not the health of thy body.
33. Be moderate in food, and drink, and exercise.
34. Now by moderation I mean what will not injure thee.
35. Accustom thyself to a style of living which is simple but not luxurious.
36. Avoid anything which can give rise to envy.

37. Spend not unseasonably as one who knows not what is right.

38. Be not niggardly nor covetous.

39. Moderation in all things is most excellent.

40. Do only those things which cannot hurt thee, and think before doing (even them).

41. Never sleep before going over the acts of the day in thy mind.

Wherein have I done wrong? What have I done? What have I left undone?

Examine thyself. If thou hast done evil, blame. And if thou hast done well, rejoice.

45. Practise thoroughly all these maxims; think on them; love them.

46. They will put thee in the way of Divine Virtue;

47. I swear it by Him who has put into our soul the Quaternion.

48. Who is the Eternal Source of Nature?

49. But go to thy work only after having prayed the gods to accomplish it.

50. Having done this, thou shalt know the constitution of the immortal Gods and of mortal men;

51. How far the different Beings extend, and what contains them and holds them together.

52. Thou shalt know also, according to right, that Nature is alike in all;

53. So that thou shalt not hope for that which thou shouldst not, and nothing shall be hidden from thee.

54. Thou shalt know also that men draw their misfortunes upon themselves of their own choice.

55. Wretches! they neither see nor understand that their Good is close at hand.

56. Few know how to free themselves from their misfortunes.

57. Such is the Fate that takes away the senses of men.

58. Some like wheels are carried in one direction, some in another, pressed down by ills innumerable.

59. For fatal strife, innate, ever following, unseen afflicts them.

60. They ought not to provoke this, but yield and so escape.

61. O Jove, mighty Father, wouldst Thou deliver them from many evils.

62. Show them what Fate is about to overtake them.

63. But be of good heart, the race of man is divine.

64. Holy Nature shews them all her mysteries.

65. If thou knowest these things, thou wilt do what I bid thee do;

66. And, having healed thy soul, thou will deliver it from these evils.

67. But abstain thou from the food, of which I have spoken, in the purifications,

68. And in the deliverance of thy Soul, decide between the courses open to you, and thoroughly examine all things.

69. Take the Supreme Mind as thy guide (who must ever direct and restrain thy course).

70. And when, after having thrown aside thy body, thou comest to the realms of most pure ether,

71. Thou shalt be a God, immortal, incorruptible.

NOTES BY A. E. A.

Suggested by the Commentaries of Hierocles and Dacier.

It is doubtful whether we have in these verses the work of the philosopher himself, for they were probably written by one of his disciples, and the ancients ascribed them to Lysis. They bear the name of Pythagoras not only because they contain his doctrines, but also because his disciples never put their names to their works, which they all imputed to their Master to do him honour and to testify their gratitude.

"Among all the Rules that contain a Summary of Philosophy, the verses of Pythagoras, called the Golden Verses, justly hold the first Rank, for they contain the general Precepts of all Philosophy, as well for what regards the Active, as the Contemplative. By their means every one may acquire Truth and Virtue, render himself pure, happily attain to the Divine Resemblance, and as is said by Plato in the *Timæus*, after having regained his Health, and recovered his Integrity and his Perfection, he may see himself again in a State of Innocence and Light."

Pythagoras begins with the precepts of active Virtue. Practical Philosophy is the mother of Virtue, as we are taught by these Verses, where practical Philosophy is called "Human Virtue" — and where the contemplative is celebrated under the name of "Divine Virtue" (45, 46).

V. i. Damascius says "God (the First Principle, that is) is raised above the reach of thought; He is an unknown and impenetrable obscurity:" while the Egyptians did not, it is said, worship this First Being, as they did not know him. And this may be the reason why, in this verse, we are bidden to worship not God, but the Sons of God.

V. ii. Pythagoras taught that God created before all things the reasonable beings: the highest and most excellent of all substances, *the Immortal Gods*, were created by his first Thought—the middle Substance, the *Heroes*, by the second Thought—the *Souls of men* by his third Thought.

V. iii. "Terrestrial"—*lit.* "under the Earth." The phrase has been explained as meaning "those who are dead after having lived a virtuous life." But Pythagoras taught that the souls of men went not under the Earth but to the *Ether*. Demons = endowed with knowledge. [The good Demons were the heads of the hierarchies of Elemental and planetary spirits.—S.A.]

V. vii. Or "Give way to thy friend by speaking to him mildly, and be kind to him."

Vv. xiii.-xvi. The school of Pythagoras accounted for the various states and conditions of men by asserting them to be the results of their first Life, which the souls had led in their spheres before bodies had been assigned to them. Jamblichus defends the Gods against the charge of injustice in the distribution of good and evil by saying that they knew the whole of the previous lives of each soul: lib. iv., cap. 4. Compare also Plato, *De Repub.*, lib. x.

V. xx. Because these evils then change their nature, for the good suffer patiently, and are supported by the certainty that divine good is reserved for the perfect. Compare Plato, *The Laws*: lib. x.

V. xxix. Compare the teaching of the Bhagavat Gita.—S.A.

Vv. xxx., xxxi. Comp. Plato, *Philebus*. The Pythagoreans called the first Cause or Principle, *Opportunity;* and the Master himself made a Precept of *Opportunity*. Plato in *Phædrus* says, "For this vicious Horse (the 'body') grows unruly and prances, his weight drawing him towards the Earth, unless the groom take care not to feed him too high."

Here, too, we find the reason for the choice of food made by Pythagoras.

V. xxxv. An effort has been lately made to form a guild of "Simple life."—S.A.

Vv. xli.-xliv. Porphyry tells us that Pythagoras advised his disciples to be particularly careful of two hours—that when they rise, and that of going to bed: of the first, to reflect on what lay before them; and of the second to give an account of the day's actions, and that he said of the first:—

"When drowsy sleep to morning Thoughts gives way,
 Think what thou hast to do th' ensuing day."

Comp. M. Aurelius at the beginning of the second book, "We ought every morning when we rise to say to ourselves, 'To-day I shall have to do with an impertinent fellow, an ungrateful person, etc.'"

V. xlvii. Quaternion, *i.e.*, the occult powers of the number 4, meaning God. How comes God to be the Quaternion? Pythagoras is said to have treated of this question in his *Treatise of the Gods*, which is now lost: in it he is also said to have explained the teaching of Orpheus, "That the essence of number was the Principle of Things, and the Root of the Gods and of the Demons." Aristotle, too, says of numbers, that they "can never be the Principles of Actions and of changes; that they may denote certain Causes, but they can never be those Causes." The Master taught that God was the unit, that all the numbers were derived from the unit, and that the finite interval of number was ten. The Power of ten is four, for before we reach the Decad, we find all the virtue and all the Perfection of the ten in the four: $1+2+3+4=10$; four is an arithmetical middle between one and seven, for the excess above one = its defect from seven. Now the unit contains the Powers of all other numbers, and the seven being a Virgin (for it produces no number between itself and ten, nor can it be produced by any of the numbers in that interval). So, too, the first solid is found in the Quaternion—for the Point answers to the Unit, the Line to a Binary, for from one Point we go to another Point; the superficies answers to the Ternary, for a Triangle is the most plain of all rectilineal Figures: but solidity is the nature of the Quaternion, for in the Four we find the Pyramid. There are Four Faculties that form a Judgment—Understanding, Knowledge, Opinion, and Sense. Aristotle teaches this, and adds Understanding answers to One, Knowledge to Two, Opinion to Three, or the Superficies, and Sense to the Quaternion or Solid. Plutarch in *The Opinions of the Philosophers*, chap. iii., explains the reasons.

Vv. lii., liii. Pythagoras and Socrates included Morality in Physics. In his commentary on these verses Hierocles plainly asserts that by Metempsychosis, Pythagoras meant that Vice changes man into the likeness of a beast, while Virtue makes him resemble God; and that he can be neither the one nor the other by his nature.

Vv. lxvii.-lxix. For an expanded statement of this teaching consult Plato, *Phædrus*.

THE SYMBOLS OF PYTHAGORAS

By Sapere Aude.

I.

Jugum ne transileas.
Go not beyond the Balance.—Dacier.
Do not exceed the necessities of the case: be accurate in judgment, and moderate in all your undertakings.
Transgress not the laws of justice.—Plutarch.
Obey not the dictates of avarice.—Athenæus.
This latter has a similar meaning, because covetousness is the common cause of injustice.
The Kabalah makes great use of this symbol of the Balance, and expatiates upon the need for equilibrium; "forces which are unbalanced, perish in the void." The kings of Edom are Kabalistic types of the results of the action of unbalanced forces.—S.A.

II.

In chœnice ne sedeto.
Sit not down upon a bushel.—Dacier.
The chœnix was a Greek measure for corn, and each slave was allowed this quantity per day; it was equivalent to a pint and a half English measure. The symbo

should mean, do not rest content with a bare subsistence.

A curious little book is *Dissertation sur le Chénix de Pythagore, par* J. Du Rondel, 1690.

III.

Coronam ne vellito.
Tear not the crown to pieces.—Dacier.
Some authors read "*vellica.*"
Do not transgress the laws of the country, for the laws are the crown.—Hierome.

Vellico, not only means to tear up, but also to *defame*, so that the symbol may mean, "do not speak evil of dignitaries;" this will be analogous to the dictum of Solomon in Ecclesiastes, c. 10, v. 20. "Curse not the king, no, not in thy thought."

IV.

Cor non comedendum.
Eat not the heart.—Dacier.
It has been suggested that this symbol means that we ought not to wear out our hearts with grief, nor to abandon ourselves to despair. Homer uses the same expression in regard to Bellerophon, "eating his own heart." The brain is usually associated with the intellect, and the heart with the emotions. Some of the ancients held that by eating the heart of an animal, man obtained a tinge of the peculiarities of that animal, in a much greater degree than by eating the flesh of other parts.

V.

Ignem gladio ne scalpas.
Stir not up fire with a sword.—Dacier.
Some old authors say that this symbol means that we ought not to inflame any further, persons who are

already at enmity. Hermetic adepts say that the true meaning is that the Elementals of the Fire should not be threatened by the use of a steel sword, for fire and iron are analogous, but that these may be coerced by the correct pentagrammatic use of the sword when it is used with a due knowledge of the correspondences. H. P. B. in *Isis Unveiled*, Vol. I. p. 247, refers to this symbol and points out that this maxim is familiar to the folk-lore of many nations, Tartars, Laplanders, Russians and the Aborigines of North and South America; see Tylor, *Primitive Culture*, who quotes *De Plano Carpini* of 1246.

VI.

Non revertendum, quum ad terminos perveneris.
When you have arrived at the end, desire not to turn back.—Dacier.

This has been applied to a human life,—when you have come nigh unto death, do not be dismayed and desire not to live. We know that an old proverb says, "*vestiga nulla retrorsum*," "no returning footsteps are visible." This symbol seems to be a statement of the law of Karma, that there is no escape from the proper reward or punishment of one's own deeds; as one has made one's bed, so one must lie upon it. A craven repentance made when one has no longer an opportunity of re-adjusting the effects of action, is of no value. As the tree has fallen so must it lie. Jamblichus gives, "Having started do not turn back, for the Furies have followed you."

VII.

Per viam publicam ne vadas.
Go not in the public way.—Dacier.

Old commentators have said that we ought not to follow public opinion, but rather the counsel of the wise. Avoid the broad way, and take instead the narrow path. Carlyle has said, "the majority of mankind are fools," and so the common procedure in any case is erroneous. Christianity teaches that "many are called but few chosen," so that one needs to be exceptional in purity and goodwill to earn the reward. Each man has a natural constitutional peculiarity, and so is suited to progress in some particular path, and not in any common mode of advancement. This assurance should lead us to be charitable in judging of the lives of others, and not to be hasty in judgment, for if one have fallen how do we know "that we could have withstood the same temptation."—S.A.

Go not into crowded places or mix freely with the multitude if you do not harmonise therewith: if you are regardless of this injunction, beware of ill effects therefrom. There are occult or astral influences emanating from all human beings: and in addition to that, astral entities love to keep men company, as they derive *vitality* from them, which is more easily effected in the contingency mentioned.—L.O.

VIII.

Domesticas Hirundines ne habeto.
Suffer no swallows about your house.—Dacier.

We may be sure that this symbol does not mean that we ought to interfere with the visits of these birds of passage, and that a philosophical maxim is here intended. Old commentators translated this symbol into the instruction:—do not encourage great talkers to visit your family. Perhaps rather, do not estimate and encourage temporary acquaintances by the standard of, and with the welcome due to familiar permanent friends. The feelings of many an old and valued companion have been hurt by effusive sympathy shown to new acquaintances.

IX.

In annulo, imaginem Dei, ne circumferto.

Wear not the image of God upon a ring.—Dacier.

We ought not to profane the name of the God we adore by speaking of Him at every turn, and before unsympathetic persons. It was, of old, deemed an offence to wear a ring, or bear a coin of the ruling monarch, when on an illegal errand, or in an unseemly place. Dion writes of a young man condemned for visiting a scandalous place while bearing a coin of the Prince of the city, Caracalla. Seneca and Suetonius report the same fact of the illegality of wearing a ring bearing the image of a king when engaged in immoral conduct. Philostratus says that one was found guilty of treason for beating a slave who bore a medal of Tiberius Cæsar.

The Hebrews were forbidden to make or wear any image of their divine Ruler. The Kabalist teaches that no representation of the Ain Soph is possible, while the emanations of the Sephiroth may be fitly typified by number, letter and word. Neither Buddhist nor Brahman makes any image of the Supreme, although numerous representations of the members of the issuant triad of Brahma, Vishnu and Siva are permissible.

N. O. M.

X.

Hominibus onus simul imponendum, non detrahendum.

Help men to burden, but not to unburden themselves.—Dacier.

Reward is not to be obtained by throwing aside responsibility, but by undertaking it. So that by relieving others of a duty, you assume their responsibility, and deprive them of an opportunity for good deeds. When one man assumes the Karma of another he does him no good service, and yet is himself answerable for the result.

XI.

Ne cuiquam dexteram facile porrigito.
Shake not hands easily with any man.—Dacier.

Or rather, do not give the right hand too freely. The right hand given to another was the special sign of suretyship. Solomon gives special warnings in the book of Proverbs, chap. vi., v. 1, and chap. xvii., v. 18, against a careless pledging of oneself to or for others, such a one, he says, is "void of understanding." But the right hand when given with due preparation is of the utmost service, for it is of the Pillar of Geburah, carrying intensity and efficiency. The instructed occultist does not shake hands readily with the chance interviewer, and the Freemason regards the giving of the right hand as a sure pledge of brotherhood.

XII.

Olla vestigium in cinere confundito.
Leave not the mark of the pot upon the ashes.—Dacier.

This symbol refers to the cooking utensil, an earthen or iron vessel, and to the ashes of a wood fire. Having cooked, remove the signs of the vessel having rested upon the heap of ashes. Having realised your aims, do not dwell upon the efforts that have been expended. Some say, that having effected a reconciliation with one who has been in enmity with you, do not again refer to the cause of your estrangement. Do not rake up old grievances. Do not add insult to the triumph you have gained over another.

XIII.

Herbam Molochen serito, ne tamen mandito.

Sow the seeds of the Mallow plant, but do not eat the fruits thereof.—Dacier.

This symbol is explained by the old commentators to mean—use mildness to others, and not to yourself; pardon offences of others, but do not overlook your own. The mallow and marsh-mallow are plants having a soothing property, and were sown and grown as medicinal herbs. Do good to others, but not for your own reward. Do not look for gratitude and expressions of thanks for good actions, and if possible, do not accept any reward for a deed done from a conscientious motive.—S. A.

Look for the medicinal virtue of the mallow plant in the leaves, not in the flowers.—L. O.

XIV.

Faculæ sedem ne extergito.

Wipe not out the place of a torch.—Dacier.

This symbol must be compared with number twelve: wipe out the mark of the pot, but do not obscure the place of the enlightenment. Do not dwell upon the history of a past success, but do not forget the Light which has illuminated you in your search for inspiration; for the same Light may illumine the path for others, but the material steps will be different for others.

XV.

Augustum annulum ne gestato.

Wear not a straight ring.—Dacier.

The translation of Dacier leaves much to be desired; in what sense can a ring be called straight? The Greek adjective is "*stenos*," not straight but narrow, confined, too tight. Still the word is used in the same sense as in the New Testament where the narrow way is called "straight." The maxim then, is "Do not wear a tight ring." Liberty of action is to be desired, and is of great advantage if liberty be not allowed to degenerate into license, and into folly, and thence into sin. Do not be fettered by custom and fashion, but do that which conscience prompts as right to be done by you. Fashion is a great slavery unto us all, brave souls alone save themselves from the current of common stupidity.

XVI.

Animalia unguicurvia ne nutrito.
Feed not animals that have crooked claws.—Dacier.

Curved claws and nails are a sign of rapacity and of such as prey upon other animals: vegetable feeders have hoofs or soft cushiony feet—among animals. Do not encourage or be familiar with anyone whom you have known to profit by an injustice to others, for such a one will one day turn and rend you also. The appetite grows by what it feeds upon. Do not hold a candle to the Devil for him to see his work by. Do not participate in ill-gotten gains.

XVII.

A fabis abstineto.
Abstain from beans.—Dacier.

This symbol has been interpreted in very various manners, as follows :—

1. In the natural sense; that Beans were a faulty article of food.
2. That Beans were a type for errors, sins, or any other impurity.
3. That Beans referred to civil offices of the state, because in elections and judgments, beans were used in voting; in a similar manner to our English form of lodge ballot by black and white balls.

Hesychius says that the bean signified the suffrages of judges, and that a synonym for a judge was a bean-caster.

4. For a theological reason in Egypt, as Herodotus tells us that the bean was sown but not eaten, and that a priest was forbidden even to look at them lest he should become unclean. See Book xi.

Hippocrates in chapter 15 of his second book on Diet, condemns beans as an article of food, calling them too astringent, and tending to cause intestinal gases.

Bonwick says that the cult of Ceres condemned the bean, and the Sabeans of Syria also refused it. There was a Sacred Egyptian Bean, which was thrown upon graves as a symbol of a renewal of life, from a notion of a sexual resemblance.

XVIII.

Melanuros ne gustato.
Eat not fish whose tails are black.—Dacier.

Melas means black, and *ouris* means tail, but it is not certain what sort of fish was so called; some say the perch, others the sea bream. This symbol has been explained, thus:—

Frequent not the company of infamous men. Black-tailed may be a fair simile for persons of seeming good aspect, who have a hidden evil side behind them, or who have left behind them an evil record.

Do not accept a doctrine which has a hidden failing, simply because its first appearance is attractive.—S.A.

Jamblichus of Chalcis, gives "Abstain from him who hath a black tail, for it belongs to the infernal gods."

N. O. M.

XIX.

Ne Erythinum edito.
Do not eat the gurnet (or gurnard—a fish).—Dacier.

It is a curious fact that so many of these symbols are apparently directions for diet. No doubt the Pythagoreans fully recognised that diet largely affected the health and tendencies of a man, and it is equally certain that these symbols have always been understood to require a double interpretation; one upon the material plane, and another of a philosophic or religious nature.

Pliny, the ancient naturalist, says that the Erythrinus was a fish all red excepting a white belly. The fish we now call gurnard is red; mediæval authors say it was an emblem of blood.

The symbol may mean, Do not shed blood, or avoid revenge which may lead to bloodshed.

I have not found that this fish was condemned as food by any other teacher than Pythagoras. Some authorities, however, read in the Greek *proslambanon* and not *esthiein*, or do not *take up*, instead of do not *eat*.

Rubrum aliquid ne suscipias; Do not undertake anything red; do not shed blood, is another reading found in *Marsilius Ficinus*.—S. A.

XX.

Animalis vulvam ne comedito.

Eat not the matrix of animals.—Dacier.

Vulva is not synonymous with matrix—the womb. The Latin should be *uterus*, not *vulva*, for the oldest Greek version reads *Metran*. The symbol may mean, avoid all that leads to sensuality; do not ponder over the ideas of sexual relation. This is almost entirely a man's failing; women are generally the victims of affection rather than passion. The apparently natural dissimilarity of the human sexes in this respect seems inexplicable.

XXI.

A morticinis abstineto.

Abstain from the flesh of animals that die of themselves.—Dacier.

On the purely material plane this rule is almost universally applied in our times; all butcher's meat is slaughtered, and presumably only healthy animals are chosen: but Christian butchers outvie the Jews in their rush for wealth, for among the Jews no meat is sold for human consumption when it is found post mortem that the animal has been suffering from disease; such carcases are handed over to the Christians, who buy them readily. Meat duly passed by the official appointed by the Rabbi is called "Kosher," that is, really fitted for use as human food. It is believed that this procedure is one reason for the smaller percentage of deaths from communicable diseases among the Hebrews.

The moral meaning of the symbol is not clear. Some old authors have said—Share not in the flesh of profane animals that are not fit for sacrifices, and renounce all dead works. Perhaps, renounce all unprofitable works; such as have no imprint of spiritual progress. Do not long follow a path which leads to no good result; or perhaps—abstain from dwelling on past events, rather look forward to future good results

S. A.

XXII.

Ab animalibus abstineto.
Abstain from eating animals.—Dacier.
There is here no necessary reference to eating. Abstain from animals is the simple translation. This might mean, spend your energies upon your fellow men and women, rather than in making pets of animals. Some have referred the word animals to unreasonable men, as animals are believed to be without reason.

XXIII.

Salem apponito.
Always put salt upon the table.—Dacier.
Provide salt, simply. The material sense may be as Dacier suggests. Salt was a Greek symbol for Justice, for as salt preserves substances, so Justice preserves the rights of men, and without Justice there is corruption. Leviticus, c. 3, v. 13, says "Thou shalt add salt to all thy offerings." Compare the old proverb concerning the spilling of salt, which was regarded as the precursor of evil.

XXIV.

Panem ne frangito.
Never break the bread.—Dacier.
What this may mean on the material plane is not clear, for bread is clearly meant to be broken, unless indeed cut, from which no gain is apparent. Greek bread was made in long portions, with surface markings dividing each loaf into four pieces. When given to the poor, it was frequently broken into these pieces and so distributed; so perhaps the meaning is, give a whole loaf, do not be mean to the poor.

Bread was also a symbol of Life, and this symbol has been interpreted, do not too much distribute your energies, but choose some good aim in life, and devote all your strength to that end.

XXV.

Sedem oleo ne abstergito.
Spill not oil upon a seat.—Dacier.
There is some error here, for "*ne abstergito*" and the original Greek "*me omorgnusthai*" both mean "do not wipe," and have no reference to "spilling."

Old authors said, *oil* was intended for praise, and *seat*

referred to official positions; their explanation was that dignitaries should not be praised The English version needs to be changed to, "Do not clean a seat with oil;" meaning, use the proper remedy in each case. Jacob at Bethel poured oil upon the stone upon which his head rested when he dreamed of the ladder to heaven, in token of his gratitude, and he did not wipe it away. Genesis, c. 28, v. 18.

XXVI.

Ne cibum iu matellam injicito.
Put not meat into a foul vessel.—Dacier.

On the material plane this is sound advice, for nothing will make meat decay so rapidly as exposure to animal excreta. A foul vessel is the symbol of a wicked man, the New Testament calls the wicked, "vessels of dishonour." It is useless, if not worse, to give to the vicious the spiritual knowledge which a good man will appreciate and be thankful for.

XXVII.

Gallum nutrito, ne sacrificato, Lunæ enim et Soli sacer est.
Feed the Cock, but sacrifice him not, for he is sacred to the Sun and the Moon.—Dacier.

The ancients used to sacrifice a cock to Æsculapius, as the thank-offering for recovery from sickness: even in our century, the great Platonist Thomas Taylor did this in pursuance of ancient usage.

The Cock was a symbol of Watchfulness and care for others. The Templar degrees of Freemasonry refer to this idea. The people of Crotona and Metapontum, colonies of Greeks among whom Pythagoras laboured, were not mindful of the maxim, for they killed him; and the Athenians sacrificed Socrates, who had been as the symbolic Cock to them. In our own days Madame

Blavatsky, who introduced to Europe the exalted ethics of the mystic East, was sacrificed in honour and reputation, if not indeed as to her life, by the modern Christian Pharisees. Jesus clearly held that the teacher should be tended by his pupils, and he sent out his disciples with orders to possess nothing themselves and to trust to sympathizers for maintenance.

XXVIII.

Dentes ne frangito.
Break not the teeth.—Dacier.
The Romans used this formula to mean "do not revile," or "avoid satire." Do not break your teeth is a wise maxim, for the teeth are necessary to good digestion, and in ethical matters a good perception must precede clear development and real progress.

XXIX.

Acetarium vas abs te removeto.
Keep the vinegar cruet far from you.—Dacier.
This is a wise maxim as to diet, and in a moral sense sourness of temper, malice and bitterness of expression ought to be avoided.

XXX.

Capillorum et Unguium tuorum præsegminia conspuito.
Spit upon the parings of your nails and the clippings of your hair.—Dacier.
The act of spitting upon anything meant the casting off and rejection of it: these parings were things of no farther use, superfluities which, if allowed to remain, would only be sources of mischief, so they are to be cast off remorselessly; this clearly must be extended to our faults, which are excrescences.

XXXI.

Pros Helion tetrammenos me ourei.   Contra Solem ne meito.
In sight of the Sun do no indecency.

No comment is needed upon this maxim, Erasmus, contrary to all rules, says Dacier, holds that this symbol means, "Do no evil Magic." Hesiod has a similar caution to men, as to public decency. The Sun as chief light-giver was also the symbol of divine purity, to which no unworthy action should appear.

XXXII.

Ad Solem versus, ne loquitur.
Speak not, facing the Sun.—Dacier.

It has been said that this maxim means, do not publish your thoughts to the world. Perhaps, do not dictate in the presence of those wiser than you are: or as the Sun was the emblem of the Greatest, the chief benefactor of the earth, do not speak when you have turned unto him, but be humble and presume not to speak.

XXXIII.

In meridie ne dormito.
We ought not to sleep at noon.—Dacier.

This symbol was considered to mean that when light is offered to you, do not accept darkness; nor ignorance, when wisdom is tendered to you.

Do not neglect opportunities, work while day is at its brightest, "for the night cometh when no man can work."

XXXIV.

Surgens e lecto, stragulam conturbato, vestigium que corporis confundito.

Stir up the bed, as soon as you have risen, and leave on it no print of your body.—Dacier.

Suffer not anything to make you remember by day, what has passed during the night, for when the night has gone, and it has become day, think not of the concerns of the darkness, but expend all your energies in attaining to the knowledge which the Light may bring.

XXXV.

Carminibus utendum ad Lyram.
Never sing but to the harp.—Dacier.

It is said that Pythagoras objected to all musical instruments but the harp. The Greek words are "Songs are suited to the Lyre." There should be a certain congruity maintained in all human concerns.

XXXVI.

Stragula semper convoluta habeto.
Always keep your things ready packed up.—Dacier.
Or, always have your coverings rolled up.

Be always ready for emergencies. The Greeks had to gather up their flowing robes in order to run. Live, so that you may be always prepared to die.

XXXVII.

Injussu Imperatoris, de Statione et præsidia, ne decedas.
Quit not your post, without the order of the General.—Dacier.

This is not only a phrasing of the well-known military rule, but also means do not take your own life, which the Divine Ruler—the General—will require of you at the proper time.

XXXVIII.

In via, ne ligna cædito.
Cut not wood by the way.—Dacier.
Do not convert to private use what is intended for the public welfare.
Otherwise, the cutting of wood was a menial task, among Greeks and also among the Hebrews; so the maxim may mean, do not be content to labour at low employments, when higher occupations are within your ability.
Stanley quotes the following meaning:—Do not disquiet your course of life with excessive cares and vain solicitude.

XXXIX.

Quod elixum est, non assato.
Roast not that which is boiled.—Dacier.
Do no things which are superfluous.

XL.

Gladium acutum avertito.
Avoid the two edged sword.—Dacier.
The words are "a sharp sword." This is a common symbol for a slanderer, who should be always avoided.

XLI.

Quæ ceciderunt e mensa, ne tollito.
Pick not up what has fallen from the table.—Dacier.
This maxim was believed to encourage charity; leave the crumbs for the birds, and the loose ears of corn for the gleaners.

XLII.

Ab arca cyparissina abstineto.
Abstain even from a cypress chest.—Dacier.

Do not provide expensive funerals.

The rich affected coffins of cypress, a very expensive wood, and one believed to tend to long preservation of a dead body. Plato and Solon also condemned expenditure on funerals.

XLIII.

Cœlestibus, imparia sacrificato; inferis vero paria.
Sacrifice an odd number to the Celestial Gods, and to the Infernal an even number.—Dacier.

Odd numbers cannot be halved and so were considered the most perfect; even numbers could be equally divided.

Deity was typified by Unity, and Matter by the Dyad.

XLIV.

Ex imputatis vitibus, ne Diis libato.
Offer not to the Gods the wine from an unpruned vine.—Dacier.

This has been rendered as an encouragement to agriculture: some have thought that "the wine of an unpruned vine" meant Blood, and that the symbol was intended to condemn the sacrifice of living animals and birds.

XLV.

Ne sine farina sacrificato.
Never sacrifice without meal (or flour).—Dacier.

Barley flour was sprinkled over the heads of animals before sacrifice. It has been suggested that the meaning is to substitute vegetable offerings for animal sacrifices. Or perhaps, as was done in Egypt, to offer a cast or mould of flour, shaped like a certain animal, rather than a living being.

XLVI.

Nudis pedibus adorato et sacrificato.
Adore the Gods, and sacrifice barefoot.—Dacier.
Reverence was indicated by the baring of the feet, by the Hebrews, Greeks and Romans. Remember the instruction to Moses. The maxim refers to spiritual humility, as well as to bodily procedure.

XLVII.

Circumactus adora.
Turn round when you worship.—Dacier.
Or rather "turn around," not alone reverse your position. This seems to mean that God is everywhere, and is not to be approached in any one place or direction; nothing but a complete circle can assimilate with His universality.

XLVIII.

Adoraturus sedeto.
Sit down when you worship.—Dacier.
Kneeling was not an accepted position for prayer among the ancient Greeks, they stood or sat. Perhaps the maxim may mean, be seated, in the sense of devote some considerable time to devotion, and do not be content with hurried prayers, it is not always the Passover.

XLIX.

Ad sacrificia ungues ne præcidito.
Pare not your nails during the sacrifice.—Dacier.
Pay attention to your devotions, and do not let the mind wander to commonplace ideas, nor carry on commonplace actions. Jamblichus reads this symbol to mean, "do not exclude poor relations from your festivals."

The following are less clearly appropriated to Pythagoras, although they have come down to us from his school of thought:

L.

Cum tonat terram tangito.
When it thunders, touch the ground.—Dacier.
Be submissive to the trials sent by the gods. Some moderns have seen in this maxim electrical reference; no doubt a recumbent posture would attract a flash of lightning less than a form erect, but any mere stooping to touch the ground with the hands would not conduce to safety.

LI.

Ad lucernam faciem in speculo ne contemplator.
Regard not yourself in the looking glass, by the light of a torch.—Dacier.
A mirror is apt to be deceptive, but the distortion is increased by artificial light. We should not estimate ourselves by fallacious standards. Jamblichus says a mirror represents only the surface of things, and the torch means opinion: do not judge by appearances aided by unlearned representations.

LII.

Unum, Duo.
One, Two.—Dacier.
By the number One was intended the Divine; by Two, Nature: if we know nothing of God, we cannot understand his works.

LIII.

Honorato imprimis habitum, tribunal et triobolum.
Honour the marks of dignity, the Throne and the Ternary.—Dacier.

The Kabalist would say, First Kether, the Crown, and then the Supernal Triad.

LIV.

Flantibus ventis, Echo adora.
When the winds blow, adore Echo.—Dacier.

Lilius Giraldus explains thus: the winds mean revolts and sedition, and Echo means a desert place, and so the maxim means, leave your homes in the towns when there are conspiracies.

Leave the room when men quarrel.

When there is disputation, the calm where an echo can be heard, is the haven of peace.

LV.

Ex curru, ne comedito.
Eat not in a chariot.—Dacier.

In the olden Greek, *currus* was *diphros*, a seat as well as a carriage.

Life may be symbolised as a drive through time, and the meaning may be that life is not for enjoyment alone.

LVI.

Dextrum pedem primum induito, sinistrum vero primum attolito. (Or *calceato* and *lavato*.)
Put on the right shoe first, but wash the left foot first.—Dacier.

Or in the first case, put on the right shoe first, but in taking shoes off, take off the left first.

Be more ready to take up rightful work than to begin a pleasure.

LVII.

Cerebrum ne edito.
Eat not the Brain.—Dacier.

Do not consume your faculties of mind by overstudy.

LVIII.

Palmam ne plantato.
Plant not the Palm tree.—Dacier.
This is supposed to mean, do not transplant a growing palm tree, but raise it from seed; because the Babylonians reckoned up 367 advantages to be derived from the Palm tree, but as a matter of experience it was known that a transplanted Palm bore fruit of no value. Do no useless works.

LIX.

Libamine Diis facito per Auriculam.
Make libations to the Gods by the ear.—Dacier.
Apollonius has it that this means that religious services should be accompanied by music and singing.

Do not make drink offerings to Gods, but rather pray so steadfastly that they may hear you.—S. A.

Some authorities give another version; "*Libamina Diis facienda juxta auriculam poculorum.*" Libations to the Gods are to be made from near the ear (or handle) of the cups.—N. O. M.

LX.

Sepiam ne edito.
Eat not the cuttle fish.—Dacier.
This animal when attacked is able to eject a black fluid which discolours the water around it, in which obscurity, the fish that attack lose its whereabouts. Have no concerns with those who revile when displeased.

LXI.

In limine non consistendum.
Stop not at the threshold.—Dacier.
Do not waver, choose one path or the other and continue upon it. Having put your hand to the plough, look not back.

LXII.

Prægredienti gregi e via cedendum.
Give way to a flock passing by.—Dacier.
Do not openly oppose the multitude.

LXIII.

Mustelam devita.
Avoid the weazel.—Dacier.
Avoid tale-tellers is said to be the meaning, referring to an old fancy that the weazel bore its young through its mouth.

LXIV.

Arma a muliere sumministrata rejice.
Reject the weapons a woman offers you —Dacier.
When your own conscience does not lead you to combat, do not consent to fight because a woman encourages you. The ancients said that woman's weakness made her more liable to be revengeful, and that men should not prove themselves weak also, by acting with impropriety at their dictation.

LXV.

Colubram intra ædes collapsum, ne perimito.
Kill not a serpent that chances to fall within your house.—Dacier.
Do not harm your enemy, when he is your guest as suppliant.

LXVI.

Lapidem in fontem jacere, scelus.
It is a crime to throw stones into fountains.—Dacier.
It is wrong to cast obloquy upon those who are doing public service.

LXVII.

Sinistrum, cibum ne sumito.
Do not feed yourself with your left hand.—Dacier.
Support yourself honourably, and not by left hand, or as we now say, by underhand devices.

LXVIII.

Sudorem ferro obstergere, tetrum nefas.
It is a horrible crime to wipe off the sweat with Iron.—Dacier.
It is wicked to take by force from another, the thing he has earned by his own exertions. Compare Ecclesiasticus, c. xxxiv., v. 21.

LXIX.

Hominis vestigia, ferro ne configito.
Stick not iron into the footsteps of a man.—Dacier.
Do not attack the character of the dead.

LXX.

In sepulchro ne dormito.
Sleep not upon a grave.—Dacier.
Do not rest content with the property left to you by parents, but make a living of your own.

LXXI.

Integrum fasciculum in ignem ne mittito.
Lay not the whole faggot upon the fire.—Dacier.
Live thriftily, and do not squander your estate. Do not put all your eggs in one basket.

LXXII.

De rheda, junctis pedibus, ne exilito.
Leap not from a chariot with your feet close together.—Dacier.
Do not make sudden changes of attitude or of occupation; unless indeed your feet are ready to support you in the new condition.

LXXIII.

In astrum ne digitum intendito.
Do not threaten the stars.—Dacier.
This is an error by Dacier; *intenta* would mean *threaten*, but *intendere digitum*, means to point with the finger at anything, as in derision.
The meaning is, do not contemn the astral influences, which you cannot evade.

LXXIV.

Candelam ad parietem ne applicato.
Place not a candle against the wall.—Dacier.
This was said to mean, do not persist in endeavours to teach those who are too stupid to understand, for they will resist your instructions even as a wall throws back the rays of the sun. Perhaps, do not apply the candle flame to the wall, for that would be a mischief and cause a blackening: so occult Light must be conferred with caution, and not be delivered to the stupid or vicious; this necessity is insisted upon by both Eastern and Western schools of Esoteric knowledge.

LXXV.

In nive ne scribito.
Write not in the snow.—Dacier.
Do no unprofitable task; the Greeks also had the maxim, Do not write upon water.

LXXVI.

Cachinno ne indulgeto.
Do not indulge in immoderate laughter.

LXXVII.

Non propter opes, ducenda uxor.
Do not marry for money.

LXXVIII.

Locum ubi humanus sanguis effusus est.
Lapidibus obruito.—J. Castalio.
Cover up with stones the place where human blood has been shed.

LXXIX.

Deum imitatus. silentium serva.—J. Castalio.
Imitate the Deity by keeping silent.
Another similar maxim is simply:—
Silentium servato.
Keep silence.

LXXX.

Templum dextra ingredito, sinistra egredito.—J. Castalio.
Enter a church by the right hand side, and leave it by the left.

LXXXI.

De rebus Divinis etsi incredibilia narrentur risu abstineto.—J. Castalio.

When Divine things are told to you, restrain from smiling, even if they are incredible. In the middle ages, it was said, *Credo quia impossibile est*, I believe *because* of its impossibility.

LXXXII.

Clara voce precandum.
You should pray in a clear voice.

LXXXIII.

In terra ne naviges.
Do not go to sea on dry land.
When at Rome do as the Romans do.

LXXXIV.

Neque in aquiminali intingendum, neque in balneo lavandum
Neither bathe in a hand basin, nor wash yourself in a bath.

There is a place for every purpose under heaven, and a place designed for one purpose should not be converted to another use.

LXXXV.

Ad fæmineam divitem ne accedito sobolis procreanda causa.

Do not give a rich woman the means of having children. Because such women are apt to think most of their pleasures and their appearance, and do but seldom give that personal attendance to children which is so necessary to the health and growth.—S. A.

LXXXVI.

Mitem neque violes neque cædas plantam.
Neither injure nor destroy the tender plant.

LXXXVII.

De Pythagoreis sine lumine, ne loquitor.
Do not criticize the (doctrines of the) Pythagoreans without light (unless you understand them).

Collectanea Hermetica

EDITED BY

W. Wynn Westcott, M.B., D.P.H.

VOLUME VI.

THE

Chaldæan Oracles

OF

Zoroaster

Edited and Revised
By SAPERE AUDE.

With an Introduction
By L. O.

THE CHALDÆAN ORACLES ATTRIBUTED TO ZOROASTER.

PREFACE

By Sapere Aude.

THESE Oracles are considered to embody many of the principal features of Chaldæan philosophy. They have come down to us through Greek translations and were held in the greatest esteem throughout antiquity, a sentiment which was shared alike by the early Christian Fathers and the later Platonists. The doctrines contained therein are attributed to Zoroaster, though to which particular Zoroaster is not known; historians give notices of as many as six different individuals all bearing that name, which was probably the title of the Prince of the Magi, and a generic term. The word Zoroaster is by various authorities differently derived: Kircher furnishes one of the most interesting derivations when he seeks to show that it comes from TzURA=a figure, and TzIUR=to fashion, ASH=fire, and STR=hidden; from these he gets the words Zairaster=fashioning images of hidden fire;—or Tzuraster=the image of secret things. Others derive it from Chaldee and Greek words meaning "a contemplator of the Stars."

It is not, of course, pretended that this collection as it stands is other than disjointed and fragmentary, and it is more than probable that the true sense of many passages has been obscured, and even in some cases hopelessly obliterated, by inadequate translation.

Where it has been possible to do so, an attempt has been made to elucidate doubtful or ambiguous expressions, either by modifying the existing translation from the Greek, where deemed permissible, or by appending annotations.

It has been suggested by some that these Oracles are of Greek invention, but it has already been pointed out by Stanley that Picus de Mirandula assured Ficinus that *he* had the Chaldee Original in his possession, "in which those things which are faulty and defective in the Greek are read perfect and entire," and Ficinus indeed states that he found this MS. upon the death of Mirandula. In addition to this, it should be noted that here and there in the original Greek version, words occur which are not of Greek extraction at all, but are Hellenised Chaldee.

Berosus is said to be the first who introduced the writings of the Chaldæans concerning Astronomy and Philosophy among the Greeks,* and it is certain that the traditions of Chaldea very largely influenced Greek thought. Taylor considers that some of these mystical utterances are the sources whence the sublime conceptions of Plato were formed, and large commentaries were written upon them by Porphyry, Iamblichus, Proclus, Pletho and Psellus. That men of such great learning and sagacity should have thought so highly of these Oracles, is a fact which in itself should commend them to our attention.

---

* Josephus, *contra Apion. I.*

The term "Oracles" was probably bestowed upon these epigrammatic utterances in order to enforce the idea of their profound and deeply mysterious nature. The Chaldæans, however, had an Oracle, which they venerated as highly as the Greeks did that at Delphi.*

We are indebted to both Psellus and Pletho, for comments at some length upon the Chaldæan Oracles, and the collection adduced by these writers has been considerably enlarged by Franciscus Patricius, who made many additions from Proclus, Hermias, Simplicius, Damascius, Synesius, Olympiodorus, Nicephorus and Arnobius; his collection, which comprised some 324 oracles under general heads, was published in Latin in 1593, and constitutes the groundwork of the later classification arrived at by Taylor and Cory; all of these editions have been utilised in producing the present revise.

A certain portion of these Oracles collected by Psellus, appear to be correctly attributed to a Chaldæan Zoroaster of very early date, and are marked "Z," following the method indicated by Taylor, with one or two exceptions. Another portion is attributed to a sect of philosophers named Theurgists, who flourished during the reign of Marcus Antoninus, upon the authority of Proclus,† and these are marked "T." Oracles additional to these two series and of less definite source are marked "Z or T." Other oracular passages from miscellaneous authors are indicated by their names.

---

* Stephanus, *De Urbibus*.

† *Vide* his Scholia on the *Cratylus* of Plato.

The printed copies of the Oracles to be found in England are the following:—

1. *Oracula Magica*, Ludovicus Tiletanus, Paris, 1563.
2. *Zoroaster et ejus 320 oracula Chaldaica;* by Franciscus Patricius. . . . 1593.
3. Fred. Morellus; *Zoroastris oracula*, 1597. *Supplies about a hundred verses.*
4. Otto Heurnius; *Barbaricæ Philosophiæ antiquitatum libri duo*, 1600.
5. Johannes Opsopoeus; *Oracula Magica Zoroastris* 1599. *This includes the Commentaries of Pletho and of Psellus in Latin.*
6. Servatus Gallœus; *Sibulliakoi Chresmoi*, 1688. *Contains a version of the Oracles.*

Thomas Stanley. *The History of the Chaldaic Philosophy*, 1701. This treatise contains the Latin of Patricius, and the Commentaries of Pletho and Psellus in English.

Johannes Alb. Fabricius, *Bibliotheca Græca*, 1705-7. *Quotes the Oracles.*

Jacobus Marthanus, 1689. This version contains the Commentary of Gemistus Pletho.

Thomas Taylor, *The Chaldæan Oracles*, in the *Monthly Magazine*, and published independently, 1806.

Bibliotheca Classica Latina; A. Lemaire, volume 124, Paris, 1823.

Isaac Preston Cory, *Ancient Fragments*, London, 1828. (A third edition of this work has been published, omitting the Oracles.)

Phœnix, New York, 1835. A collection of curious old tracts, among which are the Oracles of Zoroaster, copied from Thomas Taylor and I. P. Cory; with an essay by Edward Gibbon.

INTRODUCTION

By L. O.

It has been believed by many, and not without good reason, that these terse and enigmatic utterances enshrine a profound system of mystical philosophy, but that this system demands for its full discernment a refinement of faculty, involving, as it does, a discrete perception of immaterial essences.

It has been asserted that the Chaldæan Magi[*] preserved their occult learning among their race by continual tradition from Father to Son. Diodorus says: "They learn these things, not after the same fashion as the Greeks: for amongst the Chaldæans, philosophy is delivered by tradition in the family, the Son receiving it from his Father, being exempted from all other employment; and thus having their parents for their teachers, they learn all things fully and abundantly, believing more firmly what is communicated to them."[†]

The remains then of this oral tradition seems to exist in these Oracles, which should be studied in the light of the Kabalah and of Egyptian Theology. Students are aware that the Kabalah[‡] is susceptible

---

[*] This powerful Guild was the guardian of Chaldæan philosophy, which exceeded the bounds of their country, and diffused itself into Persia and Arabia that borders upon it; for which reason the learning of the Chaldæans, Persians and Arabians is comprehended under the general title of Chaldæan.

[†] *Diodorus, lib. I.*

[‡] *Vide Kabalah Denudata,* by MacGregor Mathers.

of extraordinary interpretation with the aid of the Tarot, resuming as the latter does, the very roots of Egyptian Theology. Had a similar course been adopted by commentators in the past, the Chaldæan system expounded in these Oracles would not have been distorted in the way it has been.

The foundation upon which the whole structure of the Hebrew Kabalah rests is an exposition of ten deific powers successively emanated by the Illimitable Light, which in their varying dispositions are considered as the key of all things. This divine procession in the form of Three Triads of Powers, synthesized in a tenth, is said to be extended through four worlds, denominated respectively Atziluth, Briah, Yetzirah and Assiah, a fourfold gradation from the subtil to the gross. This proposition in its metaphysical roots is pantheistic, though, if it may be so stated, mediately theistic; while the ultimate noumenon of all phenomena is the absolute Deity, whose ideation constitutes the objective Universe.

Now these observations apply strictly also to the Chaldæan system.

The accompanying diagrams sufficiently indicate the harmony and identity of the Chaldæan philosophy with the Hebrew Kabalah. It will be seen that the First Mind and the *Intelligible Triad*, Pater, Potentia, or Mater, and Mens, are allotted to the Intelligible World of Supramundane Light: the "First Mind" represents the archetypal intelligence as an entity in the bosom of the Paternal Depth. This concentrates by reflection into the "Second Mind" representative of the Divine Power in the Empyræan World which is identified with the second great Triad of divine powers, known as *the Intelligible and at the same time Intellectual Triad:* the Æthereal World comprises the dual third Triad denominated *Intellectual:* while the fourth or Elementary World is governed by Hypezokos, or Flower of Fire, the actual builder of the world.

CHALDÆAN SCHEME.

The Intelligibles World of Supra-mundane Light	The Paternal Depth The First Mind
	The Intelligible Triad Pater : Mater or Potentia : Mens
	The Second Mind
Intelligibles and Intellectuals in the Empyræan World	Iynges Synoches Teletarchæ
Intellectuals in the Ethereal World	(The Third Mind.) Three Cosmagogi (Intellectual guides inflexible.) Three Amilicti (Implacable thunders).
Elementary World The Demiurgos of the Material Universe	Hypezokos (Flower of Fire) Effable, Essential and Elemental Orders
	The Earth-Matter

KABALISTIC SCHEME.

World of Atziluth   The Boundless   Ain Suph.
   or of God   The Illimitable   Ain Suph Aur
                         Light
                                   A radiant triangle.

                               Kether
World of Briah   (crown)
Divine Forces   Binah   Chokmah
                  (Intelligence)   (Wisdom).

                         Geburah   Chesed
World of Yetzirah   Tiphereth
  or of Formation   Hod   Netzach
                              Yesod

World of Assiah   Malkuth
                            Ruled by
Material Form.   Adonai Melekh

                            The Earth-Matter.

CHALDÆAN SCHEME OF BEINGS.

Representatives of the previous classes guiding our universe.

    I. Hyperarchii—Archangels
   II. Azonœi—Unzoned gods
  III. Zonœi—Planetary Deities.

Higher demons: Angels

Human Souls

Lower demons, elementals
    Fiery
    Airy
    Earthy
    Watery

Evil demons
Lucifugous; the kliphoth

===

Chaldæan Theology contemplated three great divisions of supra-mundane things:—the First was *Eternal*, without beginning or end, being the "Paternal Depth," the bosom of the Deity. The Second was conceived to be that mode of being having beginning but no end; the Creative World or Empyræum falls under this head, abounding as it does in productions, but its source remaining superior to these. The third and last order of divine things had a beginning in time and will end, this is the transitory Ethereal World. Seven spheres extended through these three Worlds, *viz.*, one in the Empyræum or verging from it, three in the Ethereal and three in the Elementary Worlds, while the whole physical realm synthesized the foregoing. These seven spheres are not to be confounded with the Seven material Planets; although the latter are the physical representatives of the former, which can only be said to be material in the metaphysical sense of the term. Psellus professed to identify them but his suggestions are inadequate as Stanley pointed out. But Stanley, although disagreeing with Psellus, is nevertheless inconsistent upon this point, for although he explains the four Worlds of the Chaldæans as successively noumenal to the physical realm, he obviously contradicts this in saying that one *corporeal* world is in the Empyræum.

Prior to the supramundane Light lay the "Paternal Depth," the Absolute Deity, containing all things "*in potentia*" and eternally immanent. This is analogous to the Ain Suph Aur of the Kabalah, three words of three letters, expressing three triads of Powers, which are subsequently translated into objectivity, and constitute the great Triadic Law under the direction of the Demiurgus, or artificer of the Universe.

In considering this schema, it must be remembered that the supramundane Light was regarded as the primal radiation from the Paternal Depth and the archetypal noumenon of the Empyræum, a universal, all-pervading—and, to human comprehension—ultimate essence. The Empyræum again, is a somewhat grosser though still highly subtilized Fire and creative source, in its turn the noumenon of the Formative or Ethereal World, as the latter is the noumenon of the Elementary World. Through these graduated media the conceptions of the Paternal Mind are ultimately fulfilled in time and space.

In some respects it is probable that the Oriental mind to-day is not much altered from what it was thousands of years ago, and much that now appears to us curious and phantastic in Eastern traditions, still finds responsive echo in the hearts and minds of a vast portion of mankind. A large number of thinkers and scientists in modern times have advocated tenets which, while not exactly similar, are parallel to ancient Chaldæan conceptions; this is exemplified in the notion that the operation of natural law in the Universe is controlled or operated by conscious and discriminating power which is co-ordinate with intelligence. It is but one step further to admit that forces are entities, to people the vast spaces of the Universe with the children of phantasy. Thus history repeats itself, and the old and the new alike reflect the multiform truth.

Without entering at length into the metaphysical aspect, it is important to notice the supremacy attributed to the "Paternal Mind." The intelligence of the Universe, poetically described as "energising before energy," establishes on high the primordial types or patterns of things which are to be, and, then inscrutably latent, vests the development of these in the *Rectores Mundorum*, the divine Regents or powers already referred to. As it is said, "Mind is with Him, power with them."

The word "Intelligible" is used in the Platonic sense, to denote a mode of being, power or perception, transcending intellectual comprehension, *i.e.*, wholly distinct from, and superior to, ratiocination. The Chaldæans recognised three modes of perception, *viz*., the testimony of the various senses, the ordinary processes of intellectual activity, and the intelligible conceptions before referred to. Each of these operations is distinct from the others, and, moreover, conducted in separate matrices, or vehicula. The anatomy of the Soul was, however, carried much farther than this, and, although in its ultimate radix recognised as identical with the divinity, yet in manifested being it was conceived to be highly complex. The Oracles speak of the "Paths of the Soul," the tracings of inflexible fire by which its essential parts are associated in integrity; while its various "summits," "fountains," and "vehicula," are all traceable by analogy with universal principles. This latter fact is, indeed, not the least remarkable feature of the Chaldæan system. Like several of the ancient cosmogonies, the principal characteristic of which seems to have been a certain adaptability to introversion, Chaldæan metaphysics synthesize most clearly in the human constitution.

In each of the Chaldæan Divine Worlds a trinity of divine powers operated, which synthetically constituted a fourth term. "In every World," says the Oracle, "a Triad shineth, of which the Monad is the ruling principle." These "Monads" are the divine Vice-gerents by which the Universe was conceived to be administered. Each of the four Worlds, *viz.*, the Empyræan, Ethereal, Elementary and Material, was presided over by a Supreme Power, itself in direct *rapport* with "the Father" and "moved by unspeakable counsels." These are clearly identical with the Kabalistic conception of the presidential heads of the four letters composing the Deity name in so many different languages. A parallel tenet is conveyed in the Oracle which runs: "There is a Venerable Name projected through the Worlds with a sleepless revolution." The Kabalah again supplies the key to this utterance, by regarding the Four Worlds as under the presidency of the four letters of the Venerable Name, a certain letter of the four being allotted to each World, as also was a special mode of writing the four-lettered name appropriate thereto; and, indeed in that system it is taught that the order of the Elements, both macrocosmic and microcosmic, on every plane, is directly controlled by the "revolution of the name." That Name is associated with the Æthers of the Elements and is thus considered as a Universal Law; it is the power which marshals the creative host, summed up in the Demiurgus, Hypezokos, or Flower of Fire.

Reference may here be made to the psychic anatomy of the human being according to Plato. He places the intellect in the head; the Soul endowed with some of the passions, such as fortitude, in the heart; while another Soul, of which the appetites, desires and grosser passions are its faculties, about the stomach and the spleen.

So, the Chaldæan doctrine as recorded by Psellus, considered man to be composed of three kinds of Souls, which may respectively be called:

First, the Intelligible, or divine soul,
Second, the Intellect or rational soul, and
Third, the Irrational, or passional soul.

This latter was regarded as subject to mutation, to be dissolved and perish at the death of the body.

Of the Intelligible, or divine soul, the Oracles teach that "It is a bright fire, which, by the power of the Father, remaineth immortal, and is Mistress of Life;" its power may be dimly apprehended through regenerate phantasy and when the sphere of the Intellect has ceased to respond to the images of the passional nature.

Concerning the rational soul, the Chaldæans taught that it was possible for it to assimilate itself unto the divinity on the one hand, or the irrational soul on the other. "Things divine," we read, "cannot be obtained by mortals whose intellect is directed to the body alone, but those only who are stripped of their garments, arrive at the summit,"

To the three Souls to which reference has been made, the Chaldæans moreover allotted three distinct vehicles: that of the divine Soul was immortal, that of the rational soul by approximation became so; while to the irrational soul was allotted what was called "the image," that is, the astral form of the physical body.

Physical life thus integrates three special modes of activity, which upon the dissolution of the body are respectively involved in the web of fate consequent upon incarnate energies in three different destinies.

The Oracles urge men to devote themselves to things divine, and not to give way to the promptings of the irrational soul, for, to such as fail herein, it is significantly said, "Thy vessel the beasts of the earth shall inhabit."

The Chaldæans assigned the place of the Image, the vehicle of the irrational soul, to the Lunar Sphere; it is probable that by the Lunar Sphere was meant something more than the orb of the Moon, the whole sublunary region, of which the terrestrial earth is, as it were, the centre. At death, the rational Soul rose above the lunar influence, provided always the past permitted that happy release. Great importance was attributed to the way in which the physical life was passed during the sojourn of the Soul in the tenement of flesh, and frequent are the exhortations to rise to communion with those Divine powers, to which nought but the highest Theurgy can pretend.

"Let the immortal depth of your Soul lead you," says an Oracle, "but earnestly raise your eyes upwards." Taylor comments upon this in the following beautiful passage: "By the eyes are to be understood all the gnostic powers of the Soul, for when these are extended the Soul becomes replete with a more excellent life and divine illumination; and is, as it were, raised above itself."

Of the Chaldæan Magi it might be truly said that they "among dreams did first discriminate the truthful vision!" for they were certainly endowed with a far reaching perception both mental and spiritual; attentive to images, and fired with mystic fervours, they were something more than mere theorists, but were also practical exemplars of the philosophy they taught. Life on the plains of Chaldæa, with its mild nights and jewelled skies, tended to foster the interior unfoldment; in early life the disciples of the Magi learnt to resolve the Bonds of proscription and enter the immeasurable region. One Oracle assures us that, "The girders of the Soul, which give her breathing, are easy to be unloosed," and elsewhere we read of the "Melody of the Ether" and of the "Lunar clashings," experiences which testify to the reality of their occult methods.

The Oracles assert that the impressions of characters and other divine visions appear in the Ether. The Chaldæan philosophy recognized the ethers of the Elements as the subtil media through which the operation of the grosser elements is effected—by the grosser elements I mean what we know as Earth, Air, Water and Fire—the principles of dryness and moisture, of heat and cold. These subtil ethers are really the elements of the ancients, and seem at an early period to have been connected with the Chaldæan astrology, as the signs of the Zodiac were connected with them. The twelve signs of the Zodiac are permutations of the ethers of the elements—four elements with three variations each; and according to the preponderance of one or another elemental condition in the constitution of the individual, so were his natural inclinations deduced therefrom. Thus when in the astrological jargon it was said that a man had Aries rising, he was said to be of a fiery nature, his natural tendencies being active, energetic and fiery, for in the constitution of such a one the fiery ether predominates. And these ethers were stimulated, or endowed with a certain kind of vibration, by their Presidents, the Planets; these latter being thus suspended in orderly disposed zones. Unto the Planets, too, colour and sound were also attributed; the planetary colours are connected with the ethers, and each of the Planetary forces was said to have special dominion over, or affinity with, one or other of the Zodiacal constellations. Communion with the hierarchies of these constellations formed part of the Chaldæan theurgy, and in a curious fragment it is said: "If thou often invokest it" (the celestial constellation called the Lion) "then when no longer is visible unto thee the Vault of the Heavens, when the Stars have lost their light the lamp of the Moon is veiled, the Earth abideth not, and around thee darts the lightning flame, then all things will appear to thee in the form of a Lion!" The Chaldæans, like the Egyptians, appear to have had a highly developed appreciation of colours, an evidence of their psychic susceptibility. The use of bright colours engenders the recognition of subsisting variety and stimulates that perception of the mind which energizes through imagination, or the operation of images. The Chaldæan method of contemplation appears to have been to identify the self with the object of contemplation; this is of course identical with the process of Indian Yoga, and is an idea which appears replete with suggestion; as it is written, "He assimilates the images to himself, casting them around his own form." But we are told, "All divine natures are incorporeal, but bodies are bound in them for your sakes."

The subtil ethers, of which I have spoken, served in their turn as it were for the garment of the divine Light; for the Oracles teach that beyond these again "A solar world and endless Light subsist!" This Divine Light was the object of all veneration. Do not think that what was intended thereby was the Solar Light we know: "The inerratic sphere of the Starless above" is an unmistakable expression and therein "the more true Sun" has place: Theosophists will appreciate the significance of "the more true Sun," for according to *The Secret Doctrine* the Sun we see is but the physical vehicle of a more transcendent splendour.

Some strong Souls were able to reach up to the Light by their own power: "The mortal who approaches the fire shall have Light from the divinity, and unto the persevering mortal the blessed immortals are swift." But what of those of a lesser stature? Were they, by inability, precluded from such illumination? "Others," we read, "even when asleep, He makes fruitful from his own Strength." That is to say, some men acquire divine knowledge through communion with Divinity in sleep. This idea has given rise to some of the most magnificent contributions to later literature; it has since been thoroughly elaborated by Porphyry and Synesius. The eleventh Book of the *Metamorphoses* of Apuleius and the *Vision of Scipio* ably vindicate this; and, although no doubt every Christian has heard that "He giveth unto his beloved in sleep," few, indeed, realise the possibility underlying that conception.

What, it may be asked, were the views of the Chaldæans with respect to terrestrial life: Was it a spirit of pessimism, which led them to hold this in light esteem? Or, should we not rather say that the keynote of their philosophy was an immense spiritual optimism? It appears to me that the latter is the more true interpretation. They realised that beyond the confines of matter lay a more perfect existence, a truer realm of which terrestrial administration is but a too often travestied reflection. They sought, as we seek now, the Good, the Beautiful and the True, but they did not hasten to the Outer in the thirst for sensation, but with a finer perception realised the true Utopia to be within.

And the first step in that admirable progress was a return to the simple life; hardly, indeed, a return, for most of the Magi were thus brought up from birth.* The hardihood engendered by the rugged life, coupled with that wisdom which directed their association, rendered these children of Nature peculiarly receptive of Nature's Truths. "Stoop not down," says the Oracle, "to the darkly splendid World, For a precipice lieth beneath the Earth, a descent of seven steps, and therein is established the throne of an evil and fatal force. Stoop not down unto that darkly splendid world, Defile not thy brilliant flame with the earthly dross of matter, Stoop not down for its splendour is but seeming, It is but the habitation of the Sons of the Unhappy." No more beautiful formulation of the Great Truth that the exterior and sensuous life is death to the highest energies of the Soul could possibly have been uttered: but to such as by purification and the practice of virtue rendered themselves worthy, encouragement was given, for, we read, "The Higher powers build up the body of the holy man."

The law of Karma was as much a feature of the Chaldæan philosophy as it is of the Theosophy of to-day: from a passage in *Ficinus*, we read, "The Soul perpetually runs and passes through all things in a certain space of time, which being performed it is presently compelled to pass back again through all things and unfold a similar web of generation in the World, according to Zoroaster, who thinks that as often as the same causes return, the same effects will in like manner return."

---

* They renounced rich attire and the wearing of gold. Their raiment was white upon occasion; their beds the ground, and their food nothing but herbs, cheese and bread

This is of course the explanation of the proverb that "History repeats itself," and is very far from the superstitious view of fate. Here each one receives his deserts according to merit or demerit, and these are the bonds of life; but the Oracles say, "Enlarge not thy destiny," and they urge men to "Explore the River of the Soul, so that although you have become a servant to body, you may again rise to the Order from which you descended, joining works to sacred reason!"

To this end we are commended to learn the Intelligible which exists beyond the mind, that divine portion of the being which exists beyond Intellect: and this it is only possible to grasp with the flower of the mind. "Understand the intelligible with the extended flame of an extended intellect." To Zoroaster also was attributed the utterance "who knows himself knows all things in himself;" while it is elsewhere suggested that "The paternal Mind has sowed symbols in the Soul." But such priceless knowledge was possible only to the Theurgists Who, we are told, "fall not so as to be ranked with the herd that are in subjection to fate." The divine light cannot radiate in an imperfect microcosm, even as the Clouds obscure the Sun; for of such as make ascent to the most divine of speculations in a confused and disordered manner, with unhallowed lips, or unwashed feet, the progressions are imperfect, the impulses are vain and the paths are dark.

Although destiny, our destiny, may be "written in the Stars" yet it was the mission of the divine Soul to raise the human Soul above the circle of necessity, and the Oracles give Victory to that Masterly Will, which

> "Hews the wall with might of magic,
> Breaks the palisade in pieces,
> Hews to atoms seven pickets . . .
> Speaks the Master words of knowledge!"

The means taken to that consummation consisted in the training of the Will and the elevation of the imagination, a divine power which controls consciousness: "Believe yourself to be above body, and you are," says the Oracle; it might have added "Then shall regenerate phantasy disclose the symbols of the Soul."

But it is said "On beholding yourself fear!" *i.e.*, the imperfect self.

Everything must be viewed as ideal by him who would understand the ultimate perfection.

Will is the grand agent in the mystic progress; its rule is all potent over the nervous system. By Will the fleeting vision is fixed on the treacherous waves of the astral Light; by Will the consciousness is impelled to commune with the divinity: yet there is not One Will, but three Wills—the Wills, namely, of the Divine, the Rational and Irrational Souls—to harmonize these is the difficulty.

It is selfishness which impedes the radiation of Thought, and attaches to body. This is scientifically true and irrespective of sentiment, the selfishness which reaches beyond the necessities of body is pure vulgarity.

A picture which to the cultured eye beautifully portrays a given subject, nevertheless appears to the savage a confused patchwork of streaks, so the extended perceptions of a citizen of the Universe are not grasped by those whose thoughts dwell within the sphere of the personal life.

The road to the *Summum Bonum* lies therefore through self-sacrifice, the sacrifice of the lower to the higher, for behind that Higher Self lies the concealed form of the Antient of Days, the synthetical Being of Divine Humanity.

These things are grasped by Soul; the song of the Soul is alone heard in the adytum of God-nourished Silence!

THE ORACLES OF ZOROASTER.

CAUSE. GOD.
FATHER. MIND. FIRE.
MONAD. DYAD. TRIAD.

1. But God is He having the head of the Hawk. The same is the first, incorruptible, eternal, unbegotten, indivisible, dissimilar: the dispenser of all good; indestructible; the best of the good, the Wisest of the wise; He is the Father of Equity and Justice, self-taught, physical, perfect, and wise—He who inspires the Sacred Philosophy.
    Eusebius. *Præparatio Evangelica*, liber. I., chap. X.

This Oracle does not appear in either of the ancient collections, nor in the group of oracles given by any of the mediæval occultists. Cory seems to have been the first to discover it in the voluminous writings of Eusebius, who attributes the authorship to the Persian Zoroaster

2. Theurgists assert that He is a God and celebrate him as both older and younger, as a circulating and eternal God, as understanding the whole number of all things moving in the World, and moreover infinite through his power and energizing a spiral force.
    Proclus on the *Timæus* of Plato, 244.   Z. or T.

The Egyptian Pantheon had an Elder and a Younger Horus—a God—son of Osiris and Isis. Taylor suggests that He refers to Kronos, Time, or Chronos, as the later Platonists wrote the name. Kronos, or Saturnus, of the Romans, was son of Uranos and Gaia, husband of Rhea, father of Zeus.

---

3. The God of the Universe, eternal, limitless, both young and old, having a spiral force.

Cory includes this Oracle in his collection, but he gives no authority for it.
Lobeck doubted its authenticity.

---

4. For the Eternal Æon*—according to the Oracle—is the cause of never failing life, of unwearied power and unsluggish energy.

Taylor.—T.

* *"For the First Æon, the Eternal one," or as Taylor gives, "Eternity."*

---

5. Hence the inscrutable God is called silent by the divine ones, and is said to consent with Mind, and to be known to human souls through the power of the Mind alone.

Proclus in *Theologiam Platonis*, 321.   T.

Iuscrutable. Taylor gives "stable;" perhaps "incomprehensible" is better.

---

6. The Chaldæans call the God Dionysos (or Bacchus), Iao in the Phœnician tongue (instead of

the Intelligible Light), and he is also called Sabaoth,*
signifying that he is above the Seven poles, that is
the Demiurgos.

       Lydus, *De Mensibus*, 83. T.

* *This word is Chaldee, TzBAUT, meaning* hosts;
but there is also a word SHBOH, meaning The Seven.

---

7. Containing all things in the one summit of his
own Hyparxis, He Himself subsists wholly beyond.
    Proclus in *Theologiam Platonis*, 212. T.

*Hyparxis, is generally deemed to mean "Subsistence."
Hupar is* Reality *as distinct from* appearance; *Hup-
arche is a* Beginning.

---

8. Measuring and bounding all things.
    Proclus in *Theologiam Platonis*, 386. T.

"*Thus he speaks the words,*" *is omitted by Taylor and
Cory, but present in the Greek.*

---

9. For nothing imperfect emanates from the
Paternal Principle,
      Psellus, 38; *Pletho.* Z.

This implies—but only from a succedent emanation.

---

10. The Father effused not Fear, but He infused
persuasion.
         Pletho. Z.

11. The Father hath apprehended Himself, and
hath not restricted his Fire to his own intellectual
power.
     Psellus, 30; *Pletho*, 33. Z.

Taylor gives:—The Father hath hastily withdrawn Himself, but hath not shut up his own Fire in his intellectual power.

The Greek text has no word "hastily," and as to "withdrawn—Arpazo means, grasp or snatch, but also "apprehend with the mind."

---

12. Such is the Mind which is energized before energy, while yet it had not gone forth, but abode in the Paternal Depth, and in the Adytum of God nourished silence.
        Proc. in Tim., 167. T.

13. All things have issued from that one Fire.
The Father perfected all things, and delivered them over to the Second Mind, whom all Nations of Men call the First.
      Psellus, 24; *Pletho*, 30. Z.

14. The Second Mind conducts the Empyrean World.
       Damascius, *De Principiis*. T.

15. What the Intelligible saith, it saith by understanding.
          Psellus, 35. Z.

16. Power is with them, but Mind is from Him.
    Proclus in *Platonis Theologiam*, 365. T.

17. The Mind of the Father riding on the subtle Guiders, which glitter with the tracings of inflexible and relentless Fire.
     Proclus on the *Cratylus of Plato*. T.

18. . . . . After the Paternal Conception
I the Soul reside, a heat animating all things.
. . . . For he placed

The Intelligible in the Soul, and the Soul in dull body,
Even so the Father of Gods and Men placed them in us.

    Proclus in *Tim. Plat.*, 124. Z. or T.

19. Natural works co-exist with the intellectual light of the Father. For it is the Soul which adorned the vast Heaven, and which adorneth it after the Father, but her dominion is established on high.

    Proclus in *Tim.*, 106. Z. or T.

Dominion, krata: some copies give kerata, horns.

---

20. The Soul, being a brilliant Fire, by the power of the Father remaineth immortal, and is Mistress of Life, and filleth up the many recesses of the bosom of the World.

    Psellus, 28; *Pletho*, 11. Z.

21. The channels being intermixed, therein she performeth the works of incorruptible Fire.

    Proclus in *Politica*, p. 399. Z. or T.

22. For not in Matter did the Fire which is in the first beyond enclose His active Power, but in Mind; for the framer of the Fiery World is the Mind of Mind.

    Proclus in *Theologiam*, 333, and *Tim.*, 157. T.

23. Who first sprang from Mind, clothing the one Fire with the other Fire, binding them together, that he might mingle the fountainous craters, while preserving unsullied the brilliance of His own Fire.

    Proclus in *Parm. Platonis*. T.

24. And thence a Fiery Whirlwind drawing down the brilliance of the flashing flame, penetrating the abysses of the Universe; for from thence downwards do extend their wondrous rays.

Proclus in *Theologiam Platonis*, 171 and 172.   T.

25. The Monad first existed, and the Paternal Monad still subsists.

Proclus in *Euclidem*, 27.   T.

26. When the Monad is extended, the Dyad is generated.

Proclus in *Euclidem*, 27.   T.

Note that " What the Pythagoreans signify by Monad, Duad and Triad, or Plato by Bound, Infinite and Mixed; that the Oracles of the Gods intend by Hyparxis, Power and Energy."

Damascius *De Principiis*.   Taylor.

---

27. And beside Him is seated the Dyad which glitters with intellectual sections, to govern all things, and to order everything not ordered.

Proclus in *Platonis Theologiam*, 376.   T.

28. The Mind of the Father said that all things should be cut into Three, whose Will assented, and immediately all things were so divided.

Proclus in *Parmen.*   T.

29. The Mind of the Eternal Father said into Three, governing all things by Mind.

Proclus, *Timæus of Plato*.   T.

30. The Father mingled every Spirit from this Triad.

Lydus, *De Mensibus*, 20.   Taylor.

31. All things are supplied from the bosom of this Triad.

> Lydus, *De Mensibus*, 20. Taylor.

32. All things are governed and subsist in this Triad.

> Proclus in I. *Alcibiades*. T.

33. For thou must know that all things bow before the Three Supernals.

> Damascius, *De Principiis*. T.

34. From thence floweth forth the Form of the Triad, being preëxistent; not the first Essence, but that whereby all things are measured.

> Anon. Z. or T.

35. And there appeared in it Virtue and Wisdom, and multiscient Truth.

> Anon. Z. or T.

36. For in each World shineth the Triad, over which the Monad ruleth.

> Damascius in *Parmenidem*. T.

37. The First Course is Sacred, in the middle place courses the Sun,* in the third the Earth is heated by the internal fire.

> Anon. Z. or T.

* *Jones gives Sun from Helios, but some Greek versions give Herios, which Cory translates, air.*

---

38. Exalted upon High and animating Light, Fire Ether and Worlds.

> Simplicius in his *Physica*, 143. Z. or T.

IDEAS.

Intelligibles, Intellectuals, Iynges, Synoches, Teletarchæ, Fountains, Principles, Hecate and Dæmons.

39. The Mind of the Father whirled forth in re-echoing roar, comprehending by invincible Will Ideas omniform; which flying forth from that one fountain issued; for from the Father alike was the Will and the End (by which are they connected with the Father according to alternating life, through varying vehicles). But they were divided asunder, being by Intellectual Fire distributed into other Intellectuals. For the King of all previously placed before the polymorphous World a Type, intellectual, incorruptible, the imprint of whose form is sent forth through the World, by which the Universe shone forth decked with Ideas all various, of which the foundation is One, One and alone. From this the others rush forth distributed and separated through the various bodies of the Universe, and are borne in swarms through its vast abysses, ever whirling forth in illimitable radiation.

They are intellectual conceptions from the Paternal Fountain partaking abundantly of the brilliance of Fire in the culmination of unresting Time.

But the primary self-perfect Fountain of the Father poured forth these primogenial Ideas.

Proclus in *Parmenidem.* Z. or T.

40. These being many, descend flashingly upon the shining Worlds, and in them are contained the Three Supernals.

Damascius in *Parmenidem.* T.

41. They are the guardians of the works of the Father, and of the One Mind, the Intelligible.

        Proclus in *Theologiam Platonis*, 205. T.

42. All things subsist together in the Intelligible World.

        Damascius, *De Principiis*. T.

43. But all Intellect understandeth the Deity, for Intellect existeth not without the Intelligible, neither apart from Intellect doth the Intelligible subsist.

        Damascius. Z. or T.

44. For Intellect existeth not without the Intelligible; apart from it, it subsisteth not.

        Proclus, *Th. Pl.*, 172. Z. or T.

45. By Intellect He containeth the Intelligibles and introduceth the Soul into the Worlds.

46. By Intellect he containeth the Intelligibles, and introduceth Sense into the Worlds.

        Proclus in *Crat.* T.

47. For this Paternal Intellect, which comprehendeth the Intelligibles and adorneth things ineffable, hath sowed symbols through the World.

        Proclus in *Cratylum*. T.

48. This Order is the beginning of all section.

        Dam., *De Prin.* T.

49. The Intelligible is the principle of all section.

        Damascius, *De Principiis*. T.

50. The Intelligible is as food to that which understandeth.

        Dam., *De Prin.* T.

51. The oracles concerning the Orders exhibits It as prior to the Heavens, as ineffable, and they add— It hath Mystic Silence.

Proclus in Cratylum. T.

52. The oracle calls the Intelligible causes Swift, and asserts that, proceeding from the Father, they rush again unto Him.

Proclus in Cratylum. T.

53. Those Natures are both Intellectual and Intelligible, which, themselves possessing Intellection, are the objects of Intelligence to others.

Proclus, Theologiam Platonis. T.

The Second Order of the Platonist philosophy was the "Intelligible and Intellectual Triad." Among the Chaldæans this order includes the Iynges, Synoches and Teletarchs. The Intellectual Triad of the later Platonists corresponds to the Fountains, Fontal Fathers or Cosmagogi of the Chaldæans.

---

54. The Intelligible Iynges themselves understand from the Father; by Ineffable counsels being moved so as to understand.

Psellus, 41; *Pletho*, 31. Z.

55. Because it is the Operator, because it is the Giver of Life Bearing Fire, because it filleth the Life-producing bosom of Hecaté; and it instilleth into the Synoches the enlivening strength of Fire, endued with mighty Power.

Proclus in Tim., 128. T.

56. He gave His own Whirlwinds to guard the Supernals, mingling the proper force of His own strength in the Synoches.

Dam., De Prin. T.

57. But likewise as many as serve the material Synoches.

              T.

58. The Teletarchs are comprehended in the Synoches.

          Dam., *De Prin.* T.

59. Rhea, the Fountain and River of the Blessed Intellectuals, having first received the powers of all things in Her Ineffable Bosom, pours forth perpetual Generation upon all things.

          Proc. in *Crat.* T.

60. For it is the bound of the Paternal Depth, and the Fountain of the Intellectuals.

          Dam., *De Prin.* T.

61. For He is a Power of circumlucid strength, glittering with Intellectual Sections.

            Dam. T.

62. He glittereth with Intellectual Sections, and hath filled all things with love.

            Dam. T.

63. Unto the Intellectual Whirlings of Intellectual Fire, all things are subservient, through the persuasive counsel of the Father.

         Proc. in *Parm.* T.

64. O! how the World hath inflexible Intellectual Rulers.

65. The source of the Hecaté correspondeth with that of the Fontal Fathers.

              T.

66. From Him leap forth the Amilicti, the all-relentless thunders, and the whirlwind receiving

Bosoms of the all-splendid Strength of Hecaté Father-begotten; and He who encircleth the Brilliance of Fire; And the Strong Spirit of the Poles, all fiery beyond.

Proc. in Crat. T.

67. There is another Fountain, which leadeth the Empyræan World.

Proc. in Tim. Z. or T.

668. The Fountain of Fountains, and the boundary of all fountains.

Dam., De Prin.

69. Under two Minds the Life-generating fountain of Souls is comprehended.

Dam., De Prin. T.

70. Beneath them exists the Principal One of the Immaterials.

Dam. in Parm. Z. or T.

Following the Intellectual Triad was the Demiurgos, from whom proceeded the Effable and Essential Orders including all sorts of Dæmons, and the Elementary World.

———

71. Father begotten Light, which alone hath gathered from the strength of the Father the Flower of mind, and hath the power of understanding the Paternal mind, and doth instil into all Fountains and Principles the power of understanding and the function of ceaseless revolution.

Proc. in Tim., 242.

72. All fountains and principles whirl round and always remain in a ceaseless revolution.

Proc. in Parm. Z. or T.

73. The Principles, which have understood the Intelligible works of the Father, He hath clothed in sensible works and bodies, being intermediate links existing to connect the Father with Matter, rendering apparent the Images of unapparent Natures, and inscribing the Unapparent in the Apparent frame of the World.

Dam., De Prin. Z. or T.

74. Typhon, Echidna, and Python, being the progeny of Tartaros and Gaia, who were united by Uranos, form, as it were, a certain Chaldæan Triad, the Inspector and Guardian of all the *disordered* fabrications.

Olymp. in Phæd. T.

75. There are certain Irrational Demons (mindless elementals), which derive their subsistence from the Aërial Rulers; wherefore the Oracle saith, Being the Charioteer of the Aërial, Terrestrial and Aquatic Dogs.

Olymp. in Phæd. T.

76. The Aquatic when applied to Divine Natures signifies a Government inseparable from Water, and hence the Oracle calls the Aquatic Gods, Water Walkers.

Proc. in Tim., 270. T.

77. There are certain Water Elementals whom Orpheus calls Nereides, dwelling in the more elevated exhalations of Water, such as appear in damp, cloudy Air, whose bodies are sometimes seen (as Zoroaster taught) by more acute eyes, especially in Persia and Africa.

Ficinus de Immortalilate Animæ, 123. T.

PARTICULAR SOULS.

Soul, Life, Man.

78. The Father conceived ideas, and all mortal bodies were animated by Him.
Proc. in Tim., 336.   T.

79. For the Father of Gods and men placed the Mind (nous) in the Soul (psyche); and placed both in the (human) body.

80. The Paternal Mind hath sowed symbols in the Soul.
Psell., 26; Pletho, 6.   Z.

81. Having mingled the Vital Spark from two according substances, Mind and Divine Spirit, as a third to these He added Holy Love, the venerable Charioteer uniting all things.
Lyd. De Men., 3.

82. Filling the Soul with profound Love.
Proc. in Pl. Theol, 4.   Z or T.

83. The Soul of man does in a manner clasp God to herself. Having nothing mortal, she is wholly inebriated with God. For she glorieth in the harmony under which the mortal body subsisteth.
Psellus, 17; Pletho, 10.   Z.

84. The more powerful Souls perceive Truth through themselves, and are of a more inventive Nature. Such Souls are saved through their own strength, according to the Oracle.
Proclus in I. Alc.   Z.

85. The Oracle saith that Ascending Souls sing a Pæan.

Olymp. in *Phæd.*   Z or T.

86. Of all Souls, those certainly are superlatively blessed, which are poured forth from Heaven to Earth; and they are happy, and have ineffable stamina, as many as proceed from Thy Splendid Self, O King, or from Jove Himself, under the strong necessity of Mithus.

Synes. De Insom, 153.   Z or T.

Query Mithras.

---

87. The Souls of those who quit the body violently are most pure.

Psellus, 27.   Z.

88. The girders of the Soul, which give her breathing, are easy to be unloosed.

Psellus, 32; *Pletho*, 8.   Z.

89. For when you see a Soul set free, the Father sendeth another, that the number may be complete.

Z. or T.

90. Understanding the works of the Father, they avoid the shameless Wing of Fate; they are placed in God, drawing forth strong light-bearers, descending from the Father, from whom as they descend, the Soul gathereth of the empyræan fruits the soul-nourishing flower.

Proc. in *Tim.*, 321.   Z. or T.

91. This Animastic Spirit which blessed men have called the Pneumatic Soul, becometh a god, an all-various Dæmon, and an Image (disembodied), and in this form of Soul suffereth her punishments. The

Oracles, too, accord with this account; for they assimilate the employment of the Soul in Hades, to the delusive visions of a dream.

Synesius *De Insom.* Z. or T.

The word Dæmon in the original meaning of the term did not necessarily mean a bad Spirit, and was as often applied to pure spirits as to impure.
Compare the Eastern doctrine of Devachan, a stage of pleasing illusion after death.

---

92. One life after another, from widely distributed sources. Passing from above, through to the opposite part; through the Centre of the Earth; and to the fifth middle, fiery centre, where the life-bearing fire descendeth as far as the material world.

Z. or T.

93. Water is a symbol of life; hence Plato and the gods before Plato, call it (the Soul) at one time the whole water of vivification, and at another time a certain fountain of it.

Proc. in *Tim.*, 318. Z.

94. O Man, of a daring nature, thou subtle production.

Psell., 12; *Pletho*, 21. Z.

95. For thy vessel the beasts of the Earth shall inhabit.

Psell., 36; *Pletho*, 7. Z.

Vessel is the body in which the Nous—thou, dwellest for a time.

---

96. Since the Soul perpetually runs and passes through many experiences in a certain space of time;

which being performed, it is presently compelled to pass back again through all things, and unfold a similar web of generation in the World, according to Zoroaster, who thinketh that as often as the same causes return, the same effects will in like manner be sure to ensue.

Ficin. *De Im. An.*, 129. Z.

97. According to Zoroaster, in us the ethereal vestment of the Soul perpetually revolves (reincarnates).

Ficin. *De Im. An.*, 131. Z.

98. The Oracles delivered by the Gods celebrate the essential fountain of every Soul; the Empyrean, the Ethereal and the Material. This fountain they separate from (Zoogonothea) the vivifying Goddess (Rhea), from whom (suspending the whole of Fate) they make two series or orders; the one animastic, or belonging to the Soul, and the other belonging to Fate. They assert that the Soul is derived from the animastic series, but that sometimes it becometh subservient to Fate, when passing into an irrational condition of being, it becometh subject to Fate instead of to Providence.

Proclus *de Providentia* apud Fabricium in *Biblioth.*

Græca., vol. 8, 486. Z. or T.

MATTER.

The World—and Nature.

99. The Matrix containing all things.

T.

100. Wholly divisible, and yet indivisible.

101. Thence abundantly springeth forth the generations of multifarious Matter.

Proc. in *Tim.*, 118.   T.

102. These frame atoms, sensible forms, corporeal bodies, and things destined to matter.

Dam, *De Prin.*   T.

103. The Nymphs of the Fountains, and all the Water Spirits, and terrestrial, aërial and astral forms, are the Lunar Riders and Rulers of all Matter, the Celestial, the Starry, and that which lieth in the Abysses.

Lydus., p. 32.

104. According to the Oracles, Evil is more feeble than Non-entity.

Proc. de Prov.   Z. or T.

105. We learn that Matter pervadeth the whole world, as the Gods also assert.

Proc., Tim., 142.   Z. or T.

106. All Divine Natures are incorporeal, but bodies are bound to them for your sakes. Bodies not being able to contain incorporeals, by reason of the Corporeal Nature, in which ye are concentrated.

Proc. in *Pl. Polit.*, 359.   Z. or T.

107. For the Paternal Self-begotten Mind, understanding His works sowed in all, the fiery bonds of love, that all things might continue loving for an infinite time. That the connected series of things might intellectually remain in the Light of the Father; that the elements of the World might continue their course in mutual attraction.

Proc. in *Tim.*, 155.   T.

108. The Maker of all things, self-operating, framed the World. And there was a certain Mass of Fire: all these things Self-Operating He produced, that the Body of the Universe might be conformed, that the World might be manifest, and not appear membranous.

Proc. in Tim., 154. Z. or T.

109. For He assimilateth the images to himself, casting them around his own form.

110. For they are an imitation of his Mind, but that which is fabricated hath something of Body.

Proc. in Tim., 87. Z or. T.

111. There is a Venerable Name, with a sleepless revolution, leaping forth into the worlds, through the rapid tones of the Father.

Proc. in Crat. Z. or T.

112. The Ethers of the Elements therefore are there.

Olympiodorus in Phæd. Z. or T.

113. The Oracles assert that the types of Characters, and of other Divine visions appear in the Ether (or Astral Light).

Simp. in Phys., 144. Z. or T.

114. In this the things without figure are figured.

Simp. in Phys., 143. Z. or T.

115. The Ineffable and Effable impressions of the World.

116. The Light hating World, and the winding currents by which many are drawn down.

Proc. in Tim., 339. Z. or T.

117. He maketh the whole World of Fire, Air, Water, and Earth, and of the all-nourishing Ether.

         Z. or T.

118. Placing Earth in the middle, but Water below the Earth, and Air above both these.

         Z. or T.

119. He fixed a vast multitude of un-wandering Stars, not by a strain laborious and hurtful, but with stability void of movement, forcing Fire forward into Fire.

     Proc. in *Tim.*, 280. Z. or T.

120. The Father congregated the Seven Firmaments of the Kosmos, circumscribing the Heavens with convex form.

     Dam. in *Parm.* Z, or T.

121. He constituted a Septenary of wandering Existences (the Planetary globes).

         Z. or T.

122. Suspending their disorder in Well-disposed Zones.

         Z. or T.

123. He made them six in number, and for the Seventh He cast into the midst thereof the Fiery Sun.

     Proc. in *Tim.*, 280. Z. or T.

124. The Centre from which all (lines) which way soever are equal.

        Proc. in *Euclidem*.

125. And that the Swift Sun doth pass as ever around a Centre.

     Proc. in *Plat. Th.*, 317. Z. or T.

126. Eagerly urging itself towards that Centre of resounding Light.

      Proc. in *Tim.*, 236.   T.

127. The Vast Sun, and the Brilliant Moon.

128. As rays of Light his locks flow forth, ending in acute points.

      Proc. in *Pl. Pol.* 387.   T.

129. And of the Solar Circles, and of the Lunar, clashings, and of the Aërial Recesses; the Melody of Ether, and of the Sun, and of the phases of the Moon, and of the Air.

      Proc. in *Tim.*, 257.   Z. or T.

130. The most mystic of discourses informs us that His wholeness is in the Supra-mundane Orders: for there a Solar World and Boundless Light subsist, as the Oracles of the Chaldæans affirm.

      Proc. in *Tim.*, 264.   Z. or T.

131. The Sun more true measureth all things by time, being itself the time of time, according to the Oracle of the Gods concerning it.

      Proc. in *Tim.*, 249.   Z. or T.

132. The Disk (of the Sun) is borne in the Starless realm above the Inerratic Sphere; and hence he is not in the midst of the Planets, but of the Three Worlds, according to the telestic Hypothesis.

      Jul., *Crat.*, 5, 334.   Z. or T.

133. The Sun is a Fire, the Channel of Fire, and the dispenser of Fire.

      Proc. in *Tim.*, 141.   Z. or T.

134. Hence Kronos, The Sun as Assessor beholds the true pole.

135. The Ethereal Course, and the vast motion of the Moon, and the Aërial fluxes.

> Proclus in *Tim.*, 257. Z. or T.

136. O Ether, Sun, and Spirit of the Moon, ye are the chiefs of the Air.

> Proc. in *Tim.*, 257. Z. or T.

137. And the wide Air, and the Lunar Course, and the Pole of the Sun.

> Proc. in *Tim.*, 257. Z. or T.

138. For the Goddess bringeth forth the Vast Sun, and the lucent Moon.

139. She collecteth it, receiving the Melody of Ether, and of the Sun, and of the Moon, and of whatsoever things are contained in the Air.

140. Unwearied Nature ruleth over the Worlds and works, that the Heavens drawing downward might run an eternal course, and that the other periods of the Sun, Moon, Seasons, Night and Day, might be accomplished.

> Proc. in *Tim.*, 4, 323. Z. or T.

141. And above the shoulders of that Great Goddess, is Nature in her vastness exalted.

> Proc. in *Tim.*, 4. T.

142. The most celebrated of the Babylonians, together with Ostanes and Zoroaster, very properly call the starry Spheres "Herds"; whether because these alone among corporeal magnitudes, are perfectly carried about around a Centre, or in conformity to the Oracles, because they are considered by them

as in a certain respect the bonds and collectors of physical reasons, which they likewise call in their sacred discourse "Herds" (agelous) and by the insertion of a gamma (aggelous) Angels. Wherefore the Stars which preside over each of these herds are considered to be Deities or Dæmons, similar to the Angels, and are called Archangels; and they are seven in number.

Anon. in *Theologumenis Arithmeticis.* Z.

Daimon in Greek meant "a Spirit," not "a bad Spirit."

---

143. Zoroaster calls the congruities of material forms to the ideals of the Soul of the World—Divine Allurements.

Ficinus, *de Vit. Cœl. Comp.* Z.

MAGICAL AND PHILOSOPHICAL PRECEPTS.

144. Direct not thy mind to the vast surfaces of the Earth; for the Plant of Truth grows not upon the ground. Nor measure the motions of the Sun, collecting rules, for he is carried by the Eternal Will of the Father, and not for your sake alone. Dismiss (from your mind) the impetuous course of the Moon, for she moveth always by the power of necessity. The progression of the Stars was not generated for your sake. The wide aërial flight of birds gives no true knowledge nor the dissection of the entrails of

victims; they are all mere toys, the basis of mercenary fraud: flee from these if you would enter the sacred paradise of piety, where Virtue, Wisdom and Equity are assembled.

Psel., 4.   Z.

145. Stoop not down unto the Darkly-Splendid World; wherein continually lieth a faithless Depth, and Hades wrapped in clouds, delighting in unintelligible images, precipitous, winding, a black ever-rolling Abyss; ever espousing a Body unluminous, formless and void.

Synes., *de Insom.*, 140.   Z. or T.

146. Stoop not down, for a precipice lieth beneath the Earth, reached by a descending Ladder which hath Seven Steps, and therein is established the Throne of an evil and fatal force.

Psell., 6; *Pletho*, 2.   Z.

147. Stay not on the Precipice with the dross of Matter, for there is a place for thy Image in a realm ever splendid.

Psell., 1, 2; *Pletho*, 14; *Synesius*, 140.   Z.

148. Invoke not the visible Image of the Soul of Nature.

Psell., 15; *Pletho*, 23.   Z.

149. Look not upon Nature, for her name is fatal.

Proc. in *Plat. Th.*, 143.   Z.

150. It becometh you not to behold them before your body is initiated, since by alway alluring they seduce the souls from the sacred mysteries.

Proc. in *I. Alcib.*   Z. or T.

151.   Bring her not forth, lest in departing she retain something.

Psell., 3; *Pletho*, 15.   Z.

Taylor says that "her" refers to the human soul.

---

152.   Defile not the Spirit, nor deepen a superficies.

Psell., 19; *Pletho*, 13.   Z.

153.   Enlarge not thy Destiny.

Psell., 37; *Pletho*, 4.

154.   Not hurling, according to the Oracle, a transcendent foot towards piety.

Dam. in *Vitam Isidore. ap. Suidam*   Z. or T.

155.   Change not the barbarous Names of Evocation for there are sacred Names in every language which are given by God, having in the Sacred Rites a Power Ineffable.

Psell., 7.   Nicephotus.   Z. or T.

156.   Go not forth when the Lictor passeth by.

Picus de Mirandula, *Concl.*   Z.

157.   Let fiery hope nourish you upon the Angelic plane.

Olymp. in *Phæd.*   Proc. in *Alcib.*   Z. or T.

158.   The conception of the glowing Fire hath the first rank, for the mortal who approacheth that Fire shall have Light from God; and unto the persevering mortal the Blessed Immortals are swift.

Proc. in *Tim.*, 65.   Z. or T.

159.   The Gods exhort us to understand the radiating form of Light.

Proc. in *Crat.*   Z. or T.

160. It becometh you to hasten unto the Light, and to the Rays of the Father, from whom was sent unto you a Soul (Psyche) endued with much mind (Nous).
Psell., 33.   *Pletho*, 6.   Z.

161. Seek Paradise.
Psell., 41.   *Pletho*, 27.   Z.

162. Learn the Intelligible for it subsisteth beyond the Mind.
Psell., 41.   *Pletho*, 27.   Z.

163. There is a certain Intelligible One whom it becometh you to understand with the Flower of Mind.
Psell., 31.   *Pletho*, 28.   Z.

164. But the Paternal Mind accepteth not the aspiration of the soul until she hath passed out of her oblivious state, and pronounceth the Word, regaining the Memory of the pure paternal Symbol.
Psell., 39.   *Pletho*, 5.   Z.

165. Unto some He gives the ability to receive the Knowledge of Light; and others, even when asleep, he makes fruitful from His own strength.
Synes., *de Insomn*, 135.   Z. or T.

166. It is not proper to understand that Intelligible One with vehemence, but with the extended flame of far reaching Mind, measuring all things except that Intelligible. But it is requisite to understand this; for if thou inclinest thy Mind thou wilt understand it, not earnestly; but it is becoming to bring with thee a pure and enquiring sense, to extend the void mind of thy Soul to the Intelligible, that thou mayest learn the Intelligible, because it subsisteth beyond Mind.
Dam.   T.

167. Thou wilt not comprehend it, as when understanding some common thing.

Damascius, de primis principiis. T.

168. Ye who understand, know the Super-mundane Paternal Depth.

Dam. Z. or T.

169. Things Divine are not attainable by mortals who understand the body alone, but only by those who stripped of their garments arrive at the summit.

Proc. in *Crat.* Z. or T.

170. Having put on the completely armed-vigour of resounding Light, with triple strength fortifying the Soul and the Mind, He must put into the Mind the various Symbols, and not walk dispersedly on the empyræan path, but with concentration.

171. For being furnished with every kind of Armour, and armed, he is similar to the Goddess.

Proc. in *Pl. Th.*, 324. T.

172. Explore the River of the Soul, whence, or in what order you have come: so that although you have become a servant to the body, you may again rise to the Order from which you descended, joining works to sacred reason.

Psell., 5. *Pletho*, 1. Z.

173. Every way unto the emancipated Soul extend the rays of Fire.

Psell., 11. *Pletho*, 24. Z.

174. Let the immortal depth of your Soul lead you, but earnestly raise your eyes upwards.

Psell., 11. *Pletho*, 20.

175. Man, being an intelligent Mortal, must bridle his Soul that she may not incur terrestrial infelicity, but be saved.
Lyd., *De Men.*, 2.

176. If thou extendeth the Fiery Mind to the work of piety, thou wilt preserve the fluxible body.
Psell., 22.   Pletho, 16.   Z.

177. The telestic life through Divine Fire removeth all the stains, together with everything of a foreign and irrational nature, which the spirit of the Soul has attracted from generation, as we are taught by the Oracle to believe.
Proc. in *Tim.*, 331.   Taylor.

178. The Oracles of the Gods declare, that through purifying ceremonies, not the Soul only, but bodies themselves become worthy of receiving much assistance and health, for, say they, the mortal vestment of coarse Matter will by these means be purified." And this, the Gods, in an exhortatory manner, announce to the most holy of Theurgists.
Jul., *Crat.* v., p. 334.   Z. or T.

179. We should flee, according to the Oracle, the multitude of men going in a herd.
Proc. in *I. Alc.*   Z. or T.

180. Who knoweth himself, knoweth all things in himself.
I. Pic., p. 211.   Z.

181. The Oracles often give victory to our own choice, and not to the Order alone of the Mundane periods. As, for instance, when they say, "On beholding thyself, fear!" And again, "Believe thyself to be above the Body, and thou art so." And,

still further, when they assert, "That our voluntary sorrows germinate in us the growth of the particular life we lead."

Proc., de Prov., p. 483.   Z. or T.

182. But these are mysteries which I evolve in the profound Abyss of the Mind.

183. As the Oracle thereforth saith: God is never so turned away from man, and never so much sendeth him new paths, as when he maketh ascent to divine speculations or works in a confused or disordered manner, and as it adds, with unhallowed lips, or unwashed feet. For of those who are thus negligent, the progress is imperfect, the impulses are vain, and the paths are dark.

Proc. in *Parm.*   Z. or T.

184. Not knowing that every God is good, ye are fruitlessly vigilant.

Proc. in *Platonis Pol.*, 355.   Z. or T.

185. Theurgists fall not so as to be ranked among the herd that are in subjection to Fate.

Lyd., *De men.*   Taylor.

186. The number nine is divine, receives its completion from three triads, and attains the summits of theology, according to the Chaldaic philosophy as Porphyry informeth us.

Lyd., p. 121.

187. In the left side of Hecate is a fountain of Virtue, which remaineth entirely within her, not sending forth its virginity.

Psell., 13; *Pletho*, 9.   Z.

188. And the earth bewailed them, even unto their children.

> *Psell.*, 21 ; *Pletho*, 3. Z.

189. The Furies are the Constrainers of Men.

> *Psell.*, 26 ; *Pletho*, 19. Z.

190. Lest being baptized to the Furies of the Earth, and to the necessities of nature (as some one of the Gods saith), you should perish.

> Proc. in *Theol.*, 297. Z. or T.

191. Nature persuadeth us that there are pure Dæmons, and that evil germs of Matter may alike become useful and good.

> *Psell.*, 16 ; *Pletho*, 18. Z.

192. For three days and no longer need ye sacrifice.

> *Pic. Concl.* Z.

193. So therefore first the Priest who governeth the works of Fire, must sprinkle with the Water of the loud-resounding Sea.

> Proc. in *Crat.* Z. or T.

194. Labour thou around the Strophalos of Hecaté.

> *Psell.*, 9. Nicephorus.

195. When thou shalt see a Terrestrial Dæmon approaching, Cry aloud! and sacrifice the stone Mnizourin.

> *Psell.*, 40. Z.

196. If thou often invokest thou shalt see all things growing dark; and then when no longer is visible unto thee the High-arched Vault of Heaven, when the Stars have lost their Light and the Lamp of

the Moon is veiled, the Earth abideth not, and around thee darts the Lightning Flame and all things appear amid thunders.

Psell., 10; *Pletho*, 22.   Z.

197. From the Cavities of the Earth leap forth the terrestrial Dog-faced demons, showing no true sign unto mortal man.

Psell, 23; *Pletho*, 10.   Z.

198. A similar Fire flashingly extending through the rushings of Air, or a Fire formless whence cometh the Image of a Voice, or even a flashing Light abounding, revolving, whirling forth, crying aloud. Also there is the vision of the fire-flashing Courser of Light, or also a Child, borne aloft on the shoulders of the Celestial Steed, fiery, or clothed with gold, or naked, or shooting with the bow shafts of Light, and standing on the shoulders of the horse; then if thy meditation prolongeth itself, thou shalt unite all these Symbols into the Form of a Lion.

Proc. in *Pl. Polit.*, 380; Stanley *Hist. Philos.*
Z. or T.

199. When thou shalt behold that holy and formless Fire shining flashingly through the depths of the Universe: Hear thou the Voice of Fire.

Psell., 14; *Pletho*, 25.   Z.

ORACLES FROM PORPHYRY.

1. There is above the Celestial Lights an Incorruptible Flame always sparkling; the Spring of Life, the Formation of all Beings, the Original of all things! This Flame produceth all things, and

nothing perisheth but what it consumeth. It maketh Itself known by Itself. This Fire cannot be contained in any Place, it is without Body and without Matter. It encompasseth the Heavens. And there goeth out from it little Sparks, which make all the Fires of the *Sun*, of the *Moon*, and of the *Stars*. Behold! what I know of God! Strive not to know more of Him, for that is beyond thy capacity, how wise soever thou art. As to the rest, know that unjust and wicked Man cannot hide himself from the Presence of God!

No subtilty nor excuse can disguise anything from His piercing Eyes. All is full of God, and God is in All!

---

2. There is in God an Immense Profundity of Flame! Nevertheless, the Heart should not fear to approach this Adorable Fire, or to be touched by it; it will never be consumed by this sweet Fire, whose mild and Tranquil Heat maketh the Binding, the Harmony, and the Duration of the World. Nothing subsisteth but by this Fire, which is God Himself. No Person begat Him; He is without Mother; He knoweth all things, and can be taught nothing.

He is Infallible in His designs, and His name is unspeakable, Behold now, what God is! As for us who are His messengers, *We are but a Little Part of God.*

Collectanea Hermetica

EDITED BY

W. WYNN WESTCOTT, M.B.,

Supreme Magus of the Rosicrucian Society.

VOLUME VII.

EUPHRATES

OR THE

WATERS OF THE EAST

BY EUGENIUS PHILALETHES.

1655.

WITH A COMMENTARY BY

S. S. D. D.

EDITOR'S PREFACE.

My friend S. S. D. D. has contributed a Commentary to this very curious and highly mystical tract, which was written by that eminent Rosicrucian Adept, Thomas Vaughan, and published by him under the pseudonym of Eugenius Philalethes. The seriously minded mystical student will find much to instruct and interest in the learned comments with which this edition is enriched.

The Paragraphs of the original work have been numbered for convenience of reference, and the new notes and comments have been placed after each numbered portion.

It must be borne in mind that there is an essential difference between the meaning of the word "element" as used by Vaughan, and the modern scientific meaning of the word.

For the ancient and mediæval philosophers knew nothing of our modern theory of chemical elements; their view of the common origin of matter not recognizing such definite and independent substances.

The word "Element" as used by the learned at the period when "Euphrates" was penned, meant rather a "state" of matter, such as the hot, cold, moist and dry natures; or the solid, liquid, gaseous or ethereal conditions; or the stationary, slow, quick or instantaneous processes of change.

No alteration has been made in the text of Vaughan's work except in the mode of spelling of a few words, the omission of italics and the correction of misprints.

It is intended to issue shortly the "Lumen de Lumine" of the same author, these two volumes will be found to be mutually explanatory.

W. Wynn Westcott.

EUPHRATES,

Or the Waters of the East;

Being a short Discourse of that Secret Fountain, whose Water flows from Fire; and carries in it the Beams of the Sun and Moon.

By EUGENIUS PHILALETHES

Sadith, ex. Lib. Sacro. Dixit Deus, Cujus Nomen sanctificetur: "Fecimus ex Aqua omnem Rem."

London:
Printed for Robert Boulter at the Turk's Head in Cornhill over against the Royall Exchange, 1655.

TO THE READER.

I HAVE Reader, (and I suppose it is not unknown to thee) within these few years, in several little Tracts delivered my Judgement of Philosophie, I say of Philosophie, for Alchymie in the common acceptation, and as it is a torture of Metals, I did never believe, much less did I study it. In this print, my books being perused will give thee evidence; for there I refer thee to a subject that is universal, that is the foundation of all Nature, that is the matter whereof all things are made, and wherewith being made are nourished. This I presume can be no metal, and therefore as I ever disclaimed Alchimie in the vulgar sense, so I thought fit to let the Alchimists know it, least in the perusal of my Writings they should fix a construction to some passages, which cannot suit with the Judgement of their Author. Hence thou mayest see what my conceptions were, when I began to write, and now I must tell thee they are still the same, nor hath my long experience weakened them at all, but invincibly confirmed them. But to acquaint thee how ingenuous I am, I freely confess, that in my practise I waved my own principles, for having miscarried in my first attempts, I laid aside the true subject, and was content to follow their Noise, who will hear nothing but Metals. What a drudge I have been in this school, for three years together, I will not here tell thee, it was well that I quitted it at last, and walk'd again into that clear light, which I had foolishly forsaken. I ever conceived that in metals there were great secrets, provided they be first reduc'd by a proper dissolvent, but to seek that Dissolvent, or the matter whereof it is made, in Metals, is not only Error but Madness. I have for the Truths sake, and to justify my innocent and former Discourses, added to them this little piece; which perhaps is such, and hath in it so much, as the World hath not yet seen published. It is not indeed the tenth part of what I had first design'd, but some sober Considerations made me forbear, as my sudden and abrupt Close will inform thee. However, what I now reserve, as to the Philosophical Mysteries may be imparted hereafter in our Meteorologie; and for the Theological, we shall draw them up for our own private use in our Philosophia Gratiae. I have little more to say, but if it may add anything to thy content, I can assure thee here is nothing affirm'd, but what is the fruit of my own experience. I can truly say of my own, for with much labour have I wrung it out of the Earth, nor had I any to instruct me; for I was never so fortunate as to meet with one man, who had the ability to contribute to me in this kind. I would not have thee build mountains on the Foundation I have here laid, not especially those of Gold; But if thou dost build Physick upon it, then have I hew'd thee the Rock and the Basis of that famous art, which is so much profest, and so little understood; here thou shalt find the true subject of it demonstrated, and if thou art not very dull, sufficiently discovered; Here God himself and the Word of God leads thee to it; Here the Light shews thee Light, and here hast thou that Testimony of Iamblicus, and the Aegyptian Records cleared namely, that God sometimes delivered to the ancient Priests and Prophets a certain matter, *per beata spectacula*, and communicated it for the use of Man. I shall conclude with this Admonition; if thou would'st know Nature, take heed of Antimonie and the common metals; seek onely that very first mixture of elements, which Nature makes in the great world; seek it I say, whil'st it is fresh and new, and having found it, conceal it. As for the use of it, seek not that altogether in Books, but rather beg it at the Hands of God, for it is properly his gift, and never man attain'd to it, without a clear and sensible assistance from above; Neglect not my Advice in this, though it may seem ridiculous to those that are overwise and have the mercies of God in derision. Many men live in this World without God; they have no Visits from him, and therefore laugh at those that seek him, but much more at those that have found him. St. Paul gloried in his Revelations, but he that will do so now shall be number'd among Ranters and Anabaptists. But let not these things divert thee, if thou servest God, thou servest a good Master, and he will not keep back thy Wages. Farewell in Christ Jesus.

E. P.

OF THE ADDRESS TO THE READER.
By S. S. D. D.

Let no man take up this book in the hope of finding it to contain a treatise on the transmutation of metals. It is rather a very profitable study of the philosophy of nature and a guide to the attainment of that perfection of mind and body, which has been called by some, the achievement of Adeptship.

Thomas Vaughan, who wrote under the name of Eugenius Philalethes, the lover of truth, published this work in 1655. At a time when the struggles between Puritans and Catholics had reached an acute stage. At a time when it was dangerous to write openly, and when man was still supposed to be the end of Creation. Spinoza was writing his exposure of the ignorance of Bible commentators and of the vulgar interpretation of the Scriptures; Hume's famous essay on miracles was still unthought of; Nature was degraded as the enemy of God much in the same way as Woman was looked upon as the temptress of Man.

Luther's demand that the "sacred oracles" should be placed in the hands of the unlearned, while it exposed the restrictions of the Priestly teaching was still doing as much harm as good. For without much learning, the words of the Jewish scriptures may be twisted into enough contradictory dogmas to furnish the battle cries of opposing sects till the end of time.

It is impossible to understand the Old Testament while we are ignorant of the esoteric construction put upon it by the Jews; and this key to its secret meaning is given in the Qabalah. That Thomas Vaughan was a Qabalist there is no doubt; but he dared not openly acknowledge the fact; so that we shall find him frequently speaking in a manner that obliges him to excuse himself to the learned and acknowledge that he writes thus " for the sake of those with weak consciences."

Our author says that he treats of a " subject which is universal;" that is to say, of a subject which has its analogies on all planes, a subject " which is the *foundation* of all nature."

Now the Foundation was the special name used by English Qabalists to translate the word Jesod, which is the Ninth Sephira, or absolute emanation of the manifesting God: and the waters of the fourth river of Eden, Phrath or Euphrates, flow down through the foundation of life into the visible universe.

The Egyptians, in whose secret archives we find the origin of much of the Qabalah, considered the human principle, or Chaibt, which they represented hieroglyphically by an open fan, to imply the emanation known to moderns as the odour, or the Aura, or the sympathetic or antipathetic influence of one being upon another.

In like manner we may think of the Sephira Jesod as not only a symbol of generative force, but also of this subtle emanation acting and reacting upon all creation; some of the results of which are tides, tempests, affinities, love, friendship; which is in fact the foundation alike of the relationship of a being to its parts, and of one being to another.

This odour or aura is especially noticeable in vegetable life. It is found that the essential oil existing in the outer cells of the petals is the source of the perfume of a flower, the lower surfaces containing tannin and colouring matter. Now the first action of the Foundation of life is to emit an odorous sphere or aura or emanation of influence. From the interaction of this with the Ruach or spirit, the material body is formulated from the elements. The seed being the magnet of attraction as we shall see expressed later on in the text of this work.

Thomas Vaughan's next sentence confirms us in the conclusion that the ideas he associates with the word Foundation are strictly Qabalistic, "That is the matter whereof all things are made, and wherewith being made they are nourished."

Now there is no doubt that in whatever form we may take our food, whether as beef, rice, or green food, it is alike resolved by digestion and fermentation into a milky emulsion in which will be found the essential oils of the various ingredients we have eaten, and that occurs before it can in any way be said to nourish us.

Again Metals can be acted upon by ferments of an acid nature and so changed into their higher form or tincture, but without the aid of the external elementary substance they are in themselves incapable of regeneration.

Having said thus much in words intended to puzzle the untrained scholar, our author closes his introduction abruptly, advising the student to apply himself to physic, or the regeneration of his own nature rather than to the making of gold.

With a final warning against metals and an exhortation to seek only the first mixture of elements which nature makes, he closes his introduction.

I may here remark that after fermentation or putrefaction, an amount of a volatile oil far exceeding in quantity the original essential oil of a natural substance can be extracted from it by the usual processes of distillation, etc.

Fermentation in this sense was one of the most important processes known to the ancients.

We may I think gather that the essential oil and comprehend with it the perfume or aura, was the physical basis of life in the eyes of the ancients. Death, putrefaction or fermentation sets free large quantities of this essence which when treated by the wise, may effect the regeneration of a particular body. Bringing about by art in a short time what nature would have effected slowly.

EUPHRATES, ETC.

Paragraph I.

It is written in those living Oracles, which we have received, and believe, that there is an Angel of the Waters: and this seems to be spoken in a general sense, as if the Angel there mentioned had been President of all that Element. Elsewhere we find an Angel limited to a more particular Charge, as that which descended at a certain season, and stirred the Waters in the Pool of Bethesda. Nor is it indeed anything strange that Angels should visit and move that Element, on which the Spirit of God did move in the beginning. I cite not these places, as if they were pertinent to my purpose, or made altogether for it, though I know they make nothing against it; but I cite them as Generals, to show that God is conversant with matter, though he be not tied to it, and this is all my design. Notwithstanding I know, that Prince Avicen, hath numbered St. John the Evangelist among the Chymists: And certainly if some passages in the Revelation were urged, and that no farther than

Rev. ch. xvi. v. 5.

John, ch. v. v. 4.

Gen. ch. 1. v. 2.

Lib. de. An. ch. v. dict. 1.

their own sense would carry them, it would be somewhat difficult to repel his opinion. Surely I am one that thinks very honourably of Nature, and if I avoid such Disputes as these, it is because I would not offend weak Consciences. For there are a people, who though they dare not think the Majesty of God was diminished, in that he made the World, yet they dare think, the Majesty of His Word is much vilified, if it be applied to what he hath made. An Opinion, truly, that carries in it a most dangerous Blasphemy; namely that God's Word and God's Work should be such different things, that the one must needs disgrace the other. I must confess I am much to seek, what Scripture shall be applied to, and whom it was written for if not for us, and for our instruction; for if they that are whole (as our Saviour testifies) have no need of a Phisician, then did God cause Scripture to be written, neither for himself, nor for his Angels, but it was written for those creatures, who having lost the first estate, were since fallen into corruption. Now then if scripture was written for us, it concerns us much to know what use we shall make of it, and this we may gather from the different conditions of Man before and after his Fall. Before his fall, Man was a glorious Creature, having received from God Immortality, and perfect Knowledge; but in and after his Fall, he exchanged immortality for death, and knowledge for ignorance. Now as to our redemption from this fall, we may not

Mark i. v. 17.

(in respect of Death) expect it in this world, God having decreed, that all men should once die; But for our ignorance, we may and ought to put off in this life, forasmuch as without the Knowledge of God, no man can be saved: for, it is both the Cause and the Earnest of our future immortality. It remains then that our ignorance must be put off in part, even in this life, before we can put off our mortality; and certainly to this end was Scripture written; namely that by it we might attain to the knowledge of God, and return to him from whom we were fallen. And here let no man be angry with me, if I ask how Scripture teacheth us to know God? Doth it only tell us there is a God, and leave all the rest to our discretion? Doth it (that I may speak my mind) teach us to know God by his Works, or without his Works? If by his Works then by Natural things, for they are his Works, and none other, if without his Works, I desire to know what manner of teaching that is, for I cannot yet find it. If they say it is by Inspiration, I say too that God can teach us so, but Scripture cannot; for certainly Scripture never inspired any man, though it came itself by inspiration. But if it be replied, that in Scripture we have the testimonies of men inspired, I say this Answer is beside my Question; for I speak not here of the bare Authority or Testimony of Scripture, but I speak of that Doctrine, by which it proves what it testifies, for with such Doctrine the Scripture abounds. Sure I am, that Moses proves God by his Creation, and God proves himself to

Moses by Transmutation of his Rod into a Serpent, and of the serpent into a Rod. And to the Egyptians he gives more terrible Demonstrations of his Power and Sovereignty in Nature, by turning their Rivers into Blood, and the Dust of their Land into Lice, by a Murrain of Beasts, by Blains and Boils, and the death of their first-born. By the fever plague of Frogs, Locusts, Hail, Fire, Thunder, and Darkness; all which were but great natural works, by which he proved his Godhead, as himself hath said. And the Aegyptians shall know that I am the Lord, when I stretch forth my hand upon Aegypt.

Exod. ch. vii. v. 5.

When he reveals himself to Cyrus, he does it not by a simple affirmation that he is God, but he proves himself to be such by the World that he hath made.

I am the Lord (saith he) and there is none else; there is no God besides me; I girded thee, though thou hast not known me, I formed the Light, and create Darkness, I make Peace, and create Evil. I the Lord do all these things. I have made the earth, and created Man upon it. I even my hands have stretched out the Heavens, and all their Host have I commanded. Let any man read those Majestic and Philosophical Expostulations between God and Job; or in a word, let him read over both Testaments and he shall find, if he reads attentively, that Scripture all the way, makes use of nature, and hath indeed discovered such natural Mysteries as

Isaiah xlv.

Job. ch. xxxviii., v. 39, 40, 41.

are not to be found in any of the Philosophers; and this shall appear in the following Discourse. For my own part, I fear not to say, that Nature is so much the business of Scripture, that to me, the Spirit of God, in those sacred Oracles, seems not only to mind the Restitution of Man in particular, but even the Redemption of Nature in general. We must not therefore confine this Restitution to our own Species, unless we can confine corruption to it withal, which doubtless we cannot do; for it is evident that Corruption hath not onely Seiz'd upon Man, but on the World also for man's sake. If it be true then that man hath a Saviour, it is also as true, that the whole Creation hath the same; God having reconciled all things to himself in Christ Jesus. And if it be true, that we look for the Redemption of our Bodies, and a New man; It is equally true, that we look for a new Heaven, and a new Earth, wherein dwelleth righteousness; for it is not man alone, that is to be Renewed at the general Restauration, but even the world, as well as man, as it is written: Behold! I make all things New. I speak not this to disparage man, or to match any other creature with him: for I know he is principal in the Restauration, as he was in the Fall, the Corruption that succeeded in the Elements, being but a Chain, that this prisoner drags after him: but I speak this to show, that God minds the Restitution of Nature in general, and not man alone, who though he be the

Rev. ch., xxi. v. 5.

noblest part, yet certainly is but a small part of Nature. Is scripture then misapplied, much less vilified, when it is applied to the object of Salvation, namely to Nature, for that is it, which God would save, and redeeme from the present Deprivations, to which it is subject: verily, when I read Scripture, I can find nothing in it, but what concerns Nature and Natural things: for where it mentions Regeneration, Illumination, and Grace, or any other spiritual gift, it doth it not precisely, but in order to Nature, for what signifies all this, but a new influence of Spirit, descending from God to assist Nature, and to free us from those Corruptions, wherewith of a long time we have been opprest? I suppose it will not be denied, but God is more Metaphysical, than any Scripture can be and yet in the work of salvation, it were great impiety to separate God and Nature, for then God would have nothing to save nor indeed to work upon. How much more absurd is it in the Ministry of Salvation to separate Scripture and Nature, for to whom I beseech you doth Scripture speak? Nay, to whom is Salvation minister'd, if Nature be taken away? I doubt not but man stands in nature, not above it, and let the School-men resolve him into what parts they please, all those parts will be found natural, since God alone is truly Metaphysical. I would gladly learn of our Adversaries, how they came first to know, that Nature is Corrupted; for if Scripture taught them this physical truth, why may it not teach them more? but that Scripture taught them, is altogether undeniable; Let us fancy a Physician of such Abilities, as to state the true temperament of his patient, and wherein his Disease hath disordered it. Doth he not this to good purpose? Questionless, he doth: and to no less purpose is it in my opinion, for the spirit of God, whose patient nature is, to give us in Scripture a Character of Nature, which certainly he hath done in all points, whether we look to the past, present, or future Complexion of the World. For my own part, I have this assurance of Philosophy, that all the Mysteries of Nature consist in the knowledge of that Corruption, which is mention'd in Scripture, and which succeeded the Fall: namely to know what it is, and where it resides principally: as also to know what Substance that is, which resists it most, and rewards it, as being most free from it, for in these two consist the Advantages of life and death. To be short, Experience, and Reason grounded thereupon. I have taught me, that Philosophy and Divinity are but one, and the same science: but man hath dealt with knowledge, as he doth with Rivers, and Wells, which being drawn into several pipes are made to run several ways, and by this accident come at last to have several names. We see that God in his work, hath united spirit and matter, visibles and invisibles, and out of the union of spiritual, and natural substances riseth a perfect compound, whose very nature, and Being consists in that union. How then is it possible to demonstrate the Nature of that Compound by a divided

Theory of Spirit by itself and matter by itself? for if the nature of a Compound consists in the Composition of Spirit and matter, then must not we seek that Nature in their separation, but in their mixture and Temperature, and in their mutual mixt Actions and Passions. Besides: who hath ever seen a spirit without matter, or matter without spirit, that he should be able to give us a true Theory of both principles in their simplicity? Certainly, no man living. It is just so in Divinity, for if by evasion we confine Divinity to God in the abstract, who (say I) hath even known him so? Or, who hath received such a Theology from him, and hath not all this while delivered it unto us? Verily, if we consider God in the abstract, and as he is in himself, we can say nothing of him positively, but we may something negatively, as Dionysius hath done, that is to say, we may affirm what he is not, but we cannot affirm what he is. But if by Divinity, we understand the Doctrine of Salvation, as it is laid down in scripture, then verily it is a mixed Doctrine, involving both God and Nature. And here I doubt not to affirme That the Mystery of Salvation can never be fully understood without Philosophy, not in its just latitude, as it is an Application of God to Nature, and a Conversion of Nature to God, in which two Motions and their Means, all spiritual and natural knowledge is comprehended.

COMMENTS UPON THE FIRST PARAGRAPH.

"And I heard the Angel of the Waters say, Thou art righteous, O Lord, which art, and wast, and shalt be, because thou hast judged thus." (Rev. xiv. 5).

Here we find at once our author falling in with the "weak consciences" he expected to deal with, and for the moment taking the literal meaning of the *sacred oracles*.

"For an angel went down at a certain season into the pool and troubled the water." (St. John v. 4.)

"And the Spirit of God moved upon the face of the waters." (Gen. i. 2.)

Then he circumstantially states his opinion that God's Work does not disgrace God's Word, and his object is "to show that God is conversant with matter though he be not tied to it." It is curious to note that Professor Tyndal in his famous Belfast Address to the British Association for the Advancement of Science made an almost identical appeal to his audience saying:—

"Spirit and matter have ever been presented to us in the rudest contrast, the one as all noble, the other as all-vile. Supposing that, instead of having the foregoing antithesis of spirit and matter presented to our youthful minds, we had been taught to regard them as equally worthy and equally wonderful; to consider them as two opposite faces of the self-same mystery. . . . . Looking at matter not as brute matter but as the living garment of God; do you not think the law of relativity might have had an outcome different from its present one. Without this total Revolution of the notions now prevalent, the Evolution hypothises must stand condemned (for what is the core, the essence of this hypothesis? Strip it naked and you stand face to face with the notion that not the more ignoble forms of animalculæ but the human body, the human mind itself, emotion, intellect, will, and all their phenomena were once latent in a fiery cloud); but in many profoundly thoughtful minds such a revolution has already taken place. They degrade neither member of the mysterious duality referred to, but they exalt one of them from its abasement, and repeal the divorce hitherto existing between both. In substance, if not in words, their position as regards the relation of spirit and matter is; 'What God hath joined together let not man put asunder.'"

It is necessary in this place to make a slight digression on the nature of God according to the Ancients. "The Egyptians recognised a divinity only in those cases where they perceived a fixed law either of permanence or change. The Earth abides, so do the Heavens, Days, Months, Seasons; these show a regularity which was called Maāt. The Gods are called possessors of Maāt or subsisting through Maāt. Truth and Justice are but forms of Maāt applied to human action" (Renouf, Introduction to the *Papyrus of Ani*). Beyond these the Egyptians believed in the Unnameable One. He whose throne the plumes of Amen's headdress barely touch. (The Hebrew root Amen, AMN, signifies stability.)

Among the Jews, the "Jehovah" holy as He was, existed only as the manifesting deity taking form in the world of matter as the holy living creatures, the forces of heat, moisture, cold and dryness; or on another plane developing as spirit, soul, mind and matter. But the real Being of Deity was called "Ehyeh," the "I am that I am," and behind Him was the Potential Being or Ain Soph Aur. For it is written " His is the Mind, Theirs are the powers."

In the same way Brahma the Universe separated its body into two halves; *Viraj*, the spiritual, intelligent nature, and *Vach* or the manifest expression of the eternal divine Ideation. But this was not the same as the Great Brahm, or "Great Breath" breathing out for millions of years, and again breathing in for the same period, becoming alternately manifest and unmanifest. So far we have spoken of the Macrocosmic God or Macroprosopus. Of the Microprosopus; the Microcosmic God of the New Testament, He through whom we can approach the vast ideal which the human brain is too small to grasp, we need not here speak further.

I must now deal shortly with the occult meaning of the Fall. The Fall means more especially—fallen into generation or corruptibility. When Isis let loose Typhon after his imprisonment by Horus, her enraged son destroyed her royal diadem and cut off her head, but Thoth—in one sense the moon god, replaced it by a cow's head. That is to say, when in the course of cosmic evolution Primæval chaos seemed to return as ruler of night and winter, the child of the spirit moving on the waters of creation laid low the glorious mother who had borne him. She became the Nature Goddess of the earth the symbol of fruitfulness, the sacred cow, the increaser of harvest. Henceforth the processes of change became recognised as gods or "fixed laws;" death and corruption which for a time seem like annihilation, being some of these.

Of the teaching of the Qabalah on the Fall I have only room to quote the following paragraph from S. L. Macgregor Mathers' Introduction to the *Kabalah Unveiled*.

"The first two letters of Jehovah I and H are the father and mother of Microprosopus" (or the supernal Adam) "and the H final is his bride" (or Eve). "But in these forms is expressed the equilibrium of severity and mercy. Mercy being masuline and severity feminine. Excess of Mercy is merely weakness, but Excess of Severity calls forth the evil and oppressive force which is symbolised by Leviathan. Wherefore it is said 'Behind the shoulders of the Bride, the Serpent rears his head.' Of the Bride" (the cow-headed

Isis) "not the Supernal Mother" (Isis crowned with the Royal diadem) "for she bruises the head of the Serpent."

The serpent is the centripetal force, ever seeking to penetrate paradise, and "thereby constricting the efflux of divine radiation," which is centrifugal. The Adam Qadmon's exchange of the Garden of Eden for knowledge and death, must be taken to mean the exchange of uncreated thought into differentiation and evolution, resulting finally in the creation of a material universe.

On this subject much may be learnt from the first book of the *Divine Pymander*, published in this series; in the Seventeenth book it is written:—

"Moreover the things that are made are visible, but *He is invisible;* and for *this cause he maketh them*, that *he may be visible;* and therefore he maketh them always."

So we see that the Eternal one being defined, saw a reflection of himself; and the love he bore his image emanated as a third form, the Supernal Mother who aspireth to the Wisdom which is beyond. So is the Supernal triad formed.

In like manner the Holy Triad, reflected and defined, became the throne whereon the holy deific form was seated, and the Hexagram of the Macroprosopus was reflected unto the Heart of the Microprosopus.

And in this sense are to be understood the words written on the mummy case of Panehemisis, "The heart of Man is his own God."

Around the image in the sanctuary of our hearts is the firmament and the powers, and below are the Kerubim or Living Creatures.

In his book entitled *Lumen de Lumine*, our author laments the separation that has taken place between the Elemental, Celestial, and Spiritual Sciences, for he says, these three are branches of one tree.

"Out of one universal root, the Chaos, grew all specified natures and their individuals."

I must deal shortly with the nature of Chaos as understood by the ancients, because in the present volume our author evades any definite explanation of it.

Chaos, the Abyss or " Great Deep " was personified among the Egyptians by Neïth; the only one containing all—without form or sex, giving birth to itself without fecundation. She was adored under the form of a Virgin Mother. She is the Father-Mother, the immaculate Virgin. She is called the Lady of the Sycamore, and is represented as dispersing the waters of the Tree of Life. She is the Bythos of the Gnostics, The One of the Neoplatonists, The All of the German Metaphysicians, the Anaita of Assyria.

Now from this root or chaos sprang all manifestations, divine, celestial, and elemental, and these three are one, and if separated from each other are like the dead branches cut from the parent stem.

For some pages our author dwells on the exoteric meaning of the scriptures in a manner that concerns the modern thinker very little. But we must bear in memory the intolerance and bigotry that prevailed at the period, and that twenty years later Spinoza forfeited all worldly advantages by asserting that the vulgar interpretation of the Sacred Oracles had led to much error.

However, Thomas Vaughan having paid his tribute to "weak consciences," touches us all when he says, " God minds the Restitution of Nature in general, and not of Man alone, ... who is but a small part of nature. Regeneration, Illumination and Grace, signify a new influence of Spirit. If God and Nature be one, how much more shall man and nature be one."

Emerson has said in this relation, " Indeed we are but Shadows we are not endowed with real life and all that seems most real about us is but the thinnest substance of a dream, till the heart be touched by nature. That touch creates us: then we begin to be; thereby we are beings of reality and inheritors of eternity."

We acknowledge nature to be corrupt, but by the knowledge of that corruption is to be solved the riddle of the Universe.

The union of spirit and nature gives rise to a perfect compound. The Light of wisdom united by philosophy to experiment makes the perfect artist or creative adept.

Philosophy or the passion for wisdom stimulates the intellect, as religion stimulates the emotions; these passions or expansions of the Ego carry it beyond the limits of its own being, and tend to merge it in the all being. Here the centrifugal or redeeming force is free to act, and the constrictions of matter cease. When the Passions of the Emotions and the Intellect are set free, the Experience of Elemental Nature can be judged with safety. This then is the Esoteric meaning of the "Unity with God." "I am in my father, and ye in me, and I in you." (St. John x. 14-20.) Compare again, "His is the mind, theirs are the powers" of the Chaldean Oracles. For the perfect man stands between the finest ether and the coarsest matter, and his spirit must penetrate all.

For the world, religion means, as Cardinal Newman puts it, "the knowledge of God, of His will, and of our duties towards Him." Separating Him as a formal notion from His works, cutting Him off as a branch from the Tree of Life of which He is the very root and being. Therefore to the initiated it is no blasphemy to say that such religion is a vanity and vexation of spirit.

The world holds many half evolved personalities who have to live and learn much before they can be conscious of the latent complexities of their own natures. Their hour has not yet come. But for the more fully developed,—life daily sounds undreamed of harmonies. Just as in modern music the most acute emotion is produced by subtle changes of key, so the human being in passing from one aspect to another of a highly complex existence intensifies and enriches his being with experiences, undreamed of by the undeveloped man, just as little as, by the masters of the simple harmonies of ancient music.

Our author's first paragraph ends with the clear statement that without philosophy, or the passion for wisdom, salvation cannot be understood. Again he pleads for the union of the divine, the celestial, and the natural; for he says the very nature of the highest existence is the union and synthesis of the diverse products of differentiation.

Can we not dimly comprehend from this principle how it is that each day of Brahma (or manifestation of the Universe) enriches and beautifies the night of his repose; how Nirvana becomes more and more exquisite in its subtle harmonies, as beings are prepared for it by finer and finer complexities and variations of parts.

Paragraph II.

' To speak then of God without Nature, is more than we can do, for we have not known him so, and to speak of Nature without God, is more than we may do, for we should rob God of his Glory, and attribute those Effects to Nature, which belong properly to God, and to the spirit of God, which works in Nature. We shall therefore use a mean form of speech, between these extremes, and this form the Scriptures have taught us, for the Prophets and Apostles, have used no other. Let not any man therefore be offended, if in this Discourse we shall use Scripture to prove Philosophy, and Philosophy to prove Divinity, for of a truth our knowledge is such, that our Divinity is not without Nature nor our Philosophy without God. Notwithstanding, I dare not think but most men will repine at this course, though I cannot think, wherefore they should, for when I joyne Scripture and Philosophy, I do but join God and Nature, an union certainly approved of by God, though it be condemned of men. But this perverse ignorance, how bold soever it be, I shall not quarrel with, for besides Scripture, I have other grounds, that have brought me very fairly, and soberly to this Discourse.

COMMENTS UPON THE SECOND PARAGRAPH.

This is a recapitulation of the general principle that God and Nature,—Scripture and Philosophy—are to be joined together and not separated from each other in our minds.

Paragraph III.

I have sojourn'd now for some years, in this great Fabric, which the fortunate call their World: and certainly I have spent my time like a Traveller, not to purchase it, but to observe it. There is scarce anything in it, but hath given me an occasion of some thoughts; but that which took me up much, and soon, was the continuall action of fire upon water. This Speculation (I know not how) surpris'd my first youth, long before I saw the University, and certainly Nature, whose pupil I was, had even then awaken'd many notions in me, which I met with afterwards, in the Platonic Philosophy. I will not forbear to write, how I had then fancied a certain practice on water, out of which, even in those childish dayes, I expected wonders: but certainly neither gold, nor silver, for I did not so much as think of them, nor of any such covetous artifice. This Consideration of my self, when I was a Child, has made me since examine Children, namely, what thoughts they had of these elements, we see about us, and I found thus much by them, that Nature in her simplicity, is much more wise, than some men are with their acquired parts, and Sophistry, of a truth I thought my self bound to prove all things, that I might attain to my lawful desires, but least you think, I have only conversed with children I shall confess, I have convers'd with children and Fools too: that is, as I interpret it, with Children and Men, for these last are not in all things, as wise as the first. A Child, I suppose, in puris Naturalibus,

Before education alters him, and ferments him, is a Subject hath not been much consider'd, for men respect him not, till he is company for them, and then indeed they spoil him. Notwithstanding I should think, by what I have read, that the natural disposition of Children, before it is corrupted with Customs and Manners, is one of these things, about which the Antient Philosophers have busyied themselves even to some curiosity. I shall not here express what I have found by my own experience, for this is a point of foresight, and a ground by which wise men have attained to a certain Knowledge of Morals, as well as Naturals.

Paragraph IV.

But to return from this Digression, to the Principles first proposed, namely Fire and Water, I shall borrow my entrane into this discourse, from my famous Country-man Rice of Chester, who speaking of this Art, delivers himself thus.

Ars hoec (saith he), de Philosophia occulta est; est de illa parte Philosophiae quae Meteora tractat; Loquitur enim, haec Ars non solum de elevatione et depressione Elementorum, sed etiam Elementatorum. Scias H O C, quia magnum secretum est.

Paragraph V.

These words, if the Mysteries they involve and relate to were distinctly laid down, would make an endless Discourse; for they contain all that Nature doth: and all that art can do. But that we may in some order, and as far as Conscience will permit, express what they signifie: We do first say, That God is the principal and sole Author of all things, who by his Word and Spirit hath form'd and manifested those things we see, and even those things which at present we cannot see. As for the matter whereof he formed them, it being a substance pre-existent, not only to us, but to the world itself, most men may think the knowledge of it impossible, for how shall we know a thing that was so long before us, and which is not now extant with us, nor ever was (in their opinion) since the creation? To this objection, which at first sight may seem invincible, we shall return an answer that shall break it; for we will show how and by what means, we came to know this matter, and not only to know it, but after long labours to see it, handle it, and taste it. It is evidence enough that every Individual (suppose man himself) is made of a seed, and this seed when the body is perfected, appears no more, for it is altered and transformed to a body. However that self-same body does afterwards yield a seed which is the very same in nature with that original first seed whereof the body was made. I presume then, that he that would know the generation of man, needs not look back so far as Adam to know the first seed, for if Nature still affords the like, what needs that fruit less retrogradation? It is even so with the world, for it was originally made of a seed, of a seminal viscous humidity or water, but that seed (as we have said in our Aphorisms) disappeared in the Creation, for the Spirit of God that moved upon it transformed it, and made the world of it. Howsoever that very world doth now yield and bring forth out of its own body a secondary seed, which is the very same in essence and substance with that primitive general seed whereof the world was made. And if any man shall ask what use nature makes of this general seed, and wherefore she yields it; I answer, that it is not to make another world of it, but to maintain that world with it which is made already. For God Almighty hath so decreed that his creatures are nourished with the very same matter whereof they were formed, and in this is verified that maxim which otherwise would be most false: Ex iisdem nutrimur, ex quibus constamus.

We seek not much whence our own nutriment comes, nor that of beasts, for both provisions are obvious. But what is that which feeds Grass, Herbs, Corn and all sorts of trees with their fruits? What is it that restores and supplies the earth, when these copious and innumerous products have for the greatest part of the year lived sucking on her breasts and almost exhausted her? I am afraid they will speak as they think and affirm it is water, but what skilful assertors they are shall appear hereafter.

COMMENTS UPON THE FIFTH PARAGRAPH.

Thomas Vaughan begins by defining the creative deity as the formulator and manifestor of the visible world. He pictures him as an artificer working upon pre-existent substance. As I have already pointed out, this idea is that of the Jehovah of the Jews in relation to the Ehyeh and Ain Suph Aur. This latter principle must, however, be regarded by us at present as the Divine Neith or Chaos, also explained in the notes on the first paragraph. This fundamental virgin substance is only to be understood, says Vaughan, by the study of seeds.

Now if we cut open any moderate-sized seed, we shall find an outer covering, two masses of starchy matter, and a root or radicle.

In the root we have the image of the One from whom sprung the many; in the two halves the positive and negative nourishing or preserving principles; and in the coat or cover the constricting force without which manifest form is impossible, but which must be overcome for growth to take place.

The seed planted in the ground becomes a sugary fœculent mass, and in the midst of putrefaction and fermentation the new living being grows and becomes manifest. The study of embryology takes us a long way towards the solution of the mystery of life. We start with the protyle or protoplasm of modern science, we trace the beginnings of a human being through stages akin to the mollusc, the fish, the reptile, and the monkey. This protyle or secondary chaos, which so much resembles the Hyle or sediment of the waters of creation is most evident to the unscientific mind in the scum of a stagnant pool.

M. Pasteur has shewn us that the air is full of microscopic life, that it can be found everywhere, from the bloom of a peach to the liver of a pig; that it can be taken thence and made to germinate in any gelatine, syrup, or glycerine basis; that the white corpuscles of blood are minute living organisms, capable of being oxygenated, and that they, like gold, become red in the process. This is no doubt a materialistic translation of our author's meaning; but the evolution of the highest is similar to the evolution of the lowest, as is taught us by the Emerald Tablet of Hermes.

All my researches lead me to consider that the great mystery of the origin of life consists almost entirely of a measure of temperature. Life is *latent* everywhere; it merely awaits the time in the cooling of a world that is appropriate to its manifestation. Let us at the same time bear in mind the Qabalistic and mystical interpretation of the "Foundation," and its connection with the emanations of the microcosm.

Paragraph VI.

Certainly, even that which we eat ourselves, and beasts also, proceeds all of it from the same fountain, but before it comes to us it is altered, for animals feed on particulars, but vegetables abstract this sperm immediately in its heavenly universal form. Notwithstanding I would not have this so understood, as if this seed did serve only to nourish, for many things are made of it, and especially that subterraneous family of minerals and metals. For this thing is not water, otherwise than to the sight, but a coagulable fat humidity, or a mixture of fire, air and pure earth, overcast indeed with water, and therefore not seen of any nor known but to few. In vegetables it oftentimes appears, for they feed not as some think, on water, but on this seminal viscosity that is hid in the water. This indeed they attract at the roots, and from thence it ascends to the branches, but sometimes it happens by the way to break out at the bark where meeting with cold air, it subsists and congeals to a gum. This congelation is not sudden but requires some small time, for if you find while it is fresh it is of an exceedingly subtle moisture, but glutinous for it will spin into strings as small as any hair, and had it passed up to the branches, it had been formed, in time, to a plum or cherry.

This happens to it by cold, and above ground, but in the bowels of the earth it is congealed by a sulphureous heat into metals and if the place of its congelation be pure, then into a bright metal, for this sperm is impregnated with light, and is full of the star fire, from whence all metals have their lustre. The same might be said of pearls and precious stones, this starry seed being the Mother of the all, for when it is mineralised by itself and without any faeculent mixture, then,

Vomit igniculos suos

it sheds and shoots its fires, and hath so much of heaven that if we did not know the conspiracy we should wonder how it could love the earth. Let us now in a few words resume what we have said, and the rather, because we would explain our method, for we intend to follow Raymond Lullie, who in the fifth chapter of his testament hath laid down a certain figure, which fully answers to those words we have formerly cited out of Rhaesus Cestrensis.

COMMENTS UPON THE SIXTH PARAGRAPH.

This calls attention to the fact that difference of circumstance alone congeals the prima materia into metals, vegetables, or animals. We know very well that between the lowest forms of animal and vegetable life, between the small water fungi and the hydra or amœba there is very little to choose; in fact, if we look upon the brain of an animal as corresponding to the root of a tree, we shall find extraordinary similarities even in the more complex developments of the two great kingdoms. Minerals, on the other hand, are created and formulated at such high temperatures, and are so much more durable that it is not at once obvious to us that the principle of evolution is the same.

The Arabians called the prima materia, "Halicali," from Hali—summum, and Calop—bonum; but the Latin Authors corruptly write it Sal Alkali. This summum bonum is the Catholic receptacle of spirits, it is blessed and impregnated with Light from above, and was therefore styled by Magicians—Domus Signata, plena Luminis Divinitatis.

Paragraph VII.

We have already mentioned two principles, God and Nature, or God and the created world, for that third principle or chaos that was pre-existent to the world, we shall speak of no more, but in lieu of it, we shall have recourse to the secondary sperm or chaos that now is, and comes out of the visible world, for we will ground our discourse upon nothing but what is visible, and in the front of it we place the Divine Majesty who is the sole central Eternal Principle and Architect of all.

COMMENTS UPON THE SEVENTH PARAGRAPH.

Here we find our author distinctly associates his Chaos with that which is behind Kether—the first emanation of Deity; God with Chokmah or the Abba of the Kabalists; Nature with Binah or the Aima or Mother, the third emanation. Or we may put it thus; from the Chaos or Neith sprang God or the Father, and Nature or the Mother; from their union sprang the secondary Chaos or first reflected triangle. Thus completing the Hexad of the Macrocosm.

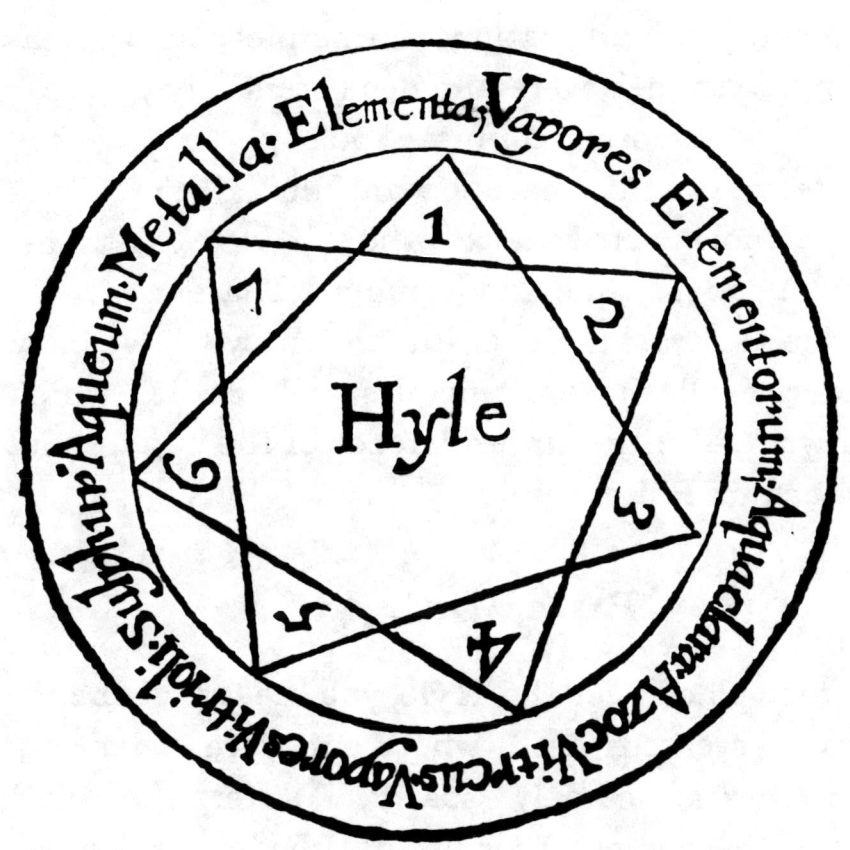

Paragraph VIII.

This Figure is Raymond Lullie's, and in the centre of it you see the first Hyle, or matter whereof the world was made. In this Hyle (saith Raymond) all the Elements and all natural Principles, as well as Means and Extremes, were mingled potentially,

in forma confusa Aquae;

and this primitive Spermatic ocean filled all that space which we now attribute to the air, for (saith he)

Attingebat usque ad circulum Lunarem.

Out of this central Hyle (with which we have now done) did rise all those Principles and Bodies which you find written in the circumference of the Figure and here begins our Philosophy.

Paragraph IX.

In the first place over the Hyle, you see the Elements of the visible created world, whose parts are commonly called Elements, namely Earth, Water, Air and Heaven, for there is no other fire but that Ignis fatuus, which Aristotle kindled under the Moon. From the elements on the right hand, by rarefaction and resolution of their substance, you see derived another Principle, namely Vapores Elementorum the Vapours of the Elements or the clouds, in which vapours the inferior and superior Natures meet and are there married, and out of their mixture results that secondary Sperm or

Chaos Philosophical, which we look for. Next to the clouds or vapours of the elements, you will find in the figure a third Principle Aqua Clara, namely a clear water, which proceeds immediately from the clouds.

Et illa est Res (saith Lullie) argento vive vivo magis propinqua, quae quidem reperitur supra terram currens, fluens.

The fourth Principle, which Nature immediately generates by congelation out of the substance or viscosity or the Aqueous universal Mercury is the glassy Azoth, which is a certain fiery sulphureous masculine Minera; and this is gold philosophical, the sulphor, the earth, and the Male, as the viscous Water is the Mercury and the female. The rest of the Principles which are ranged in the Figure, are artificial Principles, and cannot be known or manifested without art, excepting the seventh and last Principle, which is either gold or silver, for these are perfect metals and Ferments that specify the medicine which of itself is universal, and reduce it to a particular disposition and effect. Thus far we thought fit to deal plainly with you, and for the practice part of this Figure, we shall wave it, for we had rather speak nothing than to speak that we cannot be understood. I daresay there are some writers who rejoice in their own riddles, and take a special pleasure to multiply those difficulties which are numerous enough already. For my part I shall not put you to a trial of wit, you may take the rest from their author, and thus expose you to no other hazard, but what I have been formerly exposed to myself. We shall now again return to our theory and to make our entrance we say, that fire begins every motion, and motion begins generation. For if the Elements or parts of this material world did all of them stand in suis terminis (on their own bases) such a cessation would produce nothing. To prevent this, the Almighty God placed in the heart of the world, namely in the earth (as he did in the heart of every other creature) a fire-life which Paracelsus calls the Archaeus and Sendivow the Central Sun. This Fire, lest it should consume its own body the earth, he hath overcast with a thick, oily saltish water, which we call the sea, for sea water, (as we have tried) not to speak of its salt, is full of a sulphureous volatile fatness, which doth not quench fire like the common water, but feeds it. The like Providence we see in the bodies of animals whose heat or life is tempered with a sulphureous, saltish moisture, namely with blood, and the blood with the breath, as the sea is with wind and air. Over this Archaeus, or central fire, God hath placed in his heaven the sun and the stars, as he hath placed the head and the eyes over the heart. For between Man and the world there is no small accord, and he that knows not the one can never know the other. We may observe also, that the wind passeth between the inferior and superior Fires, that is between the central and celestial sun, and in man the breath hath all its liberty and motion between the heart and the eyes, that is between the fire and the light that is in us. We feel moreover in man and the world, a most even correspondency of effects, for as the blood, even so the sea hath a constant pulse or agitation, both spirits stirring and working alike in their bodies. Nor ought we to neglect another consideration, That the light of the world is in the superior parts of it, namely in the sun and stars, but the original fire from whence these sparks fly upwards appears not, but lives imprisoned in the earth, even so certainly, all the brightness of man is in his face, for there he sheds his light at the eyes, but the first source of it, namely that fire which is at the heart, is no more seen than that which is in the earth. Only this we may say, that both these imprisoned forces are manifested to reason by the same effects, namely by the pulse, that the one causeth in the blood and the other in the sea, to which may be added that transpiration or evaporation of humours, which both these spirits produce alike in their several bodies. And that we may further prove that these terms of Archaeus and Sol Centralis are not vain words, let us but consider what a strong heat is required to this sublimation of vapours and exhalations, for it is not simple water that is driven upwards, but abundance of salt and oil together with the water. If any man thinks the sun can do this, I must tell him he knows not the operations of the sun, nor for what use it serves in nature. The sun serves only to dry up the superfluous humidity which the night leaves behind her on the outside of things, for this makes all vegetables cold and flaccid, hinders their digestion and maturity. But the sun with a clear heat, taking off that extraneous moisture, forwards their concoction, and helps to ripen that which is raw. This must be done with a most gentle heat, not with such as shall make the earth to smoke and extract clouds from it, for this would not bring things to a maturity, but rather burn and calcine them. We know that if we stand long in the sun we shall grow faint, and common fire will not burn in the light of it, for the sun, which is the true element of fire, attracts it, so that by degrees it goes off and forsakes his fuel. But if you convey the fire out of the sun, then it will more strongly apply to the fuel and unite itself to it and burn it. It is just so with the earth, for while the heat of the sun is present the heat of the earth is more busy with the sun than with its own body. For as Sendevow hath well written, In superficie Terrae Radii radiis junguntur.

In the face of the earth the beams of both luminaries meet, and there is such a conspiracy between fire and fire that the central breaking forth to meet the celestial suffers a kind of extasy and doth not much mind his own body. Give me leave to speak thus, for there is such an affinity between these two, that they had rather join with one another than with any third nature, but that is it which cannot but be in part and by way of influence, God having confined the one to the centre, and the other to the circumference. I could demonstrate this sympathy by a most noble magnetism, which I have seen to my admiration, between the sun and sweet oil, or rather the fire and soul of Nitre, and here I shall tell you that the earth is full of nitre, nay I must affirm that pure earth is nothing else but Nitre, whose belly is full of wind, air and fire, and which differs no more from heaven than the root of a tree that lodgeth in the dirt, doth from the branches of it that grow in the sunshine. This attraction of fire by fire is the true cause why the heat of the earth is so weak in summer, and so strong in winter, for in the winter when the sun is absent, the central fire keeps altogether within the earth, and being irritated by an hostile invasion of cold, heats the waters much more vigorously, so that exhalations and clouds are far more copious in the winter than they are in the summer, which could not be if the sun were the cause of them. Add to this, that an outward dry heat, as that of the sun is, falling immediately on the earth, must needs burn the earth before it can make it smoke, but an inward fire, that is mingled with the moisture of the earth, cannot burn, be it never so intense, for it is qualified with the water, and tempered to a moist heat, and without doubt such a fire may very naturally resolve some parts of the earth, and cause them to exhale as our own inward heat, being moisened with the blood, makes us sweat without any violence. To reduce all this to a Corrollary we say that in the winter God seals the face of the earth with frost and cold, as a man would seal a glass, and this is to keep in the congelative Spermatic Humidity, which otherwise might ascend with the more crude vapours that break out copiously at that time and filling the sphere of the air take in, like so many sponges, the celestial vital influences. For we must know, that nature begins to impregnate the earth about the end of autumn, and continues it all winter, the fiery, subtle influx of the heavens being then condensed by the cold and moisture of the moon, who is regent all the winter and elevated above the sun. This you may see in snow, which falls in hard frost, which being taken up while it is fresh, and digested in a Blind Glass in ashes for twenty-four hours, if then you open the glass whilst the solution is warm, you shall perceive in the breath of the water all the odours of the world, and certainly far more pleasant than they are in the flowers at May. Look into the bottom of the glass and you shall find there a fat grey slime, not unlike to Castile soap, separate the phlegm from it by a soft distillation in balneo, and put the residue in a Boltshead well stopped, in a dry heat of ashes, keep it then warm for an hour or two, and suddenly the glass will fly to pieces, for the wind, the life or spirit, is not well fetled in the body. Here you may see the first attempts of nature, but if you know how to work upon the water you shall find greater things than I have told you.

COMMENTS UPON THE NINTH PARAGRAPH.

Our author calls the elements, Earth, Water, Air, and Heaven or Fiery Water.

From these by digestion and sublimation the gases, vapours, and clouds are derived. This is what in ordinary occult language is called the firmament, the Yetziratic or formative world.

From this is distilled a clear water of the nature of wine or alcohol.

By congelation is obtained a fiery sulphurous substance as wine becomes acid vinegar by exposure to a certain heat, this acetate will run into an oily burning gum or glass when duly concentrated.

Vitriol vapour and liquid sulphur are not dealt with in this volume.

I will now supply a scale of attribution and analogies between the Macrocosm and the Microcosm.

The sun and moon are allotted by Cornelius Agrippa to the eyes, as being the lights of the greater and lesser worlds.

The other planets to the nostrils, mouth, and ears.

These, then, typify the parts of the Spiritual Consciousness or divine in man.

The lungs are the seat of the firmament, and in them circulates the air we breathe.

The heart, the central fire, the Archæus. The blood with its constant pulse, the sea full of sulphurous volatile fatness.

Our author next points out that the interior heat is greatest when the light is latent.

He then says clearly that Pure Earth is Nitre, better known to us as saltpetre—a white powder which attracts moisture, and by eliminating the mineral potash forms nitric acid, one of the most corrosive acids that we have. (Of course I need not point out that another proportion of oxygen and nitrogen gives us the ordinary air we breathe.) He then shows that the latent heat contained in snow will, if hermetically sealed, cause a glass to break more rapidly than the latent heat in ordinary water.

Paragraph X.

The Magnesia then (as Sendivow hath written) is generated in winter, and not without reason, for then the heat of the earth is strongest, and best able to digest the nutriment that comes down from heaven, and concoct it to a viscous Sperme. But in the spring and summer seasons, when the sun hath chased off the frost, and the central and celestial luminaries have, by their mutual mixture and conflux of beams, relaxed and dilated the pores of the earth, then there is a way made for the Sperme to ascend more freely, which subliming upwards is attracted and sublimated by the vegetable Kingdom, whose immediate aliment it is.

COMMENTS ON THE TENTH PARAGRAPH.

The sap restrained by the cold of winter doubtless accumulates force proportionate to the strength of its prison walls. Like an arrow released it flies further, according to the weight of the bow which propels it.

Paragraph XI.

To return then to those first words of Rhæsus Cestrensis, we say, this Sperm is made of the vapours or clouds, and the vapours are made by elevation and depression of elements, and not only of the elements, but (as he saith) of elementates also, that is of bodies compounded of the elements, and this bears a double sense. For we must know that the earth is charged with many particular natures, as minerals of all sorts and cadaverous reliques, for our bodies also lodge in the earth when the Spirit of Life hath left them. All these, as well as the earth itself, suffer a rarefaction, and resolution of substance, for into these vapours, saith Raymond Lully, Omnia corpora elementata resolvantur ad intrandum, novam generationem [all elementary bodies are resolved, when a further new development is to take place].

This puts me in mind of an opinion I have read sometimes in the Cabalists; namely that this bulk or body we have attained to by attraction and transmutation of nutriment, riseth not in the resurrection, but out of that seminal particle, which originally attracting the nutriment, did overcast itself therewith, there shall spring another new body, and this seminal particle (say they) lurketh somewhere in the bones, not in that part which moulders into dust. Of a truth we see that bones are very permanent and lasting, and this Joseph was not ignorant of, when dying in Egypt, he gave that charge to his brethren, Ye shall carry up my bones from hence. We know that the Israelites were bondmen in Egypt near four hundred years after Joseph's death, yet all that time his bones were not consumed, but were carried away to the Land of Canaan, as it is written, And Moses took the bones of Joseph with him, for he had straightly sworn the Children of Israel, saying, God will surely visit you, you shall carry up my bones hence with you. Certainly if we judge rightly, we must confess that this seminal particle is our only original fundamental matter, the rest being but an accretion that comes from the extraneous substance of meat and drink. What loss is it then if we lay by this corrupt accretion or access of matter, for cannot He that made us at first of the seminal particle, make us of it again? From this opinion St. Paul, in my judgement, abhors not, in that speech of his to the Corinthians, where he would show them the manner of the Resurrection, and with what bodies the dead rise. Thou fool (saith he) that which thou sowest, is not quickened except it die, and that which thou sowest, thou sowest not that body which shall be, but bare grain, it may chance of wheat or some other grain, but God giveth it a body as it hath pleased him, and to every seed a body which is proper for it, for so signifieth the original. And here you that are angry readers, let me be excused, for I deliver this not as my own sentiment, but as the

Gen. ch. l. v. 25.

tradition of the Jews, who were sometimes a very learned people, and knew more of the mysteries of God and nature than any other nation whatsoever. But to begin again where we left, you must know that when the central Sun sublimes the vapours, those vapours partake not only of the nature of the Earth and Water, but of divers other particular minerals whereof the earth and water are full.

COMMENTS UPON THE ELEVENTH PARAGRAPH.

Vaughan here returns to Mr. Rice. of Chester, or Rhæsus Cestrensis, whose Latin aphorism was quoted in the third paragraph, and deals with the meaning of the word elementates or secondary elements, which are generated in the same manner as simple elements by the application of a gentle heat and moisture.

Then our author is reminded of the association of the reincarnating ego with the os coccygis by the Jews; after a lengthy digression on this subject, he hints that particular minerals are to be regenerated in the same way as universal elements; we presume he wishes to point out that in the same way as simple life is generated, so a complex being can also be regenerated.

It is worthy of note that phosphorus discovered by Brand in 1669, is prepared from bones, and has many properties in common with the secret fire of the Alchemists.

Paragraph XII.

To make this more clear, the vapours properly so called, rise from the sea, and from all fresh waters. These partake of the substance and qualities of such minerals as are in the water, some of them being bituminous, some saltish, some mercurial and all of them moist and phlegmatic. On the contrary, those exhalations that come from the earth are dry, for the earth is more hot and mineral than the water. These fiery earth fumes meeting with the cold vapours of the water, oftentimes produce most terrible tempests, some of these being nitrous, some arsenical, some sulphurous and all hot, and some by reason of their copious sulphur, inflammable. Both these, I mean the earthly exhalations and the watery vapour, meet in that vast circulatory of the air, where their contrary complexions of heat and cold are mingled together like agent and patient, or sulphur and mercury, and the particular Natures and Vapours which they acquired from the minerals, are resolved by the wind, and totally reduced into general principles. It is strange to consider what a powerful resolving faculty there is in wind or air, for wind is no other thing than air stirred, and that by fire, as we feel in man, that the motion of the breath is caused by heat, as well as that of the blood, both proceeding from the same hot principle of life. So certainly the life of the world causeth wind or a commotion in the air as well as a flux in the sea, for both these are seas, and have their fluxes, as we shall prove elsewhere more fully. Air then, as we have said, resolves all things, and especially wind, for it resolves all salts into water, and if this solution be distilled, we shall find some part of the salt reduced into fresh water. As for the residue, if it be exposed to the wind, it will resolve again, and you may distil it the second time. In a word, if you repeat this process, you will bring the whole body of the salt into a volatile fresh water, nothing different from the common either in sight or taste. And here you must not think your salt is lost, for if you know how to congeal the water, you will find it again, but so altered from what it was, that you will wonder to see it. This practice, if well understood, sufficiently declares the nature of air; but he that knows where to find congealed air, and can dissolve it by heat to a viscous water, he hath attained to something that is excellent. Much more I could say of this wonderful and spiritual element, whose penetrating, resolving faculty I have sometimes contemplated in this following and simple experiment. Common quicksilver hath a miraculous union of parts, and of all compounds is the strongest excepting gold; for if you distil it by retort a hundred times, it will be quicksilver still notwithstanding all those reiterated rarefactions of his body. But if you take a thousand weight of it, and vapour them away but once in the open air, it will never come to quicksilver again; for the fumes will be lifted up to the wind, where they will suffer a total dissolution, and will come down as mere rain-water. This is the very reason why also the vapours of the elements are lifted up to the middle region of the air; for there the wind is most cold, and hath most liberty, and in no other place can their resolution, which Nature intends, be perfected. This if understood, is a most noble secret of Nature: nor was Job ignorant of it, when complaining of the decays of his own body, he delivered himself thus.

Ch. xxx. v. 22.
"Thou lifteth me up to the wind, Thou causeth me to ride upon it, and dissolveth my substance."

COMMENTS UPON THE TWELFTH PARAGRAPH.

Vaughan points out that the vapours of the sea are bituminous, saltish, mercurial, moist and phlegmatic. The exhalations of the earth are hot and mineral, nitrous, arsenical, sulphurous; and in the air all these things are mixed together and resolved.

He then points out that salts tend to liquefy if left in moist air. That quicksilver volatilizes, and on being divided into minute particles loses its identity in the atmosphere; but it is to be presumed that it merely turns into an oxide of mercury and falls to the earth, as many other matters do under the corrosive influence of oxygen.

Paragraph XIII.

We have hitherto shown you how fire rarefies all things, and how wind and air resolve them yet further

Anima Magica than fire, as we have exemplified in quicksilver. And this is it we have delivered elsewhere in more envious terms, namely that Circumferences dilate, and Centres contract; That superiors dissolve, and inferiors coagulate; That we should make use of an indeterminate Agent, till we can find a determinate one. For true it is, that the mercurial dissolving faculty is in the air, and in airy things; and the sulphureous congealing virtue is in the earth, that is to say, in some mineral natures and substances which God hath hid in the earth. Take therefore water of air, which is a great dissolvent, and ferment it with earth, and on the contrary, earth with water; or to speak more obscurely, ferment mercury with sulphur, and sulphur with mercury. And know that this congenial faculty is much adjuvated by heat; especially in such places where the sperm cannot exhale, and where the heat is temperate; but if the place be open, and the heat excessive, then it dissipates. It remains now that we speak something of the two passive material elements, namely of earth and water; for these are the bodies that suffer by fire, and whose parts are perpetually regenerated by a circular rarefaction, and condensation.

COMMENTS UPON THE THIRTEENTH PARAGRAPH.

The action of Fire tends to overcome what we call the gravitation of matter. The action of air is to transmute or oxgyenize matter. To congeal and coagulate gravitation and magnetism must be brought to bear on the substance.

Paragraph XIV.

It is the advice of the Brothers of the R. C. that those who would be proficients in this art should study the elements and their operation before they seek after the tinctures of metals. It is to be wished indeed that men would do so, for then we should not have so many broilers, and so few philosophers. But here it may be questioned, who is he that studies the elements for any such end as to observe and imitate their operations? For in the Universities, we study them only to attain to a false book theory, whereof no use can be made but quacking, disputing, and making a noise. Verily the doctrine of the Schoolmen hath allayed and perverted even that desire of knowledge which God planted in man. For the traditions we receive there, coming from our superiors, carry with them the awe of the tutor, and this breeds in us an opinion of their certainty; so that a University man cannot in all his lifetime, attain to so much reason and confidence as to look beyond his lesson. I have often wondered that any sober spirits can think Aristotle's philosophy perfect, when it consists in mere words without any further effects; for of a truth the falsity and insufficiency of a mere notional knowledge is so apparent that no wise man will assert it. This is best known to the physicians, who when they have been initiated in this whirligig, are forced at last to leave it, and to assume new principles, if they will be such as their profession requires they should be. Aristotle will very gravely tell us: Ubi definit Philosophus, ibi incipit Medicus; But I admire what assistance a physician can receive from this philosopher, whose science tells us: Scientia non est particularium; for without particulars a physician can do nothing. But in good earnest, did not Aristotle's science (if he had any) arise from particulars, or did it descend immediately from universals? If from universals, how came he to be acquainted with them? did he know the genus, before he knew the species, or the species before the individuals? I think not; he knew the individual first, and having observed his nature and propriety, he applied that to the whole species; or to speak sense, to all individuals of that kind: and this application made that knowledge general, which at first was particular, as being deduced from a particular object. This is true, and Aristotle will tell us so, though he give himself the lie; for elsewhere he affirms, Nihil esse in intellectu, quod non fuit prius in sensu. Which if it be true then "Scientia non est particularium" is false. But I have done with him at present, and for my own part I have learnt long ago not of Aristotle but of Roger Bacon, Quod communia pauci sunt valoris, nec proprie sequenda, nisi propter particularia. And this is evident in all practices and professions that conduce anything to the benefit of man. For Nature herself hath imprinted the Universal notions and conceptions in every soul, whether learned or unlearned, so that we need not study Universals, and this our Friar had observed; for saith he. In communibus Animi conceptionibus vulgus concordat cum sapientibus; in particularibus vero, et propiis errat et discordat. And for this very reason, he condemns Aristotle and Galen. Quia in communibus et universalibus se occupaverunt, et perducti sunt ad senectutem, vitam consumentes in pejoribus et vulgatis, nec vias ad haec secreta magna perceperunt. Let not us do as those Hebrews did, though in this very point the greatest part of the world follows them. Let us rather follow where Nature leads; for the having impressed these Universals in our mind, hath not done it in vain, but to the end we should apply them to outward sensible particulars, and so attain to a true experimental knowledge, which in this life is our only crown and perfection. If a man should rest in the bare theory of husbandry, and only read Virgil's Georgics, never putting his hand to the plough, I suppose this theory could not help him to his daily bread: and if we rest in the notions and names of things never touching the things themselves, we are like to produce no effects, nor to cure any diseases, without which performances philosophy is useless, and not to be numbered amongst our necessities. But how false this is, God knows and man also may know it if he considers but those two obstructions of life, sickness and poverty. But they are not only effects that are wanting to Aristotle's philosophy but even his theory is for the most part false, and where it is true, it is so slight and superficial that it doth not further us at all. He is none of our auxiliaries who believes it, but the very Remora to all natural discoveries, and he hath for many ages, not only obstructed but extinguished the Truth. Much might be said of this fellow and his ignorance, which is not more gross than perverse: I omit to speak of his Atheism and eminency of his malice, which was not only destructive to the Fane of the old Philosophers, whose books this scribbler burned, but even to the happiness and progress of posterity whom he robbed of those more ancient, more excellent and invaluable monuments.

COMMENTS UPON THE FOURTEENTH PARAGRAPH.

Study, search, think, and experiment for yourselves. So only can you find the light that will make your particular life a living reality. To accept a ready-made belief blindly is to commit mental and moral suicide. You must slay the delusions, the constrictive forces by which you find yourself surrounded when you start on your search for light. You must fight and conquer the dragons of habit and custom which stultify your spiritual consciousness; kill them and wash yourself in their blood, like the heroes of old. You must fail, and fall, and then rise again; you must strip yourself of all idolatrous shams, until you find the vivifying idea or light which shall render your life fruitful. Each man or woman must do this for him or herself. This is the teaching of the Brothers of the Rosy Cross, and it is the only living truth, for it has no finality; and the Nemesis of all reformers is finality.

But this truth has never more than half dawned upon the world; the leader of each wave of evolution looks upon those who went before him as having erred. But the Heroic Man is always right for the time he lives in. Dante was right in the age when Catholicism was a living force; Shakespere was right when feudalism was a living force. So Luther was right when only the husk of a religion was left, and Cromwell was in the right when the belief in the divine right of kings had died out in his race.

When we have found the constructive faith that has the inherent force to carry us onwards, we shall be right. But what that is, only the heart of each man can tell him.

In the midst of the Renaissance, through the Reformation, and Civil Wars, and after the narrowing fights of the schoolmen, Bacon called on all men to weigh and consider for themselves.

Vaughan was echoing this cry when he hurled abuse at the critic and exalted the artist and craftsman, for Aristotle must ever be the type of the former, as Plato is the type of the latter.

But we must not forget in reading the works of Vaughan, that the dawn of experimental science had scarcely appeared when they were written. For much that is a commonplace to us, would have been considered a miracle at that time; and we must appreciate the vigour of his intellect when we find him saying so much in 1655 that is still being said by those who have thought out for themselves a complete theory of life based upon a clear knowledge of its possibilities and its limitations. Not a little of Vaughan's wisdom might be well accepted by those who study the metaphysical side of life; but who disdain to put in practice any of the theories they are so busy in promulgating.

For, as he says, "without effect, Philosophy is useless and not to be numbered among our necessities."

Paragraph XV.

I have digressed thus far to correct this scabby sheep, who hath spoiled a numerous flock; and the rather, because of a late creeping attempt of some of his friends, who acknowledge him their Dictator, and the father of their human wisdom, and such indeed he is. But when they tell us, who write against him, that we do but restore old heresies, when indeed we oppose an atheist, and one that denied the creation of the world, and the dear immortality of our souls: they must give us leave to be a little angry with them, since we must lay the heretic at their doors, for they are the men that maintain him. In the mean time, if they are in earnest and think us guilty of any heresy, let them publicly show wherein, and we shall not fail to give them an account of our sense and their misinterpretations. For our part, we had not troubled them at this time had not one of them darkly and timorously signified, that we teach a new physic, new philosophy, and new divinity. To whom I shall return no answer but this: that before he undertakes to judge what philosophy or divinity is new, he should first endeavour to understand the old. But this is a step out of my way, and that I may return.

T. P.

Paragraph XVI.

I shall now resume my discourse on Earth and Water. and those sure are sensible substances, not Universals and chimeras, such as the Peripatetics fancy, when they couple Nature and Nothing.

Paragraph XVII.

By earth, I understand not this impure faeculent body, on which we tread, but a more simple pure element, namely, the natural central salt nitre. This salt is fixed or permanent in the fire, and it is the sulphur of Nature, by which she retains and congeals her mercury. When these two meet, I mean the pure earth and the water, then the earth thickens the water, and on the contrary, the water subtilates the earth, and from these two there riseth a third thing, not so thick as earth, not so thin as water, but of a mean, viscous complexion, and this is called mercury, which is nothing else but a composition of water and salt. For we must know, that these two are the prime materials of Nature, without which she can make no sperm or seed; nor is that all, for when the seed is made, it will never grow to a body, nor can it be resolved and disposed to a further generation, unless these two are present and also co-operate with it. This we may see all the year round by a frequent and daily experience, for when it rains, this heavenly water meets with the nitre that is in the earth, and dissolves it, and the nitre with his acrimony sharpens the water, so that this nitrous water fertilises all the seeds that are in the ground; and thus solution is the key of generation, not only in our art but in Nature also, which is the art of God. We need not speak much more of the earth, for these few words, if rightly understood, are sufficient, and carry in them a deeper sense than an ordinary reader will perceive. I know there is another Solar Oriental Earth, which is all golden and sulphurous and yet is not gold, but a base contemptible thing that costs nothing, for it may be had for the taking up. This is the earth of Aethiopia, that hath all colours in it: this is that Androdamas of Democritus, the green Duenech and Sulphur that never touched the fire, which if it be resolved, then it is our glassy Azoth, or vitriol of Venus philosophical.

COMMENTS ON THE SEVENTEENTH PARAGRAPH.

By earth our author understands nitre, salt-petre, etc. It may be suggestive to point out that in all alchemical receipts we find nitre and sea-salt (symbolised by a circle divided by a vertical or a horizontal line respectively), as the two essential constituents of the materia magica. And that aqua regia or the acid which alone can resolve gold, is made of a mixture of nitric and hydrochloric acids.

The Solar Oriental Earth is probably orpiment or some mixture of antimony, for although pure antimony is of little use in transmutation there is no doubt that it contains, under certain conditions, native properties not to be found in other substances.

Paragraph XVIII.

This is enough as to the nature of the earth, and now we will speak of the water. This element is the deferent, or Vehiculum of all influences whatsoever: for what efflux so ever it be that proceeds from the terrestrial centre, the same ascends and is carried up in her to the air. And on the contrary all that comes from Heaven descends in her to the earth, for in her belly the inferior and superior natures meet and mingle, nor can they be manifested without a singular artifice. Hence it is that whatsoever is pure in the earth, all that she receives from the water: and here I mean such pure substances as are called by the philosophers Decomposita; for the eagle leaves her egg, that is to say, the water leaves her Limosity in the earth, and this limosity is connected into nitre, and to other innumerous minerals. We have formerly told you of two suns or fires, the celestial and the central. Now both these dispense their effluxions, or influences, and they meet in the vapour of the water; for the Vulcan, or earthly sun, makes the water ascend to the region of the air, and here the water is spread under the superior fires, for she is exposed to the eye of the sun, and to the pointed ejaculations of all the fixed stars and planets, and this in a naked, rarefied, opened body. The air, of a truth, is that temple, where inferiors are married to their superiors; for to this place the heavenly light descends, and is united to the aereal oleous humidity, which is hid in the belly of the water; this light being hotter than the water, makes her turgid and vital, and increaseth her seminal viscous moisture; so that she is ready to depose her sperm or limosity, were she but united to her proper male. But this cannot be unless she returns to her own country, I mean the earth, for here the collastrum, or male resides. To this purpose she descends hither again, and immediately the male lays hold upon her, and his fiery sulphureous substance unites to her limosity. And here observe that this sulphur is the father in all metallic generations, for he gives the masculine fiery soul, and the water gives the body, namely, the limosity or heavenly aqueous nitre, whereof the body, by coagulation is made. We must know, moreover, that in this sulphur there is an impure extraneous heat, which gnaws and corrodes this watery Venus, endeavouring to turn her to an impure sulphur, such as his own body is; but this cannot be, because of the heavenly seed or light hid in the aqueous nitre, which will permit no such thing, for as soon as the sulphureous terrestrial heat begins to work, so soon it awakes and stirs up the heavenly light, which, being now fortified with the masculine tincture, or pure fire of the sulphur, begins to work on its own body, namely, on the aqueous nitre, and separates from it, the feculent extraneous parts of the sulphur, and so remains by itself a bright celestial metalline body. Observe then, that the tincture or soul of the sulphur cannot be regenerated in its own impure body, but it must forsake that dark and earthy carcase, and put on a new purified body before it can be united to the light of Heaven. This new body springs out of the water, for the water brought it down from Heaven, and certainly by water and spirit we must be all regenerated; which made some learned divines affirm that the element of water was not cured, but only that of the earth. Nor can I here omit the doctrine of St. John, who makes the water one of those three witnesses which attest God here on earth. And much to this purpose is that speech of St. Paul: How that God in times past suffered all nations to walk in their own ways, but nevertheless (saith he), he left not himself without a witness, inasmuch as he gave them rain from Heaven, etc.

The benedictions or blessings that descend from God, are not a form of words, like the benedictions of men; they are all spirit and essence, and their Deferents are natural visible substances, and these are the blessings which the Patriarch wished to his son: "God give thee of the dew of Heaven from above, and of the fatness of the earth from beneath." He was not ignorant of those blessings, which the God of Nature had enclosed in those natural things; and therefore He saith in the same place:

Gen.

"The smell of my son is like the smell of a field, which the Lord hath blessed." And St. Paul in his epistle to the Hebrews tells us: "That the earth, which drinketh in the rain, that cometh oft upon it, receiveth blessing from God: but that which beareth thorns and briars is rejected and nigh unto cursing, whose end is to be burnt."

COMMENTS UPON THE EIGHTEENTH PARAGRAPH.

The whole of this paragraph is worthy of the most attentive study, and may be interpreted on all planes, with advantage to the student of occultism. Taking for instance the

	Natural.	*Philosophical.*	*Religious*
Passion (expansion)	Fire	The flash of an idea	Enthusiasm, impulse
Intuition (instinct)	Water	Creative imagination (Nourishing the idea)	Aspiration
Vehicle (the medium)	Air	Formulative intelligence (The word)	Emotional energy
The nourisher (the manifestor)	Earth	The completed work	Complete communion

The three alchemical principles may be taken as the principles of centrifugal, centripetal and circulatory motion; or as corroding, penetrating, and preserving, according to the commonly understood characteristics of sulphur, mercury and salt.

Paragraph XIX.

But to explain what this blessing is, we remember we have written elsewhere, that water is of a double complexion, circumferential and central. In the circumference she is crude, volatile and phlegmatic; but in the centre she is better concocted, viscous, aereal, and fiery. This central part is soft and saltish, outwardly white and lunar, but inwardly red and solar, nor can it be well extracted without a lunar or solar magnet, whose proper element it is, and with which it has a wonderful sympathy. Hence that obscure saying of the philosophers, who when they describe unto us their mercury, give it this character as most natural, Quod adhaeret corporibus. That it adheres to the bodies or metals. And as Pythagoras saith in the Turba, Suum absque igne consequitur socium. And therefore it is written in the same book, Magna est propinquitas inter magnesiam et ferrum. We see indeed by a vulgar experience, that if any ordinary stone stands long but in common water there sticks to it a certain limosity, which the water deposeth. But notwithstanding all this, and all they say, we must needs affirm, that even their mercury adheres not to the vulgar metals; and in this word mercury, as in all other terms, they are not a little ambiguous and subtle. There is indeed a mystery of theirs in water, and a knotty one, with which many

[margin: Anthrop.]

learned men have been gravelled; and now since we have mentioned it, we care not much if we speak soberly of it.

Paragraph XX.

There is nothing so frequent, and indeed nothing so considerable in their books as fire and water, but the reciprocal and confused use of both terms, puzzles much, as when they tell us that their water is their fire. Of this they have written so strangely, that I have sometimes been angry with them; but amongst them all, I found one had a good will to satisfy me. This author confessed he miscarried two hundred times, notwithstanding his knowledge of the true matter, and this because he did not know the fire or agent by which the matter is altered. These misfortunes of his own moved him it seems, to a commiseration of posterity; but I must needs affirm he hath taken his liberty, and expressed his own mind after his own way. "Our fire (saith he) is mineral, equal, continual; it vapours not unless the heat be too great; it participates of sulphur; it dissolves, calcines, and congeals all; it is artificial to find, and not chargeable, and it is taken elsewhere than from the matter." To all this he adds that at last, whereof he would have us take notice. "This fire (saith he) is not altered or transmuted with the matter." He thought certainly he had spoken enough, and truly so he hath but it is to such as know it already.

COMMENTS UPON THE TWENTIETH PARAGRAPH.

Deals with the nature of philosophical fire, that it is moist and invisible as the heat of a hot-bed or forcing-house; or a humid, tepid fire, blood warm.

There are different degrees of heat for the black, white, and red stages of the work, but the first must be gentle and moist. Here again we have the symbolism of thought and gentle melancholy, purity, and finally practical power.

Paragraph XXI.

For my own part I have found a certain mineral stinking water, which partakes of the nature of sulphur, and whose preparation is artificial, which is not of the essential parts of the matter, but accidental and extraneous, which vapours not unless it be overheated, which dissolves, calcines, and congeals all, but is not congealed; for it is expelled at last by the fire of nature, and goes off in windy fumes. This menstruous sulphureous fire against nature hath taught me how natural our work is; for it doth that here, which common water doth in the great world. In this respect it is called of some philosophers phlegma, ros, aqua nubium; not certainly that it is such, and therefore let us not deceive ourselves with misconstructions. He that would know the reason of those terms, let him take this account from a most learned philosopher. Aqua Nubium vocatur (saith he) quia distillata, est velus ros Maii, tenuissimarum partium. Est quoque eadem aqua acetum acerrimum, quod corpus fecit merum spiritum. Ut enim acetum diversarum qualitatum est, nempe ut in profundum penetret, et astringat, sit haec aqua solvit, et coagulat, non autem coagulatur, quia non est de subjecto proprio. Thus much as to the terms, and now let us return to the thing itself. I said this fire effects that in the glass which common water doth in the great world; for as this phlegmatic element coagulates not, nor is it at all diminished, notwithstanding that infinite number of individuals which Nature still produceth, even so it is so in our work; for our water also alters not, though the matter be altered in her belly, and our very principles generated there, namely, sulphur and mercury philosophical. Nor should any man wonder that I affirm common water to be incoagulable by heat at least, for in this I speak not unadvisedly. I know there are in water some natures coagulable, but they are not parts of the water, but are other elements; nor will I deny but some phlegm, nay, a very great quantity, and sometimes all, may be retained by mixture with other natures, and seem to be coagulated into stones, and those sometimes transparent; but coagulation in this sense, namely, by mixture of parts, as in meal and water, I mind not; but by coagulation I understand a transmutation of the substance of mere water into earth or air, and this in simple water cannot be. I know there is a water, that of itself, without all extraneous additions will coagulate in a soft heat to a fusible salt more precious than gold; but this is not any water that the eye sees, but another invisible humidity, which is indeed everywhere, sed non videtur (saith Sendivow) donec artifici placeat. This might satisfy as to this point, but I will add something more, lest I speak without reason, especially to those, who are not willing to allow others a better judgments than they have themselves.

COMMENTS UPON THE TWENTY-FIRST PARAGRAPH.

Deals with the putrefying agent as a centrifugal energy, for until the elements have fallen out among themselves the celestial influence cannot descend.

Until we are conscious of our present imperfections, we cannot receive the perfecting influence.

Paragraph XXII.

The commerce that is maintained between Heaven and earth by the ascent and volatility of water may sufficiently inform us of what dangerous consequence, the coagulation of this element would be. It is improbable then that the wise god of Nature should make that humidity coagulable, whose very use and office requires it should be otherwise; for if in the essence of water, as it is simple water, there were an astringent congealing faculty, it would by degrees attain to a total fixation, and then there could be no further generation, either of sperms or bodies; reason for it is this, if the water were fixed there would be no vapour or cloud, and there being no vapour there could be no sperm, for the elements cannot meet to make the sperm but in a vapour. For example, the earth cannot ascend, unless the water be first rarefied, for in the belly of the water is the earth carried up: and if the earth ascends not, having put off her gross body and being subtilated and purged with the water, then will not the air incorporate with it, for the moisture of the water introduceth the air into the rarefied and dissolved earth. And here again as the water reconciled the air to the earth, so doth the air reconcile the water to the fire, as if it would requite one courtesy with another; for the air with its unctuosity and fatness introduceth the fire unto the water, the fire following the air, and sticking to it as to its fuel and element. It remains now, that we observe, that the vapour of the water was the locus or matrix, wherein the other three elements did meet, and without which they had never come together; for this vapour was the deferend that carried up the pure virgin earth to be married to the sun and the moon, and now again she brings her down in her belly impregnated with the milk of the one and the blood of the other, namely, with air and fire, which principles are predominant in those two superior luminaries. But some wise ones, they argue and tell me, that this vapour being thus impregnated may now be coagulated, and fixed, by help of those hot principles of air and fire. To this I answer that the viscous seminal part of the water may, but the phlegm never, and I will show as much by example. When this vapour is fully impregnated it stays no longer in that region, but returns presently to the earth from which it ascended. But how doth it return? But certainly not in a violent stormy precipitation like rain, but as I have written elsewhere, it steals down invisibly and silently; even if it be a vapour, such as I speak of, In quo est imaginatum semen astrale certi ponderis, then it is neither heard of nor seen till a long time after. But to proceed in what I have promised to do, I shall instance in common dew: for dew hath in it some small dose of the star fire. We see therefore that this humidity comes down silently, for its enclosed fire keeps it rarefied in the form of air, and will not suffer it to condense to water at that height as the vapour of rain doth, but when it is descended near the earth it mingles with other crude vapours, and borrowing from them a great quantity of phlegm settles at last into drops. But before we go any further let us here consider those words of the son of Sirach. "Look (saith he) on all the works of the Most High, and there are two and two, one against the other." In this he agrees with that little fragment which goes under the name of Moses, where God teacheth him thus.

Lumen de lumine.

Scias, quod unicuique Creaturae, et compar, et contrarium creavi. I will not peremptorily affirm that Moses is the author of this piece, or that God taught him in those very words, but I affirm that those words express the truth of God, and point at some great mysteries of His wisdom. Nor will I here omit a circumstance, namely, that this piece hath in it some Hebrew words, and this proves that the author was a Jew if not Moses. But to pass by the author and come to the sense; I say that God created water to oppose it to the earth, and this appears by their different complexions and qualities; for the earth is gross and solid, the water, subtil and fluid; and the earth hath in her the coagulating, astringent power, as the water hath partly in it the softening dissolving faculty. The earth then shuts up herself and in herself the fire so that there can be no generation or vegetation, unless the earth be opened, that the fire may be at liberty to work. This we may see in a grain of corn, where the astringent earthly faculty hath bound up all the other elements, and terminated them to a dry compacted body. Now this body, as long as it is dry, or as Our Saviour saith, as long as it abideth alone; that is to say as long as it is without water, so long it can bear no fruit; but if it falls into the ground and dies, that is to say, if it be dissolved there by the humidity of Heaven (for death is but dissolution) then it will bring forth much fruit, as Our Saviour testifieth. It is the water then that dissolves, and life followeth the dissolution; for no sooner is the body opened, but the spirit stirs in it, perceiving in the dissolvent or dewy water, another spirit, to which he desires to be united. This spirit is the air enclosed in the dew or water, which air is called in the philosopher's books Aqua maris nostri, aqua vitae manus non madefaciens. But who will believe that there is a dry water hid in the moist? certainly few: and this Sendivow tells us of some Sophisters of his acquaintance. Non credebant aquam esse in mari nostro, et tamen philosophi videri volebant. I have myself known many such philosophers, and of whom I say the very same. But to return to our business; it is called aqua vitae, because this air involves in itself a fire, which is life Universal: not yet specified, and therefore it agrees with all particular lives, and is amicable to all kinds of creatures.

Now the particular specified fire, or life of the grain, which is the vegetable magnet, attracts to himself the universal fire or life, which is hid in the water, and with the fire he attracts the air which is the vestiment or body of the fire, called by the Platonics, currus Anima, and sometimes Nimbus ignis descendentis. Here then is the ground upon which the whole mystery of natural augmentation and multiplication is built; for the body of the grain of corn is augmented with the aliment of air, not simple but decomponded, which air is carried in the water, and is a kind of volatile sweet salt; but the fire or life of the grain, is fortified with the universal fire, and this fire is involved in the air, as tne air is in the water. And here we may observe that it is not water only that conduces to the generation or regeneration of things, but water and fire; that is water and spirit, or water that hath life in it and this, if rightly understood, is a great manuduction to divinity.

COMMENTS UPON THE TWENTY-SECOND PARAGRAPH.

It is not the vehicle that coagulates, but the matter borne in the vehicle. Here it will be well to remember the Qabalistic definitions of the parts of the Soul. The Earth or The Nephesh is the aura or lower astral. The Water or The Neshamah is the throne of the spirit. The Fire or The Chiah, and Neshamah form the Wheels and the Throne of the Incarnating Ego (Yechidah) or the real spirit of the Triple Fire. While the air, or the human Ego, is the meeting place of the other forces.

Paragraph XXIII.

To conclude, the sum of all we would say is this, the roots and seeds of all vegetables are traced in the earth, in the midst of this dewy fountain, as a lamp is placed in the midst of oil; and the fire or life of the seeds attracts to itself the abryssach or leffa, I mean the juice or gum of the water, as the fire of a lamp attracts the oil that is round about it. Now when all the air is drawn out of the water then the traction ceaseth, and concoction or transmutation begins, but if the crude water, which was the vehiculum of the air stays with the seeds, then it hinders concoction, and therefore the sun and the archeus jointly expel her, so that she takes wing and returns to the region of the air, where again she fills her belly with that starry milk, and then descends as before. This is the reason why there is in nature such a vicissitude of showers and sunshine, for the showers bring down the aereal nutriment, and when the plants have attracted it, then the sunshine calls up the crude water, which otherwise would hinder digestion and coagulation. This then is the trade that common water drives, but if she could be coagulated, this trade would cease, and all life would cease with it. I have for many years looked upon her as on a bird that flies to her nest, and from it again, feeding her young ones, and fetching food for them. Now is this a new fancy of mine, for some learned men considered as much before; in which respect that milky moisture which is found in her crystal breasts is called by some of them Lac volatilium, the milk of birds, and they have left it written, that birds do bring their stone unto them.

Paragraph XXIV.

To make an end, observe that there is a great difference between this common water, and our chymical ater or fire, mentioned formerly out of Pontanus, for our water helps coagulation and this hinders it. For if the phlegm, or crude spirit stays with the air, the air will never congeal; and therefore said Sendivow, omnis aqua congelatur calido, si est sine spiritu, and thus have I demonstrated my position, namely that common water is not congealable.

Paragraph XXV.

Nothing now remains, not is there anything hinders, but that we may safely and infallibly conclude, that simple crude water feeds nothing; but the gum of congealable part of it feeds all things; for this is the astral balsam and the elemental, radical humidity, which being compounded of inferiors and superiors, is a restorative both of spirits and bodies. This is the general vital element which God Himself provides for all His creatures, and which is yearly produced and manifested in the elements, by the invisible operation of his spirit, that works all in all. This hath in it the whole anatomy of Heaven and earth, whose belly is full of light and life, and when it enters into these lower parts of the world, it overcasts them with a certain virility, makes them break forth into flowers, and presents us with something that is very like to the paradise we have lost. In a word this is no human confection, but a thing prepared by the Divine Spirit;

nor is it made for vegetables only, but for man also, whom God did sometimes feed with it. This the Scripture tells us, whose authority is above Aristotle and Galen; for thus I read in Exod. "And it came to pass that at even, the quails came up and covered the camp, and in the morning the dew lay round about the host. And when the dew that lay was gone up, behold upon the face of the wilderness there lay around small thing, as small as the hoar frost on the ground, and when the children of Israel saw it, they said one to another, it is manna; for they wist not what it was, and Moses said unto them 'this is the bread which the Lord hath given you to eat.'" Every child knows that dew settles into round drops; and here Moses tells us that when the phlegmatic humidity was gone up, the congelative part that stayed behind, was a round small thing, for it retained still the figure of the drop, in whose belly it was hid. This coagulative part is oleous and fusible, and with this also the Scripture accords, telling us, that when the sun waxed hot, it melted. It is with all of a most facile quick alteration, and therefore easily transmutable or convertible into any form; and for this reason Moses charged the people to leave none of it till the morning; but some of them (saith the text) left of it till the morning, and it bred worms and stank; whence we may gather, that it is in some degree animal. We feel then that the Spirit of God is still busy with water, and to this hour moves not only upon

(marginal note: Chap. xvi. 13, 14, 15.)

it but in it, nor do I doubt but this is the ground of that deep question, which amongst many others God proposed to Job. "Hath the rain a father, or who hath begotten the drops of dew?" it is worth our observation that the children of Israel, when they saw this thing (though they knew it not) said one to another: it is Manna; for what argues this, but that Manna (as the words imports) was some secret gift of God, which they knew not, but had formerly heard of by tradition from their fathers; and perhaps by such a description as Hermes gives it in the Zaradi, namely, that it ascends from the earth to Heaven and descends again from Heaven to the earth; and this might make them call it Manna, because it descended with the dew. I question not but Moses knew it well, though the common people wist not what it was; for the golden calf could not be burned to powder with common fire, but with the fire of the altar, which was not that of the kitchen. This is plain out of the Machabees, where it is written, that this fire was hid in a pit, and that for many years it was there kept safe during the captivity. But who is so mad as to hide common fire in a pit, and to expect he shall find it there many years after? is it not the best course to quench it, and rather drown it in a well than bury it in a pit. We doubt not for our part, but this fire was far different from the common, and this the text also tells us, for when it was brought out of the pit it was not fire, but a thick water. The truth

Chap. xxxviii. v. 28.

Magia Adamioa is that this mystery belonged to the Jewish Church: the priests and prophets having received it from the patriarchs, I mean from Abraham, Isaac and Jacob, and they from Noah, and all of them from Adam, as we have proved elsewhere. These indeed were the men that planted the world, and instructed posterity: and these and none other must be those ancient and first philosophers, whom Zadith calls Avos Mundi, some of whose terms are cited by him.

COMMENTS UPON THE TWENTY-FIFTH PARAGRAPH.

But the gum or jelly of water feeds all things. Manna is a translation of the Hebrew word Man, meaning occultly the mixture of the upper and lower waters; the waters of creation in the chariot of the waters of the floods.

The fire that was hid in the pit, the fire of the altar, may, of course, have been any inflammable spirit or oil, such as spirits of wine, petroleum or a preparation of phosphorus, limelight or even an application of electrical force. But there is a deeper meaning to be looked for in the passage quoted from Maccabees.

This paragraph ends with an apology for the Jews, whom, it must remembered, were at this time, still looked upon with loathing by the Christians.

Paragraph XXVI.

We shall now (before we make an end) repeat all we have said and that in a few words, such as shall be agreeable to Nature and to the parts of the world as they have been manifested to us by experience.

We have certainly found, that there is nothing above but the very same is also here beneath, but in a more gross material complexion; for God hath ordained, that the gross and corpulent sperm of inferiors, should afford a body to the animating and subtle influx of their superiors. Now God hath decreed no union of sperms but of such as proceed from bodies that are of the same nature and kind, for his own word bears him witness that he hates confusion or a mixture of seeds that are different or of a diverse kind. Not unadvisably then did the priests, or (as Proclus tells us, the founders of the ancient priesthood affirm, Coelum esse in Terra sed modo Terrestri, et Terram esse in Coelo sed modo Coelesti; for otherwise they could not be of a kind. We say therefore, that in this universe, there are four luminaries, whereof two are coelestial and two are central. The celestial are the sun and moon, and they are known to all the world; the central indeed are not known, and therefore not believed, for the one is overcast with earth, and the other with water. In the centre then of the earth, there is hid a fire, which is of Nature solar, but more gross than that which is in the sun; and in the belly of the water, there is carried a viscous gross air, of a menstrous lunar nature, but not so bright and subtle as that which is in the moon. To be short, the central sun casts into the belly of the

Levit. xix. 7, 19.

water a masculine hot salt; and the water receiving it, adds to it her seminal feminine limosity, and carries it upon her wings into the region of the air. Thus we see how the material part of the seed is made, and now to this body of it the heaven gives life, the moon giving it spirit, and the sun giving it soul; and thus are the four lunaries brought together, the superior contributing that to the seed, which is subtle and vital; and the inferior that which is corpulent and material. This seed is carried invisibly in the belly of the wind, and it is manifested in water, I say in water as clear as crystal, and out of water it must be drawn, for there is not under heaven, any other body where it may be found. I have sought it myself in the common metals, in quicksilver, in antimone, and in regulus of antimony also in regulus of Mars, Venus, and Saturn, and of all the bodies; but I lost my labour, for I sought it where it was not. All these errors did I run into after I had known true matter; for having mis-carried in my first attempts upon it, I left it as a thing untractable; and this tergiversation of mine, brought me many inconveniences. I conceived indeed, that a vitriol made of those four imperfect bodies, antimony, lead and copper might be that glassy Azoth of Lullie, whose spirit or water, he has so magnified in his testament.

COMMENTS UPON THE TWENTY-SIXTH PARAGRAPH.

We now come to the connecting link between the parts of this volume. We have here a series of actual quotations from the Emerald Tablet of Chiram Trismegistus, or as he is commonly called, Hermes.

Of the four luminaries I may here quote a passage from our author's book called *Lumen de Lumine*.

"' It is most certain that no Astrabolism takes place without some grievous corruption and alteration in the Patient, for Nature works not but in loose moyst discomposed Elements. When the Elements fall out among themselves, the Celestial Fire reconciles them and generates some new Form, seeing the old one could consist no longer. . . . The body must be reduced to sperm, which receives the Impress of the Stars, and must immediately be exposed to the fire of Nature.' . . . When she had thus said she took out two Miraculous Medals. I did not conceive there was in Nature such glorious substances, she called them the Saphirics of the Sun and Moon."

The sun and the moon are the Cœlestial luminaries, but the central ones are a fire hidden in the earth or nitre, and an airy lunar nature in the water.

These two mixed natures are known to us as the desires of the flesh and the phantasies of the imagination: in their transmutation by consecration of the desires and purification of the thoughts, lies the pathway to wisdom.

The will and the imagination of an adept are symbolised by the Urim and Thummim of the High Priest; with this key read the paragraph carefully, and it will give you food for much profitable reflection.

Paragraph XXVII.

This indeed clinks finely, and may so swell a young head as to make him turn poet, and like the Delphic devil, tell a lie in heroics. No less obstructive to me was that speech of Parmenides, in the Turba. "Aes aut plumbum, pro pinguedine vel nigredine, et stannum pro liquefactione sumite." What can this signify at first sight but Antimony? and what can this stannum, that comes from it by liquefaction be, but Regulus.

This made me labour for a long time on this feculent and unprofitable body, supposing of a truth, that Regulus of antimony was white lead or tin philosophical. But that we be not deceived, all these parables relate to another mineral, and not to common antimony, which the Turba condemns in these words. Notandum est quod invidi lapidem antimonium nuncupârunt. Note (saith Cambar) or observe that the envious call the stone antimony. But what the envious call it, that certainly it is not and Basil Valentine in his Currus Triumphalis, which he hath written in the praise of antimony, tells us: non tantum illi a Deo concessum est ut in, vel ex Antimonio inventatur Mercurius philosophicus, primum Ens, Argentum vivum, et aqua prima metallorum perfectorum, ex qua sit magnus lapis antiquorum philosophorum, sed hoc primum Ens in Alio Minerali invenitur, in quo metallica ratione operatio altior est, quam stibii. And the

(margin: Camba in Turba.)

same Basil a little afterwards, speaking of Stella martis, delivers himself thus: Plerique putarunt hanc stellam esse materiam veram lapidis philosophorum, cogitantes se veraciter hoc imaginari, quia natura stellam hanc sponte sua formavit; Ego vero nego; hi viri, Regia via relicta, per avias rapes, ubi Ibices habitant, et prædatrices Aves nidificant, iter instituunt; non id debetur huic stellæ, ut materia sit lapidis nobilissimi, licet in eo latet medicina optima. It remains then, reader that, we lay aside all common metals, as gold, silver, copper, iron, tin, lead, antimony and quicksilver. For if we seek the sperm in any of these, we shall never find it, because we seek it in metallis vulgi, in quibus non est, as Sendivow hath told us. We must therefore seek another body, which is not common, nor is it made by mixture or otherwise, of any metal that is common; but is a certain black sulphur made by nature, and which never touched the fire. This is that body whereof Albertus Magnus has thus written: Datur in Rerum natura corpus metallicum quoddam, facilis solutionis, facilisque putrefactionis, si praeparationem ejus nosti, felix Medicus eris. And after him, his disciple Thomas Aquinas speaking of the same minera, cites these notable words out of another philosopher; est quaedam species metalli, quam gens nunquam invenit. This is the metal we must seek for and it is hard to find, because we must not dig to come at it, for if we know where it is, we need no more but stoop and take it up gratis. Yet it is neither Glauber's antimony, nor common lead, nor is it a flintstone, not the marle of Peter Faber, who after he had wearied himself, and deceived his readers with discourses of antimony, and sublimate with salts of common metals, sulphur at last in this Clod, or Marga as he calls it. But to pass by these fooleries and come to a conclusion: I say that this black sulphur is the male, which being found, we are in the next place to seek the female; and here observe, that God Almighty hath in particular bodies made no differences of sexes, but only in the animal kingdom, for in vegetables and minerals there is no such thing. We see that in grains of corn (suppose of wheat) there is no division into males and females, for the truth is they are all males, and God hath allowed them no female but the universal one, namely water, whose viscous general seed joining with the particular seed and spirit that is in the grain, is therewith fermented and congealed into the same nature with the grain itself, and so propagates and multiplies corn: even so it is in metals, for every one of them is masculine, sulphureous, choleric, nor hath God ordained that any of them should propagate and multiply the other either naturally or artificially though we deny not but that they may be multiplied by help of that seed, wherein God hath placed the blessing of multiplication. In metals then, there is no distinction or differences of sexes, so that out of them it is impossible to extract masculine and feminine sperms, for such cannot be extracted but from bodies that are male or female, which metals are not, for if they were, they would propagate without art, God having so ordained it. It is plain then, that metals (being not male and female) breed within themselves no seed, and by consequence cannot give which they have not; for the truth is, the seed whereof they spring, is that general seed of the elements, namely a certain humidity, which appears (as Sendivow tells us) in forma aquae pinguis, that is in the form of a fat water. This water is their seed, their mother and their female, for of this they were originally made, and if in this they be again resolved then the child will attract the mother to it, and convert her totally to his own nature; and on the contrary, the spirit of the mother will multiply the spirit of the child and exalt it to a perfection more than ordinary. This is the way, and besides it there is none; for there is no water under Heaven, from what bodies soever it be extracted, that hath in it the multiplying virtue, but this one water which God hath blessed. And here, though I seem to speak indifferently of metals, yet do not I: mind the common, for their spirits have been mortified in the fire. Take therefore our sulphur which never touched the fire, and whose whole life is whole in Him: join this living male to a living female, for in this (as I have elsewhere intimated) lies all the mystery,

<small>Anima Magica.</small> namely in the union of a particular spirit to the universal, by which means Nature is strangely exalted and multiplied. Labour therefore to unite these two substantially

and thoroughly, and thou canst not miss, if thou knowest the applications; for suffer me to tell thee a secret; that the application of actives to passives, I mean the manner of it, is the greatest difficulty in all the art. Farewell reader, and enjoy these my labours which I freely communicate to thee: not I assure thee out of any design, for I seek not my own glory but that of God and thy benefit.

COMMENTS UPON THE TWENTY-SEVENTH PARAGRAPH.

This points out that the only means of multiplying metallic natures is to apply their sulphurous nature to the universal feminine fat water; the oxide or tincture of a metal if dealt with according to art with a careful adjustment of temperature, may then be treated as a ferment.

But as I have said from the beginning, the author is too vague for us to derive any clue to practical alchemy from his work, and I will content myself by pointing out that the human passions, Pride, Envy, Anger, Sloth, Avarice, Gluttony, Lust, have long been associated with the seven gross metals, and that the oxidised metals may be regarded as symbolic of their saving virtues, Humility, Love, Patience, Fortitude, Compassion, Temperance and Chastity.

The Union of a particular to a universal exalts and multiplies strongly. Here is the final lesson then. Let us recognise that only the merging of our human wills with the Universal Will can result in hastening the day of our perfection. It we labour against the World's Will we shall fail, and our work will vanish from off the face of the earth.

SHORT APPENDIX BY WAY OF ADMONITION TO THE READER.

It was not my intention to add anything unto what has been already written: but when I reflect on those vexations I have endured myself in the pursuit of this science, I begin to think I have not said enough. To be a little more plain, know reader, that whosoever seeks the philosopher's mercury in metals, of what kind soever they be, is already out of the way: for that philosophic mercury so much talked of, is a water, and in metal, water there is none; for the sulphur hath not only congealed it there, but hath withal dried it up. This is evident in common quicksilver and antimony, which of all metalline bodies, are the most crude, and yet as crude as they are, their water is exsiccated by their fire; for if we force them into a fume, that fume settles not to a liquid spirit, but into dried flowers. This made the philosophers seek a more crude mineral whose fume was moist, and would settle into water, as being not yet mastered by the sulphur. Such there was none but the mother of mercury, or the first matter, whereof Nature makes the common mercury, and this also they call quicksilver, and a viscous water, for such it is. In this minera the mercurial vapour was not so dry, but it would settle into water, and with this water, they dissolve the metalline bodies; for the moist fume of this minera reduced the metalline dry fumes, so that both turned into one water, and this called mercury philosophical, and duplicated mercury. In this point I need not say more, and if they be not wilfully blind, here is light enough for our metalmongers, and especially for those confident roasters of antimony, who over the smoke of that drug dream of mysteries, as if they were transported into a certain capnonancy. For my part I deny not but antimony may be reduced to a mercurial water, though I know not to what purpose, for neither our mercury nor our tincture riseth from it, if Basil Valentine may be believed. True it is, that the philosophers use it, but as a mere instrument that goes off again, and so they use even kitchen fire, but it is not their matter or subject, and much less is it common gold, as some ignorants would have it. There is indeed another antimony, which is our sulphur, and the subject of the whole art; but this is so hard to find, and when it is found, so hard to prepare, that it had almost cast me into despair. Howsoever if thou dost seriously consider what I have written, and what hath fallen from me in some places with as much purpose as caution, then verily neither the thing itself not the preparation of it can be hid from thee. To make an end, know that the philosophers have two mercuries or waters, the first and second, their first is the spirit of our antimony and here understand me rightly; their second is that of mercury and Venus philosophical, and this of itself is all sufficient; but to shorten time, the philosophers ferment it with common gold. I have now spoken more than discretion can well allow of, but the sense of those difficulties I have met withal, have carried me thus far. Howsoever be thou cautious in thy construction, lest the name of antimony deceive thee, for so thou mayest run into a fruitless expense of time and substance. This is all I have to say, and now what use to make of it is in thy power; if thou canst believe, it is well; if not, forbear from this art altogether, or thou wilt live to punish thy own incredulity.

COMMENTS UPON THE APPENDIX.

I will end as I began by saying, I have read many Alchemical Treatises, but never one of less use to the practical Alchemist, than this. At the same time I have come across few occult works that have helped me more in my search for the secrets of these Great Adepts—who are the Masters of our Race.

S. S. D. D.

"Alas, Alas, that all men should possess the Master-soul, be one with the World-soul, and that possessing it, the Master-soul should so little avail them."

The Book of Golden Precepts.

FINIS.